LIBRARY OF NEW TESTAMENT STUDIES

678

Formerly the Journal for the Study of the New Testament Supplement series

Editor
Chris Keith

Editorial Board
Dale C. Allison, Lynn H. Cohick, R. Alan Culpepper, Craig A. Evans, Jennifer Eyl,
Robert Fowler, Simon J. Gathercole, Juan Hernández Jr., John S. Kloppenborg,
Michael Labahn, Matthew V. Novenson, Love L. Sechrest, Robert Wall,
Catrin H. Williams, Brittany E. Wilson

Image © Benedictine Sisters of Turvey Abbey

Markan Typology

*Miracle, Scripture and Christology
in Mark 4:35–6:45*

Jonathan Rivett Robinson

LONDON • NEW YORK • OXFORD • NEW DELHI • SYDNEY

T&T CLARK
Bloomsbury Publishing Plc
50 Bedford Square, London, WC1B 3DP, UK
1385 Broadway, New York, NY 10018, USA
29 Earlsfort Terrace, Dublin 2, Ireland

BLOCMSBURY, T&T CLARK and the T&T Clark logo are trademarks of Bloomsbury Publishing Plc

First published in Great Britain 2023
Paperback edition published 2024

Copyright © Jonathan Rivett Robinson, 2023, 2024

Jonathan Rivett Robinson has asserted his right under the Copyright, Designs
and Patents Act, 1988, to be identified as Author of this work.

For legal purposes the Acknowledgements on p. xii constitute an extension of this copyright page.

All rights reserved. No part of this publication may be reproduced or transmitted in any form or by any
means, electronic or mechanical, including photocopying, recording, or any information storage or
retrieval system, without prior permission in writing from the publishers.

Bloomsbury Publishing Plc does not have any control over, or responsibility for, any third-party websites
referred to or in this book. All internet addresses given in this book were correct at the time of going to
press. The author and publisher regret any inconvenience caused if addresses have changed or sites
have ceased to exist, but can accept no responsibility for any such changes.

A catalogue record for this book is available from the British Library.

Library of Congress Cataloging-in-Publication Data

Names: Robinson, Jonathan Rivett, author.
Title: Markan typology : miracle, scripture and Christology in Mark 4:35-6:45 /
by Jonathan Rivett Robinson.
Description: London ; New York : T&T Clark, 2022. | Series: The library of New Testament studies ;
2513-8790, volume 678 | Includes bibliographical references and index. | Summary: "Responding
to the belief that typology was a later development of the early church, and not applicable to the
earliest canonical Gospel, Jonathan Robinson stresses that typology has deep Jewish roots, and
that typological modes of thought were a significant part of the Gospel's historical and cultural
background. He brings this insight to bear on four of the most dramatic miracles in Mark's
Gospel, discovering a surprisingly consistent typological approach." – Provided by publisher.
Identifiers: LCCN 2022013526 (print) | LCCN 2022013527 (ebook) | ISBN 9781441131607 (hb) |
ISBN 9781441165329 (pb) | ISBN 9781441123824 (ebook) | ISBN 9781441100238 (epdf)
Subjects: LCSH: Bible. Mark, IV, XXXV-VI, XL–Criticism, interpretation, etc. | Typology (Theology)
Classification: LCC BS2585.52 .R625 2022 (print) | LCC BS2585.52 (ebook) |
DDC 226.3/06—dc23/eng/20220708
LC record available at https://lccn.loc.gov/2022013526
LC ebook record available at https://lccn.loc.gov/2022013527

ISBN:	HB:	978-0-5677-0871-7
	PB:	978-0-5677-0875-5
	ePDF:	978-0-5677-0872-4
	eBook:	978-0-5677-0874-8

Series: Library of New Testament Studies, volume 678
ISSN 2513-8790

Typeset by RefineCatch Limited, Bungay, Suffolk

To find out more about our authors and books visit www.bloomsbury.com
and sign up for our newsletters.

Contents

List of tables	x
Preface	xi
Acknowledgements	xii
Note on the text	xiv

§1	Introduction		1
	§1.1	The thesis question	1
	§1.2	What is typology and why would Mark use it?	2
		§1.2.1 The theological motivation for typology	5
		§1.2.2 From typology to christology	7
	§1.3	Why these miracles?	8
	§1.4	Miracle, scripture and christology in Mark	9
		§1.4.1 The place of miracle in Mark	9
		§1.4.2 Scripture in Mark and the miracles	11
		§1.4.3 Christology in Mark and the miracles	12
		§1.4.4 Richard Bauckham's divine identity	13
		§1.4.5 Daniel Kirk's category of exalted human figures	15
	§1.5	Reading Mark as narrative literature	16
		§1.5.1 Genre	18
		§1.5.2 Implied/Ideal reader	19
		§1.5.3 Intertextuality	21
		§1.5.4 Terminology of textual relationships	22
		§1.5.5 Narrative allusions	24
	§1.6	Reception history and Markan typology	25
	§1.7	Procedure	26
§2	Reading Mark's miracles typologically		29
	§2.1	The question of plausibility: Typology before Mark	29
	§2.2	Josephus as a witness to first-century typology	29
		§2.2.1 The sign-prophets	29
		§2.2.2 Divine providence	32
		§2.2.3 Josephus and the Prophet Jeremiah	33
		§2.2.4 Typology in Josephus	34

	§2.3	Typology in early Jewish literature	34
		§2.3.1 Hebrew scriptures	34
		§2.3.2 Tobit	38
		§2.3.3 1 Maccabees	39
		§2.3.4 Liber Antiquitatum Biblicarum	40
	§2.4	Typology in the earlier New Testament	43
	§2.5	Scriptural conflation	46
	§2.6	Graeco-Roman Mimesis	47
	§2.7	Conclusion	49
§3	Typology and christology in the context of Mark's Gospel		51
	§3.1	The Son of God appears: Typology and christology in Mark 1:1–15	51
		§3.1.1 The way of the Lord	52
		§3.1.2 Divine identity in Mark 1:2–3?	52
		§3.1.3 God's beloved son: Isaac Typology at the Baptism	53
	§3.2	The mountain transfiguration: Typology and christology in Mark 9:2–8	56
		§3.2.1 The typology of Jesus' transfiguration	56
		§3.2.2 Isaac typology on the mountain	59
		§3.2.3 The transfiguration and Jesus' ontology	60
	§3.3	Judgement on the Temple: Typology and christology in Mark 11–12	63
		§3.3.1 Typology of the withered fig tree	64
		§3.3.2 God's only beloved son: Typology in the Parable of the tenants	65
	§3.4	The son is slain: Typology and christology in Mark 14–15	68
		§3.4.1 Jesus as type of Passover	68
		§3.4.2 Isaac typlogy in the crucifixion	69
	§3.5	The King of the Jews: Davidic royal typology in Mark 11–15	71
		§3.5.1 Zechariah's Davidic Messiah in the Passion	72
		§3.5.2 Jesus and David, the twice-anointed Kings	73
		§3.5.3 Typological betrayal	74
		§3.5.4 The coronation of the Davidic Messiah	76
		§3.5.5 Divine identity in the trial of Jesus?	77
	§3.5	Conclusion	79
§4	Jonah typology in Mark 4:35–41		81
	§4.1	More than a 'Simple Miracle Story'	81
	§4.2	Exploring the conventions: Miraculous sea rescues in antiquity	82

		§4.3	Psalm 107 (LXX 106)	83
		§4.4	Jonah 1	86
			§4.4.1 Narrative correspondence	87
			§4.4.2 Lexical coherence	88
			§4.4.3 Thematic inversion	89
			§4.4.4 Contextual evidence for the link	89
			§4.4.5 A deliberate typological reference	91
		§4.5	Reading Mark 4:35–41 with Jonah 1	91
			§4.5.1 Jesus as a greater Jonah	91
			§4.5.2 Kirk and Young's early Jewish paradigm of water miracles	92
			§4.5.3 Jesus as Jonah's God?	93
			§4.5.4 Bauckham's divine identity and Mark's storm stilling	97
			§4.5.5 Jesus and his mission	98
		§4.6	Conclusion	98
§5	Elisha typology in Mark 5:21–43			101
		§5.1	A story within a story	101
		§5.2	Exploring the conventions	103
			§5.2.1 Ancient healing miracles	103
			§5.2.2 Ancient resurrection miracles	105
		§5.3	Elisha, 2 Kings 4:18–37	106
			§5.3.1 Narrative correspondences	109
			§5.3.2 Lexical correspondences	109
			§5.3.3 Thematic inversion	110
			§5.3.4 Unique indicators	111
			§5.3.5 A deliberate reference	111
		§5.4	Reading Mark 5:21–43 with 2 Kgs 4:18–37	113
			§5.4.1 Jesus as a greater Elisha	113
			§5.4.2 Kirk's common framework of empowered prophet as healer	116
			§5.4.3 Jesus, prayer and divinity	119
			§5.4.1 Hays' discussion of Mark 5:21–43	121
			§5.4.2 Jesus and the Gentiles	121
		§5.5	Conclusion	121
§6	David (and Goliath) typology in Mark 5:1–20			123
		§6.1	'A Strange Story'	123
		§6.2	Exploring the conventions	125
		§6.3	Isaiah 65:3–5 (LXX)	127

	§6.4	The watcher tradition		129
	§6.5	1 Samuel 16:14–18:9		133
		§6.5.1	David the Exorcist	133
		§6.5.2	Goliath the Nephilim	135
		§6.5.3	Narrative coherence	136
		§6.5.4	Lexical coherence	137
		§6.5.5	Thematic inversion	138
		§6.5.6	Unique identifier	138
		§6.5.7	Summary	139
	§6.6	Reading Mark 5:1–20 with 1 Samuel 16–18		140
		§6.6.1	Jesus as a greater David	141
		§6.6.2	Kirk's royal framework for Jesus' exorcisms	144
		§6.6.3	Jesus as the Lord of Hosts	145
		§6.6.4	Jesus and the Gentile mission	149
	§6.7	Conclusion		150
§7	Shepherd, Moses and Elisha typology in Mark 6:30–44 and 8:1–10			153
	§7.1	Mark's miraculous meals		154
	§7.2	Exploring the conventions		156
	§7.3	The banquet of death		157
	§7.4	A revolutionary gathering?		159
	§7.5	Transformation of a revolution		161
	§7.6	The repeated miracle		162
	§7.7	2 Kgs 4:42–44		164
	§7.8	The shepherd motif		165
	§7.9	Moses		168
		§7.9.1	A unique indicator	170
	§7.10	Reading Mark 6:30–44 and 8:1–10 with Elisha/Moses/Joshua Typology		171
		§7.10.1	Jesus as a greater Elisha and Moses	171
		§7.10.2	Kirk's paradigm of messianic banquets	173
		§7.10.3	Jesus and the God of Israel	174
		§7.10.4	Divine identity in the feeding miracles	175
		§7.10.5	Jesus and the Gentile mission	176
	§7.11	Conclusion		180
§8	Mark's typological christology			181
	§8.1	Summary of results		181
		§8.1.1	Jesus as typological fulfilment of human agents of salvation history	181

	§8.1.2	Jesus as typologically theomorphic	182
	§8.1.3	Jesus' prototypical Gentile mission	183
	§8.1.4	The function of typology in the Gospel of Mark	184
§8.2	Regarding previous approaches to divinity in Mark's miracles		185
	§8.2.1	Mark's Jesus does not fit the paradigm of exalted human figure	185
	§8.2.2	Mark's Jesus does not fit the category of divine identity	186
	§8.2.3	Pre-existent christology in Mark's miracle accounts	187
	§8.2.4	Typology and pre-existence	188
§8.3	Mark's typological portrayal of Jesus' divinity		190
	§8.3.1	How does typology portray divinity?	190
	§8.3.2	The divinity of Mark's human Christ	192
	§8.3.3	Mark's Divine Jesus and Jewish monotheism	194
§8.4	Conclusion		195

Bibliography	197
Scripture Index	223
Index of Other Ancient Sources	230
Author Index	234
Subject Index	238

Tables

1	Reference congruence Mark 4:35–41; Mark 6:45–52	96
2	Plot comparison of 2 Kgs 4:18–37 and Mark 5:21–43	112
3	Intertextual summary Mark 5:1–20 against 1 Samuel 16–18	140
4	Parallelism in Mark 5:19 and 20	146
5	Comparison of Mark's feeding miracles and Elisha's feeding miracle	165

Preface

In this study I argue for the presence of typological scripture use in the composition of four adjacent miracle accounts in Mark's Gospel (4:35–41; 5:1–20; 5:21–43; 6:30–45). These episodes make sustained use of literary-narrative allusion to corresponding miracle accounts from the Jewish scriptures. While some of these allusions have been suggested before, this study argues for hitherto unnoticed allusions, as well as a consistent typological approach within Mark's Gospel over several miracles. These miracle accounts contain verbal, narrative and thematic correspondences that, I will argue, are best explained by the presence of a scriptural typology. This compositional approach, which is here called *literary typology*, also reveals underlying theological and Christological convictions. These convictions situate Mark's Jesus firstly as the denouement of salvation history through, what I will call, *fulfilment typology*; and secondly identify him with the God of Israel, which is expressed by, what I will call, *theomorphic typology*.

Following an introductory chapter, I will show that elements of this typological approach are evident in several early Jewish texts prior to or contemporaneous with Mark, in order to demonstrate the historical plausibility of Mark employing such an approach. Then, a chapter will argue that this typological approach to scripture use is congruent with scripture use in other Christologically significant episodes of Mark's Gospel. Following, the heart of this study consists of four exegetical chapters which argue for literary, fulfilment and theomorphic typologies in the four miracle accounts considered. These will suggest extended typological allusions to the scriptural narratives of Jonah, David, Elisha and Moses. They will also discuss the Christological significance of recognizing each miracle's implicit typology. Finally, the results of this study will be considered within the contemporary early high Christology debate, focusing especially on the work of Richard Bauckham, Richard Hays and Daniel Kirk. The applicability of their respective early Jewish paradigms of 'divine identity' and 'exalted human figures' to the Gospel of Mark will be evaluated, as well as suggestions of pre-existence Christology. The study will conclude that the presentation of Jesus in Mark's Gospel is best understood according to its own categories and not according to those distilled from the diverse corpus of extant early Jewish writings. This study exposes a startlingly creative approach to scriptural typology which presents Mark's Jesus as God's unique eschatological representative, typologically figured as both servant and son, both human and divine. Thus, this study seeks to make an original contribution to the scholarly understanding of miracles, use of scripture and Christology in the Gospel of Mark.

Acknowledgements

Heartfelt thanks go to Paul Trebilco and James Harding, my supervisors for this project, from whom I have learned a huge amount and who have both continually challenged me to improve my work at the same time as encouraging me that my work was worth doing! The Theology Programme at Otago was a fantastic place to study and the collegiality of both staff and students greatly contributed to a positive experience of doing the PhD. Friday afternoon seminars, usually followed by trips to the pub, were a real highlight, as were our lunchtime German and Greek translation groups. I will not mention you all by name, but you know who you are, and thanks. A special mention does go to Jason Picard who shared not one but three different offices with me over the last three years and was a model office mate. Deane Galbraith from the Religion Programme at Otago also took a welcome interest in my work and parts of the thesis benefited from several conversations and suggestions from him. Finally, the library staff at Otago sourced many volumes and articles from around the world and in various languages for me and never once questioned any of my more obscure or esoteric requests.

The Otago University Doctoral Scholarship paid my fees and provided a stipend for the duration. Additional financial support from the university allowed me to attend a number of events. I am grateful to have presented my work outside the university at the Aotearoa New Zealand Association of Biblical Studies, the British New Testament Society, the Australia and New Zealand Association of Theological Schools, Carey Baptist College, Laidlaw College, Bishopsdale College and Alpha Crusis. At each one I've appreciated the encouragement and critique of fellow scholars – again, you know who you are.

A number of my church family at Musselburgh Baptist Church are distinguished academics in different fields, and I was frequently encouraged in my work by their interest, prayers and support – especially when facing the vagaries of peer review!

I would also like to thank my darling Rachel, who said 'yes' to this opportunity and to bringing the family on an adventure to Dunedin. Both in-law and out-law parents supported us morally and financially over this time – thanks to them. I would also like to acknowledge my beloved offspring, Charlotte, Katherine, Elisha and Lucy, who made everything more difficult for me, but also a lot more fun. I reassure the reader that my family were not harmed or inconvenienced in the making of this PhD – it was certainly the other way around.

In the final push Winsome Parnell and Cameron Coombe did yeoman-like service in proofreading and hugely improved the manuscript. It was an absolute privilege to have my thesis examined by Craig Evans, Sarah Harris and Graham Twelftree. Their insights and comments were and are invaluable. I am also indebted to the team at Bloomsbury T&T Clark, Chris Keith, Sarah Blake, the anonymous reviewers and the editorial staff. I am sure I do not need to point out that, despite the group effort nature of this thesis, all remaining mistakes, errors, blind spots, pig-headedness, split infinitives, oddities, convolutions, gaps-in-the-literature, distortions, grammatical inconcinnities and semantic abominations are my entirely my own, and for which I unreservedly apologize in advance.

Studying the Bible is a natural outgrowth of my Christian faith, which I received through my parents, and have continued to wrestle with over the last four decades. The germ of this project was a sermon on Jonah 1 at Blockhouse Bay Baptist Church in Auckland. A number of Jonah commentaries pointed out the similarity to the storm stilling in Mark 4:35–41. What was the connection between Jonah and Jesus and what did it mean? When the time came to put together a thesis proposal, this was the one idea that appealed. I could not have known what a fruitful line of enquiry it would turn out to be. At points in this project I have felt a sense of divine guidance and inspiration, at others I have felt strong doubts and confusion. I have mixed feeling about bringing this project, or at least this stage of it, to an end. They do say, 'A PhD is never finished, only abandoned'! I certainly do not claim divine inspiration for my work, but I do want to give thanks for the experience of God's guidance, sustenance and prevenient grace during this time. If there is anything useful, insightful or beneficial in my work, I give the credit to God's kindness.

Having witnessed Jesus calm a storm, the terrified disciples ask, 'Who is this?' The mystery of Jesus Christ's identity continues to intrigue both believer and sceptic today. This thesis solves no such mystery, but it does discover new ways of appreciating how that mystery is presented in Mark's Gospel. It has been an enriching journey for me and if you should read this project, I hope it will be for you too. Thanks for reading. *Pax vobis.*

Jonathan Robinson
Dunedin, New Zealand, February 2022

Note on the text

Abbreviations follow the SBL Style Guide, second edition.

§1

Introduction

History never repeats itself, but the kaleidoscopic combinations of the pictured present often seem to be constructed out of the broken fragments of antique legends.[1]

History doesn't repeat itself, but sometimes it rhymes.[2]

§1.1 The thesis question

Leonhard Goppelt, in his seminal work on New Testament (NT) typology, remarked regarding the Gospels that, 'On the whole, it is impossible to detect that the OT [Old Testament] miracle stories have had any significant influence on Jesus' saving acts or on the Gospel accounts'.[3] Subsequent scholarship has not accepted this conclusion and the influence of the Jewish scriptures on miracles recounted in the NT has continued to be discussed, with varying results.[4] This study seeks to break new ground by arguing for a consistent approach to the use of scripture in the composition of four adjacent miracle accounts in Mark's Gospel (4:35–41; 5:1–20; 5:21–43; 6:30–45). I will argue that these have been modelled on corresponding miracle stories from the Jewish scriptures. This compositional method, which I will call *literary typology*, also reveals theological and Christological convictions. These situate Jesus of Nazareth as the denouement of salvation history through, what I will call, *fulfilment typology*. And they identify him to an unprecedented extent with God, which is expressed by, what I will call, *theomorphic typology*.

Having established the presence of a theomorphic typology in the selected Markan miracle accounts, the remainder of the study will be devoted to analysing this presentation of Jesus' divinity; that is, to examine how far this narrative presentation of Jesus acting as God allows us to assert Jesus' divinity with reference to conceptions of

---

[1] Clemens and Warner 1874: 430.
[2] Unattested quote, frequently attributed to Mark Twain (Samuel L. Clemens).
[3] Goppelt 1982: 73.
[4] From the perspective of the Gospel of Mark, written long before the formation of a Christian New Testament, the terminology of 'Old Testament' is inappropriate. Likewise, the expressions 'Bible' and 'biblical' impose 'on pre-canonical data a canonical label that implies a place in a closed list of books'. Instead, the terms 'Jewish scripture' and 'scripture' will be employed to refer to 'Israel's traditions that had both general and focussed authority at various times' (Brooke 2009: 21–2). See also Thompson 1998: 262–3; Stamps 2006: 11; Watts 2020: 165.

divinity that were operating in Jewish literature in the milieu of Mark's Gospel. This chapter will require engagement with some key figures in the contemporary early high Christology debate, especially Richard Bauckham (and Richard Hays' use of Bauckham) and Daniel Kirk. These scholars have used Mark's Gospel within their respective arguments and their results regarding Mark are called into question by this study. I will conclude that neither divine identity (Bauckham, Hays) nor idealized human figures (Kirk) are sufficient or accurate categories for Mark's presentation of Jesus in the miracle accounts. Rather, Mark's presentation of Jesus is extraordinary precisely because, with the exception of Mark 9:1–7, it lacks those visual markers of divinity (e.g. radiating light) that are present in Jewish texts which portray or discuss ontological divinity. For Mark, Jesus' particular and historical human life and actions personify God, yet Jesus' humanity is not altered. Mark's Jesus demands a new category of divinity in humanity that is not derivable from earlier Jewish writings. Instead, we must work to derive our categories from Mark's own account.

This study will thus contribute to the discussion of Mark's use of scripture and to the debate over the nature of Mark's Christology. I hope that it will complement other studies on NT typology and contribute to our awareness of early Christian typology. Indirectly, it may also contribute to current discussions regarding figurative exegesis and theological interpretation for contemporary Christian theology in church and academy.[5]

§1.2 What is typology and why would Mark use it?

Typology is a contested term with various definitions. It is important to recognize that the term *typology* as a description of a hermeneutical practice of the New Testament is to some extent anachronistic. It did not become a technical term until much later, and the way it is often used in modern discourse in opposition to *allegory* (i.e. a symbolic use of the words of a text without concern for their literal or historical meaning) is still more anachronistic.[6] Nonetheless, use of the term *typology* in this study follows the definition of Frances Young: "'typology' may be usefully used as a heuristic term to distinguish interpretive or compositional strategies which highlight correspondences, not just at the verbal level, but at the level of mimetic sign".[7]

Young builds her understanding of typology on the work of Michael Fishbane, who writes,

> inner-biblical typologies constitute a literary-historical phenomenon which isolates perceived correlations between specific events, persons, or places early in time with their later correspondents ... they will never be precisely identical with their prototype, but inevitably stand in a *hermeneutical* relationship with them.[8]

---

[5] E.g. Frei 1974; Steinmetz 1980; Lindbeck 1984; Treier 2003; Hays 2016; Millay 2017.
[6] Dawson 1992: 15–17; Frances Young 1997: 120; Martens 2008: 283–317.
[7] Frances Young 1997a: 200; also Ounsworth 2012: 4, 33.
[8] Fishbane 1985: 351, emphasis original.

Likewise, Allison states that typology is 'extended assimilation (of characters and events)' which can 'convey much meaning' and can serve ethical, poetic and theological purposes.[9]

Young's definition is chosen here to avoid anachronistic categorical precision. When applied to ancient authors, distinctions between allegory, typology or analogy create unnecessary and potentially misleading analytical categories.[10] Correspondences of all kinds were potentially significant and could be employed. Thus, the term typology is here intended to be *heuristic*.

I am not claiming that Mark or any other ancient author thought of some of their scripture use as typological in opposition to any other method or approach.[11] As Richard Ounsworth writes, typology 'describes a mode of relationship between events, persons, places and practices that they [the original NT audience] would have been able to infer, whether or not they would have labelled it "typology"'.[12] Rather, I am claiming that Mark and other ancient writers used *correspondences* between characters and events in their narratives and characters and events in earlier scriptural narratives as part of a *compositional strategy*. This *compositional strategy* was also an act of scripture *interpretation* and thus meaningful to the author, and so is not a simple borrowing of otherwise unconnected sources.

In this limited sense, a Markan *type* is a correspondence between persons or events in the Gospel with persons or events from scripture which Mark has used in the composition of the Gospel and which can be expected to contain hermeneutical significance.

This typological approach was integral to much scripture composition and interpretation found in Jewish writings of the Second Temple period. Thus, it would be natural for Mark to employ an approach which was visible in the scriptures and also in the wider religio-cultural environment. As with other scripture usage in the Gospel, Mark would have used typology rhetorically to further the agenda of the Gospel. As Christopher Stanley argues, most Jewish and Christian scripture use 'is part of a broader argument designed to convince others to believe or act in a certain way'.[13]

---

[9] Allison 1993: 13–16.
[10] This point has been repeatedly and convincingly argued by Young (1987: 113; 1989: 188; 1997a: 189–96; 1997b: 120; 1999: 7).
[11] Here, and throughout this study, 'Mark' denotes the Gospel's implied author. This expression 'serves as a way of describing or even personifying the text and is a summary of the kinds of things the text itself reveals ... [It] focuses on the "intention" of the text rather than on the conscious intent of the flesh-and-blood author or composer' (Donahue and Harrington 2005: 20). What I intend to show, over the course of the thesis, is that the texts of four of Mark's miracles are suggestive of a consistent approach to their composition using language, themes and structures of their scriptural counterparts in a Christologically meaningful way. While, for the sake of readable prose, I will attribute this to 'Mark' I do not thereby foreclose the question of whether this consistent approach is the work of an individual author or editor, a group, a traditioning process, spiritual or religious inspiration, or a combination of some or all of the foregoing. In this study, Mark is the author that the work implies and may or may not correspond to a historical person or persons. See also Guelich 1989: xix; Focant 2012: 3.
[12] Ounsworth 2012: 4.
[13] Stanley 1997: 44.

Once typology is identified as a literary feature (literary typology) it becomes possible to be more precise in recognizing how and why that typology is being employed. As Ounsworth argues, for the ancient author the 'verbal' (i.e. literary) correspondence is of less importance than the 'real' or 'ontological' correspondence.[14] One such 'real' relationship emerges from 'the shape of salvation history' as it 'is formed by the nature of God and his providential love for his people'.[15] Meaningful similarities between God's salvific actions could be inferred by early Jews without being first associated in a text. Correspondences 'are not created, as it were artificially, by a literary device, but only brought to light by verbal similarities'.[16] Thus we can look beyond the literary effect to what *real* relationship connects the types. Such real relationships can exist in a variety of ways.

Michael Goulder has argued that typology takes three explicit forms in the NT.[17] What Goulder terms 'scriptural types' are when scriptural characters or events are shown to correspond to NT characters and events. For example, Adam corresponds to Christ (Rom 5:12-21) and Elijah corresponds to John the Baptist (Mark 9:13). Then there are 'types within a Gospel'. For example, in John the resurrection of Lazarus (John 11) corresponds to the raising of Christ (John 20), and in Luke the transfiguration (Luke 9:28-36) corresponds to the ascension (Luke 24:50-53; Acts 1:9-11). In Mark, John the Baptist's passion (Mark 6:14-29) corresponds to that of Jesus (9:11-13).[18] Finally, Goulder discusses 'eschatological types' where NT events anticipate events still to come. For example, the Last Supper anticipates the messianic banquet (Mark 14:25) and the resurrection of Christ anticipates the resurrection of the church (1 Cor 15:12-20). All three of the kinds of typology identified by Goulder are thus visible in Mark's Gospel, as well as the wider NT, demonstrating the applicability of typology to the Gospel.

This study is concerned with the first category, typology of scriptural characters and events. Goulder's terminology, however, is not specific enough for my purposes. A scriptural typology may be a typology of *recurrence*, when situations or characters resemble previous ones, such as the succession of deliverers in the book of Judges (e.g. Judg 3:7-11, 12-30) or the way that Elisha's miracles emulate Elijah's (e.g. 1 Kgs 17:17-24; 2 Kgs 4:18-37). These later types do not, however, imply that the first type (*prototype*) has reached its culmination in the latter occurrence (as an *antitype*). Often, the recurrence is of a weaker variety: for example, the kings that emulated their ancestor David (1 Kgs 15:11; 2 Kgs 18:13; 22:2).

Because Jesus is not simply another Adam in an ongoing line of Adams, but is the 'last Adam' (Rom 5:12-21), and because John is not the latest Elijah in a recurring sequence, but is the eschatological fulfilment of the scriptural promise that Elijah will

---

[14] To avoid confusion with discussions of Jesus' divine ontology later in this study, the terminology of 'real' typology will be preferred. That is, to indicate a typological correspondence that could be perceived by an early Jewish Christ-believer to exist in fact, with or without a literary correspondence to indicate it.
[15] Ounsworth 2012: 6.
[16] Ounsworth 2012: 4.
[17] Goulder 1964: 1.
[18] Best 1990: 119-20; Pesch 1979: 1.344.

come (Mark 9:13), these typologies are more than simple recurrence. They escalate the type. Jesus is Adam's antitype and John is Elijah's. The last is greater than the first. The typology has reached its climactic conclusion in its antitype. These examples can thus be termed *fulfilment* typology.

The concept of fulfilment applies when Jesus is presented as the antitype of a scriptural character like Moses or David. However, I will later argue that sometimes Jesus is presented in the narrative role of Israel's God. In such circumstances Jesus cannot be said to be God's antitype. Instead the literary typology alerts us to an identification of Jesus with God, an assimilation of Jesus' narrative form to the narrative form of the divine Lord in the scriptures. This is best understood not as an escalation or fulfilment, but as a *theomorphic* typology in which the Gospel narrative causes Jesus to resemble God.[19] Recurrence and fulfilment typologies take place on a horizontal plane, diachronically, within history. Theomorphic typology, although in literary terms it relates Jesus to past events, serves to relate Jesus to the God of Israel. It creates a synchronous, vertical typology, establishing Jesus as God's earthly counterpart.

§1.2.1 The theological motivation for typology

Typology functions as an identifiable literary technique (literary typology) that is reflective of a particular interpretation of texts and/or events. Exegesis is not complete if we only identify typology as a literary feature without also seeking its 'theological value', so that we do not only 'enjoy Scripture's own artfulness', but 'engage the Bible on its own hermeneutical terms'.[20] While individual typologies will reflect specific concerns, the use of typology in itself is suggestive of certain theological assumptions.

There is an ethical-rhetorical function to typology whereby associations with an established authoritative figure can be transferred to the new one. This extends to the cultural authority of established scriptural texts.[21] The 'perceived need to provide authority and legitimacy for a new work' is a recognized possible motivation for the use of older texts by later ones within the Hebrew Bible.[22] Likewise, Markan typology serves to situate Mark's account alongside the older Jewish scriptures, to 'enlist' their 'authority' and to 'reinforce' Mark's own 'content'.[23] Importantly, such typology does not have to be explicit. Dawson argues 'oblique, sometimes nearly subliminal, echoes of the old story' can be the most effective in gaining the sympathy and support of the reader.[24]

---

[19] 'Theomorphic'; that is, 'having divine form : formed in the image of deity : endued with a divine aspect', https://www.merriam-webster.com/dictionary/theomorphic, accessed 17/10/2019; not to be confused with Theomorphism, the fifth-century heresy that the Son ceased to be God in the incarnation, described by Cyril of Alexandria. On which, see King 2014: 44–6.
[20] Emadi 2015: 21.
[21] See, e.g., Stamps 2006: 26–32.
[22] Moyise 2020: 20.
[23] Young 1997a: 130. See also Hays 1989: 155; Dawson 1992: 2–3; Moyise 2000: 18–19; Moyise 2020: 20. A similar impulse can be seen in the Jewish scriptures. See, e.g., Levinson 1997: 148–50, Sommer 1998: 158.
[24] Dawson 1992: 130; see also Fisk 2001: 109; Hays 2005: 17, 33.

The use of typology implies that Mark wants to present the Gospel as a new authoritative text, which co-opts the authority of the scriptures.

Typology is also an understandable reflex when interpreting new situations and personalities.[25] To what else would a first-century Jew compare a new religious leader and significant events, either positively or negatively, other than to the characters and events described in their scriptures?[26] Typology is thus one way of interpreting authoritative texts from another time for the author's present.[27] In parallel with legal language, a historical *precedent* is set by earlier types and so by analogy they may elucidate subsequent acts of God.[28] The use of typology allows recent, current or future events to be identified with scriptural types, or, conversely, scriptural types can be specified or modernized by identification with recent, current or future events (*contemporizing* typology).

Typology may also reveal a belief in providence, a guiding hand on history, whose characteristic ways can be discerned by the faithful.[29] As Fishbane writes, typology 'reveals unexpected unity in historical experience and providential continuity ... [it is] a disclosure of the plenitude and mysterious working of divine activity in history'.[30] Or put more simply by Allison, 'when history's tumult throws up two things alike, they intimate a third thing, the cause of their likeness—for the believer, God'.[31] Indeed, Rikk Watts has argued that 'the NT authors' fundamental hermeneutical assumption in reading scripture is the faithfulness of Yahweh's unchanging character'.[32]

The scriptures are the subtext for Mark's own narrative, and so it is not just the authority of the scriptures but their narrative arc that is invoked. The Gospel becomes a continuation of the Jewish scriptures. Heike Omerzu writes:

> Dass Jesus der 'geliebte Sohn' ist, der am Kreuz leiden musste, aber von den Toten auferweckt wurde, kann für Markus nicht (allein) angemessen durch Titel und Formeln ausgedrückt werden, vielmehr greift er auf den Modus der Erzählung zurück und stellt sich damit in die Tradition Israels. Er schreibt damit jüdische

---

[25] The key events and person that Mark wrestles to interpret are the life, death and resurrection of Jesus of Nazareth (see Juel 1992). The debates around whether Mark was composed before or after the destruction of the Temple, or whether the Gospel was written in Rome, Syria or Palestine, are to a large extent underdetermined by the text, hence the ongoing discussion. The literary features that this study is focused upon are not substantially affected by theories of date or provenance. Moreover, when turbulent current events have left such little impression on the text, it seems reasonable to conclude that the author is more concerned with preserving the gospel of Jesus Christ as they have received it than commenting on his community's immediate situation (see further Baarlink 1977: 196–7, 295; Bauckham 1998: 9–48).

[26] Foulkes 1994: 357.

[27] Hays 1989: 33; Evans 1992: 862; Ounsworth 2012: 48.

[28] Watts 2020: 174.

[29] Evans 1992: 863, 'Emphasis on the unity of Scripture and history is the distinctive of typological interpretation. What God has done in the past (as presented in Scripture), he continues to do in the present (or will do in the future).'

[30] Fishbane 1985: 352.

[31] Allison 1993: 14–15; Lampe 1965: 18.

[32] Watts 2020: 169.

Geschichte – teils in unbedingter Zustimmung, teils in kritischer Distanz (vgl. Torahauslegung) – fort als Geschichte Jesu, die u.a. Teil der Geschichte des Elia, Mose und Jesaja ist, und konstituiert damit zugleich die Geschichte seiner Adressaten.[33]

For Mark, the recent and current events of Jesus and the early church are not novel occurrences but connected to types in sacred history that reveal the deeper meanings of particular events (fulfilment typology).[34]

§1.2.2 From typology to christology

The author of Ephesians writes that God's plan (οἰκονομία) is being brought to fullness (πλήρωμα) as Christ recapitulates (ἀνακεφαλαιόω) all things (Eph 1:10). What is explicit in Ephesians is implicit in the Gospel of Mark through the use of typology. In Mark's Gospel, Jesus recapitulates many key events of scripture. He fulfils them, revealing that he is the decisive act of God's salvation-historical plan.

Markan fulfilment typology compares Jesus to previous biblical characters and compares his acts to earlier acts of God in salvation history. In doing so Mark presents Jesus as being in a line of scriptural characters and events, to be superior to earlier types, and to fulfil their deeper meaning – that is, their meaning in relation to the salvation-historical substructure of the scriptures.[35]

Thus, the theological motivation for typology extends to embrace Christological purpose, because the focus of Mark's scriptural typology is Jesus, his acts and the events surrounding his ministry, death and resurrection. Jesus is shown to be the superlative example among God's servants, God's ongoing providence, the denouement of God's salvation-historical plan and the climax of the scriptural story.

However, even that last sentence fails to do justice to Mark's Jesus. When read typologically, I will argue, Mark's Jesus is identified, not just with God's plan, but with God himself. In the miracle accounts of Mark 4:35–6:44, Jesus is the one who commands wind and sea, the one in whose name battles are won, the one who heals his daughter Israel and the one who gives miracle bread in the wilderness.

If fulfilment typology relates Jesus to the prior events of salvation history, then Jesus' narrative assimilation to the God of Israel from those same scriptures must be understood differently. Jesus can be the new David or the new Moses, but he cannot be the new God. Equally, Jesus can be a greater David or a greater Moses, but he cannot

---

[33] 'That Jesus is the "beloved Son" who suffered on the cross but was raised from the dead cannot be adequately expressed for Mark by titles and formulas alone; rather, he resorts to the narrative mode and thereby places himself in the tradition of Israel. He therefore updates Jewish history – partly in unconditional approval, partly in critical distance (see the interpretation of Torah) – as the story of Jesus, which amongst other things is part of the story of Elijah, Moses, and Isaiah, and thus at the same time constitutes the history of its addressees' (Omerzu 2011: 99–100).

[34] This coheres with the use of typology described by, inter alia, Fishbane 1985; Allison 1993: 16; Young 1997a: 199.

[35] France 1971 78–9; see also Evans 1999: 376–80.

be a greater God of Israel – at least not without completely abrogating what we understand of early Jewish monotheism.

What I aim to demonstrate is that Mark employs a *theomorphic* typology, where Jesus is typologically presented in the corresponding narrative role, the narrative *form*, of God from certain scriptural stories. The literary technique is the same as in fulfilment typology but the hermeneutical import is harder to discern. In what sense does Mark's literary strategy reveal a 'divine christology'? Is it best described according to a paradigm of 'divine identity'?[36] Or, is Jesus better understood as an 'idealised human figure'?[37] How does a typological reading impact on the argument around Jesus' pre-existence in Mark?[38] Are our established ways of analysing a text's Christology appropriate for Mark? Considering these questions will be the focus of the last chapter of this study.

§1.3 Why these miracles?

This thesis will consider four miracle pericopae: the calming of the storm (Mark 4:35–41); the exorcism of Legion (5:1–20); the healing of Jairus' daughter and the woman in the crowd (5:21–43); and the feeding of the five thousand (6:30–45). They are selected for a variety of reasons.

First, they are all extended narratives and so provide ample opportunity for typological crafting. Whereas in a short passage a typology may be present but will remain ambiguous due to the inevitably small number of correspondences, in these longer passages a stronger case can be made for typologies that are present throughout the episode.

Second, the chosen miracles bear an initial clear resemblance to a scriptural miracle: a calming of a storm, control of an evil spirit, a resurrection of a child and a feeding of a multitude. As Rudolf Pesch observes, 'Alle sind aus jüdischer bzw. judenchristlicher Perspektive erzält, haben einen deutlichen atl. Hintergrund, der in Anspielungen, Motivaufnahmen und insbesondere im Überbietungsmotiv erkennbar ist.'[39] That is, the exegete does not have to search inventively for a corresponding story that might fit. There is an immediate surface correspondence for anyone familiar with the Jewish scriptures. The Gospel's later miracles are not as strongly suggestive of scriptural miracles, although they may well still contain correspondences.

Third, these stories occur together in the second quarter of the Gospel, leading up to the Christological confession of Peter (Mark 8:29).[40] It seems likely then, that they

---

[36] Bauckham 2008: 4.
[37] Kirk 2016: 3–4.
[38] See, e.g., Gathercole 2006; Bird 2017.
[39] 'All [these miracle stories] are told from a Jewish or Jewish Christian perspective, having a clear Old Testament background, which can be recognized in allusions, inclusion of motifs and especially in the motif of escalation' (Pesch 1979: 1.278).
[40] For significance of Mark 8:39 see Guelich 1989: xxxvi. There is no consensus as to Mark's outline, although many plausible outlines have been proposed (E.g. Gnilka 1998: 1.25–32; Marcus 2000: 62–4; France: 2002: 11–15; Boring 2006: 4–6). A precise outline is not determinative for this study.

have been positioned in the Gospel narrative in order to explain and give content to Peter's confession. Subsequently, as the Gospel continues, miracles have a more minor role. In regards to Jesus' public works of power, these four constitute the climactic section.[41]

Fourth, these four miracles are representative of all of Jesus' miracles. They cover the categories of healing, exorcism, nature and gift miracles.[42] As Rupert Feneberg states, 'Die Reihe der Wunder enthält alle Bereiche der Welt und des menschlichen Lebens, in denen sich die umfassende Macht Gottes bewährt'.[43] They are the longest and most detailed examples within the Gospel of their individual categories, the 'Höhepunkte des Wunderwirkens Jesu'.[44] They may well provide an interpretive key for the significance of miracles in Jesus' ministry in general.

Finally, these four miracles comprise the first pre-Markan catena of miracles identified by redaction critic Paul Achtemeier or, as my discussion will also include Mark 6:45-52 and 8:1-10, the six miracles of the 'die vormarkinische Wundergeschichtensammlung' discussed by Pesch, and so may have existed as a unit prior to the composition of Mark's Gospel.[45]

§1.4 Miracle, scripture and christology in Mark

§1.4.1 The place of miracle in Mark

Miracles comprise the most prominent feature of the Markan narrative.[46] However, their function within the Gospel is disputed. David Strauss argued that the miracles served to confirm Jesus' messianic identity, because in the Jewish context the messiah was expected to conform to 'Old Testament types and declarations', particularly the miracles of Moses and Elisha and the prophecy of Isa 35:5-6.[47] While Strauss buttresses his claim with references to Matthew and John,[48] as James Dunn has observed, 'According to Mark, not one of the miracles performed publicly led the spectators to conclude that Jesus was the Messiah'.[49] Indeed, it is unclear whether the diversity of early Jewish messianic speculation contained any expectation that the messiah would perform healings and exorcisms.[50]

---

[41] '[N]owhere else in the gospel do we find such a group of spectacular miracles' (Fisher 1981: 14).
[42] Pesch 1979: 1.279.
[43] 'The series of miracles contains all areas of the world and of human life in which the comprehensive power of God proves itself' (Feneberg 2000: 135).
[44] Pesch 1979: 1.267.
[45] Achtemeier 1970: 291; Pesch 1979: 1.277-281.
[46] By some counts, as much as 31 per cent of the total Gospel material, or 47 per cent of the material outside of the passion account is miracle stories. See Twelftree 1999: 57; 2003: 108 n. 19; following Richardson 1941: 36. A more conservative estimate is produced by counting lines of text in Nestle-Aland, which produces 377 of 1430 total lines in the Gospel (26 per cent) for miracle accounts and summaries, by comparison with 263/1430 (18 per cent) for the passion account. See Schmücker 1993. 3. Of course, such estimates are only indicative.
[47] Strauss 1846: 413.
[48] Strauss 1846: 414-15.
[49] Dunn 1970: 94.
[50] Evans 2001: 220-2; Kee 1987: 187.

Rudolf Bultmann's form criticism understood Mark's miracles as depicting a Hellenistic 'divine man' (θεῖος ἀνήρ) Christology that emphasized his supernatural power in order to appeal to a Greek religious world used to legends of powerful demigods.[51] However, the divine-man hypothesis of Ludwig Bieler which Bultmann employed has since been heavily criticized as lacking any historical basis.[52]

Redaction criticism sought to identify an authorial theology behind the Gospel's collection and arrangement of traditions. Following Theodore Weeden this miraculous divine-man Christology was usually pitted against another Markan theme, the suffering Son of Man and the cross, where the Gospel author used the latter to refute the former.[53] More recently, narrative criticism has rightly problematized the idea that the Gospel author presents a negative view of the miracles or that the miracles compete with or contradict other Christological themes in the Gospel. However, as Adam Winn argues, narrative critics tend to downplay the Christological significance of the miracles and to focus on other aspects, such as characterization.[54]

This thesis will nuance Strauss's insight that the miracles were anticipated by 'Old Testament types and declarations'.[55] Contrary to Strauss, these particular types were not part of messianic expectation prior to Jesus. Rather, as the early church reflected on the life, death and resurrection of Jesus they interpreted these events through the Jewish scriptures, and vice versa.[56]

Winn's recent attempt to demonstrate how the Christological themes of power and suffering in Mark's Gospel 'find unity in the realm of Roman political ideology'[57] is convincing in terms of a historically located reader-response for the first-century Christian community in Rome, but does not explain Mark's composition from an Early Jewish perspective.[58] On the other hand, Winn is essentially correct in arguing that Jesus's suffering is given meaning by recognizing who it is that suffers and the recognition that such suffering is undergone willingly. As one of the Gospel's principal means of establishing Jesus's Christological identity, the miracles are an essential interpretive context for Jesus' trial under the Sanhedrin and execution by the Romans (Mark 14:43–15:39). They show that Jesus is not simply another tragic victim of religious and political forces, but the powerful Son of God and eschatological Son of Man who

---

[51] Bultmann 1952: 1.131–32; see also Dibelius 1971: 96.
[52] Bieler 1967; for a comprehesive critique see Blackburn 1991.
[53] The most prominent example of this is Weeden 1971. For further discussion see Broadhead 1992: 17–21; Twelftree 1999: 57–58.
[54] Winn 2016: 14–20. Examples of this emphasis on characterization are Rhoads and Michie 1982: 103–16; Malbon 2014.
[55] Strauss 1846: 413.
[56] Hengel 1976; Juel 1992; Bauckham 2008.
[57] Winn 2016: 164.
[58] A shorter treatment of Mark's Gospel as a response to Roman imperial propaganda, but which gives more attention to Jewish traditions, is Evans 2006. Arguably, however, Jewish Christ-believers would have been motivated to show that Jesus was the fulfilment of scripture with or without the need to counter imperial propaganda. This is not to deny this Roman background or its influence, but to place it in relation, as Evans does, to the ongoing tradition of scripture interpretation, rather than simply as an ad hoc response to current events.

undergoes these events as the scriptures have foretold (Mark 14:21) and in accordance with his Father's will (14:36).

§1.4.2 Scripture in Mark and the miracles

Two critical and overlapping concerns in the study of Mark's Gospel are Mark's Christology and Mark's use of Scripture. Because the Gospel primarily uses the Jewish scriptures with regard to and as a way of interpreting Jesus, the Gospel's Christology and use of scripture are intimately connected.

Mark's use of scripture has been extensively studied. While Mark's explicit uses of scripture have received the most attention,[59] a significant issue has been the presence or absence of scriptural allusion especially in the Passion account. For example, the influence of Isaiah 53 on the Markan passion, despite the absence of clear quotations, has been vigorously argued and is accepted by many commentators.[60] The theme of 'new exodus' from Deutero-Isaiah is also argued by Watts to be a significant allusive background to much of the Gospel.[61] However, Kelli O'Brien has recently challenged the legitimacy of recognizing allusions that lack significant lexical correspondence.[62]

There is a spectrum among Markan scholars as to the extent to which they are willing to acknowledge scriptural references that are not explicitly indicated in the text. The Markan miracle accounts contain no clear quotations of scripture, and so are sometimes not discussed at all in regard to Mark's use of scripture.[63] Despite this, the observable trend in recent critical commentaries is to recognize the significance of scriptural allusions and parallels in locating the meaning and purpose of Mark's miracle accounts.[64]

In this study, the thesis of a literary typology within the miracle accounts leads to a simple argument: a correlation between one miracle story from the scriptures and another from the Gospel. The literary typology will be argued for by detailed attention to both texts. Relevant Jewish traditions will also be considered. Greater attention and significance are given to those which are likely to precede or be contemporary with Mark. Finally, the paradigm of typology will be based on models that can be seen to be operating in early Hellenistic Judaism, rather than on models based primarily on Greek rhetoric.

As I aim to demonstrate, some of Mark's miracles make deliberate and sustained use of literary narrative allusion to the scriptures. While some of these allusions have been suggested before, this study aims to be the most comprehensive analysis to date and the first to argue for a consistent exegetical approach by the Gospel author over several

---

[59] E.g. Lindars 1961; Dodd 1965; Watts 2007.
[60] Marcus 1992. For the influence and use of the Isaianic servant songs in the canonical gospels and the Jesus tradition see Moo 1983: 79–172.
[61] Watts 1997, 2004.
[62] O'Brien 2010. A shorter critique is offered by Foster 2015.
[63] E.g. Watts 2007.
[64] Notable in this regard are Garland 1996; Marcus 2000; Donahue and Harrington 2005; Boring 2006; Collins 2007.

miracles. Although I consider it possible for narrative allusions to be present without specific lexical correspondences, the Markan miracles considered all contain distinctive verbal correspondences that are best explained by the presence of a scriptural (literary) typology that reflects underlying fulfilment and theomorphic typologies.

§1.4.3 Christology in Mark and the miracles

Understandably, Mark's Christology has been a 'preoccupation' of Markan scholars.[65] With the recognition that the miracles contribute to the Gospel's christological agenda the challenge becomes defining and analysing what that contribution is. Wilhelm Wrede's influential *Das Messiasgeheimnis in den Evangelien* (1901) moved the focus of scholarship from the historicity of the miracles to their Christological implications.[66] In Wrede's analysis the Markan miracles revealed Jesus' identity as Son of God and Messiah, but this identity and the miracles were kept secret until after the resurrection.[67] Following Wrede, Dibelius modified the messianic secret into a way of resolving the apparent tension between the powerful Jesus of the miracles and the suffering Jesus of the cross.[68] Theodore Weeden then extended this idea by arguing that the powerful Jesus was an apostolic heresy which the Gospel contradicts by subordinating it to an alternative tradition based on the suffering Jesus.[69]

Edwin Broadhead argues, 'Because form and redaction studies ultimately seek an object behind the text, these approaches have failed to give proper attention to the narrative form and function of the Gospel stories'.[70] Broadhead's own study uses narrative analysis to maintain a focus on the text of the Gospel and understands the Gospel text as the 'Christian kerygma' itself, not something from which the kerygma has to be distilled.[71] He also recognizes that the miracle accounts are not focused on acts of power but oriented to other concerns: 'a dynamic and multifaceted characterization of Jesus' and 'corollary issues of discipleship and opposition to Jesus'.[72] Broadhead's monograph covers all the Markan miracles and so is not able to give detailed attention to each miracle. He also does not systematically consider possible scriptural backgrounds for the miracles.

This study will focus on the 'dynamic and multifaceted characterization of Jesus' within the the Markan miracles, but with detailed attention to the scriptural background of that characterization. In this way, Mark's characterization of Jesus ceases to be simply the manner in which Jesus is portrayed as an actor in the Gospel narrative but becomes a means of asserting Jesus' eschatological and theomorphic identity via typological allusion to the scriptures.

---

[65] Telford 2009: 17.
[66] Wrede 1901/1971.
[67] Wrede 1971: 80, 114.
[68] Dibelius 1971: 230–1.
[69] Weeden 1971: 159–62.
[70] Broadhead 1992: 22.
[71] Broadhead 1992: 24.
[72] Broadhead 1992: 216.

Equally, Mark's Gospel and its miracle accounts have often had a pivotal role in more general discussion of New Testament Christology. This study seeks to engage the contemporary early high Christology debate at the point where Mark's miracles play an important role. This is most apparent in the work of Richard Bauckham,[73] and, directly contesting Bauckham's work, Daniel Kirk.[74] The methods of Bauckham and Kirk are similar, in that they both construct a paradigm from Jewish literature to then apply to Mark. I will argue that when these paradigms are applied in exegesis of Mark's Gospel they can obscure features of the Markan text and mislead the exegete from their stated goals. So, this study will examine and critique the use of Mark's Gospel's miracle accounts in the current early high Christology debate and attempt to offer a constructive way forward.

A brief orientation to the approaches of Bauckham and Kirk regarding the Christology of Mark is now in order.

§1.4.4 Richard Bauckham's divine identity

Bauckham, in his seminal study *God Crucified*, republished in *Jesus and the God of Israel*, seeks to move beyond the traditional Christological categories of 'functional' and 'ontic', and proposes the category of 'divine identity'.[75] For Bauckham, the early Jews understood there to be an 'absolute distinction between God and all other reality'.[76] This is primarily God's unique status as creator and sovereign,[77] thus 'the highest possible Christology [is] the inclusion of Jesus in the unique divine identity'.[78] Importantly, divine identity focuses on *who* God is rather than *what* God is; that is, identity as opposed to divine nature or essence.[79]

In Bauckham's discussion of the Gospel of Mark he writes, 'A purely functional account of Jesus' divinity in this Gospel is not adequate; rather Mark shares with early Christian writers in general … a Christology of divine identity'.[80] He also writes, 'Throughout the narrative, Mark provides indications for his readers that Jesus does not merely act on God's behalf … but actually belongs to the divine identity'.[81]

For Bauckham,

> The culmination of these indications comes in Jesus' words to the high priest (14:62), where Jesus' claim to be seated beside God on the cosmic throne from which God rules all things can only be, from a Jewish theological perspective, a claim to share in the unique divine identity of the God who alone rules over all things.[82]

---

[73] Bauckham 2008, 2017.
[74] Kirk and Young 2014; Kirk 2016.
[75] Bauckham 2008: x.
[76] Bauckham 2008: 20, 157.
[77] Bauckham 2004: 208, 211; 2008: 19, 154.
[78] Bauckham 2008: 19.
[79] Bauckham 2008: 154.
[80] Bauckham 2008: 264–5.
[81] Bauckham 2008: 265.
[82] Bauckham 2008: 265.

Bauckham's comments on Mark are, unfortunately, brief and Mark's Gospel is not a primary focus in his work. At this point it suffices to observe that Bauckham argues for the category of *divine identity*, which he considers to be representative of the early Jewish theological perspective, and proposes that membership of this category is indicated in texts by the twin criteria of creation and sovereignty. It must then be asked whether such a paradigm is applicable to Mark's miracles.

In Mark's depiction, Jesus transcends ordinary humanity. He is able to command demons and angels (Mark 5:1–20; 13:27), to shine with heavenly glory (9:2–7; 13:26), and has a unique and privileged position at the eschaton (8:38–9:1; 14:62). For Bauckham, and other proponents of divine identity Christology, Jesus' divinity in Mark is not simply that of an exalted human, however highly exalted, but is a divinity that brings Jesus into the identity of Israel's God. In this conception, there is all of heaven and earth, including angels and patriarchs, on one side of the line, and then on the other side there is God and Jesus of Nazareth. Jesus, if divine, is not a second creator god, but shares in the God of Israel's divine identity.[83]

Prior to Mark at least some Christians were redefining the *Shema* to incorporate Jesus (1 Cor. 8:6). This redefinition included Jesus in the sovereignty of Israel's God ('one Lord, Jesus Christ'), in the creation of heaven and earth ('Jesus Christ, through whom are all things'), and even sustaining of existence ('and through whom we exist').[84] The same thought is apparent in Col 1:15–20 and Heb 1:1–3. In all three passages there is no sense that something controversial is being promoted or defended. Rather these assertions of Jesus' inclusion in the divine identity are given as the premises on which further arguments will be made.[85]

On the one hand, such statements exalt Jesus' status well beyond the pattern of the divine men of Jewish traditions (e.g. Moses in Philo [e.g. *QE* 2.29, 40] or Simon ben Onias in Sirach [e.g. Sir 50:1–20]). On the other hand, such statements resemble, even if they exceed, Jewish concepts such as wisdom, Logos and Metatron, and the Angel of the Lord. While there may be an objective difference between a personification and an entity, in the imagination of early Jews there is no reason why a literary personification could not come to be interpreted as either an actual entity or serve as a model for another person.[86]

So Bauckham argues that Jesus becomes included in the creator God's identity in such texts as John 10:30; 1 Cor 8:6; Heb 1:1–4; Col 1:15–20.[87] Jesus is not presented as a creature but is instead the one through whom the creator makes all things, an essential aspect of the creator's identity. But can we make a similar argument from the Gospel of Mark?

Bauckham's writing on Mark is limited to a few brief treatments. However, his concept of divine identity has been applied to Mark's miracles by other scholars, the most pertinent of whom for this study is Richard Hays.

---

[83] Bauckham 2008: x; Grindheim 2012: 149.
[84] Capes 2018: 120, 137; Tilling 2015: 82–6; Bauckham 2008: 97–104, 141, 210–18.
[85] Chester 2011: 36–7.
[86] Contra Gathercole 2006: 209.
[87] Bauckham 2004: 220–8.

Hays applies his intertextual method developed in his earlier work on Paul to the four canonical Gospels.[88] Hays argues that Mark's Christology cannot be reduced to propositional assertions. He writes: '[Jesus'] mysterious identity is suggested through narrative figuration rather than asserted by means of direct statement.'[89] As a result,

> The 'meaning' of Mark's portrayal of the identity of Jesus cannot be rightly stated in flat propositional language; instead, it can be disclosed only gradually in the form of narrative, through hints and allusions that project the story of Jesus onto the background of Israel's story.[90]

Hays is also explicit that his work is not a defence of an 'early high Christology'.[91] However, he does employ Bauckham's category of divine identity in his interpretation of individual Gospel episodes. Consequently, Bauckham, among others, considers Hay's work to be a vindication of the divine identity hypothesis. Bauckham states,

> One of the most important aspects of Richard Hays's new book is his demonstration, on the basis of the scriptural echoes in each Gospel, that all four canonical Gospels propound a 'high' Christology or, it would be better to say, a Christology of divine identity.[92]

I will argue, however, that Hays' study of Mark's use of scripture is hindered by his use of the category of divine identity and the results do not so much demonstrate divine identity Christology in Mark's miracles, but rather call into question its applicability to Mark.[93]

§1.4.5 Daniel Kirk's category of exalted human figures

Daniel Kirk's book *A Man Attested by God* (2016) is positioned against divine identity Christology.[94] He argues for 'an alternative paradigm for assessing the Christology of the Synoptic Tradition', which recognizes that in early Jewish literature God can share divine roles and humans can participate in the divine identity.[95] Kirk states that his exalted human Christology should be considered a 'high' Christology 'because humans can be depicted as the very embodiment of God, God's visible representative, God's voice, the exhibition of God's rule and majesty'.[96] Likewise it can be considered a 'divine' Christology because of humanity being made in God's image.[97] However, Kirk's usage

---

[88] Hays 2016; for his earlier works on Paul see Hays 1989, 2005.
[89] Hays 2016: 76.
[90] Hays 2016: 103.
[91] Hays 2016: 7.
[92] Bauckham 2017a: 21.
[93] No judgement about Hays' wider work and/or divine identity regarding the other canonical Gospels is implied here, as to do so would go well beyond the scope of this study.
[94] See especially his critiques of recent High Christology proposals, Kirk 2016: 16–38.
[95] Kirk 2016: 2.
[96] Kirk 2016: 4.
[97] Kirk 2016: 4.

is to 'restrict the label "divine Christology" to the position that sees Jesus as inherently constitutive of God, rather than contingently entailed in God through special creation or anointing'.[98]

Thus, Kirk's approach seeks to fit the synoptic Gospels within a substantially different framework of divinity to Bauckham. In this framework, human beings are already, to a limited extent, divine, and can become or be made more divine in the right circumstances. Thus, while Bauckham's paradigm of divinity is a binary concept, Kirk's paradigm presumes a gradient divinity. Within that gradient divinity, however, there is still a binary distinction to be made: Jesus is divine only as a matter of degree, but not in the absolute sense of divine identity. Jesus may be more divine than a regular human, but not as divine as God. Because of this Jesus remains essentially human. Kirk seeks to demonstrate this by reference to other human figures who were given divine attributes in early Jewish literature, and presents Jesus as one of a type of idealized, exalted human figures.

While Kirk analyses the three synoptic Gospels, my focus here is limited to his work on Mark. Kirk's discussion of the Gospel of Mark concludes:

> I have tried to establish throughout that for Mark's Jesus the 'secret' of his identity is truly a messianic secret and not a divine secret . . . Jesus exorcises, heals, and rules the created order. The son of man is the Human One who exercises the wide-ranging rule originally envisioned for Adam and then David and Israel. The kingdom of God draws near when Jesus comes on the scene as the human king of the kingdom.[99]

Note the significance of exorcism, healing and nature miracles to Kirk's account of Mark. He recognizes the Christological centrality of the miracles in Mark's Gospel. For Kirk these manifest not Jesus' divininty but his humanity as fulfilment of Adam and David. Thus, the question is raised as to whether Kirk's category does justice to Mark's presentation of Jesus. I will argue that Kirk's paradigm serves to obscure Mark's particular scriptural allusions and is not sufficient to explain Mark's portrayal of Jesus.

§1.5 Reading Mark as narrative literature

In arguing for the significance of typology to the Gospel of Mark an implicit claim is made regarding the nature of the Gospel as a work of literature. For much of the history of critical scholarship Mark was considered to be 'basically an unlettered religious enthusiast who wrote in simple Greek'.[100] James Edwards has compiled a revealing selection of judgements on Mark's literary merits:[101] For Günther Dehn, Mark was 'neither a historian nor an author. He assembled his material in the simplest manner

---

[98] Kirk 2016: 4.
[99] Kirk 2016: 574.
[100] Donahue and Harrington 2005: 12.
[101] Edwards 1989: 194.

thinkable.'¹⁰² For Rudolf Bultmann, 'Mark is not sufficiently master of his material to be able to venture on a systematic construction himself'.¹⁰³ And still into the seventies, Etienne Trocmé could write: 'The point is settled: the author of Mark was a clumsy writer unworthy of mention in any history of literature.'¹⁰⁴ To those three, I would add Wrede's excoriation: '[Mark] did not think through from one point in his presentation to the next ... Not by a single syllable does he indicate that he desires to see two facts brought into connection which he happens to tell one after the other.'¹⁰⁵

On the other hand, as early as 1959 the literary critic Helen Gardner wrote of a recent development that 'the literary problems of the New Testament are discussed in terms in which poetry is discussed, and we have recently been asked to consider St. Mark ... as having written what is from the literary point of view, "more of a poem than a treatise".'¹⁰⁶ In the late seventies a decisive point was reached when Norman Perrin, a highly regarded redaction critic, admitted that 'less than justice is being done to the text of the Gospel as a coherent text with its own internal dynamics'.¹⁰⁷ Instead he argued for a literary critical approach to Mark: 'One of the consequences of a literary-critical concern for the text of Mark as a totality is a concern for the meaning for Mark himself of the terms he uses and the incidents he narrates.'¹⁰⁸

Since then, such a literary critical approach has become increasingly mainstream. Telford, writing a summary of Markan scholarship in 2009, states that, 'A significant feature of Markan studies in the last quarter of the century is the emphasis on *Mark as literature,* an orientation that has rivalled, if not eclipsed, its treatment as history'.¹⁰⁹

Of course, the older methods of redaction criticism, form criticism, source criticism and composition criticism are themselves technically forms of literary criticism.¹¹⁰ Within the study of Mark's Gospel, however, 'literary criticism' usually signifies an approach which is in opposition to the way the other critical methods tend to 'break up the narrative in order to get at the questions they pursue'.¹¹¹ The other approaches mentioned are generally termed in current Markan scholarship as *historical* methods in opposition to *literary* methods.¹¹² Literary critics argue that the so-called historical

---

¹⁰² Dehn 1953: 18.
¹⁰³ Bultmann 1963: 350.
¹⁰⁴ Trocmé 1975: 72.
¹⁰⁵ Wrede 1971: 132.
¹⁰⁶ Gardner 1959: 82. She clarifies at 102–3: 'The contrast between a poem and a treatise is a contrast between one manner of discourse and another: between language used to express an imaginative apprehension, whether of events, person, or experiences, and language used for logical discourse and argument, or to give information ... [Mark] presents us with a sequence of events and sayings which combine to create in our minds a single complex and powerful symbol, a pattern of meaning ... St. Mark is called a "poet" because he was not concerned to narrate mere events, but to narrate meaningful events which compose a meaningful whole.' Although Gardner does not cite her source, the context, in which she refers several times to Austin Farrer, suggests that she is almost certainly paraphrasing Farrer 1951: 30.
¹⁰⁷ Perrin 1976: 120.
¹⁰⁸ Perrin 1976: 124.
¹⁰⁹ Telford 2009: 8.
¹¹⁰ Gardner 1959: 97; Broadhead 1992: 22.
¹¹¹ Rhoads 1982: 412; also Gardner 1959: 97–8; Marxsen 1979: 25.
¹¹² Telford 2009: 41; Winn 2016: 14.

methods' atomization of the text can work to obscure a work's narrative effect.[113] The historical methods have also been critiqued for using (often conjectural) factors from outside of the text to interpret the theological intention of the Gospel text.[114]

What Markan scholars tend to call a literary-critical approach may be more precisely termed narrative criticism, in that it seeks to treat the Gospel as a coherent unified narrative and study its structure and message as a whole work.[115] Such an approach need be no less historical than, for example, redaction criticism, since the final form of the text, the intention of its putative author, and its impact on its first audiences, are no less historical questions than that of how the work came to be.

This study does not seek to consider Mark as literature in opposition to or apart from historical concerns. It intends to apply narrative criticism within a particular historical setting to make a historical argument.[116] As will be shown in the next chapter, the literary typology I will argue for is an approach to composition observable within the historical era of Mark's composition. By observing how the Markan narrative works, by treating it as a unified and coherent whole and by paying attention to certain literary features, I hope to be able to identify what those literary features would have meant to Mark's ideal readers (discussed below) in the Gospel's historical context. In particular, like Adam Winn, 'I am committed to the notion that the theological content of Mark is embedded in and inseparable from the narrative itself'.[117] Thus the historical question of accessing the meaning of the miracle accounts requires both an understanding of the individual episodes as coherent narratives, and how they contribute to, are arranged in and informed by the larger narrative of the whole Gospel.[118]

§1.5.1 Genre

One indication of the validity of a typological approach to Mark comes through consideration of the Gospel's genre. The genre of Mark has long been a contested issue. Increasingly it has been recognized that the genre classifications of scholarship are not always well adhered to by the texts being studied.[119] Consequently, Mark's genre should not be conceived of in precise taxonomic categories. Genre categories for early Jewish and Christian works should be understood to be 'fuzzy' or prototypical rather than taxonomic.[120] Whatever led Mark to give the Gospel the form it has taken, it is not to be supposed he consciously set out to either create a new genre or conform rigidly to a pre-existing one. Rather, the particular examples of various genres which he, as a literate person, would have encountered, were models on which he could draw in the process of composition.

---

[113] Gardner 1959: 107; Petersen 1978: 118.
[114] Winn 2016: 14.
[115] Rhoads and Michie 1982: 2–4.
[116] For a similar approach see, Winn 2016: 24.
[117] Winn 2016: 24; see also Reid 1994: 427; Boring 1999: 471.
[118] Cf. Twelftree 1999: 58; Winn 2016: 15.
[119] Dell 2020: 40–1.
[120] On this distinction see Newsom 2005; Shively 2018. Both Newsom and Shively build their work on Rosch 1975.

Mark wrote a story. That story resembles in some respects a Graeco-Roman *bios*;[121] or a Graeco-Roman history;[122] in other respects, a Jewish apocalyptic work;[123] in still other respects, Jewish sacred history (i.e. the Elijah–Elisha cycle from 1–2 Kings).[124] It is not necessary to choose one over the others as Mark's genre. Rather, we can see the contributing influence of various genres as Mark writes the earliest 'Gospel'.[125] The Gospel of Mark thus becomes the prototype for a new genre.

That said, while Mark may have drawn on many genres and should not be defined by just one, Mark does clearly position his Gospel vis-à-vis a particular corpus. As Collins argues, 'the author has created an eschatological counterpart of an older biblical genre, the foundational sacred history'.[126] While Mark may have been influenced by other literature in the formation of the Gospel, there is only one group of works which is explicitly cited. In fact, Mark begins with a citation from the Jewish scriptures (Mal 3:1; LXX Isa 40:3; Mark 1:2-3) and attributes the events around Jesus, especially his climactic suffering and death, to the fulfilment of the scriptures (e.g. Mark 7:6; 9:12-13; 11:17; 14:21, 27, 49).

This is not to create an artificial division between Jewish and Graeco-Roman literature.[127] It is, however, to recognize the literary background specifically indicated by the Gospel text. In this study, Graeco-Roman miracle stories will be considered as examples of how such stories were told in the ancient world, and such conventions certainly influenced Jewish authors to varying degrees and may well have influenced Mark. Especially when these conventions are not followed, we are entitled to look for more specific influences from the Jewish scriptures.

The Gospel, then, is self-consciously positioned within a wider narrative of the Jewish scriptures and eschatological hope. Mark is not writing a commentary on the scriptures. Mark writes the story of Jesus' life and death in such a way as to portray it as a continuation and fulfilment of the scriptures. One of the ways this continuation and fulfilment is expressed is through the use of a literary typology that presents Jesus as the recapitulation and escalation of prior salvation historical events. Thus, typology complements and reinforces Mark's genre.

§1.5.2 Implied/Ideal reader

I consider typology primarily as a mode of production rather than a mode of reception.[128] Typology has meaning for the author, whether or not the audience is able to discern it. That said, Mark's Gospel implies that its expected readers had some ability to discern scriptural typology.

---

[121] Talbert 1977; Burridge 1992; Reid 1994: 431; Collins 2007: 22–33; Bond 2015: 54–56, 2019: 425–42.
[122] Reid 1994: 432; Collins 2007: 33–42.
[123] Hartman 1966; Boomershine 1989.
[124] Brodie 1981, 2000; Roth 1988; Winn 2010.
[125] Collins 2007: 42–3.
[126] Collins 2007: 1.
[127] See Foster 2015: 99.
[128] I take this distinction from the helpful discussion in Witherington 2017: 460–1.

Mark's first audience, and especially its levels of literacy and knowledge of the scriptures, is largely unknown to us. The construct of an *implied* reader serves to reveal 'the author's *perception* of the intended audience, including how that perception shaped the author's strategies for communicating with his audience'.[129] Similarly, the *ideal* reader is a literary-critical concept that 'is implicit in the text and is distinct from any actual reader, ancient or modern. The ideal reader is a reconstruction of all the appropriate responses suggested or implied by the text'.[130]

Some of the strongest clues in Mark as to the Gospel's ideal reader are moments when the Gospel narrative seems to address the reader directly: 'let the reader understand' (Mark 13:14); 'Let anyone with ears to hear listen!' (4:9). With such asides, the Gospel informs its readers to expect signification beyond the literal, surface meaning of the text. In the case of 13:14, the abomination that causes desolation is an apocalyptic scriptural symbol (Dan 9:27; 11:31; 12:11) of something the reader is supposed to be able to interpret as a sign of imminent events. In the case of 4:9, the cryptic meaning of the parable is not given to the crowd (even though it is explained in 4:10-20 to the disciples) but only to those with 'ears to hear'. Again, the elements of the parable (e.g. sower, seed, soils) symbolically represent something else (e.g. preacher, word, hearers). These symbols are likely based on Jewish traditions around God's eschatological judgement (traditions possibly also preserved in 4 Ezra 4:26-32; 8:37-45; 9:31-37),[131] in particular a tradition on Exodus theophanies where God says 'behold, I sow my Law in you' (4 Ezra 9:31).[132] The ideal reader also needs to have 'ears to hear' in order to understand the subsequent parables, which are not explained but also contain significant scriptural motifs.[133]

Joel Marcus argues that the rhetoric of the Gospel assumes Christian belief, especially as the call narratives give no motivation or benefit for following Jesus (1:16-20; 2:13-17).[134] If the Gospel assumes initiation into the Christian community, then it may also assume familiarity with the scriptures.[135] Dean Chapman points out that at the beginning of the Gospel implicit clues are given regarding the identity of John the Baptist as the new Elijah (Mal 4:5; 1 Kgs 1:8; Mark 1:1-7), and that these clues require a high level of scriptural knowledge to interpret.[136]

In both modern and ancient literary theory there is a recognized potency in 'gaps, blanks, indeterminacies, vacancies and negations' which stimulate the reader to supply meaning.[137] Repeated listening or reading allows more subtle allusions to be discovered.

---

[129] Stanley 1997: 57, emphasis original. See also Fowler 1981: 152, 1991: 33.
[130] Rhoads 1982: 422; Rhoads and Michie 1982: 137. See also Fowler 1991: 36-40.
[131] Drury 1985: 26-27, 52-53; Marcus 2000: 296.
[132] Trans. E. M. Metzger, OTP 1.545; Drury 1985: 28.
[133] E.g. Mark 4:21 alludes to Psalm 119:105; Mark 4:24-25 alludes to Prov 11:24; Mark 4:4:26-29 alludes to Isa 17:5-6; 18:5; Micah 4:12; Joel 3:13; Mark 4:30-32 alludes to Ezek 17:23; 31:6; Dan 4:18. See discussion in Marcus 2000a: 314-31.
[134] Marcus 2000: 28; also Bond 2019: 52.
[135] Exactly which scriptures they would be familiar with, is not certain, as will be discussed in the next chapter.
[136] Chapman 1993: 192.
[137] Wright 1990: 182; see also Hays 1989: 155; Moyise 2000: 18-19; Allison 2005: 76.

Such allusions, as the next chapter will discuss, are a well-attested feature of ancient Graeco-Roman and early Jewish writings.

Jesus rebukes the Sadducees in Mark 12:24, 'Is not this the reason you are wrong, that you know neither the scriptures (τὰς γραφὰς) nor the power (τὴν δύναμιν) of God?' For the reader to agree with this critique they must belong to a community that both knows the scriptures and God's power at work among them. Here, two themes of this study, scripture and miracles, are shown to belong together within the epistemology of Mark's Jesus, and consequently of Mark's ideal readers.

Mark's ideal reader is able to comprehend the symbolic and allusive significance of words and events relayed by the narrative. As Allison argues, 'an alluding text is a presuming text'.[138] Essential to this comprehension is familiarity with the Jewish scriptures, which have from the start of the Gospel been given as the key to the meaning of the unfolding narrative.[139] One way in which an event can be given a developed symbolism, or in which an allusion can be extended, is through literary typology. Mark's ideal reader would both recognize such typologies and find them meaningful. This is the kind of reader 'we must be willing to become, at least temporarily, in order to experience the narrative in the fullest measure'.[140]

§1.5.3 Intertextuality

Literary typology is a form of intertextuality, as it works to establish a relationship between two texts.[141] In the following study I will generally avoid using the word *intertextuality* because it is a contested term with a range of possible implications.[142] However, many recent works on biblical intertextuality are very useful for this project and will be used without bias.

Telford notes that within literary-critical approaches to Mark, 'Particular attention has been paid to intertextuality'.[143] The work of Richard Hays is generally credited with bringing discussion of intertextuality into the mainstream of biblical scholarship. It has been frequently noted, however, that Hays' is a particular form of intertextuality that in many ways has co-opted a *term* from literary theory and used it in a way diametrically opposed to the original intention.[144]

On the other hand, the comparison of ancient texts as parallels, influences or sources which explain or interpret features of the later text has always been a component of biblical scholarship. So, for example, the previously mentioned work of Dibelius and Bultmann argued that Gospel tradents assimilated Jesus to Hellenistic divine-men, which is to posit an intertextual relationship of influence from the Graeco-Roman

---

[138] Allison 2000: 21.
[139] Hays 2016: 10; Kirk 2016: 44.
[140] Fowler 1991: 33.
[141] Allison 1993: 6, 2000: 190–1; Young 1997a: 154.
[142] Porter 1997: 84–5.
[143] Telford 2009: 8, emphasis original.
[144] Porter 1997: 84–5; Foster 2015: 98; Dell 2020: 43. As Julia Kristeva complains, 'this term has often been understood in the banal sense of "study of sources"' (1986: 111).

myths of wonder workers on the Gospel.[145] More recently the scriptures and traditions of Second Temple Judaism are usually considered the most pertinent context.[146] But again, this approach is not new. Examples of those doing 'intertextual' work with Jewish texts before Hays' *Echoes of Scripture in the Letters of Paul* (1989) or the term was even apparently coined by Julia Kristeva (1966)[147] could be multiplied.

In Hays' work *intertextuality* denotes the capacity of texts to allude to and echo earlier texts and generate meaning by doing so. In Hays' terminology an *echo* is a lighter, more diffuse, resonance than an allusion.[148] It is this literary characteristic of allusion and echo which most biblical studies that are specifically *intertextual* focus on.[149] Mark's ideal reader, as discussed above, is assuredly an intertextual reader. That is, someone who is able and willing to interpret the Gospel in dialogue with the scriptural texts of Judaism.

That said, one significant issue with Hays' approach, is the assumption 'that Old Testament texts have a relatively stable, patent meaning, and this meaning is in view when used by New Testament authors'.[150] Rather, NT use of scripture was conditioned, as Donald Juel puts it, by 'a vast network of exegesis to which we have only limited access'.[151] Not just scriptural *texts* but Jewish *traditions* of interpretation available in the first century must be understood to be part of any intertextuality between the NT and the Jewish scriptures, if we are concerned in any way with historical authorial intent.[152] Because our access to those traditions is incomplete, conclusions regarding how those traditions influence the Gospel's use of a scriptural text will often be tentative, but they still need to be considered.

§1.5.4 Terminology of textual relationships

One perennial issue in studies of biblical intertextuality, the study of the NT's use of scripture, and related concerns, is the lack of standardized technical terms and definitions.[153] It is necessary then to specify and define the terminology that will be used with this study.

A *correspondence* denotes any similarity between two texts, whether verbal, thematic, narrative or otherwise without asserting any necessary authorial intention, audience awareness, or hermeneutical significance. For example χαλκίον only occurs in Mark 7:4 in the NT and 1 Sam 2:14 in the LXX, a distinctive lexical correspondence. In this case there is no apparent significance in the similarity beyond helping establish lexical meaning. Michael Lyons writes, 'Vocabulary shared by two texts could be due to deliberate borrowing, but it could also be due to coincidence, unconscious dependence,

---

[145] Bultmann 1963: 218–44; Dibelius 1971: 70–103; on this see Evans 2001: 245–50.
[146] Hurtado 1988: 6; Evans 2001: 213–50.
[147] Kristeva 1974: 59–60.
[148] Foster 2015: 98.
[149] Moyise 2000; Emadi 2015.
[150] Huizenga 2009: 61; see also Foster 2015: 98; Bauckham 2017a: 22.
[151] Juel 1992: 2; see also Huizenga 2009: 61; Sandmel 1962: 6.
[152] See, e.g., Juel 1992: 31–57; Kugel 1998: 1–41; Evans 2001: 157.
[153] Porter 1997: 80; Kowalski 2020: 89.

or the use of stock vocabulary associated with a particular social setting or genre'.[154] The same applies, *mutatis mutandis*, to any correspondence in motif, theme, characterization or narrative structure.

A *quotation* or *citation* denotes an explicit use of scripture. Steve Moyise writes:

> Generally a quotation involves a self-conscious break from the author's style to introduce words from another context. There is frequently an introductory formula like καθὼς γέγραπται [e.g. Mark 9:13] or Μωϋσῆς λέγει [e.g. Rom 10:19] or some grammatical clue such as the use of ὅτι.[155]

A clear example of a quotation is Mark 11:17: 'He was teaching and saying, "Is it not written, My house shall be called a house of prayer for all the nations [Isa 56:7]? But you have made it a den of robbers [Jer 7:11]."'

Quotations of scripture are not always marked, as in Mark 11:9: 'Then those who went ahead and those who followed were shouting, "Hosanna! Blessed is the one who comes in the name of the Lord!"' This use of Psalm 118:25–26 is a quotation rather than an allusion because it is a discrete unit of speech, it has not been incorporated into a new discourse, and is also marked by the presence of transliterated Hebrew, ὡσαννά from הושיעה נה.

Scripture can also be *cited* without strong verbal parallels. An example of this is Mark 2:25: 'And he said to them, "Have you never read what David did when he and his companions were hungry and in need of food?"' This is a reference to events of 1 Sam 21:1–6.

An *allusion* is defined by Steve Moyise as 'usually woven into the text rather than "quoted", and is often rather less precise in terms of wording'. He goes on, 'Naturally, there is considerable debate as to how much verbal agreement is necessary to establish the presence of an allusion'.[156] Allusions, however, are not only a verbal phenomenon.[157] The imagery, themes and order of events in a narrative can also be allusive. Because of their implicit nature, from the perspective of the exegete, allusions must be further defined by probability.[158]

While it will always remain a matter of scholarly judgement, it is possible to justify an evaluation of allusive probability: the relative distinctiveness of a proposed allusion reduces the chance of it being coincidental; an allusion's contribution to the author's apparent intention increases the likelihood the author would have chosen to use such an allusion; and the presence of a pattern of allusion within the Gospel increases the plausibility of similar allusions elsewhere. Such considerations can be used to judge an allusion in ascending probability as *unlikely, possible, plausible* or *likely*.

Hays suggests, 'Quotation, allusion, and echo may be seen as points along a spectrum of intertextual reference, moving from the explicit to the subliminal.'[159] An *echo* is

---

[154] Lyons 2015: 642.
[155] Moyise 2005: 419.
[156] Moyise 2000: 419.
[157] Allusion is also prevalent feature of ancient Greek and Latin literature. See, e.g., Garner 1990; Currie 2016; Whitlatch 2016: 807–12.
[158] Kowalski 2020: 88–9.
[159] Hays 1989: 23.

defined by Steve Moyise as 'a faint trace of a text and might be quite unconscious, emerging from minds soaked in the scriptural heritage of Israel'.[160] In this study an echo is distinguished from an allusion by the impact it has had on the text. Echoes contribute to the 'feel' of the text. They resonate as part of the 'cultural encyclopedia' behind the text.[161] An echo could arise as an unintended coincidence of poetic language. By contrast quotations, citations and allusions appear, rather, as deliberate acts of an author. An echo is far more an affinity of thought or faint correspondence that is not essential to the literary effect but contributes to it in some way. It is reader, rather than author, oriented. A faint echo can have a faint effect on the reader. Determining an echo is not a matter of presence and absence, but of strength.[162]

§1.5.5 Narrative allusions

Beate Kowalski writes, 'Allusions to an entire narrative, to a specific literary genre or narrative pattern, are the ideal case of contextual allusions'.[163] It is just such allusions to entire narratives that concerns this study. This study compares narrative episodes from the Gospel of Mark with corresponding narratives from the Jewish scriptures. These specific scriptural narratives are not cited or quoted in the Gospel. Their presence is allusive. However, several factors lend credibility to the suggestion of such allusions.

Allusion to large and complex prophetic texts like the book of Isaiah would be discernible by only the scripturally educated and would require considerable feats of memory. On the other hand, vivid and dramatic stories of scriptural miracles (Jonah and the whale, David and Goliath, etc.) would be easily remembered and could freely circulate even among the uneducated. Correspondingly, allusions to such stories would be more likely to occur to an author and would be more easily recognizable to an audience than allusions to anything other than the most well-known sections of the prophetic books.

Steve Smith offers a helpful subdivision for scriptural references concerning their 'function and not their structure'.[164] He suggests that there are essential references, enriching references, compositional references, and unintentional references. An essential reference, like Zech 13:7 in Mark 14:27, must be understood by the reader to be a reference to scripture. In that instance Mark's point depends on the audience appreciating that it is a reference to scripture which Jesus fulfils. On the other hand:

> Enriching references are those that some readers will notice, thereby adding implicatures, but which other readers will miss without causing detriment to the central message of the text. An author wants readers to notice these echoes because it increases understanding, but the contextual effects are secondary to the essential ones.[165]

---

[160] Moyise 2015: 419.
[161] Huizenga 2009: 61. 'Cultural enyclodpedia' is a term derived from Eco 1986: 69–84, 1981: 43. See also Desogus 2012: 501–21.
[162] Moyise 2020: 184.
[163] Kowalski 2020: 98.
[164] Smith 2020: 150–1.
[165] Smith 2020: 150.

Mark's miracle stories make sense, and contribute to the Gospel, without the allusions to scripture being noticed. However, I will argue that recognizing the allusions enriches our reading of the text and clarifies some disputed issues. Further, if we recognize that Mark's Gospel would have been repeatedly read and possibly explained in the context of Christian gatherings, this would mean that even very subtle allusions could operate as enriching references.[166]

Smith's category of compositional references suggests that New Testament authors could use the scriptures in composing their texts without requiring or expecting the audience to perceive that use. Even without a hermeneutic based on the conviction that Jesus of Nazareth was the fulfilment of the scriptures, a scripturally literate author might be expected to use the scriptural miracles as literary models in the crafting of their own miracle narratives.

Here a *narrative allusion* is understood to be more than the use of a motif or word from another narrative, but the *compositional* use of one scriptural narrative to shape the Gospel account in a way that *enriches* the account and contributes to the Gospel's message. Where there is a narrative allusion, then, there will be multiple correspondences and evident hermeneutic benefit. What the miracles of Mark 4:35–6:45 evidence is the use of scriptural miracle narratives to recount Jesus' own miracles. I would contend that such narrative allusions do not require any distinctive lexical correspondences to be present. However, what we find in Mark's Gospel is that many such narrative allusions have been reinforced by the presence of distinctive vocabulary from the Greek tradition of the Jewish scriptures, herein referred to as the LXX or Septuagint.

§1.6 Reception history and Markan typology

This study presents some novel readings of Mark. Many of the typologies I will describe have been observed at least in part in the work of others, but some have not been noticed before. Is it really plausible that after nearly two thousand years of Christian reading there are still some aspects of Mark left to discover?

Simply and briefly, Mark has been a marginalized book in the history of interpretation.[167] In the patristic era Mark's Gospel was far and away the least cited of the Gospels and was the subject of no commentary by a major figure.[168] As Schildgen pithily states, 'the gospel was present in the canon but essentially absent from attention'.[169] The most likely reason was the perception that reading Matthew and Luke obviated the need for reading Mark.[170] When in the sixth century a commentary was written on Mark, it mainly consisted of recycled patristic commentary on Matthew and Luke.[171] A seventh-century commentary, falsely attributed to Jerome but likely the

---

[166] Watts 2020: 170.
[167] On the textual evidence for Mark's marginalization, compared to Matthew, in the second century see Becker 2013: 15–36.
[168] Kok 2015: 1–15.
[169] Schildgen 1999: 36.
[170] Schildgen 1999: 37; Kok 2015: 11.
[171] Lamb 2012.

work of an Irish abbot, is the first work we are aware of to treat Mark as a Gospel distinct from the other synoptics, but it is incomplete and cursory.[172] There is thus no evidence of formal and sustained consideration of Mark in the patristic era, and this neglect continued through the medieval era.

With the rise of modern critical scholarship there was a surge of interest in Mark as 'a simple, objective report of things as they had come to him in the tradition'.[173] Yet this view did not allow for Mark's own creative genius. Telford summarises early twentieth-century views of Mark as 'simplistic and indeed frequently patronizing'.[174] Against such a background, any subtler points Mark's Gospel may possess were in danger of being overlooked. For example, Mark's strange word choices were unlikely to be investigated as deliberate clues indicating scriptural passages because Mark was assumed to be a poor writer making mistakes.

In the 1960s the application of literary criticism to biblical studies led to the discovery of Mark as a literary work.[175] Instead of a collection of source material inexpertly stitched together, Mark was read as a story with a consistent point of view.[176] However, in general this literary criticism was not applied until much more recently to the question of Mark's use of the scriptures.[177] Rather, literary critics have been interested in the way that the Gospel works as a narrative and the effect it is intended to have on the reader.

Hays argues that the history of interpretation 'should rarely be used as a negative test to exclude proposed echoes that commend themselves on other grounds'.[178] This applies *a fortiori* to Mark as a work largely neglected within that history.

In short, Mark has been ignored for most of Christian history and underestimated for most of the history of critical interpretation. With the present convergence of a growing appreciation of Mark's literary genius and of renewed interest in the way the scriptures function as a subtext for the NT documents we may expect to discover significance in previously overlooked textual details and literary parallels.

§1.7 Procedure

Following this introductory chapter, I will survey some early Jewish writings which demonstrate the presence of typological thought, actions and literary production prior to and contemporaneous with the writing of Mark's Gospel (§2). Then a survey of Mark's narrative-structural and Christological high points (namely Jesus' baptism, transfiguration and passion) will be undertaken to show the presence and significance

---

[172] Cahill 1998.
[173] Bartlett 1922: 29; cited in Telford 1995: 1.
[174] Telford 1995: 1.
[175] Telford 1995: 10.
[176] Guelich 1989: xxii–xxv.
[177] A related issue is the relative neglect of the Septuagint as a source for anything other than textual criticism of the Hebrew Bible. See Gheorghita 2009: 165; McLay 2003: x, 1–2; Law 2013: 2–3.
[178] Hays 1989: 31; see also Hays 2005: 41–4; and Fredriksen 2020: 311; but see qualifying comments in Allison 2015: 7–8.

of narrative typology at these key moments in the Gospel (§3). Each of our selected miracles will then be considered individually in an exegetical chapter (§§4–7). These exegetical chapters will: 1) briefly consider the narrative and relevant issues that the existing scholarship has identified; 2) examine for comparison the literary conventions around that kind of miracle; 3) examine and evaluate the case for currently suggested scriptural backgrounds; and 4) identify and examine the strongest typological background for the passage in relation to its interpretive significance. A final chapter will consider the results in the context of contemporary discussion of Mark's Christology and draw any conclusions relevant to this study (§8).

§2

Reading Mark's miracles typologically

For when our wives conceive, they will not be recognized as pregnant until three months have passed, as also our mother Tamar did . . . And her intent saved her from all danger. Now let us do the same.

LAB 9:5–6

§2.1 The question of plausibility: Typology before Mark

In judging the merits of any proposed Markan typology an appreciation of the literary context in which the Gospel emerged is essential. As Goulder writes, 'The evangelists are not alone, and are not the first, in using typology as a means to a theological end'.[1] The following brief survey of various typologies in Jewish and Christian literature prior to and contemporaneous with Mark aims to establish the plausibility of Mark employing typological composition and interpretation. Firstly, Josephus will provide evidence that first-century Jews were inclined to think typologically both in their actions and in the production of texts. This will demonstrate that typological features of miracle accounts could have been part of the intention of an original event and could also be added or reinforced as the event is recounted or as a narrative is composed or redacted. Then, other Jewish literature, including the Jewish scriptures and the letters of Paul, will be surveyed to show examples of literary typology that predate or were contemporaneous with Mark's Gospel. This will demonstrate the availability of typological thinking to an author such as Mark and delineate some of the ways in which typology could be used in composition.

§2.2 Josephus as a witness to first-century typology

§2.2.1 The sign-prophets

Josephus records a number of first-century Palestinian 'ostensible prophets who, following a more or less fixed scenario, led people into the desert, where miracles of deliverance like those of Moses and his imitator, Joshua, were to be enacted'.[2] During the procuratorship of Antonius Felix (52–60 CE), Josephus recounts:

---

[1] Goulder 1964: 13.
[2] Allison 1993: 81; see also Evans 2002: 46–7.

167 With such pollution did the deeds of the brigands (τῶν λῃστῶν) infect the city. Moreover, imposters and deceivers called upon the mob to follow them into the desert (εἰς τὴν ἐρημίαν). 168 For they said that they would show them unmistakable marvels and signs (τέρατα καὶ σημεῖα) that would be wrought in harmony with God's design (κατὰ τὴν τοῦ θεοῦ πρόνοιαν). Many were, in fact, persuaded and paid the penalty of their folly; for they were brought before Felix and he punished them.

Ant. 20:167–8[3]

Josephus' account of these would-be prophets is hardly sympathetic, yet it is revealing concerning his perception of the motivation of these 'brigands'.[4] The signs and wonders (τέρατα καὶ σημεῖα) in the wilderness (ἐρημία) arguably evoke the miracles of the Exodus (LXX Exod 7:3, τὰ σημεῖά μου καὶ τὰ τέρατα)[5] and Conquest.[6] In his account of the same events in *Jewish War*, Josephus describes deceitful men and rogues 'under the pretence of divine inspiration'[7] (ὑπὸ προσχήματι θειασμοῦ), who persuade the people to be led into the wilderness (εἰς τὴν ἐρημίαν) so that in the wilderness God will show them 'signs of freedom' (σημεῖα ἐλευθερίας, *J.W.* 2:259). Although Josephus does not specify what these 'signs of freedom' might be, it is reasonable to conclude that they would resemble the events around the great liberative moment in scriptural history, the Exodus. This becomes more apparent in Josephus' accounts of Theudas, 'the Egyptian' and others.

In *Ant.* 20:97 Josephus tells how in the time of Cuspus Fadus (44–48 CE) one Theudas (cf. Acts 5:36), another would-be prophet, persuaded a large number of people to pack up their belongings and follow him to the river Jordan. There he would command the river to divide (προστάγματι τὸν ποταμὸν σχίσας) and make a passage (δίοδον) through it. The packing up of belongings is reminiscent of the Israelites' departure from Egypt.[8] According to Josephus, Theudas appears to have conflated the Exodus where Moses and YHWH divide the sea (Exod 14:21, σχίζω) with the crossing of the Jordan where the river rises in a heap (Josh 3:14–17).[9]

A nameless 'Egyptian' rebel (cf. Acts 21:38), in the time of Antonius Felix, also assumes the role of prophet (προφήτου πίστιν ἐπιθεὶς ἑαυτῷ, *J.W.* 2:261; προφήτης εἶναι λέγων, *Ant.* 20:169). But the Egyptian leads the people *out* of the wilderness (ἐκ τῆς ἐρημίας, *J.W.* 2:262) and to the Mount of Olives in order to assault Jerusalem (*J.W.* 2:262; *Ant.* 20:169). In Zech 14:4 the Mount of Olives is identified as a place of God's decisive eschatological action which may well have given some significance to the Egyptian's choice.[10] In one account (*J.W.* 2:261–3) the Egyptian leads the people by a 'circuitous

---

[3] Trans. Feldman, *Josephus* IX, LCL, 479–81.
[4] Josephus uses the term 'brigand' or 'robber' as a polemical term for political and religious partisans. See Hengel 1989: 41.
[5] See also LXX Exod 11:9, 10; Deut 4:34; 6:22; 7:19; 11:3; 29:2; 34:11; Ps 77:43; 104:27; 134:9; cf. Mark 13:22.
[6] Eve 2002: 305.
[7] H. St. J. Thackeray, *Josephus* II, LCL, (1927/56), 425.
[8] Hengel 1989: 230; Eve 2002: 298.
[9] Horsley 1985: 457.
[10] Horsley 1985: 459; Ben-eliyahu 2016: 31.

route' (περιάγω) which was possibly meant to reflect the circuitous route taken by Israel in the Exodus (cf. Exod 13:18),[11] or the Israelites' circuits around Jericho (Josh 6),[12] or even both. And the Egyptian seems inspired by Joshua and the conquest of Jericho (Josh 6) when he promises his followers that at his command the walls of Jerusalem will fall (ὡς κελεύσαντος αὐτοῦ πίπτοι τὰ τῶν Ἱεροσολυμιτῶν τείχη, *Ant.* 20:170).[13]

In the case of both Theudas and the Egyptian, they do not seek to replicate the scriptural stories exactly, but at the same time their intended actions unmistakably display the stamp of scriptural miracles. As Horsley writes, 'These actions of deliverance are understood as new, eschatological actions that typologically correspond to or are informed by the great formative acts of deliverance led by Moses and Joshua'.[14] They anticipate that God's intervention in the present will resemble God's previous acts.

Josephus tells of an 'imposter' (τινος ἀνθρώπου γόητος) from when Porcius Festus was procurator (60–62 CE), who promises his followers 'salvation and rest from troubles'[15] (σωτηρίαν αὐτοῖς ἐπαγγελλομένου καὶ παῦλαν κακῶν) if they are willing to follow him as far as the wilderness (μέχρι τῆς ἐρημίας, *Ant.* 20:188). Although there is no specific miracle promised here, the language is again suggestive of scriptural events and promises, and not simply human warfare. The place of the wilderness also seems significant here. Although the wilderness is an obvious place from which to stage guerrilla warfare, away from Roman garrisons and collaborators, it is also closely connected to the Exodus, the location for many scriptural miracles, and a commonality with the other sign-prophets.[16] The language of 'as far as' (μέχρι) perhaps suggests that the imposter hoped that once they reached the wilderness God would intervene. In fact, for all these 'sign-prophets' it is the Romans who intervene and, excepting the Egyptian who manages to flee, all are killed by Roman forces.

Finally, a weaver called Jonathan persuaded (ἀναπείθω) a number of people to go into the desert (εἰς τὴν ἔρημον) in search of signs and portents (σημεῖα καὶ φάσματα, *J.W* 7:438). Josephus even tells how Cyrenian Jewish nobility reported Jonathan's 'exodus' (ἔξοδος) to governor Catallus (*J.W.* 7:439). What was not clear in the other accounts is explicit here: Jonathan's followers are easily overcome because they are unarmed (ὁ δ' ἱππέας τε καὶ πεζοὺς ἀποστείλας ῥᾳδίως ἐκράτησεν ἀνόπλων, *War* 7:440).[17] Horsley argues that the same is likely to be true of Theudas and the Egyptian.[18] It seems likely that this Roman suppression of non-military popular prophetic movements often provoked renewed violence from Jewish fighters (e.g. *Ant.* 20.172).

Notwithstanding, these examples show that first-century Jews might plan and attempt to carry out actions that were analogous to events in scripture.[19] They are evidence that there appears to have been a popular climate of expectation for God's

---

[11] Allison 1993: 79.
[12] Barnett 1981: 683.
[13] Horsley 1985: 548–59; Hengel 1989: 231; Eve 2002: 302.
[14] Horsley 1985: 454.
[15] Feldman, *Josephus* IX, LCL (1965), 491.
[16] Hengel 1989: 232.
[17] Hengel 1989: 233. However, see Eve 2002: 307–10 for contrary view.
[18] Horsley 1985: 460.
[19] Collins 2010: 217–19.

intervention and that this intervention was expected to resemble God's great acts of the scriptural past.[20]

§2.2.2 Divine providence

Josephus also provides evidence for the theological convictions behind such typological action. The sign-prophets hoped that signs and wonders would occur according to God's foreknowledge (κατὰ τὴν τοῦ θεοῦ πρόνοιαν, *Ant.* 20:168), or, as Louis Feldman translates, 'in harmony with God's design'.[21] Josephus uses the word πρόνοια to express that God governs (ἐπιτροπεύω) and steers (κυβερνάω) the world (κόσμος) and is the one who 'holds its reins' (ἡνίοχος, *Ant.* 10.278).[22] For Josephus, a belief in God's providence (πρόνοια) is a fundamental belief of all Jews (*Ag. Ap.* 2.180). This generalization is supported by other contemporary texts (e.g. Rom 9:11–18; Wis 14:3; Philo, *Opif* 171–2).[23]

The difficulty of assessing someone else's motivations through a polemical source like Josephus must be recognized.[24] Yet, 'Josephus does not completely obscure the Jewish apocalyptic features of these prophetic movements with his Hellenistic terminology and personal hostility'.[25] Josephus grudgingly acknowledges the piety of these prophetic groups (χειρὶ μὲν καθαρώτερον, *J.W.* 2.258) and communicates that they, in common with himself, hold a firm belief in divine providence.[26]

Josephus uses πρόνοια 160 times in his corpus, sometimes for human planning but frequently for divine providence.[27] When his life is threatened by a shipwreck (*Life* 15), a suicide pact (*J.W.* 3.391), or when denounced by rivals in Rome (*Life* 425), it is the providence (πρόνοια) of God which allows him to escape. But Josephus' belief in providence was not solely based on personal experience. In *Ant.* 10.277–80 he makes the argument (against the Epicureans) 'that Daniel's ability to predict the future demonstrates that the course of history is preordained by God'.[28] For Josephus, scriptural predictions demonstrated both God's involvement in history and God's foresight regarding history.

In the NT the exact word πρόνοια is not used,[29] but the theology is comparable. God foreknows (πρόγνωσις, Acts 2:23; προγινώσκω, Rom 8:29) and predestines (προορίζω, Acts 4:28; 1 Cor 2:7) his plan (οἰκονομία, Eph 1:10) for human history. In the Gospels the same belief is expressed in the conviction that the scriptures are being fulfilled in the life, death and resurrection of Jesus of Nazareth (e.g. Mark 1:2–3; Matt 26:24; Luke 4:21; John 12:14).

---

[20] Barnett 1981: 679–97.
[21] Feldman, *Josephus IX*, 479.
[22] Spilsbury 2003: 7.
[23] Spilsbury 2003: 7.
[24] Horsley 1985: 444; Bond 2016: 150–51.
[25] Horsley 1985: 455.
[26] Horsley 1985: 456.
[27] See also similar uses of πρόνοια in 3 Macc 5:30; 4 Macc 13:19; 17:22; Wis 14:3.
[28] Spilsbury 2003: 7.
[29] Its cognate verb, προνοέω, is only used of human provision or forethought (see Rom 12:17; 2 Cor 8:21; 1 Tim 5:8).

§2.2.3 Josephus and the Prophet Jeremiah

Although Josephus is dismissive of the sign-prophets, he engages in similar typological identification in reflecting on his own life. Rather than Moses or Joshua, Josephus sees the pattern of some other scriptural figures being re-worked in his own life.

In *J.W.* 5.391-3 he explicitly compares himself to Jeremiah as a prophet trying to warn of destruction, but (according to him) Josephus' hearers treat him worse than did Jeremiah's.[30] Shaye Cohen states that in *Antiquities* 10, which paraphrases much of the book of Jeremiah, 'Josephus stresses precisely those parts of Jeremiah's life which parallel his own'.[31] Further, David Daube argues that 'Several of [Josephus'] details about Jeremiah have no basis in scripture or tradition but are intelligible as retrojections of what he himself did or suffered'.[32]

In Jer 38:17-26 there is no mention of the Temple in Jeremiah's conversation with king Zedekiah. But when Josephus retells this conversation (*Ant.* 10.126-8) the Temple is a prominent concern, as it is in Josephus' Jeremiah-like appeal to his countrymen (*J.W.* 5.362, 391, 406, 411). In Jer 40:1-5 when the Babylonian commander gives Jeremiah his liberty there is no mention of Baruch. But when Josephus recounts the story (*Ant.* 10.156-9) Jeremiah successfully pleads for his servant Baruch, just as Josephus interceded for his family, friends and former acquaintances (*Life* 418-21). When Josephus describes Jeremiah's prophecies concerning Jerusalem, he asserts that Jeremiah spoke of both the Babylonian destruction of Jerusalem and also the Roman conquest, 'what has happened now in our time' (τὴν νῦν ἐφ᾽ ἡμῶν γενομένην, Ant. 10:79).[33] For Daube, 'It is Josephus' blurring of himself and Jeremiah that causes him to see Lamentations – and doubtless, quite a few chapters of the book of Jeremiah – as envisaging his own experiences'.[34]

Josephus also describes Jesus ben Ananias (*War.* 6.300-9), who preached in the Temple, emulating and quoting Jeremiah (Jer 7:34; 13:27) and who, like Jeremiah, was physically persecuted for his behaviour (Jer 20:1-2).[35] Trumbower writes of Jesus ben Ananias and Theudas, 'each man ... thought that an example from the biblical past was occurring again in his own day. Each man consciously based his actions on a particular understanding of that ancient tradition.'[36]

It is a commonplace, even today, that someone who has nearly died and had an unexpected reprieve feels a new sense of purpose to their lives. Josephus' three near-death experiences (*J.W.* 3.391; *Life* 15, 425) could be expected to make him relate to those in scripture whose lives were saved for a divine purpose, especially those who, like Josephus, also received and interpreted dreams (*J.W.* 3.351-4; *Life* 208-10) and rose to high rank in the courts of foreign rulers. Daube compiles a number of possible influences from Josephus' life upon the stories of Joseph, Daniel and Esther-Mordecai

---

[30] Daube 1980: 20.
[31] Cohen 1982: 368.
[32] Daube 1980: 26.
[33] Cohen 1982: 368; see also Ralph Marcus, *Josephus* VI, LCL (1937/51), 200-1 note c.
[34] Daube 1980: 27.
[35] On this see Horsley 1985: 451.
[36] Trumbower 1994: 32.

in his *Antiquities*. Most immediately compelling is Daniel's use of an intermediary, Arioch, in Josephus' version of Dan 2:16 (*Ant.* 10.198–99). This detail could well reflect the way Titus facilitated Josephus' audience with Vespasian (*J.W.* 3.392–9). Likewise, the axe-wielding guards of Ahasuerus (*Ant.* 11.205), not mentioned in Esther, could reflect Vespasian's guards, of whom Josephus had direct experience (*J.W.* 4.629).[37]

It is apparent, then, that Josephus not only describes typological thinking in those he disapproves of but also performs it himself towards different ends. As Josephus identified himself with scriptural characters, small details were added (to their lives or his) to bring the analogy closer. Thus typology could operate in Josephus as a form of literary production, as the writer sought to strengthen perceived analogies between scriptural people and events and their contemporary counterparts.

§2.2.4 Typology in Josephus

The above survey of Josephus suggests that typological thinking is not restricted to one group or expression, but was apparently widespread within first-century Palestinian Judaism. Commoners-turned-oracular-prophets (Jesus ben Ananus), leaders of mass movements (e.g. Theudas) and educated erstwhile-Pharisees (Josephus), despite their considerable differences in expression, all possess broadly comparable convictions about God's providence and scripture. These convictions could be applied to concrete religious-political action or reflected in the production of texts. Thus, it is plausible that other first-century Jews, both individuals and groups, could have acted in ways that imitated scriptural stories and might assimilate stories that they identified with scriptural miracles to those same scriptures.

To transpose this conclusion to the Gospel of Mark, it is plausible that Jesus and his disciples could have acted in ways that imitated scriptural stories and that, in the oral and written transmission of the memories and traditions of Jesus, accounts of these acts might be (further) assimilated to those scriptural miracles to which they bore some analogy.

§2.3 Typology in early Jewish literature

§2.3.1 Hebrew scriptures

The Jewish Scriptures are the primary source which Mark cites, from which Mark quotes and to which Mark makes allusions. That some of the books that constitute this source make use of typological composition and interpretation provides one possible influence on Mark's use of typology.

Within the Hebrew Scriptures, alongside atomistic reuse of individual words and phrases without much attention to their wider literary context, there are also examples of the evocation of 'wider arguments or patterns'.[38] An example of this is Michael Lyons'

---

[37] Daube 1980: 27–32.
[38] Tooman 2020: 34.

suggestion that Psalm 22 employs the argument of Isaiah 54, 56–66.[39] This explains a distinctive feature of this psalm that connects 'deliverance from suffering to an eschatological outlook'.[40]

> Although Psalm 22 contains vocabulary associated with the individual Suffering Servant figure of Isaiah 40–55, it is contextualized in the psalm in a way that has been influenced by the argument of chaps. 54, 56–66, in which a righteous community (the 'servants') will suffer and be vindicated like the individual servant.[41]

Lyons notes the following correspondences between Isaiah 54, 56–66 and Psalm 22:

1. A righteous community (the servants/offspring, Isa 57:1) or a righteous individual (Ps 22:2–22) is persecuted.
2. They are both mocked for their trust in YHWH (Isa 66:5; Ps 22:8–9).
3. They are both vindicated (Isaiah 65:13–15; 66:2, 5–6; Ps 22:22–27).
4. The language of Psalm 22:30–31, 'and the one who did not keep himself alive, offspring will serve him' (ונפשו לא חיה זרע יעבדנו), appears to draw on the language of offspring and serving in Isaiah 54, 56–66 (e.g. for זרע Isa 61:9; 65:9, 23; 66:22; for עבד 54:17; 65:8–9, 13–15; 66:14).
5. Both texts share an eschatological outlook where YHWH is recognized by the nations (Isa 66:18; Ps 22:28) and YHWH's deeds are proclaimed to them (Isa 66:19; Ps 22:31–32).

Noticeably this 'argument' in both Isaiah and the Psalm has a narrative shape. Persecution and mockery are followed by vindication, offspring, and eschatological worship and proclamation of Israel's God.

An example of a larger-scale pattern is found in Genesis 1–11. There is an initial pattern of creation (1:1–2:24), fall and exile (3:1–23), family strife and a curse (4:3–16), two genealogies (4:17–5:32) and transgressed heavenly boundaries (6:1–4). This pattern is then repeated with variation: a re-creation (Gen 6:5–9:17), family strife and a curse (9:20–27), a genealogy (10:1–32), an attempt to transgress heavenly boundaries (11:1–9) and a second genealogy (11:10–26).[42] Thus within the repeated pattern, typologies can be seen to emerge. Hence Noah is a type of Adam. And the sinful heaven-to-earth transgression of the 'sons of God' finds its counterpart in the sinful earth-to-heaven intent of the builders at Babel.

Abram and Sarai's sojourn in Egypt (Gen 12:10–13:2) contains several correspondences with the larger story of Israel's Exodus. Abram and the nation of Israel both,

1. Migrate to Egypt in time of famine, Gen 12:10; 42–46.
2. Prosper while in Egypt, Gen 12:16; Exod 1:7.

---

[39] Lyons 2015; Tooman 2020: 33.
[40] Lyons 2015: 644.
[41] Lyons 2015: 650.
[42] Walsh 2001: 111–13; Tooman 2020: 34.

3. Pharaoh is afflicted with plagues because of his treatment of Sarai/Israel, Gen 10:17; Exod 7–12.
4. As a result, Pharaoh sends them away, Gen 12:20; Exod 12:31.
5. And they both leave with wealth and possessions, Gen 13:2; Exod 12:35, 38.

A separate but related correspondence occurs between Gen 15:7 and Exod 20:2 where there is a marked similarity in language:

| Gen 15:7 | אני יהוה אשר הוצאתיך מאור כשדים | I am the LORD who brought you from Ur of the Chaldeans |
| Exod 20:2 | אנכי יהוה אלהיך אשר הוצאתיך מארץ מצרים | I am the LORD your God, who brought you out of the land of Egypt |

Regarding these correspondences Walter Moberly argues, 'The point of this choice of language is presumably typological. As YHWH brought Israel out of Egypt, so YHWH brought Abraham out of Ur. Abraham's story is seen as a parallel to Israel's story, and Abraham in some sense personifies and embodies Israel's experience'.[43]

The account of Abraham's sacrifice of Isaac is framed by two key words: God's intention to test (נסה) Abraham and the resulting discovery that Abraham fears (ירא) God (Gen 22:12). Both these terms are significant in the account of Israel's own testing and fear of God (Exod 1:4; Deut 5:29; 8:2; 10:12–22). But the only other time they occur together is Exod 20:20, after the giving of the Decalogue, where Moses says 'God has come only to test (נסה) you and to put the fear (יראה) of him upon you so that you do not sin'. Abraham also provides a model for Israel by making his sacrifice at the place of God's choosing (Gen 22:2–3), which Israel will also be commanded to do (Exod 20:24; Deut 12:5). In this instance, Abraham's sacrifice of Isaac functions as an ethical type, an exemplar for Israel to imitate, a 'typological embodiment of Israel's obedience to Torah'.[44]

Perhaps the most significant character for typology in the Hebrew Bible is Moses. Dale Allison has demonstrated the influence of Moses on the scriptural portrayals of Joshua, Gideon, Samuel, David, Elijah, Josiah, Ezekiel and Jeremiah.[45] Here, I will briefly explore the way Joshua and the conquest of Canaan typologically corresponds to Moses and the Exodus.[46]

Both Moses and Joshua:

1. send spies into the land (Num 13; Josh 2);
2. are told the inhabitants of the land fear them and are 'melting away' (Exod 15; Josh 2);

---

[43] Moberly 1992: 143.
[44] Moberly 1992: 145.
[45] Allison 1993: 11–62. Allison goes on to discuss Moses typology within 4 Ezra, 2 Baruch and Rabbinic literature, 62–95.
[46] Allison 1993: 23–28; Fishbane 1985: 358–9.

3. lead Israel to celebrate the passover (Exod 12; Josh 5:10–13);
4. experience a theophany and are told to take off their shoes because they stand on holy ground (Exod 3; Josh 5);
5. successfully intercede when Israel sins (Deut 9; Josh 7);
6. win a battle by holding a certain position with their arms (Exod 17; Josh 8);
7. deliver similar farewell speeches, with a 'two ways' conclusion (Deut 1–34; Josh 23–24);
8. mediate a covenant which the people promise to obey (Exod 24; Josh 24).

This typology is rendered explicit in the text of Josh 3:7 'I [YHWH] will be with you as I was with Moses'; 4:14 'they stood in awe of him, as they had stood in awe of Moses'; and 4:22–24 'the LORD your God dried up the waters of the Jordan for you ... as the LORD your God did to the Red Sea'. For Allison, 'Surely it would be a dull or uninformed reader who does not recognize that the life of Joshua is to a significant degree a replay of the life of Moses'.[47] Psalm 114 makes the same connection between Moses and Joshua by the repeated juxtaposition of the fleeing (נוס) sea and turning (סבב) Jordan (Ps 114:3, 5). Fishbane argues, 'for the ancient liturgist these two historical moments were not thoroughly disparate events ... [but] a remanifestation of divine redemptive power'.[48]

In the prophetic literature there is an expectation of eschatological recapitulation in the typological reappearance of heroes, institutions and events from the past: a second David (Isa 11:1–5; Jer 23:5; Ezek 34:24),[49] a second Elijah (Mal 4:5), a second Temple (Ezek 40–48), a new covenant (Isa 61:8; Jer 31:33–34; Ezek 37:26), and a new creation (Isa 65:17ff.; 66:22; 11:1ff.; 65:23ff.; Jer 31:27–28; Ezek 34:25ff.; 36:35).[50]

Arguably the most prominent typology in the prophetic books is the figuring of the rescue from exile in Babylon as a 'new exodus'. This typology is made explicit at a number of points (e.g. Isa 11:15–16; 43:16–21; 48:20–21; 51:9–11; Jer 16:14–15; 23:7–8; Ezek 20:34–36; Hosea 9:3; 11:5, 11; Micah 7:14).[51] The reflection on a past deliverance might have been intended to encourage confidence in the anticipated deliverance, but it also served as a means of contrast to highlight features of the new against the old. Isaiah 52, for example, compares Assyrian oppression to Egyptian oppression (52:4). But in contradistinction to the hasty flight of Israel from Egypt (Exod 12:11; Deut 16:3), in the new exodus, 'you shall not go out in haste, and you shall not go in flight' (52:12). As Fishbane writes, 'The new exodus will therefore not simply be a remanifestation of an older prototype, but will have qualitative distinctions of its own'.[52] Notably in this instance, the new improves upon a less desirable aspect (the hasty flight) of the old.

---

[47] Allison 1993: 26.
[48] Fishbane 1985: 359–60.
[49] Westerholm and Westerholm 2016: 42.
[50] Foulkes 1994: 358–63.
[51] Fishbane 1985: 353, 361–2; Foulkes 1994: 354–6; Westerholm and Westerholm 2016: 42.
[52] Fishbane 1985: 364; see also Foulkes 1994: 355.

The new exodus is also dramatically wider in its redeeming scope. In Isa 19:19–25 language from Exod 3:7–10; 7:27; 12:23; 8:16–24 and Josh 24:5 is used in an 'audacious inversion and transfer of a national tradition of redemption to the very people – the Egyptians – who were its original enslaver'.⁵³ Ultimately, the Egyptians and even the Assyrians are included in the blessing of being God's people alongside Israel (Isa 19:23–25). Thus, what was once an act of particular salvation for Israel from oppressive Egyptians becomes, in the typological imagination of Isaiah, the pre-figuration of a universal salvation including Israel's former oppressors the Egyptians and Assyrians.

§2.3.2 Tobit

The book of Tobit, a romance most likely dating from 250–175 BCE, uses the patriarchal stories of Genesis for its 'basic plot and substructure'.⁵⁴ It contains a 'rich matrix of allusions and narrative mimicry' reusing the stories of the patriarchs, as well as Deut 31–32 and Job.⁵⁵

Among its allusive features,⁵⁶ the book's namesake, Tobit, displays many characteristics that correspond to the biblical patriarchs:

1. Tobit walks in righteousness like Abraham (Tob 1:3; 7:7; 9:6; Gen 15:6; 17:1; 24:40).
2. Like the patriarchs, Tobit prays (Tob 3:2–6; 11:14–15; 13:1–18; Gen 15:1–5; 18:22–33; 25:21–23).
3. Like Abraham, God tests Tobit (Tob 12:14; Gen 22:1) and both are found to fear God (Tob 14:2; Gen 22:12); and both live to an impressive old age (Tob 14:1; Gen 25:7).
4. Like Isaac, Tobit suffers blindness (Tob 2:10; Gen 27:1).
5. Like Jacob, Tobit summons his family for prophecy of the future and final instructions before he passes away (Tob 14:2; Gen 48–49).⁵⁷
6. Sarah, daughter of Raguel, is beautiful like Sarah, wife of Abraham (Tob 6:12; Gen 12:14); is also childless (Tob 3:9, 15; Gen 11:30); and also suffers the reproaches of family servants (Tob 3:7; Gen 16:4).⁵⁸

A further prominent example is the way Tobit 7:3–5 (especially in G¹, the shorter recension)⁵⁹ is modelled upon Gen 29:4–6:

---

⁵³ Fishbane 1985: 367.
⁵⁴ Helyer 2000: 1238–9.
⁵⁵ Tooman 2020: 29. See also Fitzmyer 2003: 35–6; Moore 1996: 20–1.
⁵⁶ See further Nowell 2005: 3–13; Portier-Young 2005: 14–27.
⁵⁷ Nowell 2005: 4–6.
⁵⁸ Nowell 2005: 6–7.
⁵⁹ The shorter recension is now, due to the finds at Qumran (4Q196–200), overwhelmingly considered to be the later text (see Fitzmyer 2003: 4–5; Moore 1996: 53–56). This is not an issue here as, in this instance, the shorter text simplifies and clarifies the longer one. It either reveals what was originally there, or demonstrates the tendency of the redactor to further assimilate the text to the biblical story of which it was already reminiscent.

Tob 7:3 G¹	LXX Gen 29:4
³ καὶ ἠρώτησεν αὐτοὺς Ραγουηλ **πόθεν ἐστέ ἀδελφοί** καὶ **εἶπαν** αὐτῷ **ἐκ τῶν** υἱῶν Νεφθαλι τῶν αἰχμαλώτων ἐν Νινευη	⁴ εἶπεν δὲ αὐτοῖς Ιακωβ **ἀδελφοί πόθεν ἐστὲ** ὑμεῖς οἱ δὲ **εἶπαν ἐκ** Χαρραν ἐσμέν
⁴ **καὶ εἶπεν αὐτοῖς γινώσκετε** Τωβιτ τὸν ἀδελφὸν ἡμῶν **οἱ δὲ εἶπαν γινώσκομεν**	⁵ **εἶπεν δὲ αὐτοῖς γινώσκετε** Λαβαν τὸν υἱὸν Ναχωρ **οἱ δὲ εἶπαν γινώσκομεν**
⁵ **καὶ εἶπεν αὐτοῖς ὑγιαίνει οἱ δὲ εἶπαν** καὶ ζῇ καὶ **ὑγιαίνει** καὶ εἶπεν Τωβιας πατήρ μού ἐστιν	⁶ **εἶπεν δὲ αὐτοῖς ὑγιαίνει οἱ δὲ εἶπαν ὑγιαίνει** καὶ ἰδοὺ Ραχηλ ἡ θυγάτηρ αὐτοῦ ἤρχετο μετὰ τῶν προβάτων …
⁶ καὶ ἀνεπήδησεν Ραγουηλ καὶ **κατεφίλησεν** αὐτὸν καὶ **ἔκλαυσε**	¹¹ καὶ **ἐφίλησεν** Ιακωβ τὴν Ραχηλ καὶ βοήσας τῇ φωνῇ αὐτοῦ **ἔκλαυσεν**

In both form and at points in exact wording (in bold), the arrival of Tobias at Raguel's house matches that of Jacob's meeting of Rachel.[60] Notably, although the conversation follows the same pattern, the roles of guest and host are reversed in Tobit, as it is the host, Raguel, who questions the travellers, whereas in Genesis it is Jacob, the visitor, that questions the shepherds at the well. In both passages there is a movement from conversation with a group to the recognition of a special individual.

At no point is the author of Tobit explicit about these literary typologies or why they are employed. Nowell suggests that this 'brings encouragement to its audience, Jews living in the Diaspora. God's promises to the ancestors have not failed; the ancient stories are still reflected in the daily lives of faithful people.'[61] Despite its appearance as romance, in this way the story of Tobit is itself an appropriation and interpretation of the scriptures for its contemporary audience. The typology employed has no sense of eschatological fulfilment but serves an ethical-rhetorical function to portray its heroes in the mould of previous scriptural characters.

§2.3.3 1 Maccabees

1 Maccabees was most likely written between 103 and 63 BC.[62] In pursuing its agenda to support the Hasmonean dynasty as legitimate priest-kings of Israel it employs literary typology to portray the Hasmoneans in the mould of biblical heroes.

The author of 1 Maccabees explicitly corresponds Mattathias with Phineas (1 Macc 2:26; cf. Num 25:1–15). As Goldstein comments, 'Both words and content follow the model.'[63] Both Phineas and Mattathias operate at a time of God's wrath against the nation (Num 25:3; 1 Macc 1:64). On seeing wickedness, they both rise and leave (1 Macc 2:1–6; Num 25:7). They both kill a man in the act of committing an offending

---

[60] Fitzmyer (2003: 228) considers the 'phraseology of [Tobit 7:6] dependent on the Hebrew of Gen 29:11 (meeting of Jacob and Rachel); or Gen 33:4 (meeting of Esau and Jacob); or 45:14 (meeting of Joseph and Benjamin'. While this shows the evocative power of this particular phrase, the narrative form of this section of Tobit suggests that Gen 29 is the primary influence.
[61] Nowell 2005: 13.
[62] Goldstein 1976: 63.
[63] Goldstein 1976: 6.

sin (1 Macc 2:24; Num 25:8). The typology is reinforced by the explicit claim of Mattathias' descent from Eleazar and Phineas (1 Macc 2:1, 54). The typology extends to the son of Mattathias, Judas, who as a destroyer of the ungodly, like Phineas, turns God's wrath away from the people (1 Macc 3:8; Num 25:11). Considering the intended effect, Goldstein concludes, 'as Phineas was rewarded by being made the founder of a high priestly line (Num 25:12–13), so will Mattathias be rewarded'.[64]

Alongside the priestly typology of Phineas, there is another typology that biblically ratifies the Hasmonean claim to kingship. Mattathias is like David in his flight to the mountains (1 Macc 2:27–28, 42–43; 1 Sam 22:1–2; 23:14). Both flights are followed by a massacre of innocents (1 Macc 2:29–38; 1 Sam 22:7–19). Both become outlaw fugitives but still fight loyally for Israel (1 Macc 2:44–48; 1 Sam 23:1–5). Both legislate for the sake of Israel (1 Macc 2:39–41; 1 Sam 30:22–25).[65] Again the typology is extended to Judas. Judas is like Jonathan in disdaining larger forces and his confidence in winning battles 'by many or by few' (1 Macc 3:18; 1 Sam 14:6). When Judas dies Israel's mourning for Judas (1 Macc 9:21) is reminiscent of David's at Jonathan's death (2 Sam 1:19).[66]

The dying speech of Mattathias to his sons (1 Macc 2:49–70) imitates the death of Jacob (Gen 49). Both death speeches give predictions for their sons' future (Gen 49:1–28; 1 Macc 2:64–66), and instructions for what to do next (Gen 49:29; 1 Macc 2:67–68). Both Jacob and Mattathias die once their speech is finished (Gen 49:33; 1 Macc 2:69). Both speakers were buried in ancestral burial sites accompanied by national mourning (Gen 50:1–14; 1 Mac 2:70).[67] This correspondence further resonates in the next chapter when Judas, Mattathias' son, is described: 'He was like a lion in his deeds, like a lion's cub roaring for prey' (1 Macc 3:4). With Mattathias' Jacob-like speech still recent in the readers' memory it is a clear allusion to Judah's description as a lion's whelp in Jacob's speech (Gen 49:9).[68]

Within 1 Maccabees, then, there is a typological tendency to portray its heroes as recurrences of biblical characters. There is no sense of eschatological fulfilment, only the ethical-rhetorical effect of portraying these men in the mould of scriptural exemplars.

§2.3.4 Liber Antiquitatum Biblicarum

Pseudo-Philo (LAB) retells the story of Genesis–Kings but integrates many other Jewish traditions and scriptures into the narrative. Generally held to be a first-century or early second-century text,[69] it is a Jewish text roughly contemporaneous with Mark. At points it is explicitly, and at some other points implicitly, composed by conflating analogous scriptures. Moreover, in LAB the juxtaposition of scriptures without explanatory

---

[64] Goldstein 1976: 7; see also Goulder 1964: 11–12.
[65] Goldstein 1976: 7.
[66] Goulder 1964: 12.
[67] Goldstein 1976: 239.
[68] Goulder 1964: 11.
[69] Fisk 2000b: 865.

comment arguably serves interpretational aims. As Fisk writes, 'biblical allusion *functions as exegesis*'.[70] In some places this reworking displays typological tendencies.[71] As Richard Bauckham writes, 'one of the most prominent characteristics of Pseudo-Philo's work is the way he constantly draws attention to the parallels between biblical events, usually by the device of speeches which recall earlier events in the context of later events'.[72] A clear example of this is LAB 12:1, which recounts Moses' descent from Sinai.

> And Moses came down. And when he had been bathed with invisible light, he went down to the place where the light of the sun and the moon are; and the light of his face surpassed the splendour of the sun and the moon, and *he did not even know this*. And when he came down to the sons of Israel, they saw him but did not recognize him. But when he spoke, they recognized him. And this was like what happened in Egypt when *Joseph recognised his brothers but they did not recognize him*. And afterward, when Moses realized *that his face had become glorious*, he made *a veil* for himself with which to cover his face.
>
> LAB 12:1[73]

Here the retelling of Exod 34:29–35 is explicitly related to Gen 42:8, regarding Joseph (cf. LAB 8:10). In the process, the story of Moses is assimilated to that of Joseph. In Exod 34:29–35, there is no mention of Israel's inability to recognize Moses. However, the correspondence between 'all the Israelites' and the brothers of Joseph (sons of Israel) and their fear when beholding a transformed Moses/Joseph is made explicit by the phrase 'this was like what happened in Egypt', and also by the double quotation of Gen 42:8, 'but they did not recognise him'.[74]

Another explicit correspondence is made in LAB 15:6. There God recounts the crossing of the Red Sea to Moses: 'And there was never anything like this event since the day I said, "*let the waters under heaven be gathered into one place*," until this day.'[75] For Pseudo-Philo the dividing of the waters in Exodus 14 corresponds to the gathering of the waters in Gen 1:9.[76]

Similarly, in LAB 19:11, God says of Moses' staff,

> And your staff will be before me as a reminder all the days, and it will be like the bow with which I established my covenant with Noah when he went forth from the ark, saying '*I will place my bow in the cloud, and it will be a sign between me and men that never again will the flood water cover all the earth*'.[77]

---

[70] Fisk 2001: 21, emphasis original.
[71] My reading of Pseudo-Philo suggests that there are explicit typologies in LAB 9:5; 12:3; 14:6; 17:1–4; 19:11; 37:1–5; 40:2; 43:5; 53:10; 57:2; 59:4; 61:2–3. I also find implicit typologies in LAB 6:1–18; 12:7; 20:2; 31:3–9; 32:1; 38:2; 39:3; 48:1; 56:6; 61:9; 65:4–5. I can only discuss a representative sample here.
[72] Bauckham 1981: 41.
[73] OTP 2:319, italics original.
[74] Murphy 1993: 69.
[75] OTP 2:323, italics original.
[76] Jacobson 1996: 1.548; the same connection is made in the rabbinic tradition in *Exod. Rab.* 21.6; *Pirqe R. El.* 42.
[77] OTP 2:328, italics original.

Jacobson suggests Moses' rod has been conflated with Aaron's rod in Num 17:25 and is then connected to Gen 9:13 by the shared word, לאות, 'a sign for'.[78] Building on Jacobson, Fisk argues that both bow and staff are 'weighted symbols for two eternal covenants'.[79] Moses' rod, in its function as a covenant memorial and through the word לאות, corresponds in Pseudo-Philo's typological imagination to the rainbow of Gen 9:13, 15.

While these correspondences explicitly display the typological thought behind some of Pseudo-Philo's compositional and interpretational decisions there may also be more implicit typologies. In the retelling of Exod 32:19–20 (LAB 12:7), where Moses forces the Israelites to drink water with the ground-up golden calf, Pseudo-Philo elaborates, 'And if anyone had it in his will and mind that the calf be made, his tongue was cut off; but if he had been forced by fear to consent, his face shone'.[80] This tradition can be explained as an allusion to Numbers 5, a prescription for a woman accused of adultery to drink bitter water to determine her guilt and either suffer pain and infertility if guilty or immunity if innocent. It is likely a link has been made between the alleged adulteress of Numbers 5 and unfaithful Israel of Exodus 32 (cf. Ezekiel 16; Hosea 2). They share the uncertainty over their faithfulness, both drink water with something added, and consequently they both receive judgement.[81]

Another implicit typology is Phineas in LAB 48:1 who is assimilated to Elijah in being nourished by a bird at God's command and who shuts the heavens and opens them by his word (1 Kgs 17:1–7).[82] The analogy which likely allows for this assimilation of Phineas to Elijah is the appointment of a successor. As Elijah appoints Elisha (1 Kgs 19:19–21), Phineas appoints Eli (LAB 48:2).

As Jacobson summarizes, 'LAB routinely contains themes, language, and elements of plot that are not present in the corresponding biblical narrative, but which he has borrowed from "analogous" biblical contexts'.[83] Bauckham argues that behind the typology of LAB is a 'presupposition ... that there is a consistency about God's acts in the history of his people, so that similar situations and events constantly recur'.[84] Pseudo-Philo is thus another example of the use of literary typology and of the underlying belief in typological recurrence based on God's providence.

Thus, in the Second Temple period scriptural correspondences to contemporary or recent historical persons (Josephus and the sign-prophets, 1 Maccabees), folk tales (Tobit) and even to other biblical stories were noticed (HB, LAB), employed and invested with meaning by authors composing their works. Such literary typology, both in explicit references and exegetically meaningful allusions, was a live option for Jewish authors up to (and beyond) the first century, and so, at risk of labouring the point, was also for Mark's Gospel.

---

[78] Jacobson 1996: 1.638–9.
[79] Fisk 2001: 281.
[80] OTP 2:320.
[81] Fisk 2001: 184–5; Jacobson 1996: 1.495; Murphy 1993: 72; the same connection is made in the rabbinic literature in *Num Rab.* 9.45–9; *Pes Rab.* 10.8.
[82] Fisk 2001: 305.
[83] Jacobson 1996: 1.225.
[84] Bauckham 1981: 41.

§2.4 Typology in the earlier New Testament

Accepting the critical consensus that Mark is the earliest of the four canonical Gospels and written around 70 CE, the only NT works that are demonstrably earlier are the undisputed Pauline letters. Within a number of these we find typology being used. As letters, rather than narrative, the rhetorical intention of the author is generally less cryptic.

In the letter to the Galatians, Paul gives an 'allegory' (ἀλληγορέω, 4:24) of Sarah and Hagar.[85] In Paul's argument the two women correspond to two covenants and to two Jerusalems, and the correspondence is then extended to include the Galatian Christians:

1. Sarah and Hagar 'are' two covenants (εἰσιν δύο διαθῆκαι, Gal 4:24).
2. Hagar corresponds (συστοιχέω) to the 'present' (νῦν) Jerusalem because they are both slaves (4:25).
3. Sarah corresponds to Jerusalem 'above' (ἄνω) because they are both free (4:26).
4. The Galatian Christians accord with Isaac (κατὰ Ἰσαὰκ), as 'children of the promise' (4:28).
5. The Judaizers are 'just as' (ὥσπερ) Ishmael, who was born according to the flesh (ὁ κατὰ σάρκα γεννηθείς), because they both persecute the child of the Spirit (τὸν κατὰ πνεῦμα, Gal 4:29, cf. Gen 21:9).
6. Consequently, Sarah's command to Abraham to drive Ishmael out for Isaac's protection (Gen 21:10) becomes pertinent to the current situation in the Galatian church, although Paul does not go as far as commanding the Galatians to drive out the Judaizers (Gal 4:30).
7. Paul then reiterates his point, 'we are children, not of the slave but of the free woman', therefore they should not allow the Judaizers to enslave them to the law (4:31–5:1).

In current usage, allegory is usually defined as a symbolic use of the words of a text without concern for their literal or historical meaning.[86] By contrast, typology is usually defined as concerned with the analogy between facts; there is a real, not simply symbolic, correlation between the referent of the text and its interpretation.[87] Within these definitions Gal 4:24–5:1 does not contain an allegory, but a typology. Paul is not suggesting that Sarah and Hagar were not historical persons. Rather, he is drawing correspondences between the Galatian church's controversy and the biblical narrative of conflict between Sarah and Hagar. The terminology of correspondence, συστοιχέω (4:25, a NT *hapax*), and of accordance, κατὰ + Acc. (4:28–29), reveal that what Paul is doing here fits well within my earlier definition of typology. It seems likely that Paul's

---

[85] While Fung (1994: 206) prefers the NIV translation, 'These things may be taken figuratively', De Boer (2011: 294–6) considers allegory to encompass variants including historical allegory and typology of which Gal 4:24–27 is an example.
[86] E.g. Goppelt 1982: 7.
[87] On the anachronicity of this terminology and distinction see Dawson 1992: 15–17; Young 1997b: 120; Martens 2008.

explicit correspondence was intended to imply that the Judaizers should be driven out,[88] but rather than stating that outright Paul leaves the Galatians to complete the sequence of correspondences.

If Sarah and Hagar are understood here as types rather than allegories then, arguably, Paul employs a similar exegetical approach in 1 Corinthians and Romans.

Regarding 1 Corinthians 5, Jin Hwang argues that Paul recognized a 'situational similarity' between the crises recounted in Numbers and that happening within the Corinthian church, as they both feature division over leadership and problems of sexual morality and idolatry.[89] Unlike Gal 4, in 1 Corinthians Paul explicitly commands action regarding an incestuous Corinthian (1 Cor 5:1–5). He bolsters his apostolic command with a short typology:

1. The Corinthian's boasting is bad. It is like leaven, in that what seems like a small thing will affect the whole thing (1 Cor 5:6).
2. So they must 'clean out the old yeast (leaven)' which will have the effect of renewing them as 'unleavened bread' (5:7).
3. The mention of unleavened bread invokes the Passover, 'our paschal lamb, Christ, has been sacrificed' (5:7). The Passover lamb is identified as Christ.
4. 'Therefore let us celebrate the festival' (5:8). As in Gal 4, Paul refrains from spelling out the last correspondence of the typology. Here, he appears to leave open a wider application of the type to the whole of Christian conduct, beyond his already stated prescription (1 Cor 5:4–5).[90]
5. The typology is further reinforced by the Jewish technical term for communal discipline in v13, ἐξάρατε (cf. e.g. Deut 7:1; 17:7, 12; 19:19; 21:21).[91]

What begins as a metaphor of leaven and bread evolves into a typology whereby the need for holy conduct is predicated upon Christ's sacrifice – rather than only Paul's command.[92] Whereas Gal 4 is a typology on a narrative, 1 Cor 5:6–8 is a typology upon a scriptural institution. Furthermore, as Hays argues, 'The text makes sense if and only if the readers of the letter embrace the typological correspondence between themselves and Israel'.[93]

The paraenesis of 1 Cor 10:1–22 contains 'an extended typological correspondence':[94]

1. The Israelites were 'baptised into Moses' (1 Cor 10:1–2); Paul establishes a correspondence between ancient Israel and the Church via 'baptism'.[95]

---

[88] De Boer 2011: 307.
[89] Hwang 2009: 200–2.
[90] Fee 2014: 239.
[91] Hays 2005: 22; Hwang 2009: 200.
[92] It is also possible the mourning of 1 Cor 5:2 connects with the mourning of the Israelites in Num 25:6 where an Israelite had just committed conspicuous sexual sin. This is argued by Hwang 2009: 203–4.
[93] Hays 2005: 24.
[94] Hays 2005: 8.
[95] Fee 2014: 490.

2. Thus Paul also corresponds Christian baptism with the Exodus.[96]
3. Paul then corresponds the miraculous feeding of the Israelites to the Eucharist. They are both spiritual food and drink (10:3–4).[97]
4. Because the Eucharist is Christ's body and blood (1 Cor 11:23–26), that means that Christ was what the Israelites fed on and drank in the wilderness. To complete this correspondence Paul draws upon a Jewish tradition regarding a moving rock (10:4).[98]
5. Because the Israelites now correspond to the church through baptism, the Eucharist and the presence of Christ,[99] they become a negative example to the church of what happens when they disobey God: 'God was not pleased ... they were struck down ... as examples (τύποι) for us' (10:5–6).[100]
6. The following paraenesis is then explicitly based on this typology (cf. 10:11, τυπικῶς) against idolatry, sexual immorality, testing Christ and complaining, in all of which the church is to avoid the Israelites' fate by avoiding their actions (10:6–13).[101]
7. Then the typology of negative moral example 'flee idolatry' (10:14) is joined with a further Israel-church-idolatry typology of participation (10:16–21)[102] and concluded with a final Israel-church typology and the question 'are we provoking the Lord to Jealousy?' (10:22; cf. Deut 32:21; Exod 32:5).[103]

The Corinthians' lack of awareness (1 Cor 10:1) is not regarding the content of the Exodus story, but their failure to appreciate the significance of that story for their own conduct.[104] That significance emerges from the correspondences between Israel and the believers and the consequent possibility of extrapolating consequences for sin from that typology.[105]

The final example of Pauline typology is the Adam–Christ typology (1 Cor 15:21–22, 45–49; Rom 5:12–21). Fee argues that Paul's 'varied use' of this typology 'suggests that it is a commonplace with Paul'.[106] The correspondence in Paul's mind is easy to follow. Both Adam and Christ are individuals, εἷς ἄνθρωπος (Rom 5:19), whose actions have universal consequence for humanity. Through Adam come death, condemnation and sin to all. Through Christ comes life, justification and righteousness to many/all.[107]

---

[96] Fitzmyer 2008: 381.
[97] Fitzmyer 2008: 382; Fee 2014: 492–3.
[98] See LAB 10:7; Fitzmyer 2008: 382–3; Fee 2014: 495.
[99] It can be argued that Christian baptism and Eucharist themselves assume typological reasoning as 'enactment of the saving events' (Young 1997a: 209). Also, 'vv. 1–4 indicate to us that [Paul] considers baptism and participation in divine (spiritual) food and drink as the common experiences both communities share' (Hwang 2009: 199).
[100] 'Because Paul uses typoi, we can understand the foreshadowing connotations of other terms already used in this section ...' (Fitzmyer 2008: 385).
[101] Fitzmyer 2008: 387.
[102] Fee 2014: 511.
[103] Fitzmyer 2008: 394.
[104] Hays 2005: 8; Fee 2014: 488.
[105] Hays 2005: 11–12.
[106] Fee 2014: 832.
[107] While there is some debate over whether Paul intended a universal understanding of Christ's work here, the consensus view is that 'all' refers only to believers as a new humanity. See, e.g., Robert Jewett 2007: 385; Fitzmyer 2008: 570; Fee 2014: 831.

Adam was the first human and man of dust whose image all humanity bears. Correspondingly, Jesus is the heavenly human whose image all the righteous will bear.

Adam and Christ correspond at the level of individuals whose acts affect all humanity. This is a unique correspondence. We do not expect my obedience, or your acts, or even the acts of a David or a Jonah to have such universal consequences. Yet, the full significance of this correspondence, for Paul, lies in the thematic inversion within that correspondence. Where Adam was disobedient, Christ was obedient. Where Adam brought sin, condemnation and death, Christ brings righteousness, justification and resurrection life. Whereas humanity in the image of Adam is earthly, humanity in the image of Christ will be spiritual and heavenly. Christ is not simply a better version of Adam and Christ does not just restore what Adam damaged. Christ inverts and exceeds the effect of Adam's sin.[108]

Paul's Adam–Christ typology demonstrates that while typology could be used to indicate correspondences between characters and events, once those correspondences were established it could also indicate contrast. In Paul's Adam–Christ typology Jesus is both *like* Adam and *greater* than Adam. He is not a simple repeat of Adam but ὁ ἔσχατος Ἀδάμ (1 Cor 15:45). The contrast becomes the main point of the typology.

This ability of typology to reverse, invert or contrast a character or theme is significant.[109] We see here in Paul how much theological weight such a typological inversion can carry. This recognition should alert us to the potential of similarly meaningful typological inversions in Mark's use of scripture.

In summary, in Gal 4 and 1 Cor 5:6–8 Paul takes recourse to typology during a divisive situation and with the intention to expel someone from the church community. Similarly, in 1 Cor 10:1–22 Paul employs extensive and overlapping typological reasons to hammer home dire warnings. Adam–Christ typology is employed in two different letters by Paul (1 Cor 15:21–22, 45–49; Rom 5:12–21). These examples suggest that typology was an effective and compelling approach to scripture interpretation in the Pauline church communities, or at least that Paul thought it was. If typology could be used in such important situations by Paul then it is plausible, or even likely, that similar thinking could be used by the Gospel of Mark and in the early Christian communities for which Mark was written.[110]

§2.5 Scriptural conflation

Related to the question of typology is the widespread early Jewish practice conflating scriptures.[111] This technique may have its roots in the exegesis of legal texts. As George Brooke argues, 'A major feature of [the] halakhic materials [at Qumran] is the way that

---

[108] Fee 2014: 830–2, 872–8; Fitzmyer 1993: 421–2.
[109] Allison 2000: 192–6.
[110] It is a minor point, but Romans 5:14 (Ἀδάμ ὅς ἐστιν τύπος τοῦ μέλλοντος) along with 1 Cor 10:6 (τύποι) and 10:11 (τυπικῶς) suggest that my terminology of typology would have been understandable by Paul and is not absolutely anachronistic.
[111] Fisk 2001: 28–32; Goulder 1964: 8; Hays 2005: 15; Kee 1978: 179–81; Allison 2000: 204–6.

two or more scriptural passages are combined to create innovative interpretations of the tradition that permit the application of scriptural authority to new situations'.[112]

Conflation is not restricted to legal material. In LAB 6:1–18 the story of Abraham is conflated with the story of Babel. This conflation happens presumably because the stories are adjacent to each other in Genesis and so the need was perceived to relate them. However, through the word play on Ur (אור, Gen 11:31) also being the Hebrew word for fire, Abraham becomes a survivor of the 'fire' of the Chaldeans. This linkage through *fire* then provides the most likely explanation for the additional conflation of Meshach, Shadrach and Abednego's escape through fire (Dan 2:19–30) into the story of Abraham and the tower of Babel.[113] Not two, but three scriptural texts are here conflated to produce LAB's account.

Scriptures could be conflated because of a shared theme, shared words, textual proximity or simply because it suited the author's theological agenda. For example, Mal 3:1 and Isa 40:3, conflated in Mark 1:2–3, may have become associated through the distinctive phrase פנה דרך.[114] By bringing two scriptural texts together a new text was created, but with the assumed authority of the earlier texts. Such conflations may be the work of a text's author or may have been received by the author as an already authoritative tradition.

This alerts us to a characteristic of scripture use in Mark's Gospel: 'the fusion of one or more scriptural passages into one conflated citation'.[115] Such conflations are often prominent and play an important role in the narrative (e.g. Mark 1:2–3; 1:11; 11:1–11; 11:17; 12:1–12; 13:24–26; 14:62).

Where we can observe conflation of scriptures in Markan citations, we may also extrapolate the principle to narrative typologies. That is, in creating a narrative typology Mark is not restricted to only one scriptural allusion per narrative episode, or even at any one time. For example: the baptism of Jesus (Mark 1:9–11) effectively evokes the Exodus, the Flood and Isa 64:1 while verbally alluding to Ps 2:7 and Isa 42:1. In longer narrative passages there is proportionally greater opportunity for a range of allusions to different scriptural texts.

§2.6 Graeco-Roman Mimesis

Mimesis is one of the oldest and most fundamental terms in literary theory, albeit one that is fiercely contested.[116] Some recent biblical studies, which bear a strong methodological resemblance to the work in this study, have been carried out under the heading of 'mimesis'.[117] However, mimesis is not a single thing but a range of interrelated phenomena with more specific meanings in different genres, from author to author,

---

[112] Brooke 2010: 572; for further examples see the discussion of 11QTS in Kaufman 1982.
[113] Evans 2001: 154.
[114] Schneck 1994: 32; Watts 1997: 73–4.
[115] Marcus 1992: 15.
[116] Potolsky 2006: 1–7.
[117] E.g. Brodie 2000; MacDonald 2000; Winn 2010; Watts 2013.

from work to work, and even within a work. Paul Woodruff observes, 'Not even Plato is entirely consistent on the subject of mimesis'.[118]

Two of its many possible senses are analogous to early Jewish and early Christian typology. First is the sense of mimesis as positive or negative moral imitation of an exemplar (Plato, *Rep.* 393–8; cf. Aristotle, *Nic. Eth.* 1176a17f; Plutarch, *Peri*, 1.4; 2.2; *Life of Aratus* 1.5; *De cap ex inin*, 92.e–f).[119] This compares to the ethical use of τύπος in the NT (Rom 6:17; Phil 3:17; 1 Thess 1:7; 1 Tim 1:16; 4:12; 2 Tim 1:13; 1 Peter 5:3).[120] Ethical imitation creates a motive for literary assimilation. As the new hero is portrayed in the terms of an established exemplar there may be transference of esteem and they are in turn presented as someone to imitate.[121]

Second is the sense of mimesis as 'the relation of copy to model' (Plato, *Rep.* 596–9; *Tim.* 47b–c; Plutarch, *De glor. Ath.* 346f; 348b).[122] It is in this sense that the typology of Hebrews is sometimes considered Platonic. The correlation of an earthly form with a heavenly ideal relates very closely to Christian 'vertical' typology where earthly things are types of heavenly things.

However, when mimesis is invoked in biblical studies it is usually with a view to describing *rhetorical imitation* as the driving principle *in the production of literature*. While rhetorical imitation links to other senses of mimesis in terms of the relationship of a new text to a model or exemplar, a key distinction is that it concerns reproduction of style rather than content.[123] Prime examples of rhetorical imitation are Virgil's *Aeneid*, which imitates Homer's *Odyssey* and *The Iliad*, and the poetry of Horace, which imitates that of Sappho (*Ode* 4.1) and Pindar (*Ode* 4.2).[124] Discussions of such imitation can be found in many places in Greek and Roman literature (Plato, *Phaedrus*, 263–4; Isocrates, *Panegyricus* 10; Cicero, *De Oratore* I.xxxiv.156; II.xxii–xxiii.92–6; Seneca *Ep* 84; *Controversiae* 1. Praef. 6; Longinus IV.xii–xiv; Quintilian *Inst. Ora.* v.vii.28; x.ii.2–8).[125]

It may well be that Graeco-Roman rhetorical imitation influenced rewritten Bible in (Hellenized) Second Temple Judaism.[126] However, the ability and desire to imitate moral heroes, heavenly archetypes or authoritative texts was not isolated to the Greeks and Romans, but is an aspect of a more general human phenomenon (cf. Aristotle, *Poetics*, 4.1448b4–19).[127] In Mark's gospel the same data adduced for imitation of

---

[118] Woodruff 1992: 75.
[119] Potolsky 2006: 21; Fossheim 2001: 73–86; Zadorojnyi 2012: 175–6, 183–93.
[120] Ounsworth 2012: 34–5.
[121] Young 1997a: 209.
[122] Cain 2012: 189; see also Woodruff 1992: 77; Zadorojnyi 2012: 179; Potolsky 2006: 26–7, 32–46.
[123] Clark 1957: 144–76; Pitts 2016: 114; see also Halliwell 2001: 88.
[124] Potolsky, *Mimesis*, 52–6.
[125] One concern raised by Andrew Pitts in regard to the application of mimesis as rhetorical imitation to Gospel criticism is the extent to which the presence of mimesis in a narrative implies the content of that narrative is entirely invented. Pitts argues that Graeco-Roman mimesis implied no such thing: 'That Xenophon framed his Phillidas narrative using Herodotus's account of the Persian envoys does not, on its own, entail invention. In fact given what we know about mimesis in historical theory, this was one way of preserving and presenting historical tradition' (2016: 135).
[126] Pitts 2016: 107.
[127] Halliwell 2001: 88.

Graeco-Roman mimesis can be accounted for using Jewish examples of imitation and reuse (as discussed above). Given Mark's explicit quotation of and dependence on the Jewish scriptures it seems unnecessary to posit a particularly Graeco-Roman approach to the literary production of the Gospel. As Juel argues, Hellenistic literature is important to the study of the NT, 'but the particular investment in Israel's heritage and Israel's Scriptures suggests that the most helpful analogies for our studies will be other Jewish scriptural interpretation, as practiced of course, in the Hellenized world'.[128]

§2.7 Conclusion

I have attempted to demonstrate the plausibility of a literary typology being employed by a first-century Jewish-Christian author. Significant for this thesis is the evidence of Josephus, that individuals and groups could appropriate scriptural narratives as models for their own behaviour. Moreover, in Josephus, the Jewish scriptures, other early Jewish writings, and the letters of Paul, there are examples of literary typology being utilized to serve rhetorical purposes and theological convictions. Having seen examples of scriptural typology in a range of sources prior to and contemporary with Mark's Gospel we are now ready to begin to examine Mark's own use of scriptural typology.

---

[128] Donald Juel 2003: 285.

§3

Typology and christology in the context of Mark's Gospel

And the Great Glory was sitting upon it—as for his gown, which was shining more brightly than the sun, it was whiter than any snow.

1 Enoch 14:20

In this chapter I survey the three Christological high points that structure Mark's Gospel: the baptism, transfiguration and passion.[1] These three include supernatural phenomena in the sky (not caused by Jesus) and proclamations of Jesus as the son of God. They are also united by a narrative typology evoking the *Akedah* (Gen 22),[2] even as they individually allude to other scriptural narratives. The passion will be considered in three parts, extrapolating the typological themes of Jesus as Jerusalem's judge, Jesus as Son of God and Jesus as typological fulfilment of David. The purpose of this chapter is to show that, just as typological thinking is apparent in the wider early Jewish milieu, the Gospel of Mark employs scriptural typology at these key Christological moments. It then follows that Mark may also employ scriptural typology in the Gospel's miracle accounts, which will be considered subsequently.

§3.1 The Son of God appears: Typology and christology in Mark 1:1–15

Mark's identification of Jesus with Israel's God is apparent from the beginning of the Gospel. Gudrun Guttenberger argues that Jesus' designation as υἱοῦ θεοῦ in 1:1 means that to talk about God in the Gospel of Mark is to talk about him in his relationship with Jesus.[3] However, even if we were to delete that phrase from 1:1,[4] the Gospel still

---

[1] Dunn 1989: 46.
[2] Following Huizenga (2009, 76–7) I use the term *Akedah* as 'a convenient collective term designating any and all presentations of the fundamental story of Gen 22, including Gen 22, even those versions in which Isaac is not explicitly bound. Given the great variety found among the various presentations, it is better to think in terms of Wittgensteinian "family resemblances" than in terms of strict definitions and indispensable essences.'
[3] Guttenberger 2004: 56.
[4] The manuscript evidence for the inclusion of υἱοῦ θεοῦ (B D W al) and that against it (ℵ* Θ 28c al) is not decisive either way.

contains narrative acclamations of Jesus as 'my beloved son' by a heavenly voice (Mark 1:11; 9:7), and 'son of God' by evil spirits (3:11; cf. 5:7) and a centurion (15:39), and Jesus identifies himself as God's son (12:6; 13:32; 14:61-62).[5]

§3.1.1 The way of the Lord

The voice of God is first heard implicitly, in the scripture quotation in Mark 1:2-3.[6] Special significance is attached to this citation by its location at the beginning of the Gospel and because all other scripture citations in Mark appear in the mouths of human characters. Here, God appears to speak in a direct way unmediated by a human character.[7] The subject, 'I', of Mark 1:2 and its citation of Mal 3:1 can only be God, and the object, 'you', must be Christ.[8] This direct address portrays an 'extraordinary intimacy' between God and Jesus.[9] Thus the way that is to be prepared is Jesus' way. Mark 1:3, citing Isa 40:3 (LXX), calls this way 'the way of the Lord (κύριος)'. In its original context in Isaiah 'the way of the Lord' is clearly God's way. Transplanted into Mark and juxtaposed with Mal 3:1, the way of the Lord is also Jesus' way,[10] opening up the additional possibility that Jesus is the κύριος whose way it is.[11]

One way of understanding Mark's juxtaposition of scriptures here, resulting in a new definition of κύριος, is that, while Mark (presumably) recognizes that the original referent of κύριος in Isa 40:3 was God, he can associate Jesus with God through typology. Jesus does not replace God, but is seen to correspond to God in some way and so this scripture can now be applied to Jesus. Exactly what this correspondence is remains to be seen.

§3.1.2 Divine identity in Mark 1:2-3?

Bauckham argues that Mark's use of Isa 40:3 in Mark 1:2-3 'is an instance of the common early Christian practice of applying to Jesus Old Testament texts that use the divine name'.[12] Bauckham's conclusion that this necessarily places Jesus in the exclusive divine identity does not, however, necessarily follow. The context of the Isaiah and Malachi citations is eschatological deliverance. Their use by Mark requires that Jesus be seen as the manifestation of God's saving purposes. It requires that Jesus' ministry be seen as the fulfilment of God's promise to 'come to Zion'. It requires that Jesus' 'way' also be understood as God's way. It does not require that Jesus be understood to be involved in creation or universally sovereign.

---

[5] Van Iersel 1998: 91.
[6] Boring 1999: 464.
[7] Guelich 1989: 12; Van Iersel 1998: 93; Guttenberger 2004: 56.
[8] Guelich 1989: 11; Van Iersel 1998: 94.
[9] Marcus 2000: 147.
[10] Guelich 1989: 11; Omerzu 2011: 92.
[11] Kampling 1992: 38-9; Van Iersel 1998: 95; Guttenberger 2004: 66; Bauckham 2017a: 25.
[12] Bauckham 2008: 265.

§3.1.3 God's beloved son: Isaac Typology at the Baptism

Only twice in the Gospel's narrative does God feature as an overt character. However, even then God is not named but features as a voice from the sky (Mark 1:11; 9:7). The heavenly voice is God's, as both times it speaks it identifies Jesus as υἱός μου.[13] In all 42 of the occurrences of θεός in Mark it is never as an actor in the narrative but usually modifies other nouns, e.g. 'son of God' (3:11), 'kingdom of God' (9:1), and 'the commandment of God' (7:8). The heavenly voice's designation of Jesus as ὁ υἱός μου adds an element of distinction and definiteness to the identification of Jesus with God. Distinction, because Jesus is not *God*, but God's son. Definiteness, because Jesus is not *a son* of God, but the son of God.

This definiteness of Jesus' sonship is further established typologically by the evocation of the binding of Isaac, or *Akedah* both in language and narrative that is reminiscent of the account in Genesis 22 and in correspondence with features of developing Jewish traditions about Isaac.

The phrase ὁ υἱός μου ὁ ἀγαπητός (Mark 1:11) spoken over Jesus by a voice from heaven is highly evokcative of the *Akedah*. The expression 'your only/beloved son' (τὸν υἱόν σου τὸν ἀγαπητόν/τοῦ υἱοῦ σου τοῦ ἀγαπητου) occurs three times in Gen 22:2, 12 and 16, and not in any other suggested referent text of Mark 1:11.[14] The threefold repetition in Genesis 22 may be reflected in Mark's strategic placement of this phrase at three points of the Gospel (Mark 1:11; 9:7; 12:6).[15] Ἀγαπητός is a well attested early Jewish idiom for an only child (LXX Jer 6:26; Zech 12:10; Tob 3:10) and for children in general (1 Enoch 10:12; 12:6; 14:6; 99:5).[16] It is particularly associated with Isaac in Philo (*Somn.* 1.194–5; *Leg. all.* 3.203; *Deus* 1.4; *Abr.* 168, 196; *Migr.* 140). It is likely that the word had the same significance for Mark.[17] In its second appearance in the story of the *Akedah*, a voice from heaven repeats the key phrase (Gen 22:11–12) creating an even stronger correspondence with Mark 1:11 and 9:7. The words πειράζω (Gen 22:1; Mark 1:13; cf. Heb 11:17) and σχίζω (Gen 22:3: Mark 1:10) may also help reinforce a link.[18] Thus Jesus is one like Isaac, a uniquely beloved only son.[19] But significantly God, not Abraham, is his father.

If a river baptism seems far removed from a hilltop sacrifice it should be remembered that for early Christ-believers baptism signified death. In Mark 10:38 Jesus uses baptism, βάπτισμα, as a metaphor for his coming passion. In Rom 6:4 Paul talks about baptism as a burial into death. Christian baptism was also associated with resurrection (Rom 6:4; 1 Pet 3:21). Further, Best has argued that in both Judaism and early Christianity the sparing of Isaac was seen as a type of resurrection (Heb 11:17–19; *Pirqe R. El.* 31.10).[20] To state the obvious, resurrection requires a prior death.

---

[13] See further, Guelich 1989: 33–4.
[14] Stegner 1989: 17; Schnackenburg 1995: 46–7; Rindge 2012: 763.
[15] Rindge 2012: 766.
[16] See further, Guelich 1989: 34; Best 1990: 169–70; Hooker 1991: 47–8; Van Iersel 1998: 101.
[17] Rindge 2012: 764.
[18] Stegner 1985: 43; Rindge 2012: 763.
[19] Kampling 1992: 64.
[20] Best 1990: 170.

Accordingly, for Mark, Jesus' baptism prefigures his sacrificial death and resurrection and so may well also call to mind the *Akedah*.[21]

Géza Vermès has argued that in Rabbinic teaching Isaac's willing sacrifice was considered to have provided atonement for all his descendants.[22] However, dating concerns and the lack of evidence for influence on the NT limit the usefulness of such parallels.[23] It is even possible the influence goes in the other direction.[24] However, developing traditions around Isaac are clearly visible in Jubilees, Pseudo-Jubilees (4Q225), 4 Maccabees (7:14, 19; 13:12, 17; 16:20-25), Philo, Pseudo-Philo (LAB 18:5; 32:2-4; 40:2) and Josephus (*Ant.* 1.222-36), even if they do not contain all the distinctive features of later Rabbinic teaching on the *Akedah*. Several points are immediately significant for the consideration of the presentation of Jesus in Mark 1:1-15.

In Gen 22:6, 8, the repeated phrase that Abraham and Isaac walked on together 'likely suggested to later tradents that Isaac was indeed aware of the situation and willing to be sacrificed'.[25] In Pseudo-Jubilees (4Q225 2.ii.4) Fitzmyer reconstructs the text as Isaac saying, [כ]פות אותי יפה], 'Bind me fast'.[26] This would then be the earliest text which 'reveals an aspect of Isaac's cooperation with his own sacrificial death that figures often in Jewish writings of a later date'.[27] This picture of a willing and obedient Isaac then occurs more explicitly in LAB 32:3; 40:2; Philo, *Abraham* 172; 4 Macc 13:12; 16:20; Josephus, *Ant.* 1.232.[28] Isaac's willing submission to a sacrificial death by his father's and God's will in Jewish tradition thus corresponds with Jesus' willing submission to crucifixion by his father God's will as depicted in Mark (e.g. Mark 10:45; 14:36).

Huizenga suggests that the motif of seeing (ראה, Gen 22:4, 8, 13, 14), the angelic appearance (Gen 22:11, 15) and the voice of God (Gen 22:1-2) in the scriptural account of the *Akedah* are 'nascent apocalyptic elements' that could be developed by later interpreters.[29] In 4Q225 2.ii.2-7 the recounting of the Akedah includes descriptions of forces of angels of holiness, who weep for Isaac's impending death, and angels of animosity (mastema) who rejoice at it.[30] In LAB 18:5, Gen 22:17 is retold as a heavenly ascent by Abraham 'when I [i.e. God] lifted him above the firmament and showed him the arrangement of all the stars'.[31] In LAB 31:1-2 the stars of heaven fight alongside Deborah against Sisera. Deborah's following hymn then contains an account of angelic jealousy towards Abraham (LAB 32:1-2). For LAB this jealousy is what had inspired God's command to kill Isaac. In Jubilees it is Mastema that tells God to test Abraham with the offering of Isaac as a burnt offering (Jub 17:16).

---

[21] Stegner 1985: 46; Rindge 2012: 763-4.
[22] Vermès 1983: 204-8.
[23] Davies and Chilton 1978: 514-46; Dunn 1988: 1.501; Fitzmyer 1993: 531; Brown 1994: 2.1441-3; Longenecker 2016: 753-54.
[24] Segal 1984: 183; cited in Longenecker 2016: 754.
[25] Huizenga 2009: 78.
[26] Fitzmyer 2002: 218.
[27] Fitzmyer 2002: 219.
[28] Huizenga 2009: 102-28; Fisk 2000a: 494, 497.
[29] Huizenga 2009: 79.
[30] Fitzmyer 2002: 219.
[31] OTP 2.325

The apocalyptic elements in Mark's prologue, such as the torn heavens, descent of the spirit (Mark 1:10) and the voice from heaven (Mark 1:11) correspond with this escalating cosmic dimension in the retellings of the *Akedah* story. Most significant is the correspondence of angelic activity, especially in Mark 1:13 where Satan (corresponding to Mastema) tests Jesus and angels wait on him. The picture of Jesus between opposing spiritual forces corresponds to Isaac in 4Q225. The idea of Jesus being tested (πειράζω) by Satan connects to Jub 17:16. A similar correspondence occurs with Judith where, in what is most likely a reference to the *Akedah*,[32] Isaac is described as someone who was tested (ὅσα ἐπείρασεν τὸν Ισαακ, Jud 8:26).

Strikingly, in several places Philo exalts Isaac above the other patriarchs as the son of God.[33] In *Names* 131 Isaac is the innate son of God (ὁ ἐνδιάθετος υἱὸς θεοῦ). In *Worse* 124, 'God may with perfect truth be said to be Isaac's father'. In *Dreams* 1.173, God is merely Abraham's teacher but he begets Isaac (Ἰσαὰκ δὲ γεννήσας), Abraham is God's pupil but Isaac is God's son (υἱός). And in *Alleg. Interp.* 3.219, the Lord has begotten Isaac (Ἰσαὰκ ἐγέννησεν ὁ κύριος). This distinctively exalted portrayal of Isaac (whether literal or figurative) is especially intriguing because both Philo's *On Isaac* and the Akedah section of *Questions and Answers on Genesis* are lost to history, possibly as a result of Christian censorship.[34] While Philo's idiosyncratic interpretations cannot be considered to have influenced Mark, they do demonstrate the range of development that the figure of Isaac had undergone by the end of the first century and present Isaac as a potentially fertile figure for Christological typology.

As a result of these Jewish traditions around Isaac, just discussed, Mark's depiction of Jesus being declared God's beloved son and being tested, among apocalyptic signs and between angelic forces of good and evil, could well evoke the *Akedah* to any Jew familiar with the developing tradition(s) attested by the texts discussed above. Although it must be borne in mind that early Christians certainly might refer to the *Akedah* without any suggestion of developments beyond the scriptural story (e.g. Jas 2:21–23; Heb 6:13–14; 11:17–19), the argument for an allusion to the *Akedah* in Mark 1:11 does not depend on any of these developing traditions, but is only strengthened by the probability that they were available to the author of Mark.

Thus the opening verses of Mark set up the Christological terms which constitute the puzzle of Mark's Christology. Jesus' relationship to the God of Israel is defined along two axes. He is placed on these axes by means of scriptural typology in Mark's narrative. One, he is the singular son of Israel's θεός, the antitype of Isaac. This is fulfilment typology. Two, he is somehow identified with Israel's κύριος, in that the role assigned to 'the Lord' in scripture is to be accomplished by Jesus. When the Lord, κύριος, promised to return to Zion, Mark sees this fulfilled in and by Jesus, κύριος.[35]

---

[32] Huizenga 2009: 94.
[33] Huizenga 2009: 101–2.
[34] Huizenga 2009: 97–8.
[35] Guelich 1989: 46.

§3.2 The mountain transfiguration: Typology and christology in Mark 9:2–8

The transfiguration is identified as a Christological high point of the Gospel by its structural function, the heavenly phenomena, and the declaration of Jesus as God's 'beloved son'.[36]

The second half of Mark's Gospel (8:31–16:8) begins by revisiting the beginning (Mark 1:1–15).[37] There are a number of parallels. Jesus makes a new beginning, ἄρχω (8:31; cf. 1:1, ἀρχή).[38] Instead of prophetic scripture (1:2–3), Jesus prophesies (8:31–9:1). The prophet Malachi quoted in Mark 1:2 (Mal 3:1) is recalled here through the appearance of both Moses and Elijah (Mal 4:4–5, 'Remember the teaching of my servant Moses . . . I will send you the prophet Elijah . . .').[39] Satan does not test Jesus in the wilderness but in the person of his disciple, Peter (8:32–33). Like his original preaching of the gospel, Jesus teaches openly (8:32; cf. 1:14). There is a reiteration of the promised coming of the kingdom (9:1; cf. 1:15). At another symbolically significant location (this time a high mountain rather than the Jordan) a heavenly voice declares Jesus to be ὁ υἱός μου ὁ ἀγαπητός (Mark 9:7; cf. 1:10).[40] The section ends with a reference to John's arrest (9:13; cf. 1:14).

§3.2.1 The typology of Jesus' transfiguration

The ascent of a mountain to meet with God recalls two significant scriptural stories, that of Moses (Exod 24, 34) and that of Elijah (1 Kgs 19:8–18).[41] This connection can hardly be denied as Elijah and Moses are described as being present (Mark 9:4). Various Jewish writings suggest that the return of scriptural heroes would feature in the eschaton (4 Ezra 6:26; 14:9; 2 Bar 76:2; *T. Ben* 10:5–6).[42] The appearance of Elijah and Moses must carry great significance; however, their presence is not a return but only a temporary reappearance.[43]

Elijah is the first of the two prophets mentioned. With the mountaintop scene surrounded by the talk of persecution of both Jesus and his followers (Mark 8:31–38) and mention of Elijah/John the Baptist's fate (9:13), the transfiguration recalls Elijah's encounter at Mount Horeb (1 Kgs 19:11–18). Elijah was under the threat of death (1 Kgs 19:2) as is Jesus (Mark 3:6; 8:31). Both scenes take place after the death of prophets at the hands of a wicked king and queen (1 Kgs 18:4; Mark 6:14–29). Peter's presumptuous verbosity (Mark 9:5–6) contrasts with Elijah's silence (1 Kgs 19:12–13). God's voice interrogated Elijah (1 Kgs 19:13) before comforting him (19:15–18). In the

---

[36] 'Literarily speaking, Mark makes the transfiguration a kind of fulcrum for his book' (Litwa 2014a: 113).
[37] Marcus 2000: 640–1.
[38] Hooker 1992: 205; France 2002: 327, 333; Stein 2008: 401.
[39] Boring 2006: 261.
[40] On the significance of the mountain, see Gundry 1993: 457; Evans 2001: 35; Lee 2004: 14–15.
[41] Omerzu 2011: 86.
[42] Ramsey 1949: 109.
[43] Pesch 1979: 2.75.

transfiguration, God's voice declares that Jesus is his son and that the disciples should listen to him (Mark 9:7).

Jesus' transfiguration (μεταμορφόω, Mark 9:2) also evokes Moses' glorification (δοξάζω, Exod 34:29 LXX).[44] Moses' two ascents to meet with God in Exod 24:9–18 and 34:1–35 present a number of corresponding details: the otherwise puzzling Markan reference to six days (Mark 9:2; Exod 24:15–17);[45] the high mountain (Exod 24:12; 15–18; 34:3); the presence of a select group (Exod 24:1–2, 13); a transformed and radiant central character (Exod 34:29–30, 35); a fearful reaction (Exod 34:29–30); an overshadowing cloud (Exod 24:15–16; 34:5); a voice from that cloud (Exod 24:16; 34:5); and a human radiating light (Exod 34:29, 35).[46] As Donnahue and Harrington write, 'The common features are so numerous that it is hard to escape the impression that the transfiguration story presents Jesus as not only the Son of God but also a Moses figure'.[47]

However, two further features complicate the picture. The command ἀκούετε αὐτοῦ (Mark 9:7), 'listen to him', may call to mind the prophet like Moses in Deut 18:18–19, ὃς ἐὰν μὴ ἀκούσῃ ὅσα ἐὰν λαλήσῃ.[48] However, the wording is much closer to that of Exod 23:21, εἰσάκουε αὐτοῦ. These words are spoken by God regarding an angel who has a unique status, γὰρ ὄνομά μού ἐστιν ἐπ᾽ αὐτῷ (Exod. 23:21). This enigmatic angel of YHWH also appears in the Elijah/Horeb narrative. In the Jewish scriptures, this angel is an ambiguous figure whose identity often seems to fluctuate between being an agent of YHWH and YHWH himself.[49]

Crucially, in both Exodus 24 and 34 Moses ascends the mountain to *talk with* God. This is also the case in the parallel Elijah story (1 Kgs 19:8). In Exod 34:29 Moses' face is changed when he talks with God (ἐν τῷ λαλεῖν αὐτὸν αὐτῷ). Jesus, though, is not changed by talking with God. Neither, in Mark's account, does his *face* shine.[50] He is changed before the cloud appears or the heavenly voice speaks.[51] This narrative correspondence is reinforced by a distinctive word.[52] At the end of the Sinai cycle, Moses talks with YHWH (συλλαλέω, Exod 34:35), which is one of only four occurrences of the word in the LXX and the only occurrence in the Pentateuch. The only occurrence of this distinctive word in Mark is here when Elijah and Moses talk with Jesus (ἦσαν συλλαλοῦντες τῷ Ἰησοῦ, Mark 9:4).

---

[44] Dunn 1989: 47.
[45] Pesch 1979: 2.72; Evans 2001: 35; Lee 2004: 13; Donahue and Harrington 2005: 268; Boring 2006: 261.
[46] Stegner 1989: 87–91; Allison 1993: 243–8; Gnilka 1998: 2.2; Van Iersel 1998: 294; Marcus 2000b: 1114–15; Litwa 2014a: 123.
[47] Donahue and Harrington 2005: 274.
[48] Pesch 1979: 2.76; Stegner 1989: 93; Hooker 1991: 218; Marcus 2000b: 634; Boring 2006: 262.
[49] See Meier 1999; Von Heijne 2010. For a more detailed discussion of this in relation to the transfiguration, see my article '"Listen to Him!": Angelic and Divine Typology in Mark's Transfiguration Account', in *Horizons in Biblical Theology* (Robinson, forthcoming (b)).
[50] Evans 2001: 36. It is likely that Matt 17:2 and Luke 9:29 give Jesus a radiant face to further assimilate the transfiguration to Exod 34:29.
[51] Thus Litwa (2014: 139) is wrong to argue that Jesus' light is reflected from YHWH's light. There is no suggestion in the Markan text that the cloud emits light.
[52] Stegner 1997: 115.

Mark's report that Jesus' clothes are changed (9:3) perhaps 'reflects that of the clothes and hair of the aged figure who sits on the heavenly throne in the vision of Dan. 7.9 . . . For a moment, the three disciples see the Son of Man clothed with God's glory.'[53] Comparable is the description of God's cloak (περιβόλαιον) in 1 Enoch 14:20 as brighter and whiter than any snow (λαμπρότερον καὶ λευκότερον πάσης χιόνος).[54] Alternatively, the shining clothes reflect Jewish and Greek descriptions of heavenly beings, reinforced by Mark's statement that no one *on earth* could achieve such whiteness.[55] Notably, when humans become heavenly beings and put on robes of glory in early Jewish literature, these robes are always given to them.

> And the Lord said to Michael, 'Go, and extract Enoch from his earthly clothing. And anoint him with my delightful oil, and put him into clothes of my glory'. And so Michael did just as the Lord had said to him. He anointed me and he clothed me.
>
> 2 Enoch 22:8 J[56]

> Out of the love which he had for me, more than all the denizens of the heights, the Holy One, blessed be he, fashioned for me a majestic robe, in which all kinds of luminaries were set, and he clothed me in it. He fashioned for me a glorious cloak in which brightness, brilliance, splendour and lustre of every kind were fixed, and he wrapped me in it.
>
> 3 Enoch 12:1–2[57]

Although some have argued that μετεμορφώθη is a divine passive in Mark 9:2,[58] by comparison with other texts of heavenly enrobing, the lack of any description of dressing or giving of the robe in Mark 9:2 is conspicuous. The Markan text is silent as to the agent of Jesus' transformation, so the possibility remains that there is either no agent or that it is Jesus who transforms himself.

Once he is changed, then Moses and Elijah appear up the mountain and they then talk *with* Jesus, ἦσαν συλλαλοῦντες τῷ Ἰησοῦ (Mark 9:4), becoming figures in Jesus' story.[59] In the transfiguration Jesus takes on the role of the angel of the Lord and of God, in being the one that Moses and Elijah went up the mountain to talk to. By metamorphosing into radiance he is not imitating Moses whose face reflected the glory of God (δεδόξασται ἡ ὄψις τοῦ χρώματος τοῦ προσώπου αὐτοῦ (Exod 34:29)). He is imitating the one who made Moses' face shine. Note how in the Exodus passages God appears as a man (Exod 24:10; 34:5).[60]

---

[53] Van Iersel 1998: 294; also Evans 2001: 36.
[54] Rowland 1982: 367.
[55] Lee 2004: 16; Gathercole 2006: 48–49; Litwa 2014a: 134; following Bauckham 1999: 51; see also Ezek 9:2 and Rev 15:6 discussed in Stuckenbruck 1995: 226–8.
[56] OTP, 1 138.
[57] OTP, 1.265.
[58] Van Iersel 1998: 294; Stein 2008: 416.
[59] Omerzu 2011: 89.
[60] Hamori 2008: 30–2. For more discussion of this in relation to the transfiguration see Robinson, forthcoming (b).

Matthew and Luke's addition of changes to Jesus' face (Matt 17:2; Luke 9:29) renders Mark's focus on Jesus' clothes alone (τὰ ἱμάτια αὐτοῦ) distinctive. Gregory Palamas (thirteenth to fourteenth century) connects LXX 103:2, ἀναβαλλόμενος φῶς ὡς ἱμάτιον, with the transfiguration as evidence that Christ was himself God (*The Triads* 2.3.18).[61] While we must avoid importing later theological conceptions into the Markan text, Palamas' reading alerts us to another way of aligning the narrative typology. It is possible that Mark avoids describing Jesus' face as changed in order not to confuse Jesus with Moses, if his intended typological reference is not Moses but the angel of the Lord.

It is as if the disciples are witnessing a salvation-historical 'flashback' to the theophanies experienced by Moses and Elijah and seeing Jesus representing the God of Israel. Contrary to the view that the transfiguration anticipates the resurrection,[62] this reading suggests that it both anticipates the Son of Man's glory promised in Mark 8:38 and 9:1[63] and recapitulates the mountain ascents of Moses and Elijah to meet the Lord. If Moses and Elijah meet and talk with Jesus on the mountain, then Jesus is again assimilated to God by Mark's narrative. At the same time, the heavenly voice prevents a complete identification of Jesus with God. Jesus is both God's shining representative and the object of God's speech from heaven.

In the transfiguration Jesus is not the antitype of Elijah or Moses, because they are in the scene with him. Instead he is typologically patterned upon the God who they walked up the mountain to meet. Again, the two axes of Jesus' relationship to God are in evidence: the differentiation from God, as the heavenly voice again declares him to be 'my son', and the identification with God of the scriptures, as Jesus takes on the role of the Lord from scriptural narratives. At the same time, connections to the *Akedah* and the looming spectre of death keep this episode anchored in Jesus' journey to the cross.

§3.2.2 Isaac typology on the mountain

The allusion to the *Akedah* is stronger here than in Mark 1:1–15. Again, the language of 'beloved son' (Mark 9:7) recalls the *Akedah* which also takes place on a mountain (ὄρος, Gen 22:2, 14; Mark 9:2).[64] Both scenes are connected with the promise of a coming glorious kingdom (Gen 22:17–18; Mark 8:38–9:1). Jesus' sacrificial death is prominent in the context (Mark 8:31–9:1; 9:12). Ringe notes several words-in-common occurring at corresponding narrative points: ὑψηλός (Gen 22:2; Mark 9:2);[65] παραλαμβάνω (Gen 22:3; Mark 9:2); ἀναφέρω (Gen 22:2; Mark 9:2); φωνή (Gen 22:18; Mark 9:7); ὤφθη (from ὁράω, Gen 22:14; Mark 9:4); and ὑπακούω/ἀκούω (Gen 22:18; Mark 9:7).[66] These additional verbal connections are not particularly distinctive, but with the important narrative correspondences they are suggestive of how the *Akedah* tradition may have influenced the transfiguration pericope.

---

[61] Cited in Litwa 2014a: 111.
[62] E.g. Pesch 1979: 2.73; Schnackenburg 1995: 30; Litwa 2014a: 113 n. 3.
[63] Ramsey 1949: 117–18; Evans 2001: 35–36; Stein 2008: 417.
[64] Dunn 1989: 48.
[65] For Pesch (1979, 2.71) ὄρος ὑψηλόν is a *Stichwort* which evokes an Isaac typology.
[66] Rindge 2012: 766–7.

Mark 9:2–8 is thus a scene rich in multi-layered scriptural typology. At this second Christological high point of the Gospel, Jesus appears both as a theomorphic type of Israel's God and as the antitype of Isaac. Again, the two axes of God's son and one like God are contained in the same narrative episode.

§3.2.3 The transfiguration and Jesus' ontology

Having discussed the transfiguration in terms of typology, we now need to ask if Jesus' radiant metamorphosis is in itself a signal of divinity. Does Jesus' radiance indicate something of Jesus' ontology? Tyson Putthoff's recent anthropological study of Jewish ontology demonstrates that early Jews sometimes did conceptualize ontology.[67] His approach analyses mystical texts and the assumptions that such texts reveal about the ontology of humans and God.[68] He argues that 'ontology is a central element of early Jewish anthropology' and that 'ideas on the malleability of the self pervade Jewish mystical writings'.[69] As humans encounter divine space they can undergo physical changes to become angelic or godlike.[70] Among the texts Putthoff considers, *Joseph and Aseneth* and Philo are pertinent to this study.

In *Joseph and Aseneth*, Aseneth repents of her paganism and through ascetic practices is rewarded with transformation. Aseneth will be renewed (ἀνακαινίζω) re-formed (ἀναπλάσσω) and re-made-alive (ἀναζωοποιέω) and enjoy the food of life and drink the cup of immortality (ἀθανασία) and the anointing of incorruptibility (ἀφθαρσία; Jos. Asen. 15:5).[71] In Jos. Asen.16:16 an angelic man from heaven declares Aseneth is now a 'radically changed, immortal being, who serves as a mediator and protector to those who seek the Lord'.[72] Putthoff suggests that Aseneth's wedding dress, which is like lightning (ἀστραπή, Jos. Asen. 18:5) is also part of her transformation.[73] This would correspond well to Jesus' clothes in Mark 9. However, this is not clear from the text which describes it as her finest robe taken from her own clothing-chest, giving it an earthly origin. More significant is her and her father's reaction to her transfigured visage (Jos. Asen. 18:9–11).[74] This corresponds to the disciples' reaction of terror to Jesus' transformation (Mark 9:6). So Aseneth's spiritual transformation results in an ontological change which is communicated to the reader through the description of τὸ πρόσωπον αὐτῆς ὡς ὁ ἥλιος καὶ οἱ ὀφθαλμοὶ αὐτῆς ὡς ἑωσφόρος ἀνατέλλων, 'her face as the sun and eyes as the morning star rising' (Jos. Asen. 18:9).[75] Should we then understand Jesus' transfiguration as a description of ontological change, and if so what would it signify Christologically?

Aseneth's transformation to become like the sun and stars may draw on a similar understanding of human transformation found in Daniel's description of the

---

[67] Putthoff 2017; see also Himmelfarb 2013: 283–93.
[68] Putthoff 2017: 19.
[69] Putthoff 2017: 27; see also Himmelfarb 1993: 29–46.
[70] Putthoff 2017: 22–3.
[71] Putthoff 2017: 45–7.
[72] Putthoff 2017: 57. Also on the mediator figure, see Putthoff 2017: 64.
[73] Putthoff 2017: 60.
[74] Putthoff 2017: 61.
[75] OTP 2.232.

righteous.⁷⁶ 'Those who are wise shall shine like the brightness of the sky, and those who lead many to righteousness, like the stars forever and ever' (Dan 12:3). Other texts which perhaps build on Daniel's imagery are 1 Enoch 39:5-7; 104:2-4; 2 Bar 51:5-12, where the transformed nature of the righteous into heavenly beings is clear.⁷⁷

For early Jewish mystical literature such transformation is an intrinsic capacity of human beings.⁷⁸ For Philo (*Creation* 77) humanity already shares some kinship/relation to God, ὅτι τῆς αὐτοῦ συγγενείας, but God further gives them rationality, μεταδοὺς ὁ θεὸς ἀνθρώπῳ τῆς λογικῆς.⁷⁹ Putthoff argues that for Philo the rational part of the human soul is of the same ontological substance as God (*Dreams* 1.34, 'in man it is mind, a fragment of the deity', ἐν ἀνθρώπῳ δὲ νοῦς, ἀπόσπασμα θεῖον ὤν).⁸⁰ It is not God, but because it comes from God it shares in God's divinity.⁸¹ Divinity is thus conceived as a state that varies in degree. As a person performed mystical acts (in Philo's case, allegorical exegesis and philosophy) and encountered the divine they would themselves become ontologically more divine.⁸² Philo describes the transformation through philosophy as one from mortality to immortality, 'And from this philosophy took its rise, by which man, mortal though he is, is rendered immortal' (ὅθεν τὸ φιλοσοφίας ἀνεβλάστησε γένος, ὑφ᾽ οὗ καίτοι θνητὸς ὢν ἄνθρωπος ἀπαθανατίζεται, *Creation* 77).⁸³

Regarding the NT, David Burnett has argued that we find assumptions of ontological change in Paul's letters. In Rom 4:18 Burnett argues that the reference to Abraham's seed (Gen 15:5) as being like the stars is taken to be not simply quantitative but also qualitative. That is, Abraham's seed are to become like celestial beings.⁸⁴ He finds a similar interpretation is made explicitly in Philo:⁸⁵

> Well does the text say 'so' (οὕτως ἔσται) not 'so many' (τοσοῦτον) that is, 'of equal number to the stars'. For He wishes to suggest not number merely, but a multitude of other things, such as tend to happiness perfect and complete. The 'seed shall be' (οὕτως οὖν ἔσται), He says, as the ethereal sight spread out before him, celestial as that is, full of light unshadowed and pure as that is, for night is banished from heaven and darkness from ether. It shall be the very likeness of the stars.
>
> Philo, *Heir*: 86-7

Elsewhere, Philo gives an interpretation of Gen 15:5 that suggests both a numerical and qualitative interpretation of 'as the stars' (*QG* 4.181).⁸⁶ Burnett argues, 'Philo seems

---

⁷⁶ Newsom 2014: 364; Lacocque 2018: 277.
⁷⁷ Himmelfarb 2013: 287-88; Burnett 2015: 229.
⁷⁸ Himmelfarb 1993: 71; Gieschen 1998: 152-83; Lacocque 2018, 277.
⁷⁹ See further *Creation* 69, 134-5; *Planting* 17-20; *QG* 2.56; Litwa 2014b: 10.
⁸⁰ Trans. Colson and Whitaker, *Philo I*, LCL, 61-2.
⁸¹ Putthoff 2017: 76-7; Litwa 2014b: 9.
⁸² Putthoff 2017: 72.
⁸³ Trans. Colson and Whitaker, *Philo V*, LCL, 313. Bauckham (2012: 246-65) argues against deification in Philo by studying Philo's use of θεός. Bauckham finds θεός is only ever used of humans figuratively and not ontologically. His study is vitiated by only considering uses of the word θεός to describe deification, rather than considering the descriptions of transformation discussed here.
⁸⁴ Burnett 2015: 213; cf. also Origen *Comm. Rom.* 4.6.7.
⁸⁵ Burnett 2015: 215.
⁸⁶ Burnett 2015: 216.

to axiomatically employ the phrase 'so shall your seed be (οὕτως ἔσται τὸ σπέρμα σου)' as though it were to be taken as a kind of adage that was intended to denote celestial immortality'.[87] Burnett also notes how Sirach 44:21 in its apparent exegesis of Gen 22:17 sees 'becoming as the stars' as a reference to exaltation (ἀνυψῶσαι).[88] Finally, he adduces the slightly later text, *Apoc. Abr.* 20:3–5 (first to second century CE), where 'Abraham's seed is promised not merely the number of the stars, but their power, which is understood in terms of the rule over nations and men, which seem to have been allotted to the Eternal Mighty One or to Azazel and his company'.[89]

Burnett also discusses 1 Cor 15.[90] This is a disputed text, but whatever is specifically meant by Paul's categories of ψυχικός and πνευματικός bodies (15:44), Paul arguably expects a profound ontological change (ἀλλάσσω, 15:51) to occur for the believers at the resurrection.[91] What is sown perishable and mortal will be raised incorruptible and immortal, σπείρεται ἐν φθορᾷ, ἐγείρεται ἐν ἀφθαρσίᾳ (1 Cor 15:42). We will no longer resemble Adam but Christ (1 Cor 15:49). We will cease to be earthly (ἐπίγειος) bodies but become heavenly (ἐπουράνιος) bodies (15:40). With the above understanding of Rom 4:18 in mind, the references to heavenly bodies in 1 Cor 15:41 are not incidental but indicative of the believers' transformed post-resurrection celestial ontology.

It appears, then, that at least some Jews considered that exaltation also changed a human's ontology. In other words, an exalted person ceased to be human, mortal and earthly and became divine, immortal and heavenly. To disambiguate such a change from the binary ontology of divine identity, we could term it a *theio-morphology*. This recognition immediately problematizes the approach of both Bauckham and Kirk. For Bauckham the only divinity that qualifies is that of creational sovereignty. For Kirk, despite his initial recognition that humans are divine and may become more so, his analysis assumes that if Jesus is human then he cannot be fully divine. They analyse Mark according to a binary ontology, in contrast to the fluid gradient ontology observable in *Joseph and Aseneth*, Philo and Paul.

Many of the figures included in Kirk's paradigm of idealized human figures were probably not considered ontologically human in their exalted state – if their ontology was considered at all, which is by no means certain. Thus, in the few examples of Jewish discussion of ontology that we have access to, it is not clear how an exalted human could be said to differ ontologically from another divine being. Exaltation is effectively divinisation, understood within an inclusive, gradient sense: Aseneth became an angelic mediator, Moses became the Logos, and the faithful Christ-believers will become like the stars in heaven.

On the other hand, Bauckham's divine identity could be modified here to make better sense in this context. That is, if a pre-existent being which shared in the divine identity were to assume human form, there would need be nothing ontologically divine about

---

[87] Burnett 2015: 216.
[88] Burnett 2015: 216–17.
[89] Burnett 2015: 219.
[90] Burnett 2015: 225, n. 27; Burnett 2019: 200–3.
[91] Gundry 1976: 164; Pearson 1976: 23–5; Martin 1995: 123; Dunn 1998: 61; Engberg-Pedersen 2009: 125; Burnett 2019: 200.

them when they have taken on humanity. The continuity between the pre-existent divinity and the human person would be one of identity not *theio-morphology*. This is because Jewish thought could conceive of ontological change occurring to human and divine persons. But if this same pre-existent divinity was 'included in the divine identity' of the creator God, this would not change by them becoming human because that ontological distinction is to do with the creator-creation divide, not any particular form. However, it must be noted that in the Early Jewish examples discussed above, the movement is always a human becoming divine and not a divine being becoming human.

In Mark's Gospel there are no visible indications of ontological divinity, with the possible exception of the transfiguration in Mark 9:2-7. Wrede comments, 'To be sure the story of the transfiguration does show … the glory or majesty of Jesus; this is, something supramundane which has no place in the earthly life of Jesus'.[92] Mark 9:2 is the only instance where Jesus appears to give any signals as to a theio-morphology. But, its temporary nature implies it does not represent an ongoing ontological state.[93] It also highlights the lack of ontological signals in the rest of the Gospel. Jesus' transfiguration does conform to several aspects of the ontological transformations discussed above, but unlike that in *Joseph and Asenath*, Philo and Paul, Jesus' change is not given any commentary in the text. The lack of description of an agent enrobing Jesus (9:2-3) may suggest an inherent state or ability of Jesus being revealed rather than being temporarily given. In my view, this is the point in Mark's Gospel most inviting of an incarnational interpretation. Yet it must be recognized that it is only one possible implication and it is far from certain. Further, if this implication was accepted then neither is it clear who or what exactly has been incarnated, because Mark makes no reference to any pre-existent state. Despite the tantalizing hint of a divine ontology, I must conclude that Mark 9:2-7 is more interested in the scriptural typology evoked by Jesus' radiance than any possible ontological implications of it.

§3.3 Judgement on the Temple: Typology and christology in Mark 11-12

The climax of Mark's Gospel is the passion account. The passion begins with Jesus' triumphal entry into Jerusalem (Mark 11:1-11). Immediately after, Jesus performs two parabolic actions of judgement upon the religious institutions of Jerusalem (11:12-25).[94] The miracle of the withered fig tree (11:12-14, 20-25) is intercalated with Jesus' cleansing of the Temple (11:15-19) in Mark's characteristic 'sandwich' structure.[95]

---

[92] Wrede 1971: 68.
[93] Again, comparison with Moses is illuminating. In Exod 34:29-35 it appears that Moses' shining face is permanent and Moses has to wear a veil whenever he is not talking to God, in order not to frighten the Israelites. Jesus' dazzling clothes, however, do not appear to continue beyond Mark 9:7, when in 9:8 there is an implied return to normality, and Jesus' appearance is not commented on again.
[94] Barrett 1978: 14; Charlesworth 2014: 157.
[95] Edwards 1989; Marcus 2000b: 788.

§3.3.1 Typology of the withered fig tree

This is the last account of Jesus performing a miracle in the Markan narrative and the only account of Jesus performing a negative miracle in the Gospel. This episode is also anomalous among the Markan miracle episodes in that it is both intra-textually unique (all other miracles have identifiable complements within the Gospel, e.g. two water miracles or two feeding miracles), and geographically unique (the only Markan miracle to take place in Jerusalem). For these reasons this miracle presents itself as particularly significant in Mark's narrative presentation of Jesus.

Deborah Krause argues that Mark 11:12–25 owes its intercalated structure to Hosea 9:10–17.[96] For Krause the use of the fig tree as a metaphor for Israel (Hos 9:10) and the mention of Ephraim's root being dried up and never bearing fruit (Hos 9:16) relate to the fig tree cursed by Jesus (Mark 11:12–14, 20–25). Between those references lies the promise 'I will drive them out of my house' (Hos 9:15) which Krause relates to Jesus' driving out of the buyers and the sellers from the Temple (Mark 11:15–18). Krause argues that the phrase οἶκός μου serves to link Jesus' teaching in Mark 11:17 (quoting LXX Isa 56:7; Jer 7:11, οἶκός μου) with Hos. 9.15 (LXX, ἐκ τοῦ οἴκου μου ἐκβαλῶ αὐτούς). Mark's awkward reference to 'season' in 11:13 is explained by Krause as the influence of the reference to the season in Hos 9:10.[97] Both passages also share a reference to the nations in their immediate context (τοῖς ἔθνεσιν, Hos 10:17; Mark 11:17) and a reference to 'fruit' (καρπός, Hos 9:16; Mark 11:14).

Krause suggests ways that this scriptural background serves to assimilate Jesus to the God of Israel. Firstly, the agent who finds and sees (εὑρίσκω, ὁράω) the grapes/figs/Israel in Hos 9:10 is the Lord. In Mark 11:13 it is Jesus who sees and finds (ὁράω, εὑρίσκω) the fruitless fig tree.[98] She also recognizes the typological relationships established by the scriptural subtext: 'Mark's exegesis places Jesus' actions in continuity with the judgement of YHWH, and the Temple cult and its leaders in continuity with apostatising eighth-century Israel'.[99]

Arguably the language of 'continuity' is too weak to describe what Mark portrays which is Jesus acting the narrative role of God described in the scriptures. In this instance, while Hos 9:10–16 may well have provided a structural influence that generated Mark's intercalation, it is just one example of a prophetic theme that unites the destruction of Israel and the Temple with the picture of YHWH looking for figs.

In Hos 2:12 YHWH promises to 'lay waste her [unfaithful Israel's] vine and her fig trees'. In Joel 1:7 the day of YHWH's judgement on Israel results in the waste of vines and the splintering of the fig trees and in 1:12 'the vine withers and the fig tree droops'. In Hag 2:19 YHWH reveals that 'the vine, the fig tree, the pomegranate, and the olive tree still yield nothing' because God had withheld his blessing. In Isa 34:4 the withering of leaves on the vine and fruit on a fig tree is a metaphor for YHWH's destruction of the armies of the nations and heaven. Micah 7:1 is ambiguous as to whether the speaker is YHWH

---

[96] Krause 1994. See also my argument in §5 that Mark 5:21–43 owes its intercalated structure to a typological use of 2 Kgs 4:18–37.
[97] Krause 1994: 239, 241–44, 246.
[98] Krause 1994: 242.
[99] Krause 1994: 244.

or Micah, but also associates the image of someone looking for but not finding the 'first-ripe fig (בכורה / πρωτόγονος; cf. Hos 9:10) for which I hunger' with God's judgement on the 'house of the wicked' (6:10) and with those who 'lie in wait for blood' (7:2).

Most significantly, Jer 8:13 describes YHWH wanting to gather grapes and figs and finding none, as well as the motif of withered leaves (φύλλον, cf. Mark 11:13). This text is also in close proximity to the 'den of robbers' citation (Jer 7:11) found in Mark 11:17, which is at the centre of the Markan intercalation. Mark's passion resonates with a number of themes from this section of Jeremiah: the rebuke of Israel for not knowing the season (καιρός x2, Jer 8:7); ignorance of the judgement of the Lord (οὐκ ἔγνω τὰ κρίματα κυρίου, Jer 8:7); false scribes (Jer 8:8); rejection of the word of the Lord (Jer 8:9); greed for unjust gain (Jer 8:10); and a promise to overthrow (Jer 8:12). Importantly, Jeremiah's prophecy is set in the gate of 'the Lord's house', 'the Temple of the Lord', and addressed to 'you that enter these gates to worship the Lord' (Jer 7:1–4). As Juel concludes, 'In this case, the setting of the verse in Jeremiah cannot be accidental ... [It] fits perfectly into the context of the last chapters of [Mark's] Gospel'.[100]

Mark's conjunction of prophetic texts, especially those from Hosea and Jeremiah, continues the dual typological pattern discussed above. It portrays Jesus both in the mould of a scriptural human character, in this case Jeremiah prophesying to the worshippers in the Temple, and also taking on the role of the Lord, in this case from the same scripture. This time the typology is from a prophetic rather than a narrative scripture. It is not a single text that is evoked but a narrative motif of divine judgement that is present in Isaiah (34:4; 56:7), Jeremiah (Jer 7:11; 8:13), Hosea (2:12; 9:10–17), Joel (1:7), Haggai (2:19) and Micah (7:1).

§3.3.2 God's only beloved son: Typology in the Parable of the tenants

Following the cleansing of the Temple and cursing of the fig tree, Jesus' authority is challenged by the chief priests, scribes and elders (11:27–29). After Jesus' initial evasive response (11:29–30) Jesus goes on to tell the parable of the wicked tenants in which he implicitly reveals that his authority to judge the Temple is from God (12:1–12). The parable, as a response to the question of Jesus' authority, is Christological in focus. It develops scriptural themes to reveal Jesus' unique and unprecedented authority as God's Son.

In the parable of the wicked tenants (12:1–12) the son, Jesus, comes to the vineyard, Jerusalem, with a message of judgement from the Father, God, to the wicked tenants, the religious authorities. The parable is itself a message of judgement and the listening scribes, priests and elders realize this (12:12).[101] If they realize that they are the tenants they may also realize that Jesus is the 'only son'.[102]

The parable begins in Mark 12:1 with language dependent upon LXX Isa 5:1–2.[103] In both texts, the main character plants (φυτεύω) a vineyard (ἀμπελών), places

---

[100] Juel 1977: 133; also Evans 2001: 174–6.
[101] Evans 1984: 83; Buth and Kvasnica 2006: 65.
[102] Dechow 2000: 249.
[103] Buth and Kvasnica 2006: 77.

(περιτίθημι) a hedge, fence or wall (φραγμός), builds (οἰκοδομέω) a watchtower (πύργος), and digs (ὀρύσσω) a winepress (Isa 5:2, προλήνιον; Mark 12:1, ὑπολήνιον).[104] The coincidence of matching verbs and nouns is striking. An early reader of Mark observed and strengthened this connection: Luke adds a further detail from Isaiah, the landlord's question, 'What shall I do?' (Luke 20:13) which echoes Isa 5:4.[105]

There is some evidence that Jewish traditions associated these verses of Isaiah with the Temple (e.g., *Tg. Ps.-J.* Isa 5:2; 4Q500; *Tg. Isa.* 5:1–7; 1 Enoch 89:56, 66–67, 73).[106] However, the Markan context of the parable 'between chapters on the Temple cleansing (ch. 11) and the prediction of the Temple's destruction (ch. 13)' clearly alerts the reader to the probability of a Temple motif within the parable.[107] It is Jesus' authority vis-à-vis the Temple which is in question (Mark 11:27) and so the parable both justifies his actions in Mark 11 and anticipates his prophecy in Mark 13.

Klyne Snodgrass observes that this parable is 'of direct and major christological significance'.[108] The lord of the vineyard has one beloved son (ἕνα εἶχεν υἱὸν ἀγαπητόν, Mark 12:6) who represents Jesus. Again, the *Akedah* is evoked, this time by both the Septuagintal ἀγαπητός and the use of εἷς, a literal Greek equivalent of the Hebrew יחיד (Gen 22:2, 12, 16).[109]

The Psalm 118 citation confirms the theme of Temple within the parable. Psalm 118 describes the entry of a royal individual into the Temple gates to give thanks after a great deliverance (118:19–20). The verse regarding the cornerstone (118:22) comes between mentions of the Temple gates (118:19–20) and a festal procession to the altar (118:27). The cornerstone imagery, then, is inspired by and relates to the psalmist's (real or imagined) location within the Temple and its surrounding masonry.[110] The setting of the parable in the Temple (Mark 11:27) and the disciple's reflection on the Temple architecture (13:1) further reinforce the link between 'stone' and Temple.

At the same time, Ps 118:22 describes the psalmist's own experience of deliverance.[111] Jesus' appropriation of the psalm corresponds to his earlier predictions of rejection and vindication (8:31; 9:31; 10:33–34). The rejection he predicted is now taking place in the response to his parable.

There is also the strong possibility that behind the linking of the parable of the wicked tenants to the stone of Ps 118:22–23 (Mark 12:10–11) is the Hebrew wordplay between son, בן, and stone, אבן.[112] This Hebrew word play appears to have influenced

---

[104] It is hard to see why the LXX Isa has προλήνιον (the vat in front of a wine press). Generally, the LXX renders the underlying Hebrew יקב simply with ληνός (trough or winepress, see Num 18:27, 30; Deut 15:14; 16:13; 2 Kgs 6:27; Prov 3:10; Jer 48:33; Hos 9:2; Joel 2:24; 4:13). However, Isa 16:10; Hag 2:16 and Zech 14:10 all use ὑπολήνιον (the vat placed beneath a winepress). Mark may have assimilated Isa 5:2 to 16:10 here, may have made a word choice based on the practice most familiar to his readers, or may have had a different version of Isa 5:2.
[105] Brooke 1995: 283.
[106] On which see, Juel 1977: 136–7; Evans 1984: 83–4; Brooke 1995: 272; Buth and Kvasnica 2006: 75; Chilton et al. 2009: 364; Charlesworth 2014: 168–9.
[107] Evans 1984: 84.
[108] Snodgrass 2018: 276.
[109] Marcus 2000b: 803.
[110] Goldingay 2008: 361–2.
[111] Kraus 1993: 399–400; Mays 2011: 377.
[112] Moo 1983: 337; Hooker 1991: 277; Charlesworth 2014: 170; Snodgrass 2018: 290.

Aramaic speaking Jews. Josephus recounts how when Caesar was besieging Jerusalem the watchmen would cry in Aramaic, 'the son comes!' to warn of the stones which the Roman catapults hurled (*J.W.* 5.272). Likewise, *Tg. Ps.* 118:22 reads, 'The architects forsook the youth among the sons of Jesse, but he was worthy to be appointed king and ruler'.[113] The Aramaic טליא (child/youth) has replaced the Hebrew בן (stone), the most likely explanation for which is the Hebrew wordplay between בן and אבן being employed in the interpretation of the psalm.[114]

This Davidic/messianic interpretation of the 'stone' in *Tg. Ps.* 118:22 might have been inspired by Zech 4:7 which associates Zerubbabel and a cornerstone with the rebuilding of the Temple. In *Tg. Zech.* 4:7 the stone becomes the messiah, revealed by Zerubbabel.[115] Josephus and Targum Psalms thus suggest that the Hebrew wordplay between בן and אבן was known and employed in at least two very different Aramaic contexts. Additionally, *Tg. Ps.* 118 shows the messianic potential of the cornerstone motif, or is itself the product of an earlier tradition linking Ps 118:22 with the messiah. Equally, other scriptural stone texts such as Isa 28:16; 8:14; Dan 2:45 are suggestive of a stone typology.[116] Thus, in Mark 12:1–12 Jesus both identifies himself as the only beloved son of the owner of the vineyard and also as the messianic stone.

In the telling of the parable Jesus publicly announces and utilizes his status as Son of God for the first time, albeit within a parable.[117] Christologically the parable marks Jesus out from the prophets who went before him with a qualitative difference. They were slaves (δοῦλος, Mark 12:2, 4).[118] He is the only beloved son (cf. Gal 4:1–7). The son resembles the slaves in being sent in the same way. However, the son is more intimately and concretely connected to the father. The implication is not that the son is a more competent messenger and so is more likely to be listened to, but that the son more completely represents the father than the slaves. The son is functionally a type of slave, but in essence a type of the father. The son of the parable is a microcosm of the dual axes of the typological Christology of Mark.

The use of ἔσχατος (Mark 12:6) serves to underscore the significance of the son and gives an eschatological nuance to the story.[119] The son represents the father so completely that there will be no further messengers. If the tenants do not listen to the son, they will not listen to anyone. There is only judgement left.

In the final miracle of the withered fig tree and its accompanying parable, Jesus is the son, sent by the father with a message of judgement, a prophet like Jeremiah. Unlike the previous messengers, however, Jesus is the greatest and last. But Jesus is also in the role of Israel's God looking for fruit on the tree, judging the Temple and its 'tenants' and, in parabolic deed and prophetic parable, enacting and declaring their imminent destruction.

---

[113] Trans. Stec 2004: 210.
[114] Blomberg 2007: 74; Watts 2007: 213; Evans 2001: 229; Charlesworth 2014: 170–1; Snodgrass 2018: 295. 685, n. 176.
[115] Blomberg 2007: 74; Watts 2007: 213.
[116] Evans 1992: 865.
[117] Snodgrass 2018: 294.
[118] Cf. 1QpHab 7. See Charlesworth 2014: 168.
[119] Marcus 2000b: 803; Snodgrass 2018: 288–9.

§3.4 The son is slain: Typology and christology in Mark 14–15

For now, we pass over Mark 13, although I will discuss this within the next section. The conclusion of the passion marks the third and final Christological high point in the Gospel. It is a marked contrast to 1:1–15 and 9:2–8. The supernatural element remains, but is no longer glorifying, anointing and affirming Jesus, but instead brings darkness (15:33) and destruction (15:38). God's silence in Gethsemane (14:32–42) prepares us for Jesus' cry of abandonment (15:34) as Jesus goes through his arrest, trial and execution, apparently alone. Despite the absence of a heavenly voice, Jesus is twice marked as the Son of God (14:61; 15:39).

§3.4.1 Jesus as type of Passover

The imagery now moves from the *Akedah* to that of the Passover. Unlike Isaac who was spared by the provision of a ram (Gen 22:13–14), Jesus will be sacrificed. Jesus is the Passover lamb who is to be killed at the festival (Mark 14:1) and whose flesh is consumed in the Passover meal (14:22) and whose blood marks the covenant people (14:24).[120] From the point of view of the Christian reader, the parallelism between the Passover, the eve of Israel's great deliverance and the Last Supper, on the eve of Jesus' saving death, would be inescapable.[121]

However, the difference between *Akedah* and Passover traditions should not be overstated. *Jubilees* dates the Passover as the anniversary of Isaak's sacrifice (*Jub.*17:15–16; 18:3; 49:1).[122] *Jubilees* concludes that account by making the Passover connection explicit:[123]

> And he observed this festival every year (for) seven days with rejoicing. And he named it 'the feast of the Lord' according to the seven days during which he [i.e. Abraham] went and returned in peace. And thus it is ordained and written in the heavenly tablets concerning Israel and his seed to observe this festival seven days with festal joy.
>
> *Jub.* 18:18–19[124]

Jon Levenson writes:

> Jubilees seems to derive its duration, for which the Hebrew Bible gives no etiology, from Abraham's journey—three days to the mountain, three to return, and one day (the Sabbath) without travel. The journey begins on the twelfth rather than on the

---

[120] Wenham 1995: 13–14; Marcus 2000b: 964–8.
[121] Moo 1983: 324–5.
[122] Levenson 1993: 176.
[123] For a more detailed discussion of the theological linking of Akedah and Passover in Jubilees, see Huizenga 2009: 84–8.
[124] OTP 2.91.

evening after the fourteenth (i.e., the beginning of the fifteenth) precisely so that the binding of Isaac will coincide with the date on which the paschal lamb will be offered. Isaac has become the lamb of God, as it were, and Passover.[125]

The link is made widely in later Jewish literature (*Tg Ps.-J.* Exod 12:42; *Tg. Neof.* Exod 12:42; *Exod. Rab.* 15:11; *Mek. Ishmael* 11, 7; *Mek. Shimon* 6).[126] Neither is this connection without scriptural basis. In Exod 13:1, 11–16, the instructions for Passover include 'the festival of the offering of the firstborn', where God lays claim to all the firstborn males of Israel.[127] The divine claim and then deliverance of Israel's first born is clearly analogous to the divine claim and deliverance of Abraham and Sarah's firstborn. Also scriptural was the belief that the 'Mount of Moriah' of Gen 22:2, also called the 'Mount of the Lord' (Gen 22:14), was the location of Jerusalem (2 Chron 3:1; Isa 2:3; 30:29; Ps 24:3; *Jub.* 18:13; Jos. *Ant.* 1.13.2; §226; *Tg. Onq.* Gen 22:14; *Gen. Rab.* 56.10).[128]

Thus having been established as God's only beloved son and the antitype of Isaac earlier in the Gospel, the presentation of Jesus as Passover sacrifice is an extension rather than a replacement of Mark's earlier *Akedah* typology.

§3.4.2 Isaac typlogy in the crucifixion

Indeed, it is possible that the *Akedah* is alluded to in the Gethsemane account. Jesus' use of 'father' (transliterated Aramaic: ἀββά) in Mark 14:36 may reflect Isaac's use of 'father' (Hebrew אב) to address Abraham in Gen 22:7, an enduring feature in later recounting (*Jub.* 18:6; Tg. Onq. Gen 22:7; Tg. Ps.-J. Gen 22:7).[129] Although a son calling their father 'father' is hardly distinctive, its use within a narrative context of obedience unto death creates a more evocative correspondence.[130] Less generic is Jesus' following statement, 'Father, all things are possible to you' (ὁ πατήρ, πάντα δυνατά σοι, Mark 14:36). This may reflect a tradition preserved in Philo's retelling of the Akedah, where Abraham tells Isaac to 'know that all things are possible to God' (πάντα δ' ἴσθι θεῷ δυνατά, *Abr.* 1:175).[131] Matthew further assimilates Gethsemane to the Akedah from Mark 14:32, καθίσατε ὧδε, to Matt 26:36, καθίσατε αὐτοῦ, alluding to Gen 22:5, καθίσατε αὐτοῦ.[132]

Jesus' death is marked by several details. At noon darkness comes over the whole land (Mark 15:33). Darkness is a biblical image for chaos (Gen 1:2) and associated with judgement (Exod 10:21–23; Jer 15:9; Joel 2:2; Zeph 1:15) and eschatological events (Joel 2:31).[133] In particular, the phrase σκότος ἐγένετο ἐφ' ὅλην τὴν γῆν (Mark 15:33) is reminiscent of Amos 8:9, συσκοτάσει ἐπὶ τῆς γῆς.[134] In both passages the sun goes

---

[125] Levenson 1993: 177.
[126] Vermès 1983: 214–18; Levenson 1993: 180–87; Kanarek 2014: 50–2.
[127] Vermès 1983: 214.
[128] Best 1990: 172; Levenson 1993: 174; Brown 1994: 2.1438; Huizenga 2009: 82–3.
[129] Brown 1994: 2.1438; Rindge 2012: 769.
[130] Evans 2001: 413.
[131] Rindge 2012: 769.
[132] Brown 1994: 1.150.
[133] Donahue and Harrington 2005: 447; it may also evoke the 'Paschal night' (Best 1990: 177).
[134] Kee 1978: 183; Hooker 1991: 376; Brown 1994: 2.1451; Marcus 2000b 1054; Stein 2008: 715; see also Achtemeier 1963: 446–47.

down at noon. In the next verse the consequent mourning will be 'like the mourning for an only son (יָחִיד/ἀγαπητοῦ)' (Amos 8:10).¹³⁵ The significance of this is that the reference to יָחִיד/ἀγαπητοῦ takes us directly back to Gen 22:2, 12, 16 and the *Akedah*.¹³⁶ This is not to downplay Mark's depiction of Jesus' abandonment. As Rindge writes, 'in stark contrast to Genesis, Jesus—as Mark's reconfigured Isaac—will not be rescued by a divine voice'.¹³⁷ Thus the typological comparison highlights the abandonment of Jesus. This thematic inversion of the Isaac typology, abandonment instead of rescue, becomes a core theme of the crucifixion.

Jesus cries out from the cross, quoting Psalm 22 (Mark 15:34) but bystanders mistakenly think he is calling Elijah (15:35). In the reference to dividing garments (Mark 15:24; Ps 22:18) and wagging heads (Mark 15:27; Ps 22:7), Psalm 22 has already been evoked.¹³⁸ This use of this Psalm reinforces an irony.¹³⁹ It is a cry of dereliction and abandonment,¹⁴⁰ but just as the reader knows that the psalm ends in praise, confidence and completion of deliverance (Ps 22:21b–31), so too does the reader know that the crucifixion story will end in vindication, deliverance and resurrection (Mark 8:31; 9:31; 10:34).¹⁴¹ Whether or not Jesus recites the whole psalm from the cross, the features of the psalm evident in the crucifixion narrative are consistently the negative ones. The vindication of the righteous sufferer is not (yet) described in the narrative.¹⁴² In this too, the reader is reminded of the *Akedah*, where, although Abraham's obedience to God's command is total and the intention to sacrifice real, the Jewish reader knows full well that his or her ancestor survives to father the nation of Israel.

He is given vinegar, ὄξος, to drink by someone who seems to want to prolong his agony in case Elijah rescues him (Mark 15:36). This evokes another psalm of the righteous sufferer, Ps 69:21 (LXX 68:22, ὄξος).¹⁴³ The psalmist complains of being falsely accused (Ps 69:4; Mark 14:57), is shamed and derided (Ps 69:7, 11–12; Mark 15:20, 29, 32). Notably, this psalm is associated with Jesus in a different Christian tradition of the Temple clearing (John 2:17; Ps 69:9). Again, this psalm ends with praise, deliverance, and restoration (Ps 69:30–36).

With the *Akedah* imagery and the psalms of the righteous sufferer (Ps 69; 22) so prevelant, the expected narrative outcome, imitating Isaac and the two psalms, would be for the one who is both beloved son and righteous sufferer to be spared from death by God's intervention. Indeed, the one who gives Jesus the vinegar appears to be hoping for a miraculous deliverance. The reader knows what has happened to 'Elijah', that is John the Baptist (Mark 1:14; 6:14–29; 9:13). Elijah has been present at both previous Christological high points: typologically in the person of John the Baptist at Jesus' baptism (1:4–9); in the appearance of Elijah and discussion of John as Elijah at the

---

[135] One of the few Markan commentators to note this is Van Iersel 1998: 474.
[136] The word יָחִיד is only used 12 times in the Hebrew Scriptures, and nowhere else in the Pentateuch.
[137] Rindge 2012: 766.
[138] Donahue and Harrington 2005: 442–5; Janowski 2013: 336.
[139] Juel 1977: 47; Goodacre 2006: 36.
[140] 'The reality of his sense of abandonment must not be minimized' (Evans 2001: 507; also Cranfield 1972: 458; Hooker 1991: 375; Van Iersel 1998: 475).
[141] Cranfield 1972: 458–9; Marcus 1992: 180–6; Donahue and Harrington 2005: 451.
[142] Janowski 2013: 338.
[143] Van Iersel 1998: 476; Evans 2001: 508; Donahue and Harrington 2005: 448; Bock 2006: 16.

transfiguration (9:4, 13); and now here, present in the mind, as the hope of a bystander (15:36).[144] Yet no deliverance comes.

Jesus breathes his last with a loud cry and the Temple curtain is torn (σχίζω) in two. This connects back to 1:10, when the heavens are torn (σχίζω) apart. Mark calls attention to this action through the duplication of ἐσχίσθη εἰς δύο ἀπ᾽ ἄνωθεν ἕως κάτω.[145] The verb σχίζω is rare in the LXX but is used to denote God's salvific action in the parting of the Red Sea (Exod 14:21), the eschatological splitting of the Mount of Olives (Zech 14:4, this may be alluded to in Mark 11:23), and the splitting of the rock in the desert (Isa 48:21). Similarly, in Mark it only denotes the supernatural action of God.

Finally, the centurion by the cross comments, ἀληθῶς οὗτος ὁ ἄνθρωπος υἱὸς θεοῦ ἦν (Mark 15:39). As Hooker notes, 'for Mark, it is this Gentile soldier who gives to Jesus the title which hitherto has been spoken only by the heavenly voice or unclean spirits'.[146] The soldier's acclamation stands in sharp contrast to the earlier mockery (Mark 15:16–20). Yet it also serves as a climax to the passion. Immediately connected by the narrative to the tearing of the curtain (15:38) and the overshadowing darkness (15:33), it parallels the divine voice of 1:11 and 9:7 which was also preceded by supernatural events. Thus there is a discernible progression in the Gospel: the declaration of sonship that only Jesus witnesses (1:11), the declaration of sonship that the disciples witness (9:7) and finally a declaration of sonship by a Gentile (15:39). The declarations do not imply an escalation of Jesus' status as God's son, but a movement from private to public in the recognition of that status. At the same time, what God relented from asking of Abraham, God has done with God's own beloved son. The beloved son has become the Passover lamb.

§3.5 The King of the Jews: Davidic royal typology in Mark 11–15

In Mark's narrative, Jesus had previously made a typological comparison between himself and David (2:23–26). In the episode immediately prior to the triumphal entry, Jesus is twice called 'son of David' (10:47–48). Then, in Jesus' triumphal entry to Jerusalem the crowd declare: 'blessed is the coming kingdom of our ancestor David!' (11:10). The narrative is ambiguous as to how exactly or how reliably these cries relate Jesus to David,[147] but they do serve to bring David to mind and prepare the reader for more subtle David references to come.[148] At several points in the passion narrative Jesus is portrayed as a type of King David. This effect is achieved by a variety of techniques: a number of specific mentions of David, frequent references to the Davidic prophecy of Zechariah 9–14, some narrative assimilation to David, and a strong royal theme throughout the passion, in particular the crucifixion.

---

[144] Hooker 1991: 377; Donahue and Harrington 2005: 447–8.
[145] Donahue and Harrington 2005: 448.
[146] Hooker 1991: 378–9.
[147] France 2002: 434–5.
[148] Van Iersel 1998: 352.

§3.5.1 Zechariah's Davidic Messiah in the Passion

Jesus' arrival in Jerusalem on a colt, accompanied by shouting and Ps 118:25–26 (Mark 11:1–11), strongly evokes Zech 9:9 (cf. Matt 21:4–5).[149] However, Mark may already expect his readers to be alert to allusions from Zechariah 9–14. Zech 13:2 is the most likely background text for the Gospel of Mark's language of 'unclean spirit/s' and the exorcism accounts can be read as a presentation of Jesus as a Davidic messiah come to rid the land of evil in fulfilment of Zech 13:2.[150] Additionally, the 'strange' and 'excessive' geographical note that mentions the Mount of Olives in Mark 11:1 may serve to bring Zech 14:4 to mind.[151] By enacting Zech 9:9, the triumphal entry resonates with the earlier portrayal of Jesus and prepares the reader to see the following events of the passion with Zech 9–14 and Jesus' Davidic kingship in mind.

Having entered Jerusalem, Jesus performs his prophetic critique and judgement of the Temple (11:12–25).[152] When Jesus drives out those who are selling and buying (11:15) the reader may be reminded of Zech 14:21, 'and there shall no longer be traders in the house of the Lord of hosts on that day'.[153] As part of this narrative sequence Jesus tells his disciples that with faith they can command a mountain to throw itself into the sea (11:23). Some have suggested this has a background in Zech 14:4 where two halves of the Mount of Olives withdraw northwards and southwards, respectively.[154]

Jesus responds to the questioning of his authority to do 'these things' (11:27–33) with the parable of the vineyard (12:1–12). Jesus' parable of the vineyard most clearly uses Isa 5:1–7 and Ps 118:22–23. However, the reader familiar with Zech 9–14 might also note a correspondence with Zech 10:3–4, God's promise to 'punish the leaders' and to bring out of the house of Judah 'the cornerstone', two ideas also central to Mark 12:1–12.

Later, when Jesus' opponents have ceased to dare ask him questions (Mark 12:34), Jesus poses his own question regarding the relationship of the messiah to David (12:35–37). The term Χριστός is most likely to have associations with a Davidic messiah.[155] If this was not known from other sources, Jesus' question reveals the connection (12:35). For Marcus, 'the evangelist means both to affirm and qualify the idea of Davidic messianism'.[156] As France argues, 'It seems to have been an unquestioned conviction in first-century Christianity that the title "Son of David"... was appropriate for Jesus' (e.g. Matt 1:20; Luke 1:27, 32, 69; 2:4, 11; Rom 1:3–4; 2 Tim 2:8; Rev 5:5; 22:16).[157] Importantly, Jesus, while connecting David and the messiah through his question, also implies that the messiah has a higher status than David or the son of

---

[149] Bruce 1961: 339; Van Iersel 1998: 353; Marcus 2000b 778. As Marcus notes Gen 49:10–11 is also evoked by 'the otherwise superfluous note that the colt is tied (11:2, 4)'.
[150] This will be discussed in more detail in §6.
[151] De Jonge 2003: 88.
[152] As discussed above.
[153] Barrett 1978: 19; Evans 1999: 383–4; De Jonge 2003: 90–2; Bermejo-Rubio 2016: 114.
[154] Bruce 1961: 347–8; Marcus 2000b: 785; see also Van Iersel 1998: 359–60; Evans 1999: 384.
[155] Marcus 2000b: 848; 2008: 137; Collins 2010: 77–8; Johnson 2018: 271; see further Kee 1987: 188; Novenson 2012: 51.
[156] Marcus 2000b: 850.
[157] France 2002: 484.

David (12:37). As Kee writes, 'The messianic figure does not merely model the Davidic paradigm but surpasses David in a transcendent manner'.[158]

However, the Davidic messiah was generally associated with violent military victory.[159] This may have tempered Jesus' identification with David,[160] or indeed Mark's identification of Jesus with David.

As we have already noted, the Davidic messianic hope in Zechariah has a prominent role in Mark. In Mark 13 Jesus most closely resembles a prophet. The most pervasive influence on Mark 13 is the book of Daniel.[161] However, Jesus' prophetic words along with his location on the Mount of Olives also evoke the final judgement scene in Zechariah 14.[162] Mark 13:1–8 describes international war and the destruction of Jerusalem, as does Zech 14:1–2. Mark 13:3 places Jesus' prophecy as occurring on the Mount of Olives; Zech 14:4 promises YHWH's feet will stand on the Mount of Olives. This could well be a deliberate Christological device, placing Jesus in the Lord's role, as in Mark 1:2–3. In Mark 13:14–15 the inhabitants of Judea are told to flee. In Zech 14:5 those in Jerusalem are told 'you shall flee'. Zech 14:5 promises the arrival of YHWH with his 'holy ones'. Mark 13:26–27 states that the Son of Man will come in great glory and send out his angels. These angels are described as 'holy ones' in a related passage in 8:38.

While Jesus appears more as prophet than messiah in Mark 13, the messiah theme is still present, especially as Jesus affirms his status as true messiah over and against false messiahs in 13:6, 21–27, and in 13:32 refers to himself as 'the son'. The correspondences with Zechariah 14 maintain the theme of Davidic messianism within Mark 13. Additionally, David was considered to be a prophet himself (LAB 60:1–3; Acts 2:30). Jesus acting as prophet does not work against the David typology.

§3.5.2 Jesus and David, the twice-anointed Kings

Mark 14 begins with a brief account of the chief priests and scribes conspiring against Jesus (14:1–2) before Jesus is anointed at Bethany (14:3–9). Jesus has been anointed privately at the beginning of the Gospel (1:10–11).[163] David had been anointed privately, in the presence only of his family, by Samuel at the beginning of his story and 'the spirit of the Lord came mightily upon David from that day forward' (1 Sam 16:13). Jesus' second anointing (Mark 14:3–9), while explicitly for his burial, takes place openly in Bethany in Judea. David's second anointing takes place openly, when he is publicly anointed as king by the people of Judah in Hebron (2 Sam 2:4).

While many scholars see Jesus' Bethany anointing as having messianic symbolism,[164] others object. Boring argues that 'Jesus had already been anointed as the Christ by God; he does not just now become messiah by human anointing'.[165] However, if a David

---

[158] Kee 1987: 203.
[159] Hengel 1989: 298–300; Collins 2010: 78.
[160] Evans 1997: 195.
[161] Hartman 1966: 207.
[162] Bruce 1961: 348; Bermejo-Rubio 2016: 123–4.
[163] The baptism of Jesus is interpreted as an anointing in Ps. Jerome, *Com. Marcum.* 1:8. See Cahill 1998: 33.
[164] Garland 1996: 516; Evans 2001: 359–60; Donahue and Harrington 2005: 390; Collins 2007: 642.
[165] Boring 2006: 383.

typology in the passion is accepted, Boring's objection is vitiated because this second anointing does not need to be seen as the moment Jesus becomes the messiah, but only as a public recognition of the messianic status that was already his.

More critically, in this context, the verb μυρίζω (14:8) specifically implies anointing for burial, rather than χρίω which would imply anointing to an office.[166] Collins suggests that μυρίζω could evoke the Song of Solomon (1:3, 4; 2:5; 4:10, 14) and present Jesus as a bridegroom. This in turn parallels Jesus' use of bridegroom imagery in Mark 2:19–20. There, Jesus also predicts that the bridegroom will be taken away (2:20) which Collins sees paralleled in 'you will not always have me' (14:7).[167] Also, the bridegroom of the Song is Solomon, the son of David, so such a resonance would support the messianic interpretation of the anointing.

In my view, the significance of μυρίζω being used instead of χρίω has been overstated. The Gospel pericope describes the pouring of ointment upon Jesus' head towards the climax of a narrative which has identified Jesus as the messiah from the very first (Mark 1:1). Olive oil (ἔλαιον) poured (ἐπιχέω) on the head is how the kings of the OT were anointed (1 Sam 10: 1; 2 Kgs 9:3, 6). While ointment (μύρον) is not olive oil, the lavish pouring (καταχέω) of an expensive liquid over the head in Mark 14:3 is able to evoke a kingly anointing. The narrative parallels are sufficient without lexical correspondences. The interpretation that the anointing is for Jesus' burial is not given until later in the pericope (14:8). This allows for other inferences to operate earlier. The burial interpretation is significant, but likely expands the meaning of the anointing for the reader, rather than restricting it. Kee observes that the woman, by anointing Jesus for his burial, shows a better understanding of Jesus' messianic mission, and the place of his death in it, than the 'erroneous notions of messiahship' elsewhere in the Gospel (e.g. Mark 8:29; 12:35; 14:61; 15:32).[168] The story is powerful precisely because it can resonate with so many significant themes: the bridegroom, burial and royal consecration.

The stories of Jesus' and David's anointing are also linked by the anointed figure promising reward: Jesus to the woman with the jar (Mark 14:9) and David to the people of Jabesh Gilead (2 Sam 2:6–7). Most significantly the people of Jabesh Gilead are honoured for providing for the proper burial of King Saul (2 Sam 2:4–5), while the woman with the jar is honoured for providing for Jesus' burial (Mark 14:8–9). Immediately after the story of David's anointing the story of Abner's opposition to David begins (2 Sam 2:8). Similarly, immediately after the anointing of Jesus, Judas acts to betray him (Mark 14:10).

§3.5.3 Typological betrayal

During the Last Supper Jesus tells his disciples that one of those eating with him (ὁ ἐσθίων μετ' ἐμοῦ, Mark 14:18) will betray him. When he is questioned about this he confirms, 'It is one of the twelve, one who is dipping [bread] into the bowl with me'

---

[166] For χρίω, see BDAG: 1091; LSJ: 2007; GE: 2380. For μυρίζω, see BDAG: 661; LSJ: 1154; GE: 1371.
[167] Collins 2007: 642–3.
[168] Kee 1987: 200.

(Mark 14:20). Mark 14:18 most likely alludes to Ps 41:9 (LXX 40:10), ὁ ἐσθίων ἄρτους μου (cf. John 13:18).[169] The 'bosom friend' of Ps 41:9, 15 is identified in the Talmud with Ahithophel, David's betrayer in 2 Sam 15:31 (*b. Sanh.* 106b–107a; *Midr.* Ps 41:7).[170] If this connection of Psalm 41 with Ahithopel was known by Mark then the allusion connects Jesus to a particular Davidic episode (2 Sam 15). This tentative conclusion will be reinforced in consideration of the Gethsemane account after the Last Supper.

In the Didache the cup of the Last Supper is associated with David (Did 9:2, περὶ τοῦ ποτηρίου Εὐχαριστοῦμέν σοι πάτερ ἡμῶν ὑπὲρ τῆς ἁγίας ἀμπέλου Δαυεὶδ τοῦ παιδός σου). It is possible that Jesus' statement regarding the 'fruit of the vine' (Mark 14:25) evokes messianic exegesis of Psalm 80:8–18.[171] A stronger association is that the phrase 'blood of covenant' (Mark 14:24) reflects Zech 9:11.[172]

After the supper Jesus and the disciples go to the Mount of Olives (14:26). Jesus then predicts the disciples' desertion, citing Zech 13:7 (Mark 14:27).[173] With this citation Mark's Jesus presents himself as the royal Davidic messianic shepherd of Zech 13:7 (cf. also Jer 23:1–6; Ezek 34:23–24; 37:24).[174] Jesus' subsequent comment, 'But after I am raised up (ἐγείρω) I will go before (προάγω) you to Galilee', reinforces the shepherd theme. 'Going before' is how a good shepherd leads their flock (Isa 40:11; John 10:3–5). The divine passive of 'raised up' echoes other passages where God promises to raise up a shepherd (Zech 11:16, ἐγείρω; Jer 23:4, ἀνίστημι). The Zechariah citation also reminds the reader of the significance of the Mount of Olives (cf. Zech 14:4). This significance will now gain a new, but still Davidic, facet in the Gethsemane account.

Eugene Boring, among others, observes the similarity between Mark 14:10–42 and 2 Sam 15:16–31 where 'David is betrayed by a trusted friend [Ahithopel], goes to the Mount of Olives, weeps, and prays to God'.[175] These elements are also present in Jesus' portrayal in Mark 14: betrayal by a disciple (14:10–11, 18–21, 43–46); going to the Mount of Olives (14:26); grief, distress and agitation (14:33–34); and prayer (14:36, 39). Raymond Brown suggests Mark 14:29–30, where the disciples protest their loyalty to Jesus, reflects 'the theme of who would remain faithful' from 2 Sam 15:19–21.[176] Peter's declaration of loyalty to Jesus in Mark 14:29, 31 may also echo Ittai's declaration to David in 2 Sam 15:21.

The David/Ahithopel allusion suggested by Psalm 41:9 in Mark 14:18 might also bring to mind Psalm 55 (LXX 54),[177] which is likewise associated with Ahithophel's betrayal in the Targums and Rabbinic literature (*Targ.* Ps 55:13–24; *b. Sanh.* 106b; *m. Abot* 6.3; *Midr.* Ps 55:1).[178] Psalm 55 also has strong resonances with Gethsemane, particularly Mark 14:34: 'I am distraught (λυπέω)' (Ps 55:2/LXX 54:3) and 'My heart is in anguish within me, the terrors of death have fallen upon me' (Ps 55:4/LXX 54:5).

---

[169] Gnilka 1998: 2.236; Marcus 2000b: 954.
[170] Pesch 1979: 2.350; Collins 2007: 649–51; Johnson 2018: 256.
[171] Dodd 1965: 101–2.
[172] Brown 1994: 1.623; Evans 1997: 386; De Jonge 2003: 88.
[173] Bruce 1961: 340.
[174] Bruce 1961: 344; Brown 1994: 1.128–30; Evans 1997: 384; Bermejo-Rubio 2016: 120.
[175] Boring 2006: 393. Also Brown 1994: 1.125. This connection is considerably elaborated upon by Matthew's Gospel, see Johnson 2018.
[176] Brown 1994: 1.128.
[177] See Janowski 2013: 334.
[178] Johnson 2018: 256.

Thus, there are several strong narrative correspondences to David and Ahithopel alongside possible allusions to Psalms 41 and 55 in Mark's Gethsemane account. Judas' betrayal of Jesus is shown to be of a scriptural type and Jesus' messianic identity as a type of David is further confirmed.

§3.5.4 The coronation of the Davidic Messiah

At the Sanhedrin trial, Jesus admits to being the messiah, saying, ἐγώ εἰμι.[179] Although the messianic hope was variously construed, its 'common core' was Davidic.[180] In Jesus' response to the high priest's question he confirms that the messiah, the Son of God (the Blessed One) and the son of man all identify the same person, himself (Mark 14:61-62). By combining the messiah title with son of God, Mark fully establishes the royal and Davidic connotations of the term son of God.

Johnson notes several significant scriptures where the son of David is also called a son of God:[181]

- 'I will be a father to him, and he will be a son to me.' (2 Sam 7:14)
- 'You are my son; today I have begotten you.' (Ps 2:7)
- 'He shall cry to me, "You are my Father, my God, and the rock of my salvation!" I will make him the firstborn, the highest of the kings of the earth.' (Ps 89:27-28)

Thus it seems quite possible that the high priest's question, combining messiah with 'son of the blessed one', served to clarify the messiah as Davidic. Afterwards, in the trial before Pilate, Jewish terms like messiah and son of the Blessed one are not used. Pilate asks, 'Are you the King of the Jews?' To which Jesus answers, 'you say so' (Mark 15:2). The phrase ὁ βασιλεὺς τῶν Ἰουδαίων is then repeated in 15:9, 12, 18, 26 and finally Jesus is called ὁ χριστὸς ὁ βασιλεὺς Ἰσραήλ in 15:32.[182] This change of language should not obscure the fact that the paradigmatic 'king of the Jews/Israel' was David and that the anticipated royal messiah was the Son of David. Because Mark has so consistently established the David typology in the passion account thus far, references to Jesus as 'king' will continue to have a Davidic resonance.

From this point on there is no escaping the royal theme of the passion narrative. As Juel observes, 'Jesus is tried, mocked, and crucified as King'.[183] Once Pilate has passed sentence (14:15) the Roman soldiers cloak Jesus in purple, crown him with thorns, salute him, 'Hail King of the Jews!', kneel in homage to him (14:17-19), and crucify him under the inscription 'The King of the Jews' (15:26).

---

[179] Although the shorter reading, following the vast majority of manuscripts, is preferred, that does not imply, here, an allusion to the divine name, but in context is a simple elliptical affirmation. See Gundry 1993: 910; Evans, 2001: 450. The longer reading, found in Θ f13 565. 700. 2542s, is argued for by Dunn (1970: 111) and Marcus (2000b: 1005).
[180] Collins 2010: 78.
[181] Johnson 2018: 249.
[182] Dunn 1970: 107.
[183] Juel 1977: 49.

The whole scene is deeply ironic, as the Christ-believing reader knows that Jesus really is 'the king of the Jews' and that his death will not be the end of the story.[184] Even without prior knowledge of the outcome, the reader has been informed several times that Jesus would rise again after his death (8:31; 9:31; 10:34) and knows that he is the royal messiah/Christ (1:1; 8:29; 14:61–62). Thus the mocking of the soldiers (15:16–20) is also his true coronation.[185] Perhaps most ironic is the centurion's pronouncement at the moment of death. When Jesus seems at his most human, most frail and degraded, most dead, this flat character representing the Gentile Empire of Rome acknowledges the truth of Jesus' most exalted title.[186]

Jesus' cry of abandonment, 'My God, my God, why have you forsaken me?' (Mark 15:34), cites Ps 22:1, a psalm attributed to David.[187] The citation strengthens several earlier possible allusions to Psalm 22 in the crucifixion scene: the mockery in Mark 15:29, 32 may reflect Ps 22:6–7; the wagging heads of Mark 15:29 may reflect Ps 22:7; the challenge to 'save yourself' in Mark 15:30 may reflect 'let him deliver ... let him rescue' in Ps 22:8; the divided clothes and casting of lots in Mark 15:24 strongly alludes to Ps 22:19.[188]

In the passion, scriptural typology continues to play an important role in the Christological meaning of Mark's Gospel. Most prominent are the psalms of the righteous sufferer, including Psalms 22 and 41.[189] They function to portray Jesus with a 'righteous sufferer typology'.[190] In Jesus' day these Psalms were considered to be psalms of David due to the 'Davidization of the Psalter' in the Second Temple period.[191] In addition the anointing at Bethany and the Garden of Gethsemane pericopae serve to portray Jesus in terms of the David narrative, as anointed king and betrayed king. Thus Mark shows Jesus to be the antitype of David.

After Psalm 22 it is Zechariah 9–14 that 'offers the most extensive background for the passion'.[192] While Zechariah 9–14 provides the background for several disparate motifs in the passion, the themes are given unity by their connection with Davidic messianism.

In opposition to the expectation of a military leader, Jesus' messianic mission finds fulfilment in rejection, humiliation and death. However, his vindication and return in glory and power is also promised. While there is little, if any, narrative assimilation to God here, the supernatural events of the darkness and torn curtain signal to the reader that this death has a significance beyond the deaths of the prophets and kings of scripture, none of whose deaths were accompanied by such signs.

§3.5.5 Divine identity in the trial of Jesus?

For Bauckham, Mark 14:62 establishes Jesus as part of the divine identity and thus as on the creator side of the creator–creation divide.[193] However, neither the sitting at

---

[184] Marcus 2000b: 1058; Donahue and Harrington 2005: 442.
[185] Boring 2006: 425.
[186] Best 1990: 168. Bauckham 2017a: 33.
[187] Brown 1994: 2.1456; Bock 2006: 15–16; Janowski 2013: 322, 335.
[188] Bock 2006: 13–14; Janowski 2013: 336.
[189] Marcus 1992: 174; Garland 1996: 593–4; Janowski 2013: 330.
[190] Evans 1992: 864.
[191] Janowski 2013: 322.
[192] Brown 1994: 2.1451. See also Bruce 1961: 342; Dodd 1965: 107.
[193] Bauckham 2008: 265; also Bauckham 2017a: 32.

God's right hand of Ps 110:1 nor the coming with the clouds of heaven from Dan 7:13 necessarily demand Jesus' identification as creator. As Hurtado has pointed out, in Rev 3:21 'Laodicean Christians are promised a seat with Christ on his throne, which he shares with God!'[194] While it is possible this image implies divinisation of the Christians, what it does not suggest is that they are uncreated. Most notably, Dan 7:13–14 goes well beyond the explicit claims of Jesus in Mark 14:62. The kingship of the one like a son of man is universal, everlasting and indestructible, echoing the kingdom of the Most High God in Dan 4:3.[195] As Bauckham observes, 'the terms in which the sovereignty of the Son of Man are described in Daniel 7:14 are closely similar to those used elsewhere in Daniel of God's own sovereignty (Dan. 4:3; 4:34; 6:26)'.[196] Yet, there is no indication in either Daniel or Second Temple Jewish interpretation of Daniel that this redefines or challenges Jewish monotheism.[197] Within Jewish thought it was possible for someone (whether the son of man in Daniel is understood as an individual or corporate figure) to have such dominion given to them by God, without also assuming the identity of creator.

Bauckham argues that the sovereignty of the son of man in Dan 7:9 'does not describe God's permanent rule of the world, but the eschatological session of the divine court of judgement, and so could readily be understood as set on earth rather than in heaven'.[198] He also argues that in 1 Enoch 46:5; 48:5; 62:6, 9, the son of man is included in the identity of God because he both sits on God's throne and is recognized by the worship of kings and mighty ones as one 'who rules over all'.[199] When compared, Mark's use of son of man and throne imagery (e.g. Mark 14:62) corresponds to that in Daniel because it is eschatologically oriented, but not to 1 Enoch because Jesus is not worshipped. In 4 Ezra, another early Jewish text employing imagery from Dan 7,[200] a messianic one 'like a figure of a man' (4 Ezra 13:3),[201] who is also possibly termed God's son (4 Ezra 13:32, 37),[202] performs eschatological judgement upon the nations (4 Ezra 13:10–11, 37–38) without any hint of being involved in creation. Thus, considering the son of man figure in Dan 7:9, 1 Enoch and 4 Ezra suggests that the eschatological enthronement of the son of man in Mark does not require Jesus to have also had a role in creation.

After the Second Temple period, the rabbis record a controversy over the 'thrones' of Dan 7:9. Rabbi Akiva asserted that one throne beside the God's throne was for David. Rabbi Yosei objects to this on the grounds that no one could sit next to God (b. Ḥag. 14a; b. Sanh. 38b).[203] While the thrones caused controversy, which nonetheless

---

[194] Hurtado 2003: 47.
[195] Hengel 2001: 185.
[196] Bauckham 2008.
[197] A point made emphatically by Bauckham (2008: 162, 164); however, there is evidence that Dan 7:9 later became a locus of the 'two powers heresy' (e.g. Mek. R. Shimon 15; Mek. R. Yishmael 5.4; Pesiq. Rab. 21), see Segal 2002: 33–6.
[198] Bauckham 2008: 161–2; cf. 1999.
[199] Bauckham 2008: 171.
[200] Collins 1992: 461–2; Slater 1995: 196.
[201] OTP 1.551.
[202] For this argument see Collins 1992: 462–3.
[203] Hengel 2001: 194–6; Horbury 2011: 20.

demonstrates that some Jewish teachers could conceive of a human (David) exalted to sit next to God, the dominion of the Son of Man does not receive any qualification or comment, suggesting it did not present as an issue.

In a later essay Bauckham clarifies his position: 'The language of Dan 7:13-14 does not so clearly require this meaning [of divine identity], since the figure "like a human being" does not share the heavenly throne of God and is merely said to be given rule over all people on earth. It is the combination of this text with Ps 110:1 that makes this "Son of man" an unambiguously divine figure.'[204] But what does Psalm 110 add to Daniel 7 in terms of divine identity? Psalm 110 was received in early Judaism as a psalm of eschatological expectation (11QMelch [13]; *Midr. Pss, parasha* 4), which capitalized upon the psalm's association of kingship with divinity, with the king understood to be co-regent and supported by God.[205] Moreover, in Dan 7:9 there are multiple thrones, so by conflating Dan 7:13 and Ps 110:1 sitting 'at the right hand' of God does not likely imply sharing God's throne, but sitting on a throne 'next to God himself'.[206] The position of sitting at the right hand of a king is one of great prestige and authority, but as a servant of that king, not their equal in status.[207] Moreover, that same servant to the heavenly king is made a priest in Psalm 100:4, not God, but a mediator between God and the nation.[208] Finally, as Bauckham himself argues, the direction of Jesus' 'coming' in Mark 14:62 is to earth, to the thrones set up for eschatological judgement.[209] This is not to deny the exalted nature of the claim Jesus is making for himself here, but the claim is one of *eschatological* kingship and judgement. This is a claim of being empowered and approved by God, but not one requiring divine identity.

Bauckham further suggests that for Mark the title son of God 'indicates Jesus' unique relationship to God as one who participates in the divine identity'.[210] However this meaning is asserted rather than argued by Bauckham. Rather, as argued above, in Mark the language of son of God and beloved son relate primarily to Jesus as the new Isaac. This designation creates a uniquely special relationship between Jesus and God, but does not require creation or cosmic sovereignty to be attributed to Jesus.

§3.6 Conclusion

The foregoing analysis of Mark's baptism, transfiguration and passion accounts has shown how central scriptural typology is to Mark's presentation of Jesus. The *Akedah* narrative can be seen to be evoked in the baptism, transfiguration and passion narratives, as Jesus is presented as God's beloved son who journeys to Mount Moriah (Jerusalem) to die. This typology only becomes more meaningful when the Isaac narrative is inverted in Jesus' passion at the point of rescue from death, and no last-

---

[204] Bauckham 2017a: 32.
[205] Marcus 1992: 132-7, 2000b: 1007.
[206] Evans 2001: 451.
[207] Goldingay 2008: 294.
[208] Mays 1994: 351.
[209] Bauckham 2017a: 35-6.
[210] Bauckham 2008: 265.

second reprieve occurs. Jesus' sacrifice and obedience are thus shown to be more complete than Isaac's. Thus Jesus escalates and fulfils the type established by Isaac.

The narrative of David as suffering, rejected and betrayed king has a strong presence in the passion account, not only through narrative correspondences but also through the employment of Psalms which are attached to that Davidic story in Jewish tradition. Jesus is the Davidic messiah who will surpass his predecessor and be known as God's son (2 Sam 7:13–14; Mark 12:37). Thus Jesus escalates and fulfils the type established by David.

Markan typology is hence able to operate in a complex and multi-layered way, as Jesus is both a type of Issac, God's beloved only son (12:6), but also the Davidic messiah, son of the blessed one (14:61). One strong allusion does not prevent or vitiate another. Here the idea of sonship serves to unite the scriptural themes.

In addition to the typological connection of Jesus with human figures, we have also seen a correlation of Jesus with the God of Israel. Thus far we have observed Jesus as the coming Lord of Isaiah 40:3 (Mark 1:3), as the mountain top epiphany of Moses and Elijah (Mark 9:2–7), and as the divine judge of Israel/Jerusalem from the prophetic literature (Mark 11:12–25). This theomorphic typology will need much further discussion, exactly what we can infer from it will require considerable nuance, but for now it suffices to acknowledge that it is there.

We have not found a repetitive method or single approach to exegesis. The narrative allusion may be to a single episode (Gen 22), a collection of texts around a narrative event (2 Sam 15; Pss 41, 55), a collection of similar narratives (epiphanies of Moses and Elijah) or a scriptural theme found across the prophets (e.g. Jer 7:11; 8:13; Hosea 2:12; 9:10–17). What we have discovered is that Mark can use narrative scriptural typology powerfully in enriching his portrayal of Jesus. Mark presents Jesus as both in continuity and contrast with human figures from scriptural history, and identifies Jesus with Israel's God to an extraordinary extent. This pattern in the baptism, transfiguration and passion, is by no means present in every episode of the Gospel. However, Mark's most sustained and spectacular miracle accounts, when closely read alongside the Jewish scriptures they allude to, arguably also display this combination of fulfilment and theomorphic typologies. This is the argument I will now proceed to make.

§4

Jonah typology in Mark 4:35–41

Do you see how, as the green hears Caesar, the woods are silenced? Remember, despite the frantic tempest, the forest suddenly motionless, branches in repose. I said, 'A god is here, certainly a god expelled the east-wind'.[1]

In this chapter I will examine the storm stilling miracle of Mark 4:35–41, as well as its counterpart in 6:45–52. After an initial discussion of the story and then analysis of the genre of miraculous sea rescues, I will consider an ostensible allusion to the storm stilling of Psalm 107. The discussion will demonstrate that there is no narrative or lexical evidence of an allusion to Psalm 107 in the Markan miracle. By contrast, there are several distinctive narrative and lexical correspondences which strongly suggest the presence of an intentional allusion to the storm stilling of Jonah 1. This chapter concludes with a discussion of the Christology implied by the proposed allusion to Jonah in Mark's story of Jesus calming a storm.

§4.1 More than a 'Simple Miracle Story'

The ability to command wind and waves was a reputed power of both pagan rulers and Jewish rabbis, among others.[2] However, Mark 4:35–41 is more than a simple account of a sea miracle. First, Mark's rustic writing style conceals a finely crafted narrative where variation in tenses helps mark the stages of the story. Initially the historic present is used for the key verbs, but when the story reaches its climax the aorist is used indicating 'Jesus' decisive action'.[3] The final key verb of the episode is imperfect, leaving Jesus' identity a continuing question for the disciples.

Secondly, the performance of the miracle is subordinate to the dialogue between Jesus and his disciples.[4] The narrative focus is the identity of Jesus, rather than the supernatural event.[5] The Christological question of 4:41, 'Who can this be, that even the wind and the waves obey him?' is not rhetorical for the disciples; they are genuinely

---

[1] Calpurnius, *Bucolica* 4.97–100; author's translation.
[2] See the following section.
[3] France 2002: 222.
[4] Gnilka 1998: 1.194; Boring 2006: 144; Stein 2008: 239.
[5] Achtemeier 1962: 170; Koch 1975: 93; France 2002: 220; Boring 2006: 147.

bewildered by what they have witnessed.⁶ It has a second function in the text, however. It also addresses the reader,⁷ challenging them to allow this event to confront their preconceived categories of who Jesus might be.⁸ As Dechow writes, 'V.41 kann also nur gegen seinen Sinn im Kontext der Seesturmstillung als Auftakt eines Abschnitts angesehen werden, der als sein wesentliches Thema die christologische Frage behandelt.'⁹

Finally, Mark 4:35–41 is one of two miracles that occur on the Sea of Galilee in Mark's Gospel, the other being the walking on the water in Mark 6:45–52. The way one sea miracle is understood might be expected to have significance for the interpretation of the other, and this will be discussed in due course.

§4.2 Exploring the conventions: Miraculous sea rescues in antiquity

The storm stilling of Mark 4 can be considered a nature miracle (Bultmann) or a rescue miracle (Theissen).¹⁰ It seems unnecessary to choose between the two as elements of both are at work in the Markan episode.¹¹ Dibelius' category of 'tale' encompasses both as 'an epiphany of the divine on earth'.¹² Yet Heil's narrower category of 'sea rescue epiphany' is more useful in creating a workable category for comparison.¹³ However, Cotter rightly warns that with such anachronistic 'conscious classification' we must not project 'our categories and their criteria backwards'.¹⁴

The ability to calm sea storms was attributed in Hellenism to both gods and human heroes. Among the gods were Poseidon/Neptune, Aphrodite/Venus, the Dioscuri, the Samthrace deities, Isis and Serapis. Among the heroes were Orpheus, Pythagoras, Empedocles, Apollonius of Tyana, Julius Caesar and Augustus Caesar.¹⁵ Stories of divine rescue at sea follow a simple structure: a sudden and severe storm, prayers to a deity, and a sudden calm often accompanied by an equally sudden safe arrival at the supplicant's destination (e.g. Athenaeus, *Deipn.* 15.576a-b; Diodrus Siculus, *The Library of History* 4.43.1–2; Apuleius, *Metam.* 11.5; Aelius Aristides, *Regarding Serapis* 45.33). The only Jewish story that closely conforms to this structure is *y. Ber.* 9.¹⁶

---

⁶ This question and confusion over Jesus' identity forms an inclusio around the following sequence of miracles with Mark 6:3, see Dechow 2000: 197; Collins 2007: 258; Brower 2009: 305.
⁷ McInerny 1996: 258.
⁸ France 2002: 225.
⁹ 'V.41 can only be, contrary to its meaning in the context of the storm stilling, regarded as a prelude to a section that handles the Christological question as its essential theme' (Dechow 2000: 210, see also 239).
¹⁰ Bultmann 1963: 215–16; Gerd Theissen 1983: 99–100.
¹¹ However, see the caution of Meier (1991: 874), 'So variegated are the form, language, and content of these stories that one may rightly question whether, within the Four Gospels, "nature miracles" constitute a single intelligible category like exorcisms, healings, or raising the dead. The idea of a nature miracle is anything but clear and distinct.'
¹² Dibelius 1971: 94.
¹³ Heil 1981: 30.
¹⁴ Cotter 2010: 1–2.
¹⁵ See further, Cotter 1999: 13137, 142–8.
¹⁶ Cotter 1999: 142.

In relation to Mark 4:35–41 all these features are also present, if the complaint of 4:38 is interpreted as a prayer.[17] Notably, however, other elements, including Jesus' sleep and the post-miracle dialogue, are a departure from the usual simplicity of the form.

Wendy Cotter also suggests the storm stories of Levi (*Test. Naph.* 6:1–10) and Rabbi Gamaliel (*b. Meṣiʻa* 59b) as examples of the form.[18] They present fascinating departures from the convention which render them less useful as examples of it. Apart from the character of *Test. Naph.* 6:1–10 as part of a vision rather than realistic account, the boat is destroyed before Levi prays. The Talmud's *b. Meṣiʻa* 59b tells of a humorous prayer battle between two arguing rabbis. There is no actual storm, just a single rogue wave caused by the prayer of one of the rabbis.

Hellenistic narratives recounting the stilling of storms are limited to gods. Humans such as Pythagoras, Empedocles and Apollonius of Tyana are attributed with the ability to calm the sea or wind (Iamblichus, *Life of Pythagoras* 28, 135–6; Diogenes Laertius, *Empedocles* 8.59; Philostratus, *Vit. Apoll.* 4.13.5–13). However, none are recounted doing so in a narrative or as saving anyone through doing so. Julius Caesar's confidence in his own safety at sea did not result in a calming of the weather and the journey had to be abandoned (Dio Cassius, *Roman History* 46.1–4). Consequently, Mark 4:31–45 where a human figure stills a storm is easily interpreted as the portrayal of a divine figure; all the more so when juxtaposed with certain scriptural texts.

§4.3 Psalm 107 (LXX 106)

Psalm 107:23–32 (LXX Ps 106) is the most commonly cited background text for Mark 4:35–41.[19] A number of scholars argue for it, not least Richard Hays in his recent study of intertextuality in the Gospels.[20] Both Mark 4:35–41 and Psalm 107:23–32 recount a narrative where people embark on a voyage, encounter a dangerous storm and are saved when the storm is stilled.

The psalm portrays YHWH as the one whom wind and waves obey. In Ps 107:25, God speaks and the storm is raised and in 107:29 he commands (LXX: ἐπιτάσσω) or simply makes (MT: קוּם) the storm still and waves hush. When Mark 4:35–41 is read alongside Psalm 107:23–32 there is a ready answer to the disciples' question, 'Who can this be, that even the wind and the waves obey him?' Hays writes, 'for any reader versed in Israel's scripture, there can be only one possible answer: it is the Lord God of Israel.'[21] Briefly asserting that the passage 'looks very much like a midrashic narrative based on [Ps 107]', Hays then proceeds to situate the psalm in a matrix of Jewish scriptures (Job

---

[17] Which will be further discussed below.
[18] Cotter 1999: 140–1.
[19] Meye (1978) and Smothers (2013) have attempted to argue for a wider influence of Psalm 107 on this section of Mark. The case presented is tenuous at best.
[20] Hays 2016: 66; see also, e.g., Richardson 1941: 91–2; Pesch 1979: 1.272–3; Derrett 1985: 1.97; Drewermann 1989: 353; Garland 1996: 192; Twelftree 1999: 71, 373 n. 91; France 2002: 221; Brower 2009: 295; .
[21] Hays 2016: 66; see also Achtemeier 1962: 174; Geddert 2009: 122.

26 and 38; Pss 89 and 106; Isa 51) to show that calming storms is what God – and God alone – does.[22]

However, as neat a solution as this presents, several details warn against too direct an application of Psalm 107 to Mark 4:35–41. While the plots of the two passages cohere in several places, it is limited to generic correspondence which you would expect with any conventional sea calming story. There are also important differences which argue against dependence.

First, in Mark 4 the storm appears to arise independently and must be rebuked by Jesus with words reminiscent of his power encounters against demons.[23] For Mark, episodes set in the wilderness, mountain and sea serve to locate Jesus in the 'cosmic struggle' and reference the 'eschatological transformation of nature' of Isaiah 40.[24] Mark's storm narrative parricularly evokes primeval creation and flood myths, where the sea is a chaotic force to be mastered by the creator God.[25] By contrast, in Psalm 107 God both initiates the storm and stills it.

Second, in the Markan narrative, the disciples' fear of the storm is not explicit. The only description of the disciple's fear is within Jesus' rebuke, but the fear is attributed to their lack of faith, not the storm. In the psalm the narrator recounts the storm inspiring stupefying fear (Ps 107:26–27). This fear leads the travellers to turn to God. For Mark, however, the really terrifying one is Jesus.[26] The Markan narrative implies that the disciples are initially afraid of the storm, but the lack of explicit mention of this is a key point at which Mark could evoke Psalm 107:23–32 and does not. Rather, comparison of the two passages highlights how Mark foregrounds Christological revelation over the miraculous deliverance.

Third, Psalm 107's core message of the redeemed's thankfulness is completely absent from Mark 4:35–41.[27] The psalm as a whole repeatedly moves from distressed souls to the thankful redeemed. By contrast, Mark 4:35–41 moves from implied fear at the storm to 'fearing with great fear' at Jesus (4:41).

Fourth, a unique characteristic of Psalm 107 among the psalms is its 'paraenetic conclusion' (107:43) which lends it a sapiential character.[28] The psalm's narrative repeatedly shows sinners repenting and consequently being saved by the God of Israel. Thus 'those who are wise' (107:43) are to pay attention and imitate the behaviour of those who are redeemed by calling on God (107:6, 13, 19, 28) with faith in his 'steadfast love' (107:43). In contrast, Jesus' compassion is conspicuous by its absence in Mark 4:35–41. The disciples do not repent. There is no sapiential moral of the story, only fear and confusion. The disciples are rebuked for their fear and lack of faith. They are not presented as an example to be learned from.

---

[22] Hays 2016: 67.
[23] See Mark 1:25, 3:12 and 9:25; Achtemeier 1962: 176; Feneberg 2000: 132; Boring 2006: 146; Collins 2007: 261; Hartman 2010: 195.
[24] Marcus 1992: 27, 34.
[25] Achtemeier 1962; Drewermann 1989: 586.
[26] Gathercole 2006: 63.
[27] On this theme in Psalm 107 see Mays 2011: 345.
[28] Meye 1978: 9; see also Smothers 2013: 21.

Fifth, there is an incongruence with Psalm 107 and Mark's theme of the suffering messiah. Suffering in Psalm 107 is the result of sin (107:11, 17, 42). In Mark, it is a result of obedience (e.g. Mark 8:34; 14:36).

Thus, when the generic features of a sea rescue story are taken out of consideration there is no evidence of an allusion. On the other hand, there are several thematic incongruences between Psalm 107 and Mark 4:35–41 (their presentations of nature, fear, thankfulness, wisdom and suffering), all of which render it an unlikely text for Mark to have been drawing on in writing his account. These points make an appeal to Psalm 107 in solving the riddle of Mark 4:41 problematic. If Mark's narrative is supposed to make the reader think of Psalm 107 and identify Jesus with that depiction of God, then it must be noted that the only connection between Jesus and the God of Psalm 107 is that they both calm storms, which we have noted is not the focus of Mark's narrative.

By way of a counter-example, the 'sea rescue story' in the Greek *Testament of Naphtali* shares with Ps 107:23–32 the theme of a return from exile combined with a sea rescue (*T. Naph* 6:1–10). There, the patriarch Naphtali recounts a dreamlike vision (5:1; 7:1) which is preceded by explicit references to the exile and restoration of the tribes of Israel (4:1–5; 5:8). In response to the penance and prayers of a symbolic Levi (*T. Naph.* 6:8; cf. Ps 107:28) the λαίλαψ ἀνέμου μεγάλου (*T. Naph.* 6:4; cf. Mark 4:37; Ps 107:25–27), the 'great wind storm' of exile in which the tribes are scattered to the ends of the earth (*T. Naph.* 6:7; cf. Ps 107:3), is calmed. And the tribes are reunited to each other and their father Jacob (*T. Naph.* 6:9–10; compare Ps 107:30–32). Despite the considerable differences in genre, Psalm 107 and *T. Naph.* 6:1–10 have strong narrative and thematic overlaps with each other. These themes are not present in Mark 4:35–41.

The thematic dissonance between the two texts is complemented by the weakness of any corrspondences between the texts in terms of narrative or language. The embarkation, peril and cry for help only correspond in the most generic way. Between the cry to God of Ps 107:28 and the disciples' rude complaint of Mark 4:38 the correspondence is especially thin.

There is no significant lexical correspondence between Psalm 107:23–32 and Mark 4:35–41, despite several scholars implying that there could be. Hays argues Mark 4:39, where Jesus rebukes the sea and says to the wind, 'Peace, be still', reads like a 'midrash' on Ps 107:29 'he made the storm be still, and the waves of the sea were hushed'.[29] However, there is no verbal overlap between the phrases in Greek. In Mark 4:39 'Be still' is φιμόω but in Ps 107:29 it is ἵστημι. 'Hushed/quiet' is σιωπάω yet in Ps 107:29 it is σιγάω. 'Quiet/calm' is γαλήνη, while in Ps 107:30 it is ἡσυχάζω.

Comparing both pericopae Mark does not even use the same words for wind (ἄνεμος) and storm (λαῖλαψ) as Psalm 107 (LXX 106, πνεῦμα and καταιγίς). The common lexemes identified by Smothers, θάλασσα (Ps 107:23; Mark 4:39), πλοῖον (107:23; Mark 4:36) and κῦμα (Ps 107:25; Mark 4:37),[30] are so generic it is hard to imagine telling any sea story, let alone a sea rescue story, without them.

---

[29] Hays 2016: 67.
[30] Smothers 2013: 11.

Collins suggests the puzzling statement of 4:36, καὶ ἄλλα πλοῖα ἦν μετ' αὐτοῦ, could be explained by reference to Ps 107:23, οἱ καταβαίνοντες εἰς τὴν θάλασσαν ἐν πλοίοις.[31] If we assume Psalm 107 to have influenced Mark 4:35–41 then this would be a reasonable, albeit tenuous, suggestion. But none of the offered suggestions give grounds for the initial assumption. As Drewermann admits, 'die literarischen Beziehungen zwischen dem Psalm und dem Markus-Text recht zweifelhaft scheinen'.[32]

Despite the Christological appeal of this suggested textual connection there no evidence that Psalm 107 has influenced Mark 4:35–41 and a number of reasons why it is unlikely to have done so here. The foregoing points argue that an authorial allusion in Mark 4:35–41 to Psalm 107 is unlikely, without denying that many subsequent readers have made that connection. Psalm 107 may well 'echo' as a reader response to the text, but the evidence for an authorial allusion is lacking. There is, however, another scriptural sea rescue which shows far more correspondence with the one in Mark 4.

§4.4 Jonah 1

The suggestion that the sea storm story from Jonah 1 is a referent of Mark 4:35–41 is often made,[33] although it is debated[34] or ignored[35] by others and there is no consistency regarding the number and significance of the correspondences. Hartman, whilst acknowledging the parallels between the two narratives, considers it of 'doubtful' use to the interpreter and he does not think the existence of those parallels should influence interpretation.[36] In the following I wish to show that, unlike the widely accepted suggestion of Psalm 107, there is sufficient thematic, narrative and lexical correspondence between Jonah 1 and Mark 4:35–41 to render an authorially intended allusion highly likely.

The storm story in Jonah 1 is thematically and theologically profound. Jonah is commissioned to a 'Gentile mission' and attempts to escape it. The narrative affirms Israel's God as sovereign, omniscient, omnipresent, and as creator of land and sea. The Gentile sailors are portrayed as pious and undergo a kind of 'conversion' to the God of Israel. And the prophet sacrifices his life to save the sailors.[37] If there is an allusion to Jonah in Mark 4:35–41, there is certainly potential for a meaningful typology to be developed.

---

[31] Collins 2007: 258. See also Malbon 1984: 363–77, 365.
[32] 'The literary relationships between the psalm and Mark's text seem quite dubious' (Drewermann 1989: 353).
[33] E.g. Pesch 1979: 1.270–4; Goppelt 1982: 72–3; Derrett 1985: 1.97; Gnilka 1989: 1.194; Guelich 1989: 226; Marcus 2000a 337; Witherington 2001: 175–6; Du Toit 2006: 95; Powell 2007: 157–64, 160; Hartman, 2010: 195; Focant 2012: 190; Youngblood 2014: 90.
[34] Drewermann 1989: 352–3; Stein 2008: 245.
[35] Waetjen 1989: 110–12; Brower 2009: 296; Hays 2016: 66–8.
[36] Hartman 2010: 195.
[37] This interpretation is not just a Christian one but was significant in Rabbinic traditions also. For a list of sources see Aus 2000: 6.

§4.4.1 Narrative correspondence

Graham Twelftree notes, 'The remarkable parallel in this story to that of Jonah, which has long been recognised, makes it hard to avoid the conclusion that Mark had this Old Testament story in mind.'[38] As both Jonah 1 and Mark 4:35-41 are sea rescue epiphanies, they have several generic narrative features in common. A journey is verbally initiated (Jonah 1:1-2, Mark 4:35), a voyage is embarked upon (Jonah 1:3; Mark 4:36), a storm arises endangering the vessel (Jonah 1:4; Mark 4:37),[39] the storm is calmed (Jonah 1:15; Mark 4:39) and there is a response to the rescue of great fear or awe (Jonah 1:16; Mark 4:41). However, there are several distinctive narrative details between Jonah 1 and Mark 4:35-41 which suggest a closer relationship between the two stories.

1. Narratively, the voyage of Jonah 1 takes the prophet to the Gentiles of Nineveh. The crossing of Galilee in Mark 4:35-41 begins a narrative sequence where Jesus crosses the lake back and forth between Jewish and gentile territory the purpose of which is to demonstrate the significance and availability of the gospel for the Gentiles as well as the Jews.[40] The very next episode features the deliverance, conversion and commissioning to mission of a Gentile man.[41]
2. Second, the 'land-lubber' prophet sleeping through a storm while the mariners fear for their lives is a distinctive narrative element of Jonah 1. Similarly, Jesus, among a crew of experienced fishermen, sleeps undisturbed by the storm that they consider life threatening.[42] Aus argues that Jesus' sleeping in the stern implies he was under the partial deck from which the fishermen would cast their nets, meaning both he and Jonah were asleep below decks.[43] In Jonah 1, 'going down' (ירד) is a key verb reflecting Jonah's descent into Sheol away from God. This emphasis, unsurprisingly, is not reflected in Mark 4:35-41. Instead, Mark's description of Jesus asleep in the stern (πρύμνα) probably reflects the MT text's ירכה (Jonah 1:5), translated in the NRSV as 'the hold',[44] but equally able to be translated as the 'rear' (cf. Exod 26:22; 1 Sam 24:3), or in nautical terms the stern.[45] These unusual details set up a narrative connection to Jonah that is difficult to escape.[46] Indeed, Marcus considers Jesus' sleep in this story to be incredible and to cast doubt on the episode's historicity, albeit with the consequence of confirming an intentional connection with Jonah.[47] However, Marcus may be underestimating how tired a preacher can be after spending the day preaching outdoors.

---

[38] Twelftree 1999: 70-1.
[39] Pesch (1979: 1.270) considers Mark 4:37, γίνεται λαῖλαψ μεγάλη ἀνέμου, to be 'einer deutlichen Anspielung' to Jonah 1:4, ἐγένετο κλύδων μέγας ἐν τῇ θαλάσσῃ. But the correspondence is generic to sea rescue stories.
[40] Wefal 1995: 3-26; Malbon 2014: 30.
[41] Anderson 2012: 172-86.
[42] Garland 1996: 191.
[43] Aus 2000: 27; Marcus 2000a: 333.
[44] Cf. LXX τὴν κοίλην.
[45] HALOT 439. Compare Pesch's comment (1979: 1.270, also 271) that the Markan redactor has imported the idea of a bigger (Mediteranean) ship into the text in assimilating the story to Jonah 1.
[46] Stein 2008: 242.
[47] Marcus 2000a: 337.

3. Both Jonah and Jesus are awoken, not by the storm, but by their shipmates, and asked to intervene.[48]
4. In the dialogue of Jonah 1:8 the identity of the prophet is interrogated by his shipmates. This fearful questioning of a prophet resonates well with the disciples' questioning of Jesus in Mark 4:41.[49] However, in Jonah 1 there are two revelations of identity. Jonah is interrogated about who he is. Then in answering, Jonah also reveals the identity of YHWH/the Lord to the mariners. Implicit in the narrative is that the mariners had been aware that Jonah was being pursued by a certain 'YHWH/Lord', just not that YHWH/Lord happened to be the 'God of heaven, who made the sea and dry land' (Jonah 1:9–10). In Mark 4:31–45 the revelation that Jesus can command the wind and the sea (4:39) and the fear filled questioning that follows (4:41) correspond to the two revelations in Jonah 1.

§4.4.2 Lexical coherence

There are a number of verbal overlaps.[50] Many are too generic to be decisive; for example, πλοῖον (Jonah 1:3; Mark 4:36) is a common word for boat and it used several times in Mark elsewhere.[51] Likewise, κῦμα (Mark 4:37) is a common word found in Jonah 2:4 but not specifically in Jonah 1 where the LXX uses the more distinctive σάλος (Jonah 1:15). Both stories use θάλασσα for the sea, but this would be expected, especially as Mark always refers to the Galilean lake this way.[52] The expected word for sleep, καθεύδω, provides lexical coherence with the already noted shared narrative feature of a sleeping prophet on a boat in the storm. Both stories use the word κοπάζω for stopping the wind (Mark 4:39) or sea (Jonah 1:11, 12) but at different points in the narrative.

However, two lexical correspondences stand out as more decisive.

1. The disciples' complaint in Mark 4:38 might be expected to refer to the imminent likelihood of sinking, drowning or dying; instead it uses ἀπόλλυμι, perish. This is the same as the captain's complaint in Jonah 1:6 and the sailors' prayer in 1:14.[53] Thus, there is considerable narrative coherence with the protagonist being awoken with a complaint about 'perishing'. Marcus observes that in the LXX of Jonah, ἀπόλλυμι 'expresses the *leitmotiv* of the entire book, escape from destruction at the hand of God'.[54] It is thus a narratively coherent use in Mark of a thematically significant word from Jonah.[55]

---

[48] Dechow 2000: 204.
[49] Anderson 2012: 177.
[50] Boring 2006: 143. Boring also suggests 'waking up' provides verbal overlap. Jonah 1:6 LXX uses ἀνίστημι not ἐγείρω, so the correspondence is semantic but not lexical.
[51] I.e. in addition to four occurrences in Mark 4:36, 37, πλοῖον also occurs in Mark 1:19, 20; 4:1; 5:2; 18, 21; 6:32, 45, 47, 51, 54; 8:10, 14.
[52] Mark 4:39, 41, see 1:16; 2:13; 3:7; 4:1; 5:1, 13, 21; 6:47, 48, 49; 7:31.
[53] Pesch 1979: 1.272.
[54] Marcus 2000: 333.
[55] Donahue and Harrington 2005: 158; Stein 2008: 243.

2. Most significantly, ἐφοβήθησαν φόβον μέγαν must be seen as a strong lexical parallel.[56] The words appear in the same forms and order in Jonah 1:10 and Mark 4:41, and in Jonah 1:16 the only difference is that 'great fear' appears in the dative.[57] This phrase is highly distinctive in the Jewish scriptures, as the same words and construction occur elsewhere only in 1 Macc 10:8. In Mark they are unique.[58] The cognate-accusative construction reflects a 'semitic manner of intensive statement'[59] and so more easily calls to mind the Jewish scriptures. Mark's episode conflates the narrative elements from Jonah 1 of questioning the prophet's identity and of fearful worship of YHWH, and these are the same plot elements of Jonah 1 that contain this distinctive septuagintal phrase. The most likely explanation for the presence of this distinctive particular phrase at this particular point in this particular narrative is that it is a deliberate lexical allusion to the parallel narrative of Jonah 1.

§4.4.3 Thematic inversion

The narrative of Mark 4:35–41 inverts two important themes from Jonah 1. As argued earlier, in reference to Paul's Adam–Christ typology, these contrasting themes are often significant.[60] Here, the prophet, Jesus, calms the storm instead of being thrown into it like Jonah. A narrative action belonging to God in the scriptural text is enacted in the Gospel by Jesus. In the previous chapter we saw such theomorphic typology, but it was always separate from a typology based on human characters. Here the one literary typology relates Jesus both to Jonah and to YHWH.

There is also a contrast between the mariners and the disciples. In Jonah, the mariners, although afraid and pagan, are religiously devout (Jonah 1:5, 16) and show mercy by their reluctance to throw Jonah overboard even when he is identified as the source of their misfortune (Jonah 1:11–14). In Mark, the disciples do not pray to God and are characterized as cowardly.

§4.4.4 Contextual evidence for the link

In addition to the thematic and lexical parallels, three further considerations increase the probability of a deliberate reference to Jonah here. First, Jonah was considered a type of Jesus in the early church (e.g. Matt 12:38–41, 16:4; Luke 11:29; 1 Clement 7:7; Justin, *Dialogue* 107).[61] If later Christians made connections between Jonah and Jesus, then it is plausible that so did Mark.

---

[56] Witherington (2001: 176) notices this, but only labels it an 'echo'. That is to downplay the precise verbal correspondence. On the other hand, Pesch (1979: 1.273) states, 'Die *figura etymologica* ist für Jon 1 charakteristisch, unverwechselbar' ('The cognate-accusative figure is characteristic of Jonah 1, unmistakable').
[57] Both appearances of the phrase in Jonah also include οἱ ἄνδρες, but this is not significant for the purpose of establishing a parallel. See O'Brien 2010: 33–4.
[58] Only occurring elsewhere in the NT once, in the later Gospel of Luke (Luke 2:9).
[59] Achtemeier 1962: 170; Malbon 1984: 366.
[60] See §2.4.
[61] Lapide 1980: 38; Aus 2000: 5; Collins 2007: 260; Stein 2008: 244; Davidson 2014: 61–2.

Second, there are other possible narrative references to Jonah in the Gospel. McInerny posits a 'question and answer relationship' between Mark 4:35–41 and 6:45–52.[62] The miracle of 6:45–52 is parallel in many ways to 4:35–41. They both involve a 'sea' crossing by boat, the evening, Jesus and the disciples, the stopping of wind, the disciples' fear, and the disciples' incomprehension. Importantly they are the only two miracle accounts in Mark where the disciples are the sole beneficiaries of the miracle.[63] It is significant then that Pinchas Lapide finds an 'affinity of thought' between Jonah 1 and Mark 6:47–52.[64] The crew of both boats are distressed and crying out (Jonah 1:5; Mark 6:49) and straining at the oars but unable to get anywhere (Jonah 1:13; Mark 6:48).[65] Most useful, however, is his observation that whereas the storm calms when Jonah *leaves* the boat, in Mark 6:51 the wind becomes calm when Jesus *enters* the boat.[66] However, Lapide wrongly posits that Jesus was going *up* and Jonah going *down*.[67] In fact, in Mark 5:51 Jesus steps *up* (ἀναβαίνω) *into* (εἰς) the boat and in Jonah 1:15 Jonah is lifted *up* (נשׂא)[68] and cast *into* (εἰς / אל) the sea by the sailors. The shared directionality corroborates the connection. Thus, we see here a significant plot element of Jonah 1 that was missing from Mark 4:35–41 present in its mirror passage. Both Gospel passages, when read together, confirm and enhance each other's resonance with Jonah 1.

Mark 14:32–42 also deserves consideration. Garland makes the helpful observation that in 'bitter irony' Mark 4:35–41 is the reverse coin of Gethsemane. In 4:35–41 Jesus sleeps while the disciples are in distress; in 14:32–42 the disciples sleep while Jesus is in distress.[69] Thematic interplay between the passages is not limited to sleep however. They both share lexical connections to Jonah. Collins plausibly suggests that Jesus' words in Mark 14:34 refer to Ps 42–43 (LXX 41–42) and Jonah 4:9.[70] Presented alongside each other the similarities are striking:

Mark 14:34		περίλυπός	ἐστιν ἡ ψυχή	μου	ἕως θανάτου
Ps 42:6, 12; 43:5	ἵνα τί	περίλυπος	εἶ ψυχή		
Jonah 4:9	σφόδρα		λελύπημαι	ἐγώ	ἕως θανάτου

The connection is reinforced by the thematic parallels of a distressed prophet, in a garden, hoping God will change his mind. Just as Jonah mourned the loss of his reputation (Jonah 4:2) and the death of a plant (4:9), Jesus mourned his impending death (Mark 14:34). Both Jonah and Jesus are described as praying, προσεύχομαι (Jonah 4:2; Mark 14:32, 35, 38, 39). In prayer, both Jonah and Jesus ask God to take something from them (Jonah 4:3; Mark 14:36). These requests have comparable imperatival sentence constructions and the same final two words:

---

[62] McInerny 1996: 259.
[63] Du Toit 2006: 88.
[64] Lapide 1980: 38.
[65] See also Derrett 1985: 1.97.
[66] Lapide 1980: 38.
[67] Lapide 1980: 38.
[68] The present form of the LXX does not preserve this nuance in Jonah 1:15. However, it is preserved in Jonah's instructions in 1:12 (αἴρω).
[69] Garland 1996: 191. The same point is made by Dechow 2000: 207.
[70] Collins 2007: 260, 676–7.

λαβὲ τὴν ψυχήν μου ἀπ' ἐμοῦ (LXX Jonah 4:3)
παρένεγκε τὸ ποτήριον τοῦτο ἀπ' ἐμοῦ (Mark 14:36)

I have argued elsewhere that this narrative allusion between Gethsemane and Jonah 4 makes use of an allegorical interpretation of Jonah's gourd as the messianic vine.[71] However, such an interpretation is not necessary to make the case here. It is sufficient for the purposes of this study to note that Jonah is in some way evoked in the Gethsemane account, Jesus' decisive moment of obedient response to his Father's painful will. The disobedient prophet Jonah is recapitulated and fulfilled by the obedient son, Jesus. Consequently, the narrative allusion to Jonah in Mark 4:35–41 is not isolated in Mark but one instance among two others.

§4.4.5 A deliberate typological reference

In regard to the storm stilling, Stein states that there is no Jonah typology present and no authorial intention to connect the two stories because there is a lack of parallel language.[72] There is certainly less parallel language than there could be. Given the similar subject matter Mark barely needed to use a word not in Jonah 1. However, that is to make restrictive assumptions about how Mark would choose to allude to a scriptural narrative, and whether or not there may be other concerns shaping the composition of a passage. I am certainly not claiming that Mark has composed this episode exclusively from Jonah 1.

Given the strong thematic connections we have already discussed, the lexical connections adduced above present as sufficient evidence of an allusion to Jonah 1 by Mark. In my view there is both a readily apparent real correspondence between the two miraculous events and an evident literary typology generated by Mark's use of Jonah 1. An allusion is never a matter of absolute certainty, but the narrative, thematic and lexical correspondence between Jonah 1 and Mark 4:35–41 create a strong case for a deliberate and meaningful allusion that should enrich our reading of Mark's storm-stilling narrative.

§4.5 Reading Mark 4:35–41 with Jonah 1

Having argued that Mark 4:35–41 typologically alludes to Jonah 1, I will now suggest some ways in which this allusion might bear on the Christology of Mark's miracle account.

§4.5.1 Jesus as a greater Jonah

The first interpretive result of the typology is that it creates a comparison between Jesus and Jonah. Jesus is one like Jonah, and therefore a prophet, but he also surpasses Jonah

---

[71] Robinson 2021.
[72] Stein 2008: 244–5.

in obedience and power.⁷³ As Rupert Feneberg writes, 'Ein bibelkundiger Leser muss sofort mithören: Jesus ist weit größer als Jona'.⁷⁴ Mark thus agrees with the other Synoptics that 'one greater than Jonah is here!' (Luke 11:32; Matt 12:41).⁷⁵ Jesus is the antitype of Jonah.

§4.5.2 Kirk and Young's early Jewish paradigm of water miracles

Daniel Kirk and Stephen Young argue that that Psalm 89:25 is an overlooked background text for Mark 4:35–41, and Kirk later expands this argument.⁷⁶ While the discussion is detailed and interesting on its own account, two basic problems with their thesis (and Kirk's expanded version of it) are that 1) that there is no narrative or lexical indication that Mark connects Psalm 89:25 with the narrative of Mark 4:35–41, and 2) there is no evidence that Ps 89:25 was ever read as attributing miraculous power over water to the Davidic messiah.⁷⁷ This raises the question as to why the Jonah 1 parallels were ignored in Kirk and Young's exegesis. Recognizing a Jonah typology in this passage is also to recognize Jesus as an idealised (human) version of Jonah. Kirk gives no indication he is even aware of this possibility. But given its prevalence in the literature this seems unlikely.

As part of their discussion, Kirk and Young propose a category of early Jewish figures with authority over water, citing Moses, Joshua and Theudas (Josephus, *Ant.* 20.97).⁷⁸ In a later work, Kirk also includes Elijah and Elisha, the messiah in *Pesiq. Rab.* 36:1,⁷⁹ and Simon the High Priest (Sir 50:1–20).⁸⁰ The question remains as to whether Kirk and Young's paradigm (which is itself a sub-category of Kirk's paradigm of idealised human figures) is sufficient to contain Jesus' water miracles. I would argue that *if* it is a legitimate methodological approach to assemble paradigms, then there is not one (as Kirk and Young propose) but two available paradigms.

The first paradigm is that of prophets parting water for people to walk across. This would include Moses (Exod 14), Joshua (Josh 3), and Elijah and Elisha (2 Kgs 2:8–14), as well as Theudas (*Ant.* 20:97–98). The second paradigm is that of Rabbis praying for rain (or waves). This would include Honi the circle drawer (*m. Ta'an.* 3:8; *Ant.* 14.2.1 §22–24), and his grandsons Abba Hilqiah (*b. Ta'an* 23a–23b) and Hanan ha-Nehba (*b. Ta'an* 23b), and Rabbi Gamaliel (*b. Meṣi'a* 59b). The messiah in *Pesiq. Rab.* 36:1 and Simon the High Priest (Sir 50:1–20) do not fit into either of these paradigms because the first is not early Jewish (550–650 CE), and *neither describe a miracle being performed by a human.*

---

⁷³ Dunn 2003: 687; Du Toit 2006: 95.
⁷⁴ 'A biblically literate reader must immediately hear: Jesus is far greater than Jonah' (Feneberg 2000: 133).
⁷⁵ Pesch 1979: 1.269; Twelftree 1999: 71; Aus 2000: 7.
⁷⁶ Kirk and Young 2014: 333–40, 335. See also Kirk 2016: 90–2, 102–4, 434–42.
⁷⁷ I address these and other concerns in more detail in 'Reconsidering Psalm 89:25, Jewish Water Miracles, and Markan Christology', in the *Journal of the Jesus Movement in its Jewish Setting* (Robinson: forthcoming (a)).
⁷⁸ Kirk and Young 2014: 337.
⁷⁹ Kirk 2016: 436.
⁸⁰ Kirk 2016: 125.

The first paradigm, of prophets parting water, is linked to a typological expectation of God's works and is not about an individual having power but about God repeating liberative events from history. These miracles are always envisioned as climactic political moments and are anticipated in advance. Jesus' water miracles do not fit into this first paradigm because his miracles were spontaneous (ad hoc), private (only the disciples are present each time), and apolitical (in contrast to, e g., a Sabbath healing, or the cursing of the fig tree). The basic content of the miracle is also different. Jesus does not part the sea or the river and walk across on dry land as Moses and Joshua both did or as Theudas was hoping to do.

The second paradigm is that of holy men praying to God and then the elements respond, demonstrating that God has heard their prayer. There is no indication that the power resides in the individual. In fact, the exact opposite is reinforced. As John Meier argues, these pious figures whose prayers are answered by God do not really parallel Jesus the 'miracle-*worker*, *performing* miracles by his own power'.[81] Jesus' miracles do not fit into this second paradigm because his miracles do not involve prayer and they clearly portray Jesus as the source of power. It may be argued that these differences are a result of later embellishments reflecting different theological interests.[82] But as Mark tells the story, the paradigm does not fit.

Rather, as I argued earlier, the form of Jesus' water miracle in Mark 4:35–41 corresponds to Jonah 1 and, as I will argue below, Mark 6:45–52 correspond closely to Job 9. Having discounted Ps 89:25 as providing evidence of, or reason for, an early Jewish association of a Davidic messiah with the ability to control the sea in the way that Jesus does in his miracles, it can be asserted that in Mark's accounts of Jesus' water miracles Jesus is doing something that does not fit either Kirk's paradigm of early Jewish idealized figures nor the paradigm of contemporary Jewish holy men. Kirk and Young's argument that Mark's Jesus is simply operating within an established Jewish paradigm of exalted human figures with power over water does not do justice to Jesus' narrative portrayal. Rather Jesus is portrayed as neither rabbi nor prophet when he controls the water in his own power, but something else.

§4.5.3 Jesus as Jonah's God?

Comparing the two stories, Jesus plays both the role of sleeping prophet and the role of the creator God with power over the sea.[83] As Pesch argues, Jesus 'rückt in die Rolle einer Schutzgottheit ein, mehr: in Jahwes Rolle'.[84] Or as Collins put it, 'Jesus is portrayed not so much as a human being who has trust in God's power to save, but as a divine being . . . [The disciples] have God manifest in the boat with them!'[85] Jesus' identification with Jonah's God is shown in several features.

---

[81] Meier 1991: 2.356, emphasis original.
[82] Evans 2001c: 225.
[83] The argument that in Jewish literature human figures were given control over water is made by Kirk and Young 2014: 333–40, 335. See also Kirk 2016: 90–2, 102–4, 434–42. It is unpersuasive on several counts, but, simply, none of the texts adduced by Kirk and Young evidence such a human figure having power over water like that which Jesus displays. Some of their claims will be treated in the Christology chapter.
[84] 'Enters the role of a protective deity, more: it is YHWH's role' (Pesch 1979: 1.276).
[85] Collins 2007: 260; see also Garland 1996: 192; Boring 2006: 147; Stein 2008: 244.

McInerny correctly observes that this calming of the storm is of a different order from the miracles performed previously in the Gospel by Jesus. It is an 'unprecedented' act for a human miracle worker, unlike the healings and exorcisms.[86] By referencing the story of Jonah 1 – where the sailors gradually discover the identity of YHWH, Mark guides our interpretation away from questions of magnitude, 'just how powerful is Jesus?' to Mark's focus, Jesus' identity, 'just *who* is this?' The reaction of great fear, shown by the disciples, parallels the Gentiles' fear of YHWH/the Lord in Jonah 1.[87] As Gnilka writes, 'Große Furcht ist die angemessene Reaktion auf die Epifanie Gottes.'[88] As the recipient of great fear Jesus corresponds to God in Jonah 1.

Another feature of the episode highlighted by comparison with Jonah 1 is the absence of prayer. Jonah 1 describes the mariners praying to their gods and encouraging Jonah to pray to his. Jesus is sometimes found praying throughout Mark (Mark 1:35; 6:46; 14:32–39) and encourages his disciples to pray (Mark 9:29; 11:24, 25). However, 'Jesus bezwingt in Mk 4,39 den Seesturm allein durch sein Wort. Es wird nicht da von gesprochen, daß Jesus sich – etwa im Gebet – an die Macht Gottes wendet, ihn zum Eingreifen bewegt.'[89] Instead the disciples, afraid they might perish, do not follow the pattern of the mariners in Jonah 1:6 and ask Jesus to intercede for them, but seem to expect Jesus himself will be able to save them.[90] As Koch suggests, 'Ein Hilferuf ist ja gerade kein Zeichen von Unglauben, sondern des Vertrauens in die Macht des Wundertäter.'[91] Whatever they were hoping Jesus would do, what he actually does is beyond their expectations. Whether or not Jesus is here the recipient of prayer, Jesus is revealed here as one with the power and authority to answer prayer and with the power to save.

Jesus may retreat at times to pray to God (e.g. Mark 1:35), but he does not rely on prayer to perform miracles. As Gnilka observes, 'Wichtig ist zu sehen, daß die Vollmacht, die im Alten Testament Jahwe zugesprochen wird, von Jesus ausgesagt wird, der nicht wie Jona durch Gebet, sondern aus eigener Machtfülle das Wunderbare geschehen läßt.'[92] The closing question of 4:41 shows this. It is not that God answered his prayer, or stilled the storm at his need. It is that Jesus himself has authority over the wind and waves. As the one who answers prayer in extremity, Jesus corresponds to YHWH in Jonah 1.

A third feature which contributes to this assimilation of Jesus to God is the depiction of Jesus conquering the hostile sea. In Jonah 1, like Psalm 107, the sea is not hostile to God, but a great wind is hurled by God (Jonah 1:4). Relevant here is the other sea rescue narrative in Mark (6:45–52), which has been an even greater focus of intertextual

---

[86] McInerny 1996: 259.
[87] Pesch 1979: 1.273.
[88] 'Great fear is the appropriate reaction to the epiphany of God' (Gnilka 1998: 1.197).
[89] 'In Mk 4:39, Jesus conquers the storm by his word alone. It is not mentioned that Jesus turns to the power of God, for example in prayer, and moves him to intervene' (Dechow 2000: 208).
[90] Marcus 2000a: 338.
[91] 'A call for help is not a sign of unbelief at all but of trust in the power of the miracle worker' (Koch 1975: 97; also Dechow 2000: 205).
[92] 'It is important to note that the authority given in the Old Testament to Yahweh is predicated of Jesus, who brings about miracles, not through prayer like Jonah, but through his own fullness of power' (Gnilka 1998: 1.196).

Christological exegesis than 4:35–41. It is argued that παρελθεῖν (Mark 6:48) functions as a 'technical term' for an appearance of God, connecting Mark 6:45–52 with the theophany of Exod 33:17–23; 34:6 and 3 Kgdms 19:11.[93] It is also argued Jesus' words of reassurance to the disciples, ἐγώ εἰμι (Mark 6:50), evoke theophanic episodes, e.g. Exod 3:14, Deut 32:39; Isa 41:4; 51:12.[94] And 'Take heart ... do not fear' (Mark 6:50) may also evoke scriptural epiphanies (e.g., Exod 20:20, θαρσεῖτε; Judg 6:23, μὴ φοβοῦ).[95]

However, as Jens Dechow argues, 'Denn in all diesen Texten geht es darum, daß das Wasser zurückweicht und die Betreffenden auf dem Grund des Gewässers gehen, nicht aber um ein Wandeln auf dem Wasser'.[96] There is no narrative coherence bwteen these suggested allusions. Instead, a stronger narrative referent for Mark 6:45–52 is Job 9:8–13.[97] Collins observes that Job 9:11 is an 'anti-epiphany', a complaint about human inability to perceive or comprehend God.[98]

LXX Job 9:11	(NETS)
ἐὰν ὑπερβῇ με οὐ μὴ ἴδω καὶ ἐὰν παρέλθῃ με οὐδ' ὡς ἔγνων	If he passed over me, I would certainly not see him, and if he went by me, I would not even know.

Not only is this congruent with the motif of the disciples' incomprehension in Mark 6:52 (and 4:41) but this also provides an alternative source for παρέρχομαι. Semantically ὑπερβαίνω also reinforces the resonance with Mark's use of παρέρχομαι. In its literary context, Job 9:11 is sandwiched between references to God's victory over the sea/Rahab (Job 9:8, 13). Most impressively, LXX Job 9:8b describes the Lord περιπατῶν ὡς ἐπ' ἐδάφους ἐπὶ θαλάσσης, 'walking on the sea as on dry land'. Gathercole, observing the repetition of the phrase 'walking on the sea' from LXX Job 9:8 in both Mark 6:48 (περιπατῶν ἐπὶ τῆς θαλάσσης) and 6:49 (ἐπὶ τῆς θαλάσσης περιπατοῦντα), concludes Job 9:8 is 'the only real OT parallel to the event in Mark'.[99] Job 9:8b is exactly what Jesus is described as doing in Mark 6:48.[100] Thus it sets up a powerful narrative coherence and situates the miracle of walking on the sea firmly within the conceptual framework of YHWH's conflict against chaos.[101] Thus, on both lexical and thematic grounds, Job 9:8–13 presents as the strongest and most likely scriptural allusion in Mark 6:45–52.

Paul Achtemeier has argued that Babylonian and Israelite creation myths are a key background for Mark 4:35–41.[102] He suggests that we should see the conflict between Marduk and Tiamat (*Enuma Elish*), YHWH and chaos (Gen 1), and the Flood (Gen

---

[93] Dechow 2000: 220; Collins 2007: 334; Focant 2012: 264; Hays 2016: 72.
[94] Pesch 1979: 1.362; Gnilka 1998: 1.270; Focant 2012: 269; Collins 2007: 334; Hartman 2010: 267; Broadhead 1992: 125.
[95] Koch 1975: 105–6 n. 5. See also Hartman 2010: 267.
[96] 'For in all these texts the water recedes and the people walk on the riverbed/seabed, but do not walk on the water' (Dechow 2000: 220 n. 237).
[97] Collins 2007: 336–7; Hays 2016: 72.
[98] Collins 2007: 337.
[99] Gathercole, 2006: 63. See also Meier 1991: 914; Hartman 2010: 267.
[100] Schnackenburg 1995: 31.
[101] Dechow notes these things and suggests that the 'whirlwind' in Job 9:17 (MT) may provide a connection between Job 9 and the sea miracles of Mark (2000: 222).
[102] Achtemeier 1962.

7-8), as informing traditions. He highlights κοπάζω (Mark 4:39) as corresponding to the LXX of Gen 8:1 when YHWH caused the flood to cease.[103] However, as with Jonah 1:11, 12, the correspondence is reduced by the fact that in Mark 3:39 κοπάζω refers to the wind, rather than the sea as in Gen 8:1.

Other texts have similar resonance with Mark's storm stilling. In Ps 89:8 the question is asked, 'who is as mighty as you, O LORD?' Then the answer is given, 'You rule the raging of the sea; when its waves rise, you still them' (89:9). The words κῦμα, waves, and θάλασσα, sea, are shared with Mark 4:37 (LXX Ps 88:10). Then, the defeat of the mythic chaos sea dragon Rahab is celebrated, 'You crushed Rahab like a carcass' (89:10).[104] Likewise, Psalm 106:9 (LXX 105:9) personifies the sea in a recounting of the Exodus. It celebrates the God of Israel's deliverance when ἐπετίμησεν τῇ ἐρυθρᾷ θαλάσσῃ (he rebuked the Red Sea). Here, ἐπιτιμάω creates a lexical connection with Mark 4:39.[105]

As Drewermann notes, 'Das Meer als Symbol ist – ähnlich dem Symbol der Schlange – in den Mythen der Völker stets auch ein Bild für das "Chaos", den "Uranfang"'.[106] Certainly, elements of Mark 4:35-41 resonate strongly within this symbolic background; however, no particular text appears to be the focus of an allusion. However, recognizing this theme in Mark's second sea miracle reinforces these elements in the earlier one. Consequently, there is a symmetrical congruence of reference between Mark 4:35-41 and Mark 6:45-52, whereby the stronger theme in the one reinforces and confirms the weaker theme in the other. This is shown in Table 1.

Jesus is narratively portrayed as both the God of Jonah and the victor of the *Chaoscampf*. We can agree, then, with Hays, when he writes, 'Jesus steps, at least functionally, into a role given exclusively to the Lord God in the Old Testament'.[107] But Hays did not recognize Jonah 1 in his study of the same passage.[108] Have we gained anything by, as I would argue, correctly identifying the primary scriptural reference?

We have indeed gained nothing if all Mark wants to convey to us is the formula that Jesus *is* Israel's God. But Mark's Jonah 1 typology does not just associate Jesus with God. It also associates Jesus with a very human prophet: a prophet who sacrificed his life to save others (Jonah 1:12, 15), a prophet who had to go to Sheol before he saved the Gentiles (Jonah 2:2), and a Prophet who angrily remonstrated with God over the death

Table 1 Reference congruence Mark 4:35-41; Mark 6:45-52

	Mark 4:35-41	Mark 6:45-52
Jonah 1	Primary Narrative Allusion	Weaker Narrative Allusion
YWHW vs Chaos	Echo of Theme	Primary Narrative Allusion (Job 9)

---

[103] Achtemeier 1962: 175
[104] Achtemeier 1962: 172; Brower 2009: 295.
[105] Brower 2009: 296; Hays 2016: 68; Bauckham 2017a: 29.
[106] "The sea as symbol is – similar to the symbol of the serpent – in the myths of the peoples always also a picture for "chaos", the "Primordial Beginning"' (Drewermann 1989: 358 n. 16).
[107] Hays 2016: 76.
[108] Hays 2016: 66-8.

of a plant (Jonah 4:6–9). Although the Gospel episode only links verbally to the first chapter of Jonah, the real typology that has been established can evoke the wider context of Jonah's story and many other possible real typological connections then present themselves.

While both sea miracle episodes show Jesus displaying the power and prerogative of Israel's God, they also show him as the antitype of Jonah. This is not a simple equation. Jesus' humanity, his need for sleep (4:38), his frustration with the disciples (4:40), his need to seek God in prayer (6:46) and his thwarted intentions (6:48–49), are all also part of these episodes.[109] Like Jonah, Jesus is a prophet from the despised region of Galilee (2 Kgs 14:25, cf. John 7:52). Like Jonah, Jesus will give his life to save others. Like Jonah, Jesus' preaching will bear fruit among the Gentiles. Like Jonah, Jesus will have his own conflict with God's will (Mark 14:35–36) and while it is resolved in obedience it remains a distinction between Jesus and God that cannot be collapsed. Thus Mark creates a tension for his audience around the identity of Jesus. 'A functional view of the messiah'[110] simply cannot do justice to this Messiah-Son-of-God who is obeyed by the wind and the sea and walks on the sea as if it is dry land. Yet he cannot simply be equated to God. He is noticeably human.

§4.5.4 Bauckham's divine identity and Mark's storm stilling

For Bauckham, the 'almost rhetorical question' of Mark 4:41 and the 'formula of divine self-identification' in 6:50 are, among others, 'indications ... that Jesus does not merely act on God's behalf ... but actually belongs to the divine identity'.[111] These indications though, are only cryptic hints that culminate in Jesus' words to the high priest (14:62).[112] So Bauckham does not go so far as to claim that these indications establish divine identity on their own.

Following Bauckham, Hay's exegesis of Mark 4:35–41 is more detailed, and the main points of which have been discussed above regarding Psalm 107. In Hays' treatment of the calming of the storm in Mark 4:35–41 he dismisses Jonah 1 as a background text in a brief endnote.[113] This is despite the fact that it satisfies far more of Hays' own criteria for intertextuality than the scripture he does use to interpret Mark's storm stilling, Psalm 107.[114] Perplexingly, in support he cites Marcus and Pesch on Mark 4:35–41, but both these scholars advocate for the Jonah parallel.[115] For Hays, the parallel to Jonah is unconvincing, because Jesus, in calming the storm, is more similar to God than to Jonah. But this, according to my exegesis, is a key Christological point of the parallel.

If Hays had applied his own intertextual criteria to the question of Jonah 1's influence on Mark 4:35–41, they would have shown him the importance of Jonah 1 to

---

[109] See further Bayer 2008: 78.
[110] France 2002: 225.
[111] Bauckham 2008: 265.
[112] As discussed in §3.5.5.
[113] Hays 2016: 384, n. 105.
[114] These criteria are not discussed in detail in his Gospels book but see Hays 1989, 2005.
[115] Pesch 1979: 1.269; Marcus 2000a: 338; Hays 2016: 384, n. 105.

Mark 4:35–41. Instead, Hays interprets the story against a selection of scriptural texts which ascribe storm stilling and control of the sea to YHWH.[116] While his conclusion that 'Jesus somehow embodies the presence of God' is correct,[117] what has been missed is the rich allusion to Jonah and the human aspect of Jesus' portrayal. Even Jesus' very human sleeping in the boat after a hard day's preaching is made, by Hays, into a sign of his divinity, referencing Psalm 44:23, 'Rouse yourself! Why do you sleep, O Lord?'[118]

§4.5.5 Jesus and his mission

The references to Jonah also portray Jesus as the one who is sent. The salvation of Gentiles is a central issue in Jonah,[119] and the use of Jonah typology here serves to reinforce the parallel theme in Mark.[120] Jesus is sent to bring God's grace and salvation to the Gentiles, reflecting Mark's concern to validate 'the Gentile mission by relating it to the history of Israel and the ministry of Jesus'.[121] However, Jesus is also sent to preach repentance and impending doom 'to that great city' Jerusalem (Mark 13:2).[122]

This reading accords with Rudolf Pesch's description of Mark as a *Missionsbuch*.[123] Thus Jesus may be Lord of creation but he is also the servant of someone even greater, the one who sends him (Mark 9:37; 12:6), just as he himself sends out his disciples (3:14; 6:7) and will one day send the angels (13:27). Significantly, however, the initiative for the voyage is from the word of Jesus (4:35), rather than Israel's God (Jonah 1:1). Jesus is thus not the reluctant prophet, but, to borrow the words of Matthew and Luke, 'the Lord of the Harvest' (Matt 9:38; Luke 10:2).

§4.6 Conclusion

Mark 4:35–41 is a sea rescue miracle and conforms in many ways to the conventions for such stories. These conventions cause the miracle to resemble the account of Psalm 107:23–32, but there is no evidence that Mark has employed this psalm in his composition and several thematic reasons why it would be unlikely. However, the distinctive narrative motif of a prophet asleep on a boat during a fearsome storm and a dialogue focused on identity generate a strong correspondence with the storm stilling in Jonah 1. The presence of an authorial allusion is confirmed by the reuse of key terminology from the LXX of Jonah 1, especially ἐφοβήθησαν φόβον μέγαν, a

---

[116] Ps 107; Job 38:8–11; Ps 89:9; 65:7; 106:8–12; 44:23; Isa 51:9–11. See Hays 2016: 66–9.
[117] Hays 2016: 69.
[118] Hays 2016: 69.
[119] Chapman and Warner 2008: 43–69.
[120] Derrett 1985: 1.98; Marcus 2000a: 336.
[121] Senior 1984: 66.
[122] This is in harmony with Kelber's thought (1974: 45–65), whereby he argues Mark combines the miracle stories with Jesus' ferrying across the Sea of Galilee in order to widen the scope of the Christian mission to include both Jew and Gentile.
[123] Pesch 1979: 1:61, 'Die ganze Geschichte Jesu ist Inhalt des Evangeliums geworden. Das ganze Buch des Markus ist *Missionsbuch*' (emphasis original).

distinctive repeated phrase in LXX Jonah 1 and unique in Mark. This literary typology presents Jesus as the antitype of Jonah and also assimilates him to the narrative role of YHWH. As antitype of Jonah, Jesus' obedience, sacrificial death, message of judgement and mission to the Gentiles are highlighted. Assimilation to God was seen especially in the fear of the disciples/mariners, the question of identity, the theme of prayer and the idea of the *Chaoskampf*. Mark 4:35–41 shows us a Jesus who is both escalation and fulfilment of the scriptural prophet, Jonah, but who also corresponds to the scriptural God in power and authority – yet without ceasing to be human.

Next we will examine another story with a clear scriptural counterpart and see if Mark's typological approach continues in the same vein.

§5

Elisha typology in Mark 5:21–43

Yet none of the healers, magicians and wise men were able to cure him; on the contrary, the spirit afflicted all of them too, so that they fled. Then Hyrcanus came to me, asking me to come pray for the king, and to lay hands upon him and cure him – for he had seen me in a dream.

Gen. Apoc. 20:20–22

In this chapter I will examine the healing and resuscitation miracles of Mark 5:21–43. As with the previous chapter I will proceed with an initial discussion of the story and then analysis of the conventions of Jewish and Graeco-Roman healing and resuscitation/resurrection stories. As discussed in the previous chapter, the storm stilling episode of Mark 4:35–41 is often considered in relation to scriptural narratives like Psalm 107 or Jonah 1. By contrast, there is little discussion among the main commentators regarding a scriptural influence on Mark's presentation of the miracles of Mark 5:21–43. This absence is despite the raising of Jairus' daughter bearing a close resemblance to the two resurrections of children in the Jewish scriptures by Elijah and Elisha (1 Kgs 17:17–24; 2 Kgs 4:18–37, respectively). This chapter will draw on the suggestions of the few scholars who have considered this resemblance, and develop further lines of enquiry to argue for a sustained authorial allusion to Elisha's resuscitation miracle in 2 Kgs 4:18–37 in this Markan episode and double miracle. This chapter concludes with a discussion of the Christology implied by the proposed allusion to the Elisha narrative.

§5.1 A story within a story

If it cannot be denied that Mark 5:21–43 is a 'story within a story',[1] it is less clear what the significance of the intercalation is. Such a narrative sandwich is a 'distinctive literary technique [that Mark] utilizes far more than the other gospel writers'.[2] Yet Mark's reason for the insertion might be as prosaic as to fill in the time.[3] There is noticeable stylistic discontinuity between the stories. The story of Jairus's daughter contains short

---

[1] Schweizer 1970: 120.
[2] Boring 2006: 157.
[3] Bultmann 1963: 214; Schweizer 1970: 116; Edwards 1989: 195; Marcus 2000a: 364.

sentences dominated by the historical present, while the story of the woman in the crowd contains long sentences dominated by participles and the aorist. This is generally accepted to imply differing sources for the stories before Mark intercalated them.[4]

However, the Jairus story contains participles of its own and both parts make similar use of parataxis. Consequently, Gundry has argued that the differences should not be overstated.[5] Moreover, thematic connections between the stories are manifold. The word *daughter*, the number 12, the language of healing and salvation, the ignoring of uncleanness by Jesus, fear, faith, touch, the movement between private and public, movement from misunderstanding to revelation of power, and the connection between sickness and death are all themes which serve to unite the stories of the intercalation.[6] Thematically intertwined as they are, Marie-Christine Chou argues for the hermeneutical importance of reading the stories together.[7] It is apparent that, whatever their individual provenance, Mark intends them to be read, and thus interpreted, as a unit.

The passage also contains many thematic connections to the immediately preceding miracle accounts. These include falling at Jesus' feet (5:6, 22, 33), begging (5:10-12, 17-18, 23), casting out (5:8, 40), a character being 'in' an unclean state (spirit/flow of blood, 5:2, 25), the disciples' incomprehension (4:41; 5:31), Jesus ignoring uncleanness (from tombs, pigs, blood, a corpse, 5:1-43) and a fear response to Jesus' power acts (4:41; 5:15, 33).[8] Kathleen Fisher identifies 5:21-43 as the last in a sequence of spectacular miracle accounts in which the ultimate power of Jesus 'over Satan in nature, in possession, in disease, and in death is exhibited'.[9]

Chou observes that this is Mark's longest miracle account and the only miracle account to be presented intercalated.[10] Chou is not strictly correct on the latter point as the cursing of the fig tree is surely another intercalated miracle.[11] However, it is the only *healing* miracle presented in this way. Also, because most scholars would not class the clearing of the Temple as a miracle,[12] it is also safe to say that it is the only example of two miracles intercalated.

The presence of Peter, James and John, exclusive of the other disciples, also suggests some special significance for the resurrection of Jairus' daughter. This inner sanctum of Jesus' followers is the same group present for the transfiguration, final discourse and Gethsemane (Mark 9:2; 13:3; 14:33).[13]

As expressions of divine power and healing, all the healing miracles prefigure in a limited way the resurrection of Jesus. However, the raising of a dead girl surely prefigures it with the greatest clarity and force.[14] In demonstrating Jesus' power over

---

[4] Achtemeier 1970: 277; Guelich 1989: 297; Marcus 2000a 364; Collins 2007: 276.
[5] Gundry 1993: 285.
[6] Watts, 2004: 14; Boring 2006: 157, 161; Collins 2007: 276.
[7] Chou 2011: 363-90; also Broadhead 1992: 103.
[8] Guelich 1989: 293; Marcus 2000a: 359; France 2002: 235; Collins 2007: 284; Hartman 2010: 220.
[9] Fisher 1981: 15.
[10] Chou 2011: 365.
[11] As discussed in §3.3.1 above.
[12] The minority report is represented by Origen (*Comm. John* 10.16) and Heinrich Paulus as discussed in Strauss 1846: 2.214-216.
[13] Marcus 2000a: 371; France 2002: 239; Collins 2007: 285.
[14] See further John 2001: 104-5.

even death, it is the definitive miracle.[15] As such, we might anticpate Mark employing scriptural typology to inform and illuminate the significance of this extraordinary act of power.

§5.2 Exploring the conventions

With these two miracles we are dealing with two related narrative forms. The difference between a healing and a resurrection was not as pronounced in the ancient world as it is for the twenty-first century. As Pesch states, 'der Tod is der äußerste Fall der Krankenheit'.[16] Conversely, Cotter argues that a resurrection or resuscitation is 'a healing gone to its extreme'.[17] Collins outlines the conventions as follows. Typical features for a miraculous healing include: details of the illness and its unsuccessful treatment, therapeutic touch and instantaneous healing. Typical features for a resuscitation of a dead person include: the summoned healer arriving after death has occurred, dismissal of crowds, words of power in a foreign language, instantaneous resuscitation, the mention of the deceased's age and the demonstration of the miracle.[18]

§5.2.1 Ancient healing miracles

When the Greeks recounted gods healing people, it was usually through a visit to a temple of that god and often through dreams (e.g. Aelius Aristides, *Heracles* 40.12; *Inscriptiones Graecae* 4.1.121–2: Stelai 1.3, 9, 15, 18; 2.35, 36; Diodorus Siculus, *Library of History* 1.25.4–5).[19]

Closer parallels to Jesus' miracles are provided by the accounts of human healers. Diogenes Laertius recounts that Empedocles cures a woman 'who had been given up by the physicians' (Empedocles, *Lives of Eminent Philosphers* 8.69).[20] This is similar to the description of the woman in Mark 5:26. But there is no other detail given about Empedocles' healing; thus it is not clear whether this was a miracle.

In the ancient sources there is often ambiguity around medicine, magic and miracle. These categories are to a significant extent anachronistic.[21] Tobit 2:10 contains a similar polemic against the medical profession to Mark 5:26, yet when Tobit's blindness is healed on angelic advice the method bears more resemblance to either medical or magical technique (as modern categories would put it) than a divinely empowered miracle.[22]

Tacitus recounts two healings on the same occasion by the emperor Vespasian. The first was a blind man cured by the emperor's spittle and the second was a man with a

---

[15] Haenchen 1968: 211.
[16] 'Death is the ultimate case of sickness'. Pesch 1979: 1.297.
[17] Cotter 1999: 12; also Theissen 2020: 167.
[18] Collins 2007: 276–7.
[19] Cotter 1999: 11–34.
[20] Cotter 1999: 39.
[21] See especially Horsley 2014.
[22] Eve 2002: 223.

useless hand cured by the emperor stamping on his hand (*Hist.* 4.81).[23] Notably, Vespasian only performed the cures on the advice of his medical doctors, and so the cure is hardly presented as a miracle or as Vespasian's unique ability.[24] Further, he had the assurance that if he had failed it would have been the supplicants who would have appeared foolish, not him. The subsequent cures were seen as an omen of the gods' favour on Vespasian rather than evidence of an ongoing ability to heal.[25]

Philostratus recounts healings by Apollonius of a dislocated hip, of eyes and of a paralysed hand (*Vit. Apoll.* 3.39).[26] These accounts contain little detail. A more detailed story is Apollonius' healing of a boy bitten by a dog and then healing the dog itself (*Vit. Apoll.* 6:43).[27] Interestingly, as well as displaying knowledge of how to heal, Apollonius first shows awareness of the (previously unknown) identity and location of the mad dog. He then reveals that the boy has been possessed by the soul of Telephus of Mysia (on whom, see Apollodorus, *Epitome* 3.17-20), before using the dog to heal the boy with a lick, and then a draught of water to heal the dog. In this account Apollonius' real power is miraculous insight. The healings (or healing and exorcism) are achieved by otherwise mundane actions that it appears anyone could perform. Apollonius' own explanations suggest that anyone could have performed the healings if they had had the knowledge. By contrast, although Jesus does sometimes use actions like spitting in his healing (Mark 7:33; 8:23), there is never any suggestion that it is the action alone which brings the healing or that anyone else could have done it.

Marcus identifies the use of foreign languages or secret words as a feature of ancient folk healings (e.g. Lucien, *False Philosopher* 9; Philostratus, *Vit. Apoll.* 4.45).[28] Jesus' words in Mark 5:41 do not fit into this category. The words are reported and so they are not secret. And Aramaic is hardly a foreign language to the characters in the story. Further, the immediate provision of a translation removes any veneer of mystery for the Greek reader.[29]

Words of assurance are also a recurrent motif in Mark (e.g. Mark 2:5; 5:36; 6:50; 7:29; 9:23; 10:49). Theissen notes that in Hellenistic texts, assurance always comes with particular promises as to what will be done (*Vit. Apoll.* 3.38; 4.10, 45; 7.38; Lucian, *Philops.* 11; *Hymn of Isyllus* IG IV/2, 128), while in the Synoptics such assurances are always more general appeals to have faith.[30]

As a healer then, Jesus stands in contrast to the miraculous healers of Graeco-Roman literature, not because he heals people whom doctors have failed to heal, or has miraculous insight and knowledge, or channels divine power and favour, but because he is shown doing all those things consistently and in combination. His use of audible, intelligible instructions, and use of power rather than knowledge, also differentiates him from the typical human Graeco-Roman miracle healer.

---

[23] Cotter 1999: 40-1.
[24] Meier 1991: 2.595.
[25] See also Suetonius, Divine Vespasian, *Lives of the Caesars* 7.2; Dio Cassius, *Roman History* 65.8.
[26] Cotter 1999: 43.
[27] Cotter 1999: 44-5.
[28] Marcus 2000a 363; see also Pesch 1979: 1.310; Theissen 1983: 64.
[29] Guelich 1989: 302.
[30] Theissen 1983: 58-9.

Turning to Jewish examples, Abraham prays for Abimelech and he is healed (and his female slaves can then conceive) in Gen 20:17. The expansion of this story in the *Genesis Apocryphon* 20:20-22 also contains a polemic against doctors, and describes Abraham healing by laying hands on the king of Egypt as well as praying for him.[31] Jesus' touch is a significant motif in the healings of Mark 5:21-43 (5:23, 28, 31, 41). In Num 12:13 Moses prays for Miriam to be healed from leprosy and she is, after spending seven days in shameful isolation. King Hezekiah prays for the Israelites who ate the Passover without purifying themselves and they are healed (2 Chr 30:20). Notably, Jesus does not pray for those he heals. This is most apparent in the story of the boy whose evil spirit the disciples could not cast out (Mark 9:14-29). There Jesus cast out the demon *without praying*, and then tells his disciples that the reason *they* could not cast it out was their lack of prayer.

In contrast to those healings by prayer and personal physical contact, a number of healings in the Jewish scriptures are achieved by giving instructions. In these the prophets act as revealers of (divine) knowledge, not as sources of power. Moses made a bronze snake which healed snake-bitten Israelites who looked at it (Num 21:9). Samuel instructed the Philistines to return the ark of God with a suitable offering to be healed of tumours (1 Sam 6:3). Elisha healed Naaman by instructing him through a servant, Gehazi, to bathe seven times in the Jordan (2 Kgs 5:1-19). Isaiah healed Hezekiah by instructing a servant to place a cake of figs on his boil (2 Kgs 20:7). In contrast, the Markan Jesus usually engages the patient personally. However, he does heal at a distance (Mark 7:30) and by apparently automatic means (3:10; 5:27-30; 6:56). In bringing healing Jesus is never presented as having medical or 'magical' knowledge; rather, he is the source of healing power.

§5.2.2 Ancient resurrection miracles

Greek traditions around both Hercules and Isis contain accounts of them bringing people back from death. These do not have much in common with the Markan traditions around Jesus. Hercules' rescue of Alcestis from death was not achieved by a miracle of resurrection as such but by engaging Hades in personal combat (Apollodorus, *Library* 1.9.15; Euripedes, *Alc.* 1136-63). This was no doubt a sign of his divinity, but not of any healing power. Isis is recounted as having raised her son Horus from the dead by means of a drug which also granted him immortality (Diodorus Siculus, *Library* 1.25.6). Isis, a goddess, uses medical/magical means – not her own power.

The accounts of human miracle workers raising the dead show more relevance. Asclepius (as a human) is recounted as having rescued a man supposed dead from the funeral pyre, against the mourners wishes, and revives him back home with drugs (Apuleius, *Flor.* 19). In Greek legend, Asclepius' death at the hand of Zeus came about from his bringing back from death Hippolytus and/or a number of other men (Diodorus Siculus, *Library* 4.71.1-3; Apollodorus, *Library* 3.10.3-4; Philodemus, *Piety*

---

[31] Pesch 1979: 1.302; Marcus 2000a: 356.

52; Pliny the Elder, *Nat.* 29.1.3; Lucian, *Salt.* 45; Pausanias, *Descr.*1.27.4–5). However, there are no narrative accounts of the actual method of these raisings.

Similar to Asclepius, Apollonius revives an apparent corpse in a funeral procession. This one was a maiden who had just died during her wedding (Philostratus, *Vit. Apoll.* 4.45). If the age of Jairus' daughter is seen to imply that she is close to marriageable age, this account provides an interesting parallel. However, it is notable that there is no mention of a groom or dowry in the Markan passage, while these are prominent in Philostratus' account. Another common feature is ambiguity around the girls' death. Philostratus admits to doubt as to whether the girl was truly dead and the nature of the method Apollonius used to revive her. In Mark's account Jesus' comment 'the child is not dead but sleeping' (5:39) may cast doubt on whether she is truly dead.

In the Jewish scriptures there are three accounts of the dead being raised (1 Kgs 17:17–24; 2 Kgs 4:18–37; 13:20–21). These accounts bear directly on the argument of this chapter and so will be discussed in detail later. Here it is sufficient to note that these accounts are restricted to two closely related prophets, Elijah and Elisha, and that Elijah has no recorded healings otherwise.

§5.3 Elisha, 2 Kings 4:18–37

While a number of scriptural prophets performed some manner of healing,[32] Elijah and Elisha are the only prophets to raise someone from the dead. Elisha was held in high esteem as a miracle worker (Sir 48:12–14; Josephus, *Ant.* 9 §182).[33] The double portion of Elijah's spirit that Elisha asked for (2 Kgs 2:9) was understood to be substantiated in Elisha performing twice as many miracles, a fact not lost on ancient exegetes.[34]

> 12 When Elijah was enveloped in the whirlwind, Elisha was filled with his spirit. He performed twice as many signs, and marvels with every utterance of his mouth. Never in his lifetime did he tremble before any ruler, nor could anyone intimidate him at all. 13 Nothing was too hard for him, and when he was dead, his body prophesied. 14 In his life he did wonders, and in death his deeds were marvellous.
> Sir 48:12–14, NRSV

Given Mark's identification of John the Baptist as a type of Elijah (Mark 1:6; 9:13) and Jesus' receiving of the Spirit in John's baptism (Mark 1:9–11), it is a natural step to see Jesus as a type of Elisha. Importantly, because of Elisha's double portion, 'the attribution of an Elisha role to Jesus need not have been a derogation, but rather a recognition that more of the spirit of God had come upon him'.[35]

---

[32] See above.
[33] Brown 1971: 90; Blenkinsopp 1999: 76.
[34] Originally, the double portion most likely referred to the eldest son's portion of the inheritance (Deut 21:17). Lindars 1965: 73; Gray 1970: 475.
[35] Brown 1971: 88.

Unlike Elijah, Elisha is also recorded as performing a healing (2 Kgs 5). The healing of Naaman of who was 'leprous' (λεπρόομαι, 2 Kgs 5:1, 27; λέπρα, 5:3, 6, 7, 27; λεπρός, 5:11) has likely been called to mind early on in Mark's account of Jesus' ministry through the healing of the λεπρός (Mark 1:40) from the λέπρα (1:42).[36] Notably Elisha uses the Jordan to heal Naaman, while Jesus needs no living water, only his touch and word.[37]

There is also an affinity in lifestyle: whereas Elijah and John were solitary prophets out in the wilderness, Elisha and Jesus are presented as having a community of disciples and travelling among towns and villages.[38] Gerald Bostock suggests that the transfiguration account where Jesus met Moses and Elijah (Mark 9:2–8) casts Jesus as both Joshua and Elisha, the respective heirs of Moses and Elijah. And, even as Jesus and Joshua are the same Hebrew name, the name Jesus also leads to an identification with Elisha as their names are of similar meaning and construction (יהושע 'Yah saves'/ אלישע 'God is salvation').[39]

The Elijah–Elisha narrative has been argued to be an important, even the most important, literary background for Mark's gospel.[40] The Gospel's opening scripture quote from Malachi (Mark 1:2) 'opens up' the Elijah–Elisha story from the beginning of the Gospel.[41] In particular, studies by Wolfgang Roth, Thomas Brodie and most recently Adam Winn have sought to demonstrate that Mark's Gospel uses 1 Kgs 17–2 Kgs 13 as a source for structure, narrative and detail.[42] Certainly, within the Jewish scriptures, the ministry of Elisha as worker of a series of diverse miracles provides the strongest available literary parallel with the ministry of Jesus as the worker of a diverse series of miracles.[43] Hieke Omerzu observes that Mark's use of Elijah–Elisha traditions combines the stories of the righteous prophets with eschatological expectation concerning Elijah's return, but uses structural or thematic allusions to do so rather than unambiguous scripture references.[44]

It is surprising, then, that the narrative connection between the accounts of Elijah and Elisha raising the dead and Jesus raising the dead has not been explored in any depth by any of the aforementioned scholars. While Roth briefly notes a formal correspondence between the two stories, his concern is to show 2 Kgs 4:18–37 (also 1 Kgs 17:1–18:46; 1 Kgs 21:1–22:40; 2 Kgs 11:1–12:17) as the source for Mark's intercalation technique.[45] Because the examples from 1–2 Kings are not intercalations but linear narratives with multiple episodes his suggestion is not convincing.

Rudolf Pesch had earlier argued that the pre-Markan tradition of Jarius' daughter was a healing which, influenced by the Elijah and Elisha stories became a resurrection story.[46]

---

[36] Cf. Luke 4:27. Theissen 2020: 66. Theissen convincingly demonstrates biblical references to λέπρα do not refer to Hansen's disease (2020: 43–54).
[37] Theissen 2020: 63.
[38] Brown 1971: 89.
[39] Bostock 1980: 40.
[40] For comments about Jesus and Elisha in the gospels generally see Brown 1971; Bostock 1980; Brodie 1981; Blenkinsopp 1999: 58.
[41] Omerzu 2011: 83.
[42] Roth 1988; Brodie 2000; Winn 2010.
[43] Brown 1971: 98.
[44] Omerzu 2011: 84.
[45] Roth 1988: 38–9.
[46] Pesch 1979: 1.308–13.

However, Gnilka is perhaps representative of others in finding, 'Eine direkte literarische Abhängigkeit läßt sich aber nicht nachweisen'.[47] Pesch's judgement remains true: 'Die Kommentatoren unterschätzen meist den Einfluß der atl. Totenerweckungserzählungen von Elija und Elischa auf Entstehung und Ausformulierung der Erzählung von Jairi Töchterlein.'[48]

The exception to this neglect is a 1993 study by Timothy Dwyer which argues that Mark 5:21–43 is a 'midrashic' reworking of the Elijah and Elisha resurrection stories.[49] Dwyer makes some useful observations connecting the passages:

1. All three stories are of a child being raised from the dead in a room (1 Kgs 17:9; 2 Kgs 4:33; Mark 5:40).
2. Both Jairus and the Shunamite woman fall at the feet of the prophet (2 Kgs 4:27; Mark 5:22).
3. Jesus departs with Jairus (Mark 5:24) just as Elisha departs with the Shunamite (2 Kgs 4:30).
4. Just as Jesus is apparently unaware of who touched him (Mark 5:31), Elisha is unaware of the death of the Shunamite's son (2 Kings 4:27).
5. In all three stories there is a response of awe (Mark 5:42, 1 Kings 17:24, 2 Kings 4:37).

Additionally, Beavis notes that the three miracles are all performed in private.[50] To those initial observations I would add that in all three stories each prophet deals with a corpse without any indication that this causes ritual impurity for him.[51]

Josephus does not mention Elisha's resuscitation miracle in his account of Elisha (*Ant.* 9 §28–185). Eve suggests Josephus did not see the Elisha resurrection story as relevant to the political and military affairs which were most interesting to his Graeco-Roman readers.[52] However, that does not explain the inclusion of the resuscitation story in Josephus' account of Elijah. It seems more likely that Josephus omitted the second resuscitation as repetitious. Collins notes that in Josephus' retelling of 1 Kgs 17:17–24 (*Ant.* 8.13.3 §325–7) Elijah's stretching and breathing are omitted and that these actions are also not present in Mark 5:21–43.[53] Another correspondence between the resurrection accounts of *Ant.* 8 §325–27 and Mark 5:21–43 is the prophet encouraging the supplicant parent (Mark 5:36; cf. *Ant.* 8 §326, ὁ δὲ παρεκελεύετο θαρρεῖν).

Nevertheless, because 2 Kgs 4:18–37 contains a journey narrative as well as a resurrection it bears a much closer resemblance to Mark 5:21–43 than does 1 Kgs 17:17–24. Also, thematically both Mark 5:21–43 and 2 Kgs 4:18–37 present a woman as

---

[47] 'A direct literary dependence cannot be detected' (Gnilka 1998: 1.212).
[48] 'The commentators underestimate the influence of the OT resurrection narratives of Elijah and Elisha on the formation and formulation of the story of Jairus' daughter' (Pesch 1979: 1.298).
[49] Dwyer 1993: 23–30.
[50] Beavis 2010: 54.
[51] As Theissen argues at length, this does not mean that Elijah/Elisha/Jesus rejects purity concerns but that their own holiness overpoweringly removes the source of the impurity and so does not incur ritual impurity for the miracle worker (2020: 97–122, esp. 121).
[52] Eve 2002: 35–7.
[53] Collins 2007: 277.

a paradigm of effective faith, over and against the non-prophetic men in the story, a theme which is absent from 1 Kgs 17:17–24.[54]

Hartman notes that both the healing of Naaman in 2 Kgs 5:11 (LXX) and Mark 5:23 use ἐπιτίθημι, and suggests Jairus' request for Jesus to touch his daughter evokes Elijah and Elisha.[55] Both Elijah and Elisha touch the deceased in their resurrection miracles. However, France's observation that the laying on of hands is a 'natural gesture of healing' (e.g. Mark 1:31, 41; 6:5; 7:32; 8:23; 25) argues that this detail is not distinctive.[56]

Thus, Elisha's resurrection miracle presents as a significant parallel to the raising of Jairus' daughter. Analysis of the detail of the story, especially in the LXX, reveals further correspondences with Mark 5:21–43, not noted in earlier studies.

§5.3.1 Narrative correspondences

1. Both women also show faith in seeking out the prophet despite the impediment provided by others (2 Kgs 4:23, 30; Mark 5:24, 27).[57]
2. In both stories a parent goes to find a prophet to heal their child (2 Kgs 4:22–25; Mark 5:22).
3. Both the Shunamite's husband and Jairus' people try to dissuade the interceding parent from bothering the prophet (2 Kgs 4:23; Mark 5:35).[58]
4. In both stories the father and mother feature, although admittedly the mother is only briefly referred to in Mark 5:40; however, the insignificance of the mother's presence to the Markan narrative may suggest that she was only included for a reason ulterior to the narrative per se; that is, to further connect the episode to the Elisha story.
5. It is likely, although not stated, that the reader should infer that the woman in the crowd is barren. If so, this also resonates with the earlier section of the Elisha narrative where the Shunnamite is revealed to be barren (2 Kgs 4:14).

§5.3.2 Lexical correspondences

1. Both the Shunamite and the Haemorrhaging Woman are presented as having 'knowledge' (γινώσκω, 2 Kgs 4:9; Mark 5:29).[59]
2. Both Jesus and Elisha enter (εἰσπορεύομαι) the room where the miracle will take place (2 Kgs 4:10; Mark 5:40).
3. Elisha says the Shunamite has ἐξέστησας ἡμῖν πᾶσαν τὴν ἔκστασιν (2 Kgs 4:13) while the witnesses to the girl's resurrection are ἐξέστησαν [εὐθὺς] ἐκστάσει μεγάλῃ (Mark 5:42); the pattern of aorist active verb followed by singular cognate noun in Mark may reflect the same in 2 Kings (more on this below).

---

[54] For this point regarding Mark, see Collins 2007: 284.
[55] Hartman 2010: 219–20; also Guelich 1989: 295.
[56] France 2002: 236; also Bultmann 1963: 222; Theissen 1983: 92–3.
[57] Glasswell 1965: 157; Gray 1970: 498; Brueggemann 2000: 328.
[58] Brueggemann 2000: 323.
[59] The woman's knowledge should be contrasted to the professional and esoteric knowledge of the doctors and folk healers which has failed her; Fassnacht 2003: 106.

4. The Shunamite woman repeatedly states 'peace' (εἰρήνη/ שׁלוֹם) against the reality of the situation (2 Kgs 4:23, 26) and the prophet is concerned that she and her family have peace (2 Kgs 4:26 [x3]).[60] There also is possible wordplay on שׁלם in MT 4.28 where she instructs the prophet 'do not mislead (hiphil of שׁלה) me' or, as John Gray argues, "cause to be at ease", i.e. lull into complacency, a *hapax legomenon* in this sense in the Old Testament'.[61] This repeated and distinctive use of peace language lends allusive significance to Jesus bidding the haemorrhaging woman to ὕπαγε εἰς εἰρήνην (depart in(to) peace, Mark 5:34). This is the only use of εἰρήνη in Mark.
5. The Shunamite woman is twice described at Elisha's feet, in supplication (2 Kgs 4:27, ἐπελάβετο τῶν ποδῶν αὐτοῦ) and after the healing, presumably in gratitude (4:37, ἔπεσεν ἐπὶ τοὺς πόδας αὐτοῦ καὶ προσεκύνησεν ἐπὶ τὴν γῆν). Correspondingly, Jairus puts himself at Jesus' feet in supplication (Mark 5:22, πίπτει πρὸς τοὺς πόδας αὐτοῦ) and the woman falls before Jesus after she is healed (Mark 5:33, προσέπεσεν αὐτῷ).
6. Less directly, in the related story of Elisha's post-mortem performance of a resurrection miracle (2 Kgs 13:20–21) we find both the words ἅπτω and ἀνίστημι (2 Kgs 13:21). The word ἅπτω appears four times in Mark 5:21–43 (27, 28, 30, 31) out of a total of 11 times in Mark. The theme of 'touch' is also conveyed by other words in Mark 5:23 (ἐπιθῇς τὰς χεῖρας), 24 & 31 (συνθλίβω), 41 (κρατήσας τῆς χειρὸς τοῦ παιδίου). The word ἀνίστημι is used in Mark 5:42 for the girl's resurrection.

§5.3.3 Thematic inversion

The Shunamite's false declarations of peace (2 Kgs 4:23, 26) prior to the healing are thematically and chronologically inverted in Jesus' (true) declaration of peace to the haemorrhaging woman after she is healed (Mark 5:34).

Jesus appears to heal the woman in the crowd without his own volition or consent (Mark 5:30). This inverts the actions of Gehazi, who, on Elisha's instructions, attempts a miracle using Elisha's staff and this fails (2 Kings 4:29, 31).[62] This is both a failure of Gehazi but also of Elisha, whose staff and instructions are not sufficient.[63] Thus Jesus' involuntary healing via his clothes thematically inverts Elisha's attempt to heal the Shunamite's son via Gehazi and his staff. These both take place at equivalent points in the structure of their surrounding narratives.[64]

---

[60] 'In Hebrew the exchange is dominated by the term shalom' (Brueggemann 2000: 323).
[61] Gray 1970: 498; also HALOT 1503–4.
[62] 'This is an extraordinary act of self-confidence on the part of the prophet. But it does not work!' (Brueggemann 2000: 324).
[63] In Jewish tradition this was attributed to Gehazi's lack of faith and improper conduct towards the Shunamite woman (Ginzberg 1998: 4.243).
[64] Elisha's post-mortem resurrection miracle is a further example of an automatic miracle. Because the prophet is dead he cannot be said to have performed a miracle, yet it is through the prophet's personal holiness that his bones have such an effect. Others have noted how 2 Kgs 13:21 informs a reading of Mark 5:25–36 that does not require a background of Hellenistic magical practice. See Gundry 1993: 280, 359; Moss 2010: 510–11.

§5.3.4 Unique indicators

The expression ἐξέστησαν [εὐθὺς] ἐκστάσει μεγάλῃ (Mark 5:42) is especially important in the way that it corresponds to ἐξέστησας ἡμῖν πᾶσαν τὴν ἔκστασιν in 2 Kgs 4:13. The phrase is of the same cognate accusative construction as ἐφοβήθησαν φόβον μέγαν in Mark 4:41, which was so significant for connecting Mark 4:35–41 to Jonah 1 in §4, above. In this instance, there is no similar phrase elsewhere in the NT.

The phrase is also distinctive in 2 Kgs 4:13. It is the only positive use of a cognate accusative construction on ἐξίστημι in the LXX.[65] The underlying Hebrew phrase, חרדת אלינו את כל החרדה הזאת (Kgs 4:13), is based on the word חרד meaning to tremble, fear. But in 2 Kgs 4:13, it is usually translated with a more positive connotation as 'care'. This use of חרד is itself unique as all its other uses are with a negative sense of fear and trembling.[66]

Thus in 2 Kings 4:13, 'astonished with great astonishment' is lexically distinctive in both the MT and LXX. Although the internal narrative coherence is not strong, thematically it suits Mark's agenda that rather than the prophet being 'amazed with amazement' (as in 2 Kgs 4:13) it should be the witnesses to Jesus' power who are (Mark 5:42). Thus ἐξέστησαν ἐκστάσει μεγάλῃ in Mark 5:42 functions as a unique indicator of Mark's intent to allude to 2 Kings 4:8–37.

A second strong indicator is provided by εἰρήνη in Mark 5:34. While a common word in the LXX, its distinctiveness as a Markan *hapax*, the narrative correspondence (appearing in a similar position in both narratives) and the clustering of the term (x4 in 2 Kings 4:23–26; also verb שלה in MT 4:28) all argue for its significance. In particular we see a thematic inversion from the Shunamite, falsely giving and claiming peace, to Jesus, genuinely giving peace. Both these thematic inversions suit the Markan *Überbietungsmotiv* identified by Pesch.

§5.3.5 A deliberate reference

These correspondences combine to create compelling evidence for a Markan typology. As others have observed, while Elisha (and Elijah) prayed before their resurrection miracles, Jesus does not but is shown simply commanding the girl to rise. Jesus is presented here as a type of Elisha performing a resurrection miracle as Elisha did, but in a greater way. As with Jonah 1 and Mark's storm stilling account, the absence of prayer in this Gospel account is highlighted by recognizing the scriptural typology behind it.

Further, the typology provides a reason for the intercalation of the healing miracles. Rather than a disruptive insertion, the haemorrhaging woman is a vital part of Mark's

---

[65] LXX Ezekiel 26:16; 32:10 use ἐκστάσει ἐκστήσονται and 27:35 uses ἐκστάσει ἐξέστησαν. However, this is in a very different context of judgement and wrath. It describes negative fear and trembling as a result of witnessing punishment. ἐκστάσει ἐκστήσονται translates חרד in MT Ezek 26:16 but שער (suffer/bristle with horror) in MT Ezek 27:35; 32:10. There are no other occurrences of a cognate accusative construction on ἐξίστημι in the LXX.

[66] With the exception of Num 33:24–25 where it is a place name. See Gen 27:33; 1 Sam 14:15; Prov 29:25; Isa 21:4; Jer 30:5; Ezek 26:16 and Dan 10:7.

strategy to echo the scriptural story of Elisha and the Shunamite woman. There are far more connections to the scriptural text with the woman in the crowd than there would be without her. For Mark's typological agenda, their combination created a more satisfactory imitation of the narrative structure of 2 Kgs 4:18–37.[67] In particular the highly significant exchange between the Shunamite woman and Elisha, away from the home, is alluded to by the encounter between Jesus and the woman in the crowd. The role of the Shunamite mother is played in different aspects by both Jairus (as a parent with a dead child) and the woman (as a woman who meets the prophet on the way).

When we combine the observations of the scholars previously mentioned with my additional analysis we can see a remarkably comprehensive coverage of the details of the Elisha text by the Markan passage, especially from the point at which the story in 2 Kings becomes a healing story (from 4:18). This is shown in the table below.

It seems clear, then, that an allusion to 2 Kings 4:18–37 has been made by Mark in the intercalated stories of Jairus' daughter and the woman with the flow of blood. Moreover, this reference is sustained, multifaceted and arises more strongly from considering both intercalated stories together. While the Jairus story on its own would

Table 2 Plot comparison of 2 Kgs 4:18–37 and Mark 5:21–43

2 Kgs 4		Mark 5	
18	The son/child is older	42	Mention of girl's age
19–20	Son dies without knowledge of Father	35	Jairus informed daughter has died
21	Son laid in room	40	Girl laid in room
22	Journey to find Elisha	22	Implicit Jairus left house to find Jesus
23	Discouragement from bothering Elisha	35	Discouragement from bothering Jesus
24–25	Journey to find Elisha continued, mother desperate	37–38, 22–23, 25–26	Journey to daughter continued, Jairus and woman desperate
26	Do you have peace?	34	Go in peace
27	Grab hold of feet, supplication	22	Jairus at feet, supplication
28	Expression of doubt and fear	36	Exhortation to have faith
29, 31	Automatic healing attempted, fails	27–29	Automatic healing attempted, success
30	Mother goes with Elisha	24	Jairus goes with Jesus
32	Elisha enters room where child lies	40	Jesus enters room where child lies
33	Door closed, no witnesses	40	Parents, 3 disciples as only witnesses
34	Elisha touches mouth, eyes, hands	41	Jesus touches hand
35	Elisha walks about	42	The girl walks about
36	Elisha instructs mother	43	Jesus instructs witnesses
37	Mother falls at Elisha's feet after resurrection	33	Woman falls before Jesus after healing

[67] See also the discussion in §3.3.1 above, on the intercalation in Mark 11:12–25 which appears to allude to the structure of Hosea 9:10–17.

be sufficient to make the connection, the addition of the woman in the crowd creates further important resonances. Such a strong narrative coherence, combined with two significant lexical indicators, argues that Mark either intends his readers to recognize the allusion and to interpret the two Jesus stories in the light of the Elisha story, or at least that the allusion was meaningful to Mark and Mark's interpretation of Jesus.

§5.4 Reading Mark 5:21–43 with 2 Kgs 4:18–37

I have argued for a sustained and deliberate allusion to 2 Kings 4:18–37 in Mark 5:21–43. It now remains to show how such a reference might contribute to the Christology of the passage.

§5.4.1 Jesus as a greater Elisha

Several features of this story and of the wider Gospel, are suggestive of what might be the real typology behind Mark's literary allusion. In common with Elisha is Jesus' identity as a healer and his indifference towards uncleanness. However, details of the Markan miracle indicate that Jesus' ability as a healer and as a prophet who knows people's hearts render him superior to Elisha.

Much like the preceding story of the Gerasene demoniac (Mark 5:1–20), despite the many signals for uncleanness in the text, neither Jesus, nor the narrator, nor the recipients of salvation show any concern for ritual purity.[68] As Brigitte Kahl writes:

> Zwar verwendet er mit Begriffen wie *Blutfluß, Quelle des Blutes, berühren*, Schlüsselterminologie aus Lev 12 und 15. Umso erstaunlicher ist, daß der für Lev 12–15 eigentlich zentrale terminologische Bezug auf Reinheit/Unreinheit in Mk 5, 21ff mit keiner Silbe auch nur angedeutet wird. Die Krankheit der Frau wird ausschließlich in den Kategorien von Leiden, Ausweglosigkeit und sukzessiver Verarmung geschildert, ihre Heilung durch Jesus als Rettung von einer Plage und Gesundwerden beschrieben. Jeglicher Hinweis auf den kultischen Begriffsbereich des Reinheitskodex fehlt.[69]

Instead Jesus' 'touch communicates holiness and restoration to life'.[70] This, as noted above, is also a feature of the Elijah and Elisha narratives where they too show no concern about corpse uncleanness. Consequently, another possible interpretation of

---

[68] Equally, the stories of Mark 5:21–43 do not form a polemic against Jewish purity regulations or their interpretation by the Pharisees and scribes (D'Angelo 1999: 97; Theissen 2020: 69–96).

[69] 'To be sure, [Mark] uses terms such as blood flow, the source of the blood, touch, key terminology from Leviticus 12 and 15. It is all the more astonishing that there is not even a hint of a syllable of the central terminology of purity/impurity for Leviticus 12–15 in Mark 5:21ff. The illness of the woman is described exclusively in the categories of suffering, hopelessness and chronic impoverishment, describing her healing through Jesus as salvation from a plague and recovery. Any reference to the cultic domain of the Code of Purity is missing' (So Kahl 1996: 66).

[70] Boring 2006: 162; also Moss 2010: 516–17.

Jesus' often discussed remark that 'the child is not dead but sleeping' can be read as a dismissal of ritual purity concerns, rather than of the seriousness of her condition. Sleeping people are not unclean. If she had been dead, touching her would have rendered Jesus temporarily unclean, at least in the eyes of the public. By asserting that she is merely somnolent and not deceased, Jesus sidesteps the crowd's ritual purity concerns which might otherwise inhibit his ministry. By entering a room with a dead person Jesus should become unclean; instead the impurity of death is chased out and the girl returns to life.[71] Such imperviousness to sources of uncleanness when channelling the power of God in a miracle is not an innovation of Jesus but has precedent in the miracle narratives of Elijah and Elisha.

As Derrett notes, 'The claim made on behalf of Jesus that he cured persons of whom doctors had despaired is not merely an artistic exaggeration: it places Jesus both among physicians and beyond them'.[72] However, these healing stories do not only portray Jesus as a physician of individuals but also trigger a number of scriptural symbols. The repeated number twelve as well as other scriptural echoes identifies the females as representatives of Israel and Jesus as the healer of Israel.[73] This was the role of YHWH in the Jewsh scriptures and is part of both new exodus and sacred marriage paradigms (e.g. Isa 57:19; Hos 6:1–3). Yet it is also the role of Elisha, whose ministry to Israel 'gradually manifests the Lord's sovereignty'.[74] As the prophet Elisha purified a spring and a stew pot (2 Kgs 2:19–22; 4:38–41), fed the hungry (4:42–44; 7:1–2), protected the nation (3:4–27; 6:8–23; 13:14–21), brought gentiles into fellowship (5:1–19; 6:8–23), protected the widow and the foreigner (4:1–7; 8:1–6), healed the barren and the sick and raised the dead (4:8–37; 5:1–19), he represented the restorative presence of God among his people. Jesus likewise has a ministry of purification, feeding, justice, Gentile inclusion, healing and resurrection. He is thus presented as the healer of God's people.

However, within the typology, Jesus' power surpasses that demonstrated by Elisha in a critical way. Roth writes:

> To the detailed series of Elisha's actions done in the privacy of the prophet's chamber there corresponds the comparatively effortless and public activity of Jesus, climaxed in a command. Jesus' revival of the child demonstrates that he is more powerful than Elisha – evidently a qualitative heightening of the scriptural model.[75]

We can say more than this. When the two intercalated stories are considered as a unit and then compared to 2 Kgs 4:18–37, a structural correspondence between the healing of the woman and the failed healing attempted by Gehazi can be observed. Gehazi, on Elisha's orders, attempts an automatic healing. He does not pray or expect to perform the miracle himself. Instead, he conveys Elijah's staff, an inanimate quotidian object,

---

[71] Theissen 2020: 109.
[72] Derrett 1982: 481.
[73] Watts 2004: 19, 22–3.
[74] Roth 1988: 11.
[75] Roth 1988: 8.

which by association with the prophet may act as a container for some of the prophet's authority and power. However, such an approach reveals that Elisha's power is not sufficient to work in this way. The miracle is too great for the staff, and therefore Elisha cannot heal in this way, either through the object or at a distance. The account of the woman touching Jesus' clothing to be healed thus shows Jesus as greater than Elisha (Mark 5:27–29). Likewise, the account of the healing of the Syrophoenician's daughter at distance (Mark 7:24–30) invites the same comparison with the same result.

This episode additionally prepares us for Mark 6:6b–13 when Jesus will send out his disciples (with a staff, 6:8) to heal and cast out unclean spirits. They are successful (although they will not be in 9:18) and so, whereas Elisha's sending of his servant failed, Jesus' sending of his disciples successfully sees his power and authority manifested through them. Jesus is a greater healer than Elisha, healing without prayer or reinforcing actions, healing automatically through his cloak, and healing through the disciples he sends out.

Less clear is whether or not both Jesus and Elisha suffer from limited knowledge. Echoing Elisha's lack of awareness of the plight of the Shunamite's son, Jesus expresses ignorance of who it was that touched him and received the power which went out of him. Ernst Haenchen is able to suggest that, 'hat sie doch die Heilung quasi gestohlen!'[76] However, in contrast to Elisha's ignorance about the Shunamite's son, Jesus is aware of the status of Jairus' daughter. This creates a considerable irony between the intercalated stories. The two stories in Mark 5:21–43 do not appear to agree on whether Jesus has 'knowledge' or not. However, rather than blaming God for not revealing who touched him, as Elisha blames God for keeping the Shunamite's son's death from him, Jesus' question allows the woman to reveal and explain herself. As Chou plausibly suggests, 'la question qui suit n'est pas l'expression d'une véritable ignorance de la part de Jésus ... la question de Jésus est une vraie "fausse question" qui, sous son apparente banalité, fait signe vers autre chose, un procédé pédagogique qui doit amener la femme a une prise de parole'.[77]

Furthermore, his subsequent knowledge of Jairus' daughter and somewhat dissembling comment that she is only sleeping, suggests that his earlier ignorance should not be taken at face value.[78] Either the irony renders the two portrayals of Jesus inconsistent, or the stories are allowed to interpret the ambiguities in each other. It is more credible that Mark intended the stories to interpret each other in a way favourable to Jesus than that he did not notice the irony.

Comparing the Markan account with that of Elisha raises a further question. When Jesus asks, 'Who touched me?' this could be read as Jesus not having knowledge (i.e. an expression of ignorance) or as Jesus withholding from the crowd the knowledge the

---

[76] 'She virtually stole the healing!' (Haenchen 1968: 20).
[77] 'The question that follows is not the expression of true ignorance on the part of Jesus ... the question of Jesus is a true "false question" which, under its apparent banality, signifies something else, a pedagogical process that will lead the woman to speech' (Chou 2011: 377).
[78] Indeed, *Catena in Marcum* §320 takes the completely opposite meaning to be the case: 'But it is necessary to say in addition why the Saviour says "who touched me?" about the woman with a haemorrhage. This was in order that you may perceive that she received salvation from him willingly and not involuntarily. For he knew that the woman had touched him. And he asked in order that he might identify the woman who came forward, and that he might publicise her faith, and that the power which had been worked might not escape notice' (Trans. Lamb 2012: 288).

reader knows he has, just as God withheld knowledge from Elisha (2 Kgs 4:27). In literary context the preceding two episodes have established Jesus' power and authority over both the created world and spiritual forces (Mark 4:35–5:20). It goes against the grain to then suggest that Mark's Jesus has power stolen from him by an impoverished and physically unwell woman touching him against his will.[79] If Jesus can conquer a legion of demons can this woman plunder him so easily? Rather the reader is expected to assume that Jesus is in control of the situation and his question then reveals not ignorance and his own victimization but his compassionate engagement with the woman in the crowd. Jesus' comment in Mark 13:32 regarding eschatological timing does not apply to this situation, as it is clear that Jesus knows what is in people's hearts (Mark 2:6–8; 14:18, 30).[80]

Again, this conclusion is reinforced by the recognition of an Elisha typology. Elisha could read thoughts and know distant and secret events (2 Kgs 5:26; 6:12).[81] His failure to do so in 2 Kgs 4:27 is an anomaly which requires an explanation. Elisha attributes it to God's deliberate withholding of knowledge, demonstrating that Elisha's ability is dependent on God. In the Markan miracle there is no such explanation for the anomaly, leaving the reader to construct their explanation from evidence of the earlier episodes. The most likely conclusion is that whereas Elisha was truly ignorant of the Schunammite's affliction, Jesus only appears to be. Jesus is the greater Elisha.

§5.4.2 Kirk's common framework of empowered prophet as healer

Kirk's treatment of healing miracles begins by discussing 1 Kgs 17:17–24 and Elijah's raising of the widow's son. He observes that:

> The culmination of the miracle story ... is the affirmation of Elijah's identity by the woman: 'Now I know that you are a man of God, and that the word of YHWH is in your mouth is truth' (17:24). The ultimate healing miracle of raising the dead signals that God is, in fact, at work in and through the prophet who is God's agent.[82]

For Kirk, this story and that of the healing of Naaman (2 Kings 5) give a 'common framework for how a Jew might understand a miracle-worker who was, at the same time, claiming to speak for God: a uniquely empowered prophet'.[83] Although it can be questioned how far two stories from the books of Kings provide a 'common framework', the basic argument is fair enough. The problem is that Kirk has not noted that this response of recognition of a prophet (i.e. 1 Kgs 17:24; 2 Kgs 5:8) does not characterize any of the miracles in Mark. People in Mark's Gospel respond with fear, with amazement and with incomprehension (e.g. 4:41; 5:15, 20, 42), but they never behave as if the healings they have witnessed fit neatly into a 'common framework' that they already

---

[79] For a learned exploration of such a reading see Moss 2010 or, following her, Theissen 2020: 91.
[80] For a similar argument see Warrington 2015: 88.
[81] Bostock 1980: 41.
[82] Kirk 2016: 461.
[83] Kirk 2016: 462.

possess to categorize prophets or messiahs. In particular, Mark 5:21–43 does not allude to either of the stories mentioned by Kirk, but rather draws on 2 Kgs 4:8–37 which ends, not with an acknowledgement of God, but with the supplicant worshipping at the prophet's feet.

Kirk also argues that 4Q521 'clearly anticipates that this eschatological [messianic] age will entail healing [and] resurrection ... and may illustrate a messianic expectation wherein a human figure is God's agent in healing, resurrection, and feeding miracles'.[84] The pertinent lines, are 4Q521 2.II.11–13:

> And the Lord will perform marvellous acts such as have not existed, just as he sa[id,] [for] he will heal the badly wounded and will make the dead live, he will proclaim good news to the poor and [...] ... [...] he will lead the [...] ... and enrich the hungry.[85]

Kirk admits that the subject of the healing in 4Q521, whether God or the messiah, is ambiguous. Grammatically the most straightforward reading is that the 'Lord' of line 11 is the subject of line 12.[86] But following John Collins, Kirk argues that 'the action of proclaiming good news is more likely to have a human subject than divine'.[87] Collins' argument rests upon it being unlikely that God would be the one proclaiming good news (בשר) and he further cites 11Qmelch (13) II.15–16 where an anointed prophet proclaims (בשר) peace.[88] However, Grindheim notes that the *Hodayot* (4Q432 3.3; 1QH[a] X.6) clearly depicts God proclaiming (בשר) peace.[89] Given that God is depicted proclaiming in the *Hodayot*, there is little reason to go against the most straightforward reading of 4Q521 2.II.11–13. Moreover, as Lidija Novakovic argues,

> any conclusion regarding the function and the character of the Messiah in the end-time events described in 4Q521 is destined to be inconclusive because the text of this fragment neither ascribes the execution of these miracles directly to the Messiah nor, more fundamentally, clarifies the Messiah's identity in the first place.[90]

Grindheim also argues (citing Jub 23:26–30; 1 Enoch 96:3; 4 Ezra 8:52–54; 2 Bar 29:7) that the messiah was not expected to be a healer, and that this eschatological healing role was reserved for God.[91] Thus even if 4Q521 were taken to be 'clear' in favour of Kirk's view, this would only be one text against the more general trend in the Jewish literature. A common Jewish paradigm can hardly be constructed on the basis of one text that is contradicted by several others.

---

[84] Kirk 2016: 462.
[85] Trans. Martínez and Tigchelaar 2000: 2.1045.
[86] Collins 1994: 99–100; Grindheim 2011: 51.
[87] Kirk 2016: 462, also 95, 117; see further Eve 2002: 189–97.
[88] Collins 1994: 100–1; Kirk 2016: 117.
[89] Grindheim 2011: 51.
[90] Novakovic 2007: 209–10.
[91] Grindheim 2011: 50.

Kirk argues regarding the healings that, 'If the human characters in the story can perform the same actions, then those actions are no indication that Jesus is God'.[92] Again this is an imprecise analogy. Jesus' disciples heal, but they do so using a particular technique and the tool of oil (6:13). Moreover, they only do so after being given authority and instruction by Jesus (Mark 6:6–13). Additionally, the healings the disciples perform are attributed to Jesus' name (6:14).[93] One of the features noted in my analysis of Mark 5:21–43 was the absence of any mention of God and of Jesus' apparent innate power. He performs the healings without recourse to technique, tool, or to the name of God. There is thus a qualitative difference between the healings of the disciples and of Jesus.

For Kirk, in Mark 6:1–6,

> the focus on faith not only links this scene to the other healing miracles (2:5) and exorcisms (9:24), but also signals Jesus' ability to heal is not simply an innate, supernatural power, but is to some degree contingent on the disposition of the petitioner.[94]

But Kirk's thesis is contradicted by other healings in Mark. For example, the healing of the withered hand in Mark 3:1–6 does not mention faith at all, and appears to be performed as an object lesson or test for the Pharisees. In Mark 9:24–27, Jesus heals despite the limited faith of the supplicant. In Mark 7:24–30 he performs an exorcism on someone who is not even there. Perhaps most pertinently, in Mark 6:1–6, it states 'he could do no deed of power there', except that Jesus did, 'lay his hands on a few sick people and cured them'. The lack of faith did not stop him healing. Like 'all the people of Jerusalem' coming to see John the Baptist (Mark 1:5), 'no deed of power' is Markan hyperbole (cf. Matt 13:58, οὐκ ἐποίησεν ἐκεῖ δυνάμεις πολλὰς). The relationship between faith and healing power is more complicated than Kirk makes out.

This is made most apparent in Mark 5:21–43. The first supplicant, Jairus, does not receive the healing of his daughter but she dies (5:35). The second supplicant, the woman in the crowd, receives healing through the hem of Jesus' cloak (5:27–29), apparently without Jesus' knowledge or permission. While the woman is told 'your faith has made you well' (5:34), the reader is in no doubt that the power did not come from the woman's faith but came out of Jesus (5:30). The woman's faith is in Jesus (5:28) and it is her appropriation of Jesus' power through his cloak that heals her. Recognizing Mark's use of 2 Kings 4 in this narrative highlights the power of Jesus through the extension of his person in his clothing. It also sets up the comparison with Elisha, who was not able to communicate his power through his staff. Thus, Jesus is more than a mere human agent of divine power like Elisha, but is himself a source of divine power.

Jesus exhorts Jairus, upon the news of his daughter's death, 'do not fear, only believe' (5:36). We are not told whether Jairus then fears or believes, or does both. What we do

---

[92] Kirk 2016: 474.
[93] Rather than 'awkward' (Marcus 2000a: 398) or 'artificial' (France 2002: 252) the transition from Herod 'hearing of it' (ἤκουσεν), referring in present context 'to the activities of Jesus' disciples' (Marcus 2000a: 392), to a discussion of Jesus, is perfectly natural as the action of the disciples would reflect upon their teacher. Their deeds done on his orders would accrue to his fame.
[94] Kirk 2016: 473.

see is that regardless of Jairus' response to Jesus, when Jesus touches the girl and speaks to her, she rises from the dead (5:41–42). The emphasis in the story is not on Jairus' faith but on Jesus as the one who raises the dead.

Finally, it might be noted that the lack of faith response in Jesus' hometown identifies Jesus as 'the son of Mary' (6:3). They recognize him in terms of his human relationships alone, and so they do not come to him in faith to do works of power. As Jens Dechow puts it:

> Eine Verstehensmöglichkeit wird darin gesehen, daß die Nazarener Jesus in seinem Menschsein sehen, als Zimmermann und Glied seiner Familie, und daß sie darüber seine Gottessohnschaft und Hoheit nicht anzuerkennen bereit sind. Man könnte paraphrasieren: Dieser ist der Sohn der Maria – und nicht der Sohn Gottes. Der am Ende konstatierte Unglaube (V.6) ist dann der Unglaube bezüglich seiner hoheitlichen Person.[95]

Far from being proof of a human paradigm for Jesus' identity, it suggests that for Mark failure to recognize Jesus in relationship to God is to cut yourself off from Jesus' saving power.

The two-stage healing of Mark 8:22–26 is unique to Mark's Gospel. Kirk argues, 'If the purpose of the healings is to lend their weight to a composite picture of Jesus in a proto-Chalcedonian sense, this story is entirely out of place.'[96] There are various reasons why Mark includes healing stories throughout the Gospel and different stories serve different purposes in the narrative. Mark 8:22–26, like the story of Bartimaeus (10:46–52), for example, functions primarily as an enacted parable of discipleship, while the spectacular miracles of Mark 4–6 are more Christologically focused. Kirk appears to assume that all healings must fulfil the same purpose in the narrative. Mark has made the point regarding Jesus' power clearly in an earlier sequence of miracles (Mark 4–6). Why should it be repeated in chapter 8 when the focus has moved on to the disciples and their comprehension?

Here, Kirk fails to show that there is a prior paradigm of messianic human healers. Even if there was such a paradigm, he has failed to show that Mark's miracles fit within it. Rather, earlier paradigms of healing are insufficient to account for Mark's presentation of Jesus as a source of divine power for healing.

§5.4.3 Jesus, prayer and divinity

In common with preceding episodes in the Gospel, Jesus does not pray before performing miracles. Instead, others are shown beseeching him. When contrasted with

---

[95] 'One possible understanding is seen in the fact that the Nazarenes see Jesus in his humanity as a carpenter and member of his family, and that they are unwilling to acknowledge his divine sonship and sovereignty. One could paraphrase: This is the son of Mary – and not the Son of God. The unbelief (V.6) stated at the end is then the unbelief concerning his sovereign person' (Dechow 2000: 240).
[96] Kirk 2016: 476.

the Elijah and Elisha stories, the lack of prayer is even more evident. Boring observes, 'As elsewhere, the Synoptic miracle stories have some affinities with the Elijah and Elisha stories ... there is an obvious contrast: Jesus does not pray, engages in no rituals, has no "technique".'[97] Likewise, Pesch remarks, 'Jesus bedarf weder des Gebets noch umständlicher Manipulation zur Erweckung des Mädchens'.[98] The Elisha resurrection account describes Elisha as praying (2 Kgs 4:33, προσηύξατο πρὸς κύριον). The parallel Elijah miracle goes into far more detail:[99]

> He cried out to the LORD, 'O LORD my God, have you brought calamity even upon the widow with whom I am staying, by killing her son?'
>
> 1 Kgs 17:20, NRSV

In his retelling, Josephus elaborates even further:

> He cried out to God, 'It is not good to repay welcome and nourishment by taking away her son.' He begged God to again send the soul into the child and to grant him life.
>
> *Ant.* 8 §326, author's trans

This emphasis on the prayer of Elijah and Elisha, and the amplification of that prayer in Josephus' Elijah account portrays both the piety of the prophets concerned and their dependence on God for the miracle.[100] This is especially important in Elisha's case where God has been blamed for the prophet's lack of knowledge (2 Kgs 4:27) and possibly for his having been prevented from curing the boy at an earlier stage. By comparison the absence of prayer in Mark's account is startling.

There is no indication that Jesus requires prayer for his power. In fact, this is reinforced by the healing of the woman in the crowd. If we follow Derrett's suggestion that the woman's touching of Jesus' garment might evoke taking refuge with the deity (cf. Zech 8:23; Ezek 16:8),[101] the impression is compounded in what follows. Divine power comes *out* of Jesus not *through* him.[102] Chou suggests that the passive forms of ξηραίνω (to dry up) and ἰάομαι (to heal) might be indicative of divine action.[103] While it is not certain that the divine passive is intended here, such a suggestion certainly fits with the rest of the narrative. Moss observes that the woman's response of fear and trembling (Mark 5:33) is a standard response to theophany/epiphany in both biblical and Greek traditions.[104] The faith for which the woman was commended was not faith in God, who is not mentioned in the episode, but faith in Jesus. The power she received came not from heaven but from Jesus' body. Jesus is the source of power and divinity in this story.

---

[97] Boring 2006: 162.
[98] 'Jesus needs neither prayer nor cumbersome manipulation to awaken the girl' (Pesch 1979: 1.310).
[99] Fritz 2003: 252.
[100] Fritz 2003: 251–2.
[101] Derrett 1982: 497; see also Halton 2012: 35.
[102] Boring 2006: 160; also Moss, 2010: 510.
[103] Chou 2011: 376.
[104] Moss 2010: 518; also Hartman 2010: 222.

Boring states that 'Mark's dialectic of humanity and divinity are woven into this story'.[105] An important strand of this weaving is that the healing of the woman in the crowd is already preparing the reader to perceive Jesus as a source of divine power before he heals Jairus' daughter without prayer. By presenting Jesus as a type of Elisha, Mark also presents Jesus as someone unlike Elisha, because Elisha needed to pray to perform miracles. Rather, Jesus is portrayed as a recipient of people's petitions and a source of divine power. In this way he is both prophet and divinity.

§5.4.1 Hays' discussion of Mark 5:21–43

Neither Bauckham nor Hays focus on this story in terms of divine identity. In a note, Hays briefly discusses Horsley's suggestion that Elijah traditions are behind Mark 5:21–43.[106] He argues that the identification of Jesus with Elijah is both present but also mistaken. In this regard he cites Mark 6:14–16 and 8:27–30, and argues that, for Mark, John the Baptist is the new Elijah (citing 9:9–13). He does not discuss the text beyond this, nor does he explain how Mark 5:21–43 is to be understood in light of the Elijah background. Hays' objection to an Elijah identification may be mitigated by the recognition that Elisha follows Elijah (as Jesus follows John) and that, as argued above, Elisha's raising of the Shunammite's son is behind the Markan story, not Elijah's raising of the widow's son.

§5.4.2 Jesus and the Gentiles

A distinctive feature of Elisha's ministry in 2 Kings is the two positive miraculous interactions with Gentiles, the healing of Naaman (5:1–27) and the sparing and feeding of the blinded Aramean army (6:20–23). The Shunamite is presumably an Israelite, although the remark in 4:13, 'I live among my own people', may indicate otherwise. Shunem was in the north of Israel within the region later known as Galilee.[107] No specific location is given for Mark 5:21–43.

Having established the Elisha typology in Mark 5:21–43, Jesus' healing of a Gentile woman's daughter in Mark 7:24–30 is also reminiscent of Elisha's healing of Naaman. The theme of Elisha healing and saving Gentiles is thus complementary to the earlier noted theme of Jonah's mission to the Gentiles and Jesus' saving of a Gentile demoniac (Mark 5:1–20), as well as the positive examples of Gentile faith in Mark (Mark 7:24–30, 31–37; 15:39).

§5.5 Conclusion

Despite a lack of scholarly exploration of the connection, there is a clear surface resemblance between Mark 5:21–43 and the resurrection miracles of Elijah and Elisha.

---

[105] Boring 2006: 160.
[106] Horsley 2001: 231–53; Hays 2016: 379 n. 60.
[107] Brueggemann 2000: 323; Fritz 2003: 250.

The foregoing narrative and lexical analysis reveals an authorial allusion to 2 Kgs 4:18–37 sustained throughout the Markan episode and indicated both by the distinctive phrase, ἐξέστησαν ἐκστάσει μεγάλῃ, and the only Markan use of εἰρήνη (a word used repeatedly in the Elisha narrative). This literary typology most likely indicates a perceived connection between Elisha and Jesus as the (double portion) successor to Elijah/John the Baptist, as healer, prophet, and as one impervious to impurity. However, in showing greater power and authority to heal automatically and at a distance through his disciples, Jesus is shown to be greater than Elisha, a typology of escalation and fulfilment. In this typology there has been less apparent assimilation to God than was observed in the sea stilling miracles; however, the typology does highlight Jesus as a source of divine power, recipient of supplication, and as one who heals without praying, contributing to the portrayal of Jesus as in some sense divine.

Having argued for two scriptural narrative typologies in the miracle accounts of Mark 4:35–41 and Mark 5:21–43, we now turn to the intervening story of the Gerasene Demoniac in Mark 5:1–20 and to a narrative allusion that has not been previously suggested in the scholarship.

§6

David (and Goliath) typology in Mark 5:1–20

But now the giants who were begotten by spirits and flesh – they will call them evil spirits on the earth.

1 Enoch 15:8

This miracle account is treated out of order for two reasons. First, the narrative typology I will argue for is more complex and esoteric than that which was argued for in the previous two chapters. Second, the narrative typology I will argue for is a more novel interpretation than that argued for in the previous two chapters. Although the presence of narrative typology in the two epsidoes surrounding Mark 5:1–20 does not necessitate that Mark 5:1–20 will contain a similar narrative typology, it does give warrant for investigating the possibility that this sequence of miracles (Mark 4:35–5:43) maintains a consistent approach to scriptural allusion as a vehicle for Christology.

In this chapter I will examine the exorcism story of Mark 5:1–20. After an initial discussion of the story and then analysis of the conventions of Jewish and Graeco-Roman exorcisms, I will examine the often-asserted allusion to LXX Isaiah 65:3–5. I will argue that there is little evidence Isaiah 65 has influenced Mark's narrative and several strong reasons why Mark would not employ this text in regard to Jesus' exorcism of Legion. Then I will assemble a new approach to Mark's use of scripture in the episode of the Gerasene Demoniac. I will survey recent scholarship on the influence of the Watcher tradition on NT demonology and this exorcism account in particular. I will then connect the Watcher tradition to traditions of David as Exorcist and Goliath as a descendant of Nephilim. These lines of enquiry will lead to examining Mark 5:1–20 for allusions to the scriptural story of David's deliverance of Saul from an evil spirit and its adjacent narrative of David's defeat of Goliath. This analysis will argue for a sustained narrative allusion to 1 Sam 16:14–18:9 within Mark 5:1–20, following a similar pattern to that found in the neighbouring Markan miracles already discussed. This chapter concludes with a discussion of the Christology implied by the proposed allusion to the David narrative.

§6.1 'A Strange Story'

There are a number of strong links between 5:1–20 and the preceding episode of Mark 4:35–41.[1] The journey anticipated in 4:5 is only completed in 5:1; the boat that is embarked

---

[1] Achtemeier 1970: 265–91, 275–6; Derrett 1979a: 2–17, 3; Collins 2007: 265.

in 4:36 is disembarked in 5:2. The exorcistic language of the stilling of the storm (4:39) is followed by an actual exorcism. The question 'who is this' of 4:41 finds an answer in the demon's cry of 5:7. Both episodes show Jesus' single-handed defeat of forces that overwhelmed others. Both demonstrate the efficacy and authority of Jesus' spoken word. And both contain a fearful response to Jesus' display of power. France argues these connections suggest a Christological question-and-answer from one episode to the other.[2]

There can be no arguing with the categorization of Mark 5:1–20 as a strange story.[3] Equally inarguably, it has also led to an impressive array of even stranger and wildly varying interpretations.[4] A number of unique and perplexing features present themselves.

Most prominent is the confusing nature of the exorcism whereby the evil spirit(s) adjure Jesus by God not to torment them. To begin with, in both Jewish and Greek exorcisms the exorcist was the one that adjured the demon (compare, e.g., Josephus *Ant.* 8.2.5. §45–49. Lucian, *Philops.* 15–16).[5] To compound the confusion, at the end of the episode Jesus is asked to depart and does so![6]

This is the longest exorcism or miracle account of any kind in Mark and also contains the most detail.[7] The level of detail of the description of the demoniac in particular has been considered by most scholars to warrant some attempt at explanation. 'Die Besonderheit und Schwere des Falles (vgl. Zu 5,25f) von Besessenheit wird breit und umständlich erzählt.'[8] On the other hand the disciples, who played such a key role in the preceding episode, are now conspicuous by their absence.[9] They do not even appear to get out of the boat. The focus on the demoniac and the narrative absence of the disciples sets the scene for an epic contest between Jesus and the Demoniac and has 'all the characteristics of a single combat'.[10]

In the narrative, Mark relates events out of order (5:6, 8), allowing temporary ambiguity as to the progress of the exorcism.[11] The time the exorcism takes and the conversation of which it consists give the appearance of genuine struggle. What does this say about Jesus' power? Is it, as Derrett suggests, 'to indicate that Jesus's initial command is not his final offer!' or just for the reader to 'enjoy the bargaining'?[12]

The destruction of the vast herd of pigs is both a unique feature and a source of considerable interpretational uncertainty.[13] Is it evidence of a successful exorcism,[14] or part of the cure?[15] What does it entail for the demons?

---

[2] France 2002: 226.
[3] 'This is one of the strangest stories in Mark' (Schweizer 1970: 111).
[4] For a representative sample, see the summary in Aus 2003: 97–9.
[5] France 2002: 228; Stein 2008: 254; Focant 2012: 198; Elder 2016: 430–47, 431; Nyström 2016: 78.
[6] Donahue and Harrington 2005: 165.
[7] Koch 1975: 62; Gnilka 1998: 1.200.
[8] 'The peculiarity and severity of the case (compare 5:25–26) of possession is broadly and laboriously narrated' (Pesch 1979: 1.285).
[9] Aus 2003: 69.
[10] Starobinski 1973: 340; similarly, Carter 2014: 148.
[11] Marcus 2000a: 347. For Schweizer these out of sequence verses are a sign of 'the narrator's lack of skill' and of 'some narrator that did not understand that demons experience agony by merely being in the presence of Jesus' (1970: 112). This is to fail to note the purpose of these narrative devices.
[12] Derrett 1979b: 286–93, 288.
[13] Moscicke 2019: 363–4.
[14] Dibelius 1971: 89; Gundry 1993: 252; Collins 2007: 271.
[15] Bultmann 1963: 225; Twelftree 1993: 75; Moscicke 2019: 370.

Finally, it is not clear what we are to make of the explicit Christological statements. Is the demonic address of 5:7 a trustworthy confession? If so how does it add to our knowledge of who Jesus is? Is the failure of the healed demoniac to follow Jesus' exact instructions in 5:19–20 a mistake or an example to follow?

Despite these difficulties, it has been suggested that the episode is a microcosm of a New Testament Gospel.[16] Jesus arrives, is declared to be the son of God, defeats the strong man, restores and heals, and then departs victorious, commissioning the saved to announce the good news among the nations. Despite the areas of confusion and ambiguity, Mark's careful crafting of the story can still be discerned in subtle changes of tense as the focus of the story moves.[17] Even the prepositions seem to be carefully arranged: Ann-Janine Morey observes how, 'The first half of the narrative is built on "out"; the second half is built on "in".'[18]

§6.2 Exploring the conventions

Exorcism in the Synoptic Gospels is the verbal casting out of evil or unclean spirits (also called demons) from individuals being afflicted and possessed by them. This exact form of exorcism is unattested prior to the NT. However, there are other accounts of attempts to control, banish and influence personal spirits in antiquity, where individuals demonstrate their power over spirits.[19] As will be discussed below, δαιμόνιον and its cognates do not necessarily refer to such personal spirits so discussion will be limited to relevant narratives, not to every instance of the word δαιμόνιον.

Plutarch records that evil spirits were feared (*Def. Orac.* 417C, D, E). Falling over (cf. Mark 3:11; 5:6; 9:18) could be a sign of affliction by a spirit (Plutarch, *Marc.* 20.5f; Lucian, *Philops.* 16). Plutarch's account of Nicias' manifestation of spirit possession is striking in its graphic detail and parallels to the gospel accounts (falling down, affected voice, drives the victim out and indecent dress), but also shows that enacting spirit possession could advantage an individual – in this case avoiding arrest (*Marc.* 20.5f). Conversely, exorcisms could be performed for financial gain (Origen, *Cels.* 1.68; Lucian, *Philops.* 16).

As well as verbal exorcisms, spirits could be threatened by letter (Philostratus, *Vit. Apoll.* 3.38). Spirits could challenge holy men (*Vit. Apoll.* 4.20) as they do in the Synoptic Gospels and Acts. Another feature is the evidence of the spirit's departure, either through manipulation of a physical object (Jos. *Ant.* 8.46–49; Philostratus, *Vit. Apoll.* 4.20) or by a visible apparition (Lucian, *Philops.* 16). The rush of the pigs in Mark 5:13 may function to provide similar evidence.[20]

Apollonius is not described as performing any exorcisms but does identify and drive off malignant spirits (Philostratus, *Vit. Apoll.* 2.4; 4.25). In one account, 'the phantom pretended to weep and prayed him not to torture her nor to compel her to

---

[16] Starobinski 1973: 346–7.
[17] Marcus 2000a: 345; France 2002: 232.
[18] Morey 1990: 172.
[19] See the survey in Twelftree 1993: 22–47.
[20] Strauss 1846: 430–1; Dibelius 1971: 89; Gundry 1993: 252; Collins 2007: 271.

confess what she really was' (Philostratus, *Vit. Apoll.* 4.25).[21] This parallels the demons' fear and begging in Mark 1:24; 5:7.

Josephus recounts how Solomon was a powerful exorcist who drove demons out 'never to return'. Solomon left behind 'forms of exorcisms with which those possessed by demons drive them out' (Jospehus, *Ant.* 8.44–45). He then goes on to describe one such exorcism by Eleazar who, by use of a ring containing special roots, draws a demon out through the nose of a man who then falls down. Eleazar adjures the demon not to return, 'speaking Solomon's name and reciting the incantations which he had composed' (Josephus, *Ant.* 8.46–49).

For many Jews and Greeks in antiquity exorcism was primarily a form of healing; that is, it was not associated with any specific cosmology or eschatological expectation (1 Sam 16:14–23; Josephus, *Ant.* 6.116–69; LAB 60; Tobit 6).[22] In the rabbinic literature, Ḥanina ben Dosa's encounter with the demon queen Agrath (*b. Pesaḥ.* 112b) and Simeon ben Yose's exorcism of Ben Temalion (*b. Me'il.* 17b) feature confrontations with evil spirits which have no eschatological significance.[23] *Genesis Apocryphon* 20, where Abraham delivers Abimelech from a pestilential spirit provides another example of an evil spirit without eschatological significance. The evil spirit is sent by God, not Satan, and the spirit is not personal, there is no speech interaction with the spirit.

In Mark, however, the exorcisms relate to a dualistic cosmology where Satan is the primary power behind the evil spirits (3:22–23) and connect to an eschatological expectation of judgement for evil (1:24; 5:7; cf. 1 Enoch 55:4).[24] This renders Mark's exorcism accounts an apparently unprecedented hybrid between eschatological evil spirits (serving Satan, offspring of fallen angels, destined for destruction) like those of 1 Enoch and Jubilees, and traditional exorcisms (healing/deliverance of afflicted individuals) like those recounted in 1 Sam 16:14–23 and Tobit 6.[25]

The two exorcisms in Acts 16:16–24 and 19:11–20 appear to lose the apocalyptic elements of the Gospel exorcisms. There are no indications of a connection to Satan or of the evil spirits fearing destruction. Acts 19:11–20 features an overpoweringly strong demoniac who has spiritual knowledge of Jesus and Paul. This is similar to Mark 5:4 in terms of physical strength and to 5:7 in terms of knowledge. In Acts 16:16–24 the slave girl's spirit is not explicitly identified as evil and is not apparently harmful to the girl. Furthermore, the spirit identifies Paul and his companions without making reference to Jesus. Yet, in both stories the name of Jesus is the 'source of power-authority' for the exorcists.[26]

Almost all the features of Markan exorcisms find a place within the conventional stories of holy men healing those afflicted by spirits. Only Mark's explicitly eschatological features do not fit, and these probably relate to the same Jewish traditions preserved in 1 Enoch and Jubilees (as will be discussed below). Mark 5:1–20 makes sense in its first-

---

[21] See also discussion in Twelftree 1993: 25–7.
[22] Cotter 1999: 84, 97; Horsley 2014: 9–10.
[23] For discussion see Twelftree 1993: 22–3.
[24] Gundry, *Mark*, 75.
[25] On this see Twelftree (1993: 217–24) who argues this, and that this connection between exorcism and eschatology can be traced back to the historical Jesus.
[26] Twelftree 1993: 34.

century context as a healing narrative. However, when read against certain Jewish scriptures some features of Mark 5:1-20 take on special significance both in relation to those scriptures and in relation to Mark's Gospel as a whole.

§6.3 Isaiah 65:3-5 (LXX)

The most cited background scripture for Mark 5:1-20 is LXX Isa 65:3-5.[27] Donahue and Harrington argue that the rebellious Israelites of Isaiah 65,

> sacrifice on the hills (65:7, 11) to gods who are demons (65:3), sleep in tombs (65:4; *mnēmasin* = Mark 5:5), and eat swine's flesh. Though the situations are different ('rebellious' Israelites in Isaiah and a mad Gentile in Mark), the similarity is that for both Isaiah and Mark spending nights in the mountain tombs is a sign of pagan behaviour.[28]

In the same vein Watts writes,

> It is most probably this linking of idols, demons, and pigs in the ancient world that forms the backdrop of the Markan account and which, along with the tomb dwelling, suggests that he uses Isaiah 65 as the horizon for his story thereby linking the powerful forces of 'Legion' with typical images of anti-idol polemic such that Jesus' victory over the demonic host corresponds to the end of the idols' power.[29]

However, Mark shows no interest in paganism or idol worship.[30] Neither does the Gospel link demons or demonization with idol worship or paganism at any other point. To say that false gods are demons (LXX Lev 17:7; Deut 32:16-17; Ps 95:5; cf. 1 Cor 10:20) is not the same as saying all demons are pagan gods or that all demonized people are idolaters. Indeed, in both Early Jewish and Graeco-Roman literature the word demon (i.e. δαιμόνιον and its cognates) could refer to a wide range of spiritual beings.[31] This is illustrated by Josephus, who at different points uses δαιμόνιον for deity, divine power, destiny, bad luck, evil spirits, and good spirits (Josephus *J.W.* 1.69; 1.233; 1.613; 7.182; *Ant.* 8.44-45; 16.20).[32]

For Greeks generally, a δαιμόνιον was a spirit or minor divinity of benign or neutral character.[33] The adoption of the same word by the LXX to denote foreign gods

---

[27] E.g. Annen 1976: 182-4; Derrett 1979a: 9-10; Pesch 1979: 1.286; Schneck 1994: 137-43; Wefal 1995: 15-16; Garland 1996: 207-8; Watts 1997: 157-64; Gnilka 1998: 1.203-4; Twelftree 1999: 72; Feneberg 2000: 143; Marcus 2000a: 348; Focant 2012: 203.
[28] Donahue and Harrington 2005: 164.
[29] Watts 1997: 159.
[30] Klinghardt 2007: 43.
[31] See, e.g., Homer, *The Iliad* 1.222; Plato, *Cratylus* 398 b; *Symposium*, 202d-e; Plutarch, *Def. orac.* 417, 419; Josephus, *J.W.* 1.69, 613; 7.185; *Ag. Ap.* 2.263; Philo, *Good Person* 130; *Gig.* 16; LXX Ps 90:6; LXX Isa 13:21; 34:14; 65:11.
[32] Cotter 1999: 96.
[33] See entires on 'δαιμονίον' in BDAG, 210; LSJ, 365; GE, 450; also Frieder. 1990: 44.

introduced a negative connotation to the word.³⁴ In early Judaism the type of demons who would be idolatrously worshipped were specifically territorial spiritual powers (Deut 32:8, 17; Ps 106:37; Sir 17:17).³⁵ Importantly, it is against idolaters that the polemic of Isaiah 65 is directed. We see this same use of the word δαιμόνιον in the NT in 1 Corinthians 10:20-21 where idolatry is also the concern.

Some readings of Mark 5:1-20 thus interpret Legion, especially with his request not to be sent out of the country (5:10), as such a territorial spirit. Jesus' exorcism is thus a defeat of the territorial gentile gods.³⁶ However, the evil spirits that possess individual people depicted in the Gospels are conceptually distinct from territorial spiritual powers.³⁷ The problem posed by demons in the Gospels is not idolatry but possession. This is manifested in seizures, self-harm, mental instability and social isolation. The possessed in Mark do not need to be rebuked for idolatry but delivered from evil.

In the Gospel of Mark we thus encounter a distinct third usage of the word demon for a spirit which afflicts an individual. For Ken Frieden this use in the Gospels of *demon* to denote independent evil spirits is 'a substantial linguistic and theological novelty'.³⁸ This is an overstatement, the demon/evil spirit in Tobit being one obvious counter-example.³⁹ Yet the distinction between demons as foreign gods (as in the LXX and 1 Cor 10:20) and demons as individual afflicting evil spirits (Tobit, Gospels) remains a valid and important one that has been frequently overlooked.

Thus, the connection of Isa 65:3-5 to Mark 5:1-20 via δαιμόνιον is potentially misleading, as the same word is able to refer to substantially different entities depending on context.⁴⁰ Despite Mark 5:10, there is no indication that Mark considers these demons to be spiritual powers over a particular territory. Their influence and presence are restricted to the single tormented individual. There is no suggestion that these demons are the recipients of worship by either the demoniac or the local population. As Matthew Theissen notes, 'the hostility [demons] show to humans has no explicit connection to divine judgement for sinful behaviour'.⁴¹ Rather, the narrative presents the demoniac as someone in need of healing and deliverance. He is not presented as a pagan who needs to repent of idolatry.

Other considerations also problematise the suggested reference to Isaiah 65. Regardless of the semantic range of δαιμόνιον, a reader of the LXX of Isa 65:3 should note that those sacrifices are made to demons *that do not exist* (τοῖς δαιμονίοις ἃ οὐκ ἔστιν). By contrast the demons in Mark's narrative are very real, as evidenced both by the man's supernatural strength and the behaviour of the pigs. Why would Mark reference a scripture that denies the existence of demons in an account intending to display Jesus' superlatively greater strength than those demons? There is no merit in

---

³⁴ Frieden 1990: 45.
³⁵ Martin 2010: 667.
³⁶ Derrett 1979a: 9-10; Wefal 1995: 14; Twelftree 1999: 72; Moscicke 2019: 378.
³⁷ Wright 2016: 231.
³⁸ Frieden 1990: 45.
³⁹ Tobit 3:8, 17; 6:8, 15, 16, 17; 8:3.
⁴⁰ The reader is referred to Dale Martin's impressive and convincing study (2010) of the divergent uses and meanings of 'demon' in Graeco-Roman and Jewish traditions and the development of Christian demonology in and after the New Testament.
⁴¹ Theissen 2020: 140.

being stronger than something which does not exist.⁴² The demonologies of Mark 5 and Isaiah 65 are not only different, they serve contradictory rhetorical purposes.

There is no indication that the demoniac has eaten the swine and brought the demon possession upon himself.⁴³ This is evident from the absence of the swine in the description of the demoniac. He is not associated with them; rather, they are described as happening to be there later in the story, once they become relevant to it (Mark 5:11). They are not mentioned earlier because they are not indicative of the man's condition. If the demons had entered the man through eating unclean pork would not other pig-eaters in the vicinity be similarly afflicted?

Further, there is no hint of demon possession in LXX Isa 65:3–5, rather it is a description of deliberate and hypocritical idolaters of whom God goes on to say, 'I will repay their works into their bosom' (ἀποδώσω τὰ ἔργα αὐτῶν εἰς τὸν κόλπον αὐτῶν, Isa 65:7). Yet the demoniac in Mark 5:1–20 does not receive judgement but mercy (5:19) and it is the demons who receive repayment for their evil (5:13).

The lexical links between the passages are also slight, giving no support for influence. LXX Isa 65:3 has δαιμόνιον while Mark 5:2, 8 use πνεῦμα ἀκάθαρτον. Isa 65:4 has κρέα ὕεια for pig's flesh, while Mark 5:11 uses χοῖρος for pig. Mountain, ὄρος (Mark 5:11), occurs later in the Isaiah passage (Isa 65:7). The only exact lexical correspondence is μνῆμα (Isa 65:4; Mark 5:3, 5). So, while there is some semantic correspondence, there is no significant lexical or narrative correspondence between Mark 5:1–20 and Isa 65:3–5 so as to indicate influence. In Mark's account the demons are not worshipped. They are very real. And the pigs are uneaten. The shared references to tombs, swine, mountains and demons in Isa 65:3–5 are best considered coincidental. However, if the reader remains attached to Isaiah 65:3–5 as an allusion in or background for Mark 5:1–20, then I ask them to bear in mind the comparative weight of evidence that will be brought to bear on my alternative proposal.

§6.4 The watcher tradition

More recently, several exegetical studies have argued for the relevance of the Watcher tradition to the demons in Mark's Gospel and particularly for the account of the Gerasene Demoniac.⁴⁴ In some Jewish traditions evil spirits were connected with the Nephilim (Gen 6:1–4; 1 Enoch 6–11; 15:3–4; Jub 7:21; 10:1; *T. Sol* 5:2–3).⁴⁵ The 'sons of God' (Watchers) 'went in' to human women (Gen 6:4) and the resultant offspring, the Nephilim, were גברים – mighty men or, in the LXX, γίγαντες – giants. According to the *Book of Watchers* (1 Enoch 1–31), when these giants drowned in the flood, or were otherwise killed, their bodies were destroyed but their spirits continued. As an unholy mix of angelic and human parentage, these became unclean spirits, which would desire new homes in the bodies of others. From the perspective of this tradition, the evil

---

[42] Theissen (2020: 149) cogently makes this point in regard to both evil spirits and ritual impurity.
[43] As noted by Stein 2008: 253.
[44] Elder 2016; Murcia 2016: 123–64; Moscicke 2019.
[45] Collins 2007: 167–8.

spirits of the Gospels and the Nephilim giants would be the same entities in different forms. Evil spirits were just dead giants looking for a warm body to call home.[46] Several correspondences connect this tradition with Mark 5:1–20.

1. *Mark's use of 'unclean spirit' rather than 'demon'.* Elder argues Mark's terminology recalls Enoch and the uncleanness of the Watchers due to their boundary-breaking sexual relationships with human women.[47]
2. *The evil spirits' recognition of Jesus as 'Son of the Most High God'.* The Book of Watchers depicts previous mediatorial figures binding and destroying nephilim/giants/unclean spirits and the spirits awaiting a final eschatological judgement. Therefore, the evil spirits recognize Jesus as such a figure. 'Most High' is used as a title for YHWH in 1 Enoch 9:4 and, 10:1.[48]
3. *The significance of the demoniac's dwelling in tombs.* κατοίκησις is used four times in 1 Enoch 15:7–10 (cf. Mark 5:3). In 1 Enoch 10:5 YHWH has Asael sent to the desert of Dadouel, to dwell (οἰκησάτω) and wait for a 'resurrection to judgment'.[49]
4. *Sharp Stones.* YHWH also commands rough and sharp rocks (λίθους τραχείς καί ὀξείς) to be placed on Asael which may have influenced the sharp stones the Demoniac cuts himself with in Mark 5:5 (κατακόπτων ἑαυτὸν λίθοις).[50]
5. *The theme of swearing on a mountain.* In 1 Enoch 6 the Watchers swear to bind themselves to all commit the sin of taking wives and having children on Mount Hermon. This may explain why in Mark 5:1–20 the demon and not the exorcist is the one adjuring.[51]
6. *The theme of binding.* In answer to the puzzle of Mark's uncharacteristically detailed description of the demoniac, Elder suggests the emphasis on *binding* in the Book of Watchers has influenced Mark 5:1–20. YHWH's first word concerning the Watchers' sin in 1 Enoch 10:4 is δῆσον (bind). In 10:11–13, YHWH commands the binding of the Watchers for seventy generations in the valleys of the earth, where they will await final and eternal judgment. The terms κατοίκησιν, ἅλυσις, πέδη, διασπᾶν, and δαμάζειν are all associated with binding and are also found in 1 Enoch 1–31.[52] I would suggest a closer, and complementary, parallel is Jubiliees 10:7–9 where after the flood nine-tenths of the evil spirits are bound in order to protect the living, while a tenth remain unbound to help Satan in his work (see also *T. Sol.* 5:6).
7. *The theme of drowning.* Elder observes, 'In the Book of Watchers, the origins of evil spirits are explained as the result of the giants drowning in the flood. Mark then provides the *Endzeit* typology that corresponds to the *Book of Watchers' Urzeit* typology: just as the spirits have their origins by drowning, so also their

---

[46] Elder 2016: 431.
[47] Elder 2016: 434–6; Moscicke 2019: 365; cf. Wright 2016: 235 n. 74.
[48] Elder 2016: 438–9; Moscicke 2019: 365; also Collins 2007: 213–14, 268.
[49] Elder 2016: 440–2; Moscicke 2019: 365.
[50] Elder 2016: 441–2; Moscicke 2019: 365.
[51] Elder 2016: 442; Moscicke 2019: 365.
[52] Elder 2016: 443–4; Moscicke 2019: 365.

destruction comes by drowning. [As in Mark 5:1-20] This destruction leads to healing...'[53]
8. *Transgressive Sex.* Some scholars note the possible sexual imagery in Mark of the expression 'entering pigs', where 'entering' is a euphemism for coitus or rape, and 'pig' for female genitalia.[54] The unholy union that produced the giants is then reflected in the unclean spirits' continuing desire for unholy sexual congress.[55] This desire, as with the Nephilim, leads ultimately (although more quickly in this instance) to their destruction in water. I do not consider this image to be present as there are no other signals in the text to suggest it and it would seem unlikely that Mark's Jesus would allow such an action. Wright helpfully observes that the language of entering (εἰσελθεῖν) is simply the opposite of the exorcist's command to exit (ἐξέλθε).[56] Thus, I would argue, no sexual connotation is implied.
9. *Jewish Scapegoat Traditions.* The transfer of demons into the pigs corresponds to the transfer of sins to the scapegoat in Lev 16:21.[57] The demoniac's self-affliction with stones (Mark 5.5) recalls the desolate, rocky place of the scapegoat's sending (Lev 16:22, ארץ גזרה; cf. גזר, 'portion' or 'cut').[58] The cutting with stones of Mark 5:3 may then recall the sharp-stone-wilderness of Lev 16:22. The pigs' descent from a cliff (Mark 5:13) corresponds to Second Temple traditions where the scapegoat was thrown from a cliff (Philo, *Plant.* 61; *m. Yoma* 6.6).[59] Moscicke argues further that in the Second Temple period Asael of the Watcher myth was identified with Azazel of Leviticus 16:8 (*Book of Giants*, 4Q203 7A; *Apoc. Ab.* 14:6).[60] The account of Asael's punishment in 1 Enoch 10 is a 'cosmic enactment of the scapegoat rite, in which the source of sin/evil is physically banished and disposed of in the netherworld'.[61] Thus, 'The transference of the Gerasene demons into the pigs is like the transference of sins onto the scapegoat, in that the demons personify iniquity. The disposal of Legion corresponds to the banishment of Asael/Azazel, since it involves the dispatch of personified evil into the subterranean realm.'[62]

Elder does not argue for direct literary dependence.[63] But Murcia concludes, 'L'ensemble de ces éléments paraît bien montrer ... une connaissance précise du cycle d'Azazel consigné dans la littérature hénochienne.'[64]

---

[53] Elder 2016: 445; also Stuckenbruck 1997: 39-40; Moscicke 2019: 365.
[54] Derrett 1979b: 290; Derrett 1985: 1.102; Marcus 2000a: 345; Carter 2014: 151-3.
[55] Moscicke 2019: 373.
[56] Wright 2016: 236-7
[57] Murcia 2016: 152-3; Moscicke 2019: 367.
[58] Murcia 2016: 155; Moscicke 2019: 367. This seems especially tenuous to me and probably an etymological fallacy. Either way, it is not reflected in the LXX of Lev 16:22 which simply renders it ἄβατος.
[59] Murcia 2016: 152-3; Moscicke 2019: 367.
[60] Moscicke 2019: 371; also Stuckenbruck 1997: 78, 81, 108.
[61] Moscicke 2019: 370.
[62] Moscicke 2019: 371.
[63] Elder 2016: 433 n. 9.
[64] 'All these elements seem to show ... a precise knowledge of the cycle of Azazel recorded in the Enochic literature' (Murcia 2016: 157-8).

The thematic and lexical parallels adduced above come from various, albeit tightly grouped, places in 1 Enoch and do not suggest that one narrative episode has influenced the account of Mark 5:1–20. Indeed, while many connections have been made, few succeed in making much sense of the Markan episode as it now stands. #1, 2 and 3 are not distinctive and could easily be coincidence. The attempts to connect the demoniac's stones (Mark 5:5) with an aspect of the Asael story make no narrative sense (#4). In 1 Enoch 10:5 the angel Raphael throws sharp stones onto Azazel. But in Mark 5:5 the demoniac wounds himself (κατακόπτων ἑαυτὸν λίθοις). The emphasis in Mark is not on the stones but the demoniac's behaviour. Likewise, the Watchers adjuring each other on Mount Hermon does not really explain the demon adjuring Jesus at the bottom of a mountain (#5). Neither does the successful angelic binding of the evil spirits in the Watcher tradition correspond meaningfully to the unsuccessful human attempts to bind the demoniac (#6). Mark 5:4 focuses on the human futility of trying to restrain such evil spirits in order to enhance the impression of Jesus' exorcism.

That said, the Watcher tradition does appear significant for Mark 5:1–20 in some ways. The descent of the pigs into the water is given two plausible symbolic meanings: the recapitulation of the primeval flood (#7) and the re-enactment of the eschatological scapegoat (#9). As Moscicke argues, these two interpretations are not mutually exclusive but complement each other.[65] They all contribute to the symbolic background of purging evil enemies. They help interpret the pigs as a type of scapegoat and the water as the cleansing destruction of the demons.

Further, Archie Wright suggests that 4Q510 and 4Q511 are examples of Qumram texts that give 'a clear indication that at least some strands/groups of Second Temple Judaism believed in the ongoing activity of the evil spirits of the Watcher tradition'.[66] The spirits within the tradition appear to operate by attacking people's minds (Jub 10:1; 1QS 3:20–24). Thus a background of the Watcher tradition is historically plausible and consistent with the presentation of the demoniac in Mark 5:1–20 as suffering from considerable mental stress. However, it should be noted that neither 1 Enoch, Jubilees nor 1QS have any concept of possession, but only that evil spirits cause people to sin and lead them astray.

While it is hard to gauge how influential such a mythology would have been, certainly it was popular enough that Philo of Alexandria felt the need to rebut it with his own treatment of Gen 6:1–4, *De Gigantibus*. The Mishnah and Pseudo Philo show evidence of other early traditions regarding the creation of evil spirits by God (*P. Avot* 5:6; LAB 60:2–3), but their influence on Mark is not evident.

Thus, the Watcher tradition, including its use of the scapegoat motif, appears significant for the interpretation of the pigs and their drowning (Mark 5:11–13). Further, the Watcher tradition provides a thematic link to a scriptural figure who, uniquely in the Jewish scriptures, both delivered someone from an evil spirit and singlehandedly routed an army.

---

[65] Moscicke 2019: 373.
[66] Wright 2016: 233–4.

§6.5 1 Samuel 16:14–18:9

The next stage of my argument is relatively straightforward. Mark has, I have argued, compared Jesus to scriptural characters Jonah (Mark 4:35–41) and Elisha (Mark 5:21–43), through narrative typology connecting miracles from the scriptures to stories in the Gospel. This typology is aided by an initial resemblance between miracles, whether a storm stilling or a raising of a dead child. So, the first move is to note that the only comparable miracle in the Jewish scriptures to Jesus' exorcisms is David's deliverance of Saul from an evil spirit. Given the other elements of David typology noted in Mark's Gospel (see Chapter 3) it seems pertinent to examine this story as possible background for Mark's exorcisms. Next, bearing in mind both the propensity for Jewish exegetes to conflate scriptural passages and the genetic link between giants and evil spirits in the Watcher tradition, further analysis will show that significant correspondences also exist between the episode of the Gerasene Demoniac and that of David and Goliath.

§6.5.1 David the Exorcist

John Collins argues that by the first century CE a number of exegetical traditions in early Judaism expected a 'warlike Davidic messiah' and, while we cannot know how popular these traditions were in general, when messianic expectations arose these ideas were available to give expression to it.[67] Evans judges the David tradition to be the 'single most important factor' in the eschatology of the Dead Sea Scrolls.[68] With the Gospel's novel combination of personal evil spirits afflicting individuals in an eschatological context, David's eschatological connotations as messianic forebear, combined with his distinctiveness as the only scriptural exorcist, render it likely that David's deliverance of Saul would have been a scripture of interest to Christ-believers, just as it clearly was to other early Jews.

Key evidence for this interest comes from Qumran. Four songs to charm the demon possessed are attributed to David and a reference to songs that 'aid the stricken' also likely refers to helping those troubled by evil spirits (11Q5 XXVII.2–11).[69] In 11QApPs a psalm attributed to David (11Q11 V.4) is given to invoke the name of YHWH when visited by an evil spirit in the night. This spirit is addressed as '[offspring of] man and the seed of the ho[ly] ones' (11Q11 V.6).[70] This combination of David as exorcist with the Watcher tradition of the mixed descent of evil spirits, provides an important precedent for what we find in Mark 5:1–20.

Two further sources testify to this interest. In LAB 60:1–3, David's deliverance of Saul is expanded with a song, which specifically addresses the evil spirit. Furthermore, Josephus provides evidence of an ongoing Jewish tradition that both David and Solomon (the son of David) were exorcists (Josephus, *Ant.* 8:45).[71]

---

[67] Collins 2010: 77–8; see also Evans 1997: 194–5; Atkinson 2000: 106–23.
[68] Evans 1997: 191.
[69] Evans 1997: 191; Martínez and Tigchelaar 2000: 2.1179.
[70] Martínez and Tigchelaar 2000: 2.1203; see also Chilton et al. 2010: 190.
[71] Kirk 2016: 207.

It is strange, then, that Goppelt states that exorcisms 'have no parallel in the OT'.[72] Likewise, Bauckham asserts, 'there is no scriptural precedent for an exorcism'.[73] Would not a reader of the scriptures expecting a Davidic messiah see in the act of exorcism by a messianic figure a correspondence with David's ministry to Saul in 1 Sam 16:14–23?[74] This is the only act comparable to an exorcism in the Jewish scriptures. There, an evil spirit from God would afflict Saul, David would play his lyre and it would depart, leaving Saul in peace, temporarily.

1 Sam 16:14–23 is primarily an account of how David came to be at Saul's court, as well as demonstrating God's displeasure with Saul. However, it could still serve as a model account of an exorcism, containing five features which are also characteristic of Markan exorcism accounts. A five-part structure can be discerned in the exorcism in 1 Samuel 16. These parts are the spirit described, the exorcist arrives, the exorcism itself, the sufferer healed and the spirit departs. It is noticeable that Mark uses the same elements but in a consistently different order. However, as discussed earlier, these features are conventional, it would be hard to tell an exorcism story without them. What they demonstrate, rather, is how similar 1 Sam 16:14–23 is to a Gospel exorcism, even if it is not technically an exorcism itself. The surface similarity between a Gospel exorcism and David's deliverance of Saul should be readily apparent.

Lastly, in regard to David as exorcist, we note the earlier discussion that Mark's distinctive terminology for demons requires some explanation.[75] Without discounting the resonance with *1 Enoch* 1–31, there is an earlier messianic text with clearer and weightier textual links in Mark that uses the language of 'unclean spirit' (τὸ πνεῦμα τὸ ἀκάθαρτον), Zech 13:2.[76] As discussed in §3.5.1, Zechariah is cited and alluded to several times in Mark especially during the passion narrative.

The imagery of Zech 9–14 juxtaposes a victorious conquering Davidic messianism with suffering and rejection. These themes resonate well with the passion in Mark.[77] The figurative use of shepherd imagery for kingship (both good and bad), common in the scriptures, is continued by Zechariah. Mark makes use of this motif in the passion, which to a large extent is also a coronation. Jesus' arrival in Jerusalem, and subsequent actions and events, establish Jesus as the promised shepherd king who will establish the kingdom of God (Zech 14:9).[78] Mark 5:1–20 contains many of these themes in microcosm. Jesus both conquers the unclean Legion and is rejected by the region's inhabitants. Similar to the clearing of the Temple, Jesus drives out (ἐκβάλλω, Mark 11:15)[79] those standing against the reign of God. This is the promise of Zech 13:2 fulfilled.

Given that Mark 1:26, 5:8 and Zech 13:2 share precisely the same construction for 'unclean spirit', then Zech 13:2 is a stronger candidate to be the source of Mark's terminology than the *Book of Watchers*. Therefore Zech 13:2 is an important background

---

[72] Goppelt 1982: 70.
[73] Bauckham 2017a: 30.
[74] Derrett 1979a: 3; Kirk 2016: 416.
[75] Elder 2016: 434. See discussion above.
[76] Derrett 1979a: 9.
[77] Marcus 1992: 161–3.
[78] Goppelt 1982: 87.
[79] Cf. Mark 1:34, 39; 3:15, 22, 23; 6:13; 7:26; 9:18, 28, 38.

text for Mark 5:1–20, especially in regard to the expectation of a Davidic messiah who would rid the land of evil.[80] Jesus' exorcism could relate him to David both in imitation of 1 Sam 16:14–23 and in respect of the eschatological expectation of Zech 13:2.

§6.5.2 Goliath the Nephilim

Despite these similarities between Jesus' exorcisms in Mark and David's deliverance of Saul, the casting out of demons in Mark presents qualitatively different narratives to the repetitive therapeutic musical ministry of David to Saul. Jesus' casting out of Legion, in particular, bears greater resemblance to a more combative event,[81] like the story of David and Goliath which follows Saul's deliverance from the spirit. Indeed, these adjacent stories in 1 Samuel could be linked in tradition by more than just literary context.

It is uncertain when Goliath achieved his great height. The LXX, Dead Sea Scrolls and Josephus all record his height as 'four cubits and a span', extremely tall but not supernaturally so,[82] but the MT adds an extra two cubits, making him gigantic.[83] The increase from two to three metres in the MT simply reflects his gigantesque features in the narrative: his strength, shouting, immense armour and weapons, and his ability to single-handedly intimidate an entire army (1 Sam 17:4–11). Additionally, there are texts that associate the inhabitants of Canaan, and the Philistines in particular, with being descendants of giants (e.g. Num 13:25–33; 2 Sam 21:15–22).

In Second Temple literature there is an observed tendency to 'reconceptualise these references [to giants in the Jewish scriptures] within the ideological framework of the Enochic story-line'.[84] This reconceptualization should not be overstated, however, since to some extent the links were already there. The Watcher tradition provides a genetic link between giants and evil spirits in Second Temple thought. This might then lead to the adjacent stories of David and Saul (1 Sam 16) and David and Goliath (1 Sam 17) being conceptually connected via this tradition. If so, not just David's exorcism, but also David's combat with Goliath, may be a significant background for Mark 5:1–20. To an early Jew familiar with the Watcher tradition, Goliath the giant/Nephilim was, to all intents and purposes, simply another evil spirit that had not yet had its body taken away.

This conceptual link would have been reinforced for a Jewish exegete by the stories' proximity to each other in scripture. There is considerable evidence in ancient biblical rewriting of 'the assumption that adjacent scriptural episodes were meaningfully related and thus mutually illuminating'.[85] For example, Jubilees 24:2–3 gives the reason for Esau's hunger in Gen 25:29–34 as being from the famine of Gen 26:1. LAB 6:3–18 retells the tower of Babel (Gen 11) as part of the story of Abraham (Gen 12).[86] Thus it is entirely plausible that at some point the two adjacent scriptural stories of 1 Sam

---

[80] Collins 2010: 28.
[81] Starobinski 1973: 340; Carter 2014: 148.
[82] The author of this present work is only 8 cm shorter.
[83] NB: a number of MT verses are not present in the LXX, 17:12–31, 17:41, 17:50; 18:1–5.
[84] DiTomasso 2009: 202.
[85] Fisk 2000: 951.
[86] For further examples see Fishbane 1985: 399–403.

16:14–23 and 1 Sam 17:1–18:9 might be connected, especially because of the Watcher tradition's connection between spirits and giants.

Mark's account of the Gerasene demoniac contains evidence that this connection had indeed been made because, as well as Jesus being a type of David as exorcist, the Gerasene demoniac appears to be presented as a type of Goliath as Nephilim.

§6.5.3 Narrative coherence

We examined above the resemblance between Markan exorcisms and David's deliverance of Saul. A number of narrative details also create correspondences between the account of David and Goliath and Mark 1–20:

1. 1 Samuel 17 is an account of David's victory not just over Goliath but over the army of the Philistines; hence the women can celebrate David's responsibility for the death of ten thousand (1 Sam 18:7) even though he had only killed one with his own hand. Mark 5:1–20 is an account of Jesus' victory over an army (Legion) of demons when he heals just one man. In both stories, victory over one becomes victory over many.
2. Both 1 Sam 17 and Mark 5:1–20 5–6, share a mountain setting (ὄρος, 1 Sam 17:3; Mark 5:5, 11) and the encounter between the antagonists takes place below the mountain, in a valley and beside the sea respectively. Indeed, the reference to the demoniac howling on the mountains 'night and day' (Mark 5:5) is reminiscent of Goliath shouting to the Israelites on the mountain 'morning and evening' (1 Sam 17:3, 16). This provides a fifth connection between the descriptions of Goliath and Legion.
3. Mark 5:2–5 contains a detailed introduction to the demoniac. This has usually puzzled scholars. Morna Hooker construes Mark's description of the demoniac as containing 'an embarrassing amount of detail'.[87] However, the detailed description of the demoniac can be explained as reflecting the detailed description of Goliath in 1 Sam 17:4–10. This supposition is reinforced by the lexical and narrative coherence between these descriptions which will be discussed below.
4. Both 1 Sam 17:41–47 and Mark 5:7–13 contain an extended conversation between the protagonists and also feature invocation of god/s. David comes in the name of YHWH, the Living God, and Goliath invokes the names of his gods against David (1 Sam 17:43). One theological implication of the Samuel narrative is the powerlessness of the Philistine gods against YHWH.[88] Yet the demons in Mark 5 use the name of God to adjure Jesus against tormenting them, presumably expecting that name to have some power over him.[89] This is a rather perplexing detail which will be discussed below. For now, the emphasis on names and on the invocation of God is a commonality between the two texts.
5. In both 1 Sam 17:48 and Mark 5:2, 6, the opponent runs or rushes downhill to engage the protagonist.

---

[87] Hooker 1991: 141.
[88] Avioz 2015: 64–6.
[89] Broadhead 1992: 99; Twelftree 1993: 41–42; Marcus 2000a: 351; Wright 2016: 240.

6. In 1 Sam 18:7 and Mark 5:20 both David and Jesus are praised for their deeds. As Collins writes of the exorcism of Legion, 'This is the only miracle story in the early Christian tradition in which the motif of wonder constitutes the actual conclusion'.[90] This uncharacteristic feature could be explained by the link with the story of David and Goliath.

§6.5.4 Lexical coherence

These narrative corresondences are reinforced by the presence of several lexical connections between the two stories:

1. In LXX 1 Sam 17:4 Goliath is introduced with a semitically styled Γολιαθ ὄνομα αὐτῷ ('Goliath was his name') which follows the underlying Hebrew (גלית שמו).[91] In Mark 5:9 the demon's response to Jesus shows the same semitic construction, 'My name is Legion' (Λεγεὼν ὄνομά μοι). This is distinctive in Mark because every other time someone or something is named the word order is reversed to follow a more normal Greek style (e.g. 5:22, ὀνόματι Ἰάϊρος).[92]
2. In 1 Sam 17:5 scale body armour, or chainmail (ἁλυσιδωτός), is an extremely rare word used only three other times in the LXX. In Mark 5:3-4 chain (ἅλυσις) is used three times, the only time that word is used in Mark. In the LXX ἅλυσις only occurs in Wis 17:16. It potentially creates a connection between the descriptions of the opponents.
3. In 1 Sam 17:8 Goliath shouts at the Israelites, 'Why (τίς) do you come out?'[93] In Mark 5:7 the demoniac shouts at Jesus in a great voice, 'Who (τίς) am I to you?'[94] This word is very common, but the combination of challenge, shouting and vocabulary by the protagonist's opponent is suggestive of a link.
4. 1 Sam 17:34 uses the rare word ἀγέλη. It is a strange choice as ποίμνιον (flock) would have been more natural translation of the Hebrew צאן and would be expected in this context. In the NT this word only appears in the Synoptic Gospel accounts of the expulsion of Legion. In the LXX it is used elsewhere only nine times, five of which are in the Song of Solomon. Thus, its presence in Mark 5:1-20 is suggestive of a link to 1 Sam 17.
5. In 1 Sam 17:49 Goliath is penetrated by a stone (λίθος). In Mark 5:5 the Demoniac cuts himself with stones habitually (λίθος). Perhaps the demoniac's self-harm with the stones is an identification with Goliath who was slain by a stone (λίθος)?[95]

---

[90] Collins 2007: 273.
[91] Tov 1999: 346.
[92] Mark 3:16, 17; 5:22; 14:32
[93] Also in the MT David is challenged by his brother Eliab, 'Why (המ) have you come down?' 1 Sam 17:28. The same Hebrew word is rendered by τίς in the LXX.
[94] On the use of the phrase τί ἐμοὶ καὶ σοί, 'every synoptic use of this idiom involves the recognition of the divine nature of Jesus by demons or by persons possessed by demons' (Maynard 1985: 584). Note that David speaks with this uncommon idiom twice (2 Sam 16:10; 19:22).
[95] René Girard (1990: 82-4) finds the 'autolapidation' of the demoniac fascinating, and questions whether it is in anticipation or avoidance of being stoned by the community. Equally, then, I would argue, it could be in anticipation or avoidance of being stoned by the eschatological Davidic messiah.

6. In 1 Sam 17:51-53 after Goliath's death the Philistines flee (ἔφυγον). In Mark 5:13-14 after the death of the demons the herders flee (ἔφυγον). Again, this is a common word but used in a significant parallel place in the narratives.

These six lexical connections are of varying strength and none would be individually decisive. However, four of them relate to Goliath and the demoniac who are connected by the words ἅλυσις and λίθος, by confronting the hero with a question (τίς), and by the same Hebraic construction introducing their names. This consistency in characterization is highly suggestive of an allusion.[96]

§6.5.5 Thematic inversion

A further feature of Mark 5:1-20 is its apparent inversion of some of the themes of 1 Sam 16-18:

1. The protagonists promise to give each other's flesh to wild animals in 1 Sam 17:44-46; whereas Jesus gives the pigs, domesticated animals, to the unclean spirits, Mark 5:12-13.
2. In the MT of 1 Sam 18:2 Saul would not let David return to his father's house; whereas in Mark 5:18-19, Jesus sends the demoniac back to his family. Both Saul and the demoniac want to remain with their deliverer, but whereas Saul detains David, Jesus releases the demoniac into proclamatory mission.
3. In 1 Sam 18:6-7, women come out of the towns to meet Saul and David to celebrate the victory; whereas in Mark 5:14-16, the Geresenes come out of their town to witness the victory and then ask Jesus to leave. Equally, Jesus' rejection may be in parallel to Saul's anger at David's victory in 1 Sam 18:8-9.
4. In 1 Sam 16:14, 15, the evil spirit torments (πνίγω) Saul; whereas in Mark 5:7, the unclean spirits beg Jesus: 'don't torment me!' (βασανίζω). The evil spirit's torment of Saul is inverted into the spirit's fear of messianic torment. Tenuously, the use of βασανίζω may even reflect another reference to the stone that killed Goliath, from βάσανος, touchstone (cf. use of βασανίζω in Mark 6:48).

§6.5.6 Unique identifier

This last thematic inversion is more significant than it at first appears, however, and leads towards significant yet cryptic lexical parallel. The unclean spirits in Mark are fearful of torment (βασανίζω) but in fact their ultimate destiny is to drown in the sea.

---

[96] As F. F. Bruce notes, 'As the Qumran commentators found in the prophetic oracles references to the Teacher's opponents as well as to the Teacher himself, so the early Christians, having found in the crucified and exalted Jesus the one who fulfilled the OT, had little difficulty in recognizing allusions to his enemies – to Judas in Pss. 69:25 and 109:8 (Acts 1:20) and to Herod and Pontius Pilate with their associates in Ps. 2:1, 2 (Acts 4:25-28)' (1981: 97). As will be discussed in the next chapter, Herod and Herodias are also likewise styled after Ahab and Jezebel in Mark 6. Thus, the styling of this fearsome demoniac upon Goliath, for which I am arguing, is part of a wider typological tendency.

However, Mark selected a strange word to describe this drowning. In Mark 5:13 the demonized pigs do not drown (βυθίζω as in 1 Tim 6:9, καταποντίζω as in Ex 15:4/Matt 18:6, or καταπίνω as in Heb 11:29) but in fact choke (πνίγω, Mark 5:13) in the sea.[97] Why does he choose this odd word?

In 1 Samuel 16:14–18:9 the evil spirit and Goliath are parallel afflictions, one torments Saul and the other terrifies the Israelites. David, as secretly anointed king, is the answer to both problems. In 1 Sam 16:14–15 the evil spirit torments Saul and the LXX translates this bizarrely with the word (πνίγω, 1 Sam 16:14) to choke.[98] This is the only use of this word in the LXX and it is a noticeably odd translation of the Hebrew בעת (piel: to terrify),[99] which is never translated to indicate choking in the 14 other occurrences of בעת in the Hebrew scriptures.

Moreover, it is the only use of this word in Mark. In the NT it only occurs elsewhere in Matt 13:7 and 18:28, where in one case thorns 'choke' the crop, and in the other a slave 'chokes' another who owes him money. Matthew's straightforward use of πνιγω illusrates its oddity in Mark's account and in 1 Samuel.

I suggest that with this word choice Mark provides an extremely subtle clue, for someone intimately familiar with the scriptures, to connect these stories by using a rare word strangely in his own text, which had also been used strangely in the parallel LXX text. The word πνίγω is so rare, and its use in both instances so unusual and unnecessary, that it constitutes strong evidence that the thematic parallels are not coincidental or unconscious but that Mark is deliberately alluding to 1 Samuel 16–18.

Finally, this connection is not just a word play but exegetically meaningful. In 1 Sam 16:14–15 Saul is tormented by the evil spirit, but in Mark 5:7 the unclean spirits beg Jesus not to torment them. This torment is to be understood within Mark's eschatological framework as the end-time destruction of the demons. We have already noted the mythological *urzeit endzeit* correspondence with destruction by water for evil spirits, but with this use of πνίγω Mark signals that the torment the unclean spirits begged to avoid in fact comes upon them. Without this connection, the pigs are simply understood to be choking in the water. By lexically connecting the destruction of the swine to Saul's torment Mark reinforces the implication that as the pigs choke the demons experience the torment that signals their long-awaited destruction.

§6.5.7 Summary

In my view, Jesus is thus described by Mark as a type of David; his defeat of Legion shows typological correspondence with David's defeat of Goliath and the Philistine army. But unlike David he does not receive immediate recognition; instead he is

---

[97] While πνίγω was occasionally used in contexts of drowning, its primary meaning is to choke, or strangle. See BDAG, 838; LSJ, 1425; GE, 1690. Moscicke (2019: 376) considers the word was chosen to reflect 'a violent connotation'. He notes it is also used in 1 Sam 16:14–15 but does not comment any further. Both Matthew and Luke modify Mark's word choice (Matt 8:32, ἀποθνῄσκω; Luke 8:33, ἀποπνίγω) further suggesting that Mark's word choice was unconventional, or at least inelegant.

[98] Notably Josephus retains this word in his account of the episode, τὸν Σαοῦλον δὲ περιήρχετο πάθη τινὰ καὶ δαιμόνια πνιγμοὺς αὐτῷ καὶ στραγγάλας ἐπιφέροντα (*Ant.* 6.166). Hence, πνίγω is attached to this David tradition beyond the LXX.

[99] HALOT, 147.

Table 3 Intertextual summary Mark 5:1-20 against 1 Samuel 16-18

Mark 5	1 Sam 16-18	
Mark 5:1	1 Sam 16:21; 17:20	Protagonist/exorcist arrives
Mark 5:2	1 Sam 16:14-15	Evil spirit described
Mark 5:2-5	1 Sam 17:4-10	Detailed introduction to opponent, λίθος, ἁλυσιδωτός/ἅλυσις, Γολιαθ ὄνομα αὐτω/Λεγεών ὄνομά μοι
Mark 5:5-6	1 Sam 17:3-4, 48	Mountain setting, running/rushing to encounter
Mark 5:7	1 Sam 17:8	Shouting, challenge, τίς
Mark 5:7, 13	1 Sam 16:14,15	Torments (πνίγω) Saul/ 'don't torment me!' (βασανίζω)/ choking (πνίγω) in the sea (inversion/unique indentifier)
Mark 5:8	1 Sam 16:23b	Exorcism
Mark 5:7-13	1 Sam 17:41-47	Conversation between protagonists
Mark 5:11-12	1 Sam 17:24	ἀγέλη
Mark 5:12-13	1 Sam 17:44-46	Giving the enemy to the wild animals/ giving domesticated animals to the enemy (inversion)
Mark 5:13	1 Sam 16:23d	Spirit/s departs
Mark 5:13-14	1 Sam 17:51-53	Fleeing Philistines/pig herders, ἔφυγον
Mark 5:14-17	1 Sam 18:6-7	Women come out of towns to celebrate David/ Geresenes come out of town to reject Jesus (inversion)
Mark 5:15	1 Sam 16:23c	Sufferer healed
Mark 5:18-19	1 Sam 18:2	Saul prevents David from returning home/ Jesus sends demoniac back to his family (inversion)
Mark 5:20	1 Sam 18:7	Protagonist praised for their deeds

rejected by the people. As an exorcist Jesus is clearly greater than David, in the quantity, type and permanency of his exorcisms. The ways in which the Markan episode references the Samuel account are summarised in the above table.

The David story by no means provides for every detail of Mark 5:1-20 and other scriptural allusions and echoes may inform exegesis of this episode. The Samuel text is far larger and structurally more complicated than the Markan story, even without the MT additions. Nonetheless, it is surely indicative that every verse of Mark 5:1-20 finds some parallel in 1 Sam 16:14-18:9. The sheer number of correspondences and the comprehensive coverage of the whole episode thus suggest that within Mark 5:1-20 there is a deliberate allusion to the stories of David as exorcist and defeating Goliath. While it is possible that Mark also has the Watcher tradition and/or Isaiah 65 in mind as well, the textual data contain overwhelmingly more evidence of influence from the David tradition (interpreted through the Watcher tradition) than for either of the other suggestions.

§6.6 Reading Mark 5:1-20 with 1 Samuel 16-18

At the surface level the main point of Mark 5:1-20 is Jesus' great power. The scriptural allusions argued for above both confirm and nuance this theme. The previous episode (4:35-41) left us with the question of Jesus' identity prompted by his miraculous authority over the wind and waves. This authority continues to be the concern in this episode. Reading Mark 5:1-20 as a typology of David and Goliath reveals a subtle and complex Christology of authority and identity, beyond a simple equation of 'who is the stronger?'

§6.6.1 Jesus as a greater David

Mark's literary typology reflects a real typology whereby Jesus is a greater David. Like David, he is shepherd, conqueror and 'a man after God's own heart'. But in all these, Jesus escalates and fulfils the type.

The theme of Jesus as shepherd is at its clearest in Mark in the feeding miracles, as will be discussed in the next chapter. However, the figuring of Jesus as David here anticipates this connection. When David is introduced to Saul for the purposes of the combat with Goliath, he is introduced as a shepherd, ποιμαίνων ἦν ὁ δοῦλός σου τῷ πατρὶ αὐτοῦ ἐν τῷ ποιμνίῳ (1 Sam 17:34). The verb ποιμαίνω is also closely associated with ruling and kingship (e.g. LXX 2 Sam 7:7; Ps 2:9; Mic 7:14; Rev 2:7). It is the same word used throughout LXX Zechariah 11. Having argued that LXX Zech 13:2 is the source of Mark's terminology of 'unclean spirit', Zechariah's own combination of the Davidic messianic hope with deliverance from an unclean spirit further strengthens the scriptural connection between the eschatological Davidic shepherd and exorcism.

It is with the techniques of a shepherd, rather than of a warrior, that David dispatches Goliath. Thus Jesus, in Mark 5:1–20, is not primarily engaging in a power encounter with evil. He is primarily acting as a messianic shepherd. He is caring for God's eschatological people, rescuing the lost sheep. David looks after the flocks for his father. Zechariah's shepherd looks after the flocks of Israel for God. Jesus too is working for his father, the God of Israel.

David's victory was not only with sling and stone but 'in the name of the LORD of hosts, the God of the armies of Israel' (1 Sam 17:45). Likewise, it is Jesus' authority and not his technique which overcome Legion.[100] Jesus' power and his exercise of it are not just of a different magnitude to the demons' great physical strength, but of a different kind altogether. The frightening physical strength of the demoniac, which is the focus of Mark 5:3–5, is at no point engaged by Jesus to show which of them is the stronger.[101] Instead Jesus deals with the demoniac on the level of authority, the very same level on which the demoniac attempts to engage Jesus (5:7). Indeed, references to authority bookend the initial exorcism account in Mark 1:21–28 and this implication of exorcism should be understood to continue throughout the Gospel, including Mark 5:1–20.

Like David, Jesus also conquers the opposing army. Feneberg, among others, states 'Die Dämonen bei den Heiden werden also nicht nur einfach ausgetrieben . . . sondern sie vernichten sich letztlich selbst.'[102] Recognition of the David typology contributes further evidence for this view. David was remembered as a victorious military leader and the new David would likewise bring decisive eschatological victory (1QM 11.1–2; 4Q161; 4Q285).[103]

---

[100] Lahurd 1990: 158.
[101] Guth 2008: 67.
[102] 'The demons among the Gentiles are not just simply cast out ... but they ultimately destroy themselves'. Feneberg 2000: 143; also Hooker 1991: 141, 144; Hartman 2010: 218; *pace* Twelftree 1993: 86; France 2002: 231.
[103] Evans 1997: 185–6.

In 1 Sam 17:46 David promises to give the bodies of the Philistines to the animals of the land (τοῖς θηρίοις τῆς γῆς), a promise he only partially fulfils.[104] In Mark 5:11-13 Jesus gives the demons to the pigs of the land which promptly results in their destruction.[105] Just as David destroys the Philistine army without a battle, Jesus destroys the *Überdämon* without the physical conflict with which the Gerasenes had attempted to subdue Legion previously.[106]

The torment of the demons is often overlooked, but the implication of the imperfect of πνίγω (5:13) is not a sudden drowning beneath the waves but a continuing choking in the water (it also echoes the imperfect in 1 Sam 16:14).[107] Likewise 1 Enoch 55:4 promises that 'the messianic age will bring destruction to demonic world'.[108] In the Qumran Hodayot there is a strong connection between the sea and Sheol, Abaddon and the Abyss, where 'the doors of the pit close upon the one expectant with injustice, and everlasting bolts upon all the spirits of the serpent' (1QH^a [35] XI:15-18; 4QH^f [432] 4.I.3-7).[109] With these backgrounds in view, France is wrong to suggest that the demons are not destroyed by the water or that Jesus was as surprised as anyone else by the behaviour of the pigs.[110] As Collins argues, either Jesus destroys the demons or at least sends them to *Sheol*.[111] Lahurd observes Mark's focus on this point in contrast to Matthew and Luke.[112]

The narrated intention of David's action in defeating Goliath was that the assembly (ἐκκλησία) of Israel would know that the war belongs to the Lord (ὅτι τοῦ κυρίου ὁ πόλεμος, 1 Sam 17:47). A reader in the early Christian church would surely come to the same conclusion about Jesus' victory in Mark 5:1-20. The plunder (שׁסס) of the Philistine camp (1 Sam 17:53) is mirrored in Mark 3:27 where Jesus declares himself the burglar who has tied up Beelzebub in order to plunder his house.[113]

A less obvious, but intriguing, connection of the typology relates to the reference to 1 Sam 21:1-8 in Mark 2:23-28.[114] In the Samuel narrative, David's access to the holy bread is dependent on his internal purity. It is not just the exigency of his circumstances which allow him to break the ceremonial law regarding the bread but his internal spiritual purity. In David's conversation with Ahimelech his purity is ascertained by his abstinence from sex, but in the David narrative at large it is that David is 'a man after God's own heart' (1 Sam 13:14, 16:7; see also Acts 13:22) and his secret identity as anointed king. The pure heart of the anointed king, rather than his abstinence, is

---

[104] The implication of 1 Sam 17:52 is that only the wounded Philistines were killed by the pursuing Israelites, the rest fled.
[105] Cotter (1999: 120) suggests that demons cannot be destroyed as they are spirits, yet that is clearly not the opinion of the spirits in Mark 1:24.
[106] Haenchen 1968: 194.
[107] See Wallace 1996: 542.
[108] Gundry 1993: 75.
[109] Martínez and Tigchelaar 2000: 1.165, 2.907; see also Chilton et al. 2009: 182, 222.
[110] France 2002: 231.
[111] Collins 2007: 271. The link between the sea and Sheol is well established in Jonah 2:2, and could well be present as an idea here due to the use of Jonah 1 in the immediately preceding episode. See also Luke 8 31-33.
[112] Lahurd 1990: 157.
[113] In the LXX the Israelites only trample (καταπατέω) the Philistine camp.
[114] For discussion and literature around Mark 2:25-26 see Botner 2018: 484-99.

presumably why God himself does not object to David's otherwise sacrilegious act, not to mention his deception of the priest. Likewise, in Mark 2:23–28 Jesus' appeal to David's example cannot be based on sharing exigent circumstances. His disciples are simply grazing, not running on urgent matters. It is Jesus as a type of David who is allowed to operate as David did,[115] ignoring ceremonial restrictions because of his own personal purity, relationship with God and identity as anointed messiah (Mark 1:10).

With regard to Mark 5:1–20, a number of commentators recognize many signals of uncleanness in the text. The Gentile location, the tombs, the pigs and the word 'legion' (as Roman legions carried scalps as trophies and boar heads as standards) all serve to situate the episode within the context of uncleanness.[116] However, in Mark's narrative none of these external markers are addressed in Jesus' saving work. The removal of the pigs, for example, does not address any uncleanness they had ostensibly caused. Indeed, as pigs were unclean food, the would not transmit impurity when alive, but only when dead.[117] Rather, it is the internal change, the removal of the unclean spirits, which brings the man to wholeness and reorients his life to the kingdom. This is entirely consistent with Jesus' explicit teaching in Mark 7:1–23, 'evil things come from within, and they defile a person' (7:23).[118]

In Mark 5:1–20, Jesus as a type of David again cuts through ceremonial regulation and external conceptions of uncleanness to bring internal spiritual cleanness to the demoniac by virtue of his own inherent holiness, connection to God, and messianic rank, and not by any external form or ceremony. This is a consistent pattern in Mark, e.g. the healing of the leper (1:41) or the bleeding woman (5:27–29), where Jesus not only touches what should technically make him unclean but instead this contact transmits Jesus' wholeness and purity in the other direction.[119]

The Son-of-David was a familiar messianic title in Judaism but it is seldom found in the Gospels and is never used by Jesus or his disciples, but only by other people or a Gospel writer, e.g. Matt. 1:1. In Mark 10:46–52 Bartimaeus' use of this Christological title is, in Mark, 'a misunderstanding of his true identity'.[120] For Goppelt, this is 'characteristic of the way all of the ideas related to this theme are used with reference to Jesus'.[121]

There has already been a son-of-David who was, in the tradition, an exorcist. But while the exorcisms attributed to both David (with a lyre) and Solomon (with roots and incantations and Solomon's name)[122] were done using instrumental means, Jesus' exorcism was done only by his authority.[123]

---

[115] Goppelt 1982: 85; Schnackenburg 1995: 62.
[116] E.g. Derrett 1985: 1.101; Schneck 1994: 141–3; Aus 2000: 10–18; Marcus 2000a: 342; Collins 2007: 269.
[117] Theissen 2020: 188.
[118] See further Lahurd 1990: 157–8.
[119] Dawson 2008: 85–86; Theissen 2020: *passim*.
[120] Boring (2006: 305) makes a concise and convincing argument, '(1) The "Son of David" was expected to come from Bethlehem . . . Yet Bethlehem is never mentioned in Mark . . (2) Bartimaeus designates Jesus as "son [sic] of David" while he is still blind . . . (3) He makes this acclamation while seated beside the way [see Mark 4:4, 15] . . . (4) Mark elsewhere is suspicious of "Son of David" as a proper title for Jesus [see 11:10; 12:35–37]'. See also, Malbon 2014: 89.
[121] Goppelt 1982: 83.
[122] Josephus, *Ant.* 8.2.5 §§45–9.
[123] See further Nyström 2016: 69–92.

The *Davidssohnfrage* is thus not straightforward.[124] While Mark downplays and qualifies Jesus' connection to David as 'son' (certainly in comparison to Matthew), David typology is used in Mark 5:1–20; 2:23–28 and extensively in the passion account.

Matthew 12:42 makes Jesus' superiority to Solomon, the son-of-David, explicit, but it is not so far beneath the surface in many Markan passages, e.g. Mark 12:35–37. As an exorcist Jesus surpasses both David and Solomon. Jesus' defeat of Legion also surpasses David's defeat of Goliath. David defeats one giant; Jesus defeats about two thousand spirits of giants. The Philistines flee from David and have their tents plundered; the demons flee from Jesus and are destroyed utterly in the sea. Jesus plunders the house of Satan. Thus, Jesus is the antitype of David, but fulfils the promise of a Davidic messiah through spiritual, rather than a physical, warfare.

§6.6.2 Kirk's royal framework for Jesus' exorcisms

Although Kirk does not focus specifically upon Mark 5:1–20, he does discuss exorcisms in general and specifically in Mark.[125] Kirk argues that a central function of the exorcism stories is to demonstrate Jesus' authority (cf. Mark 1:27).[126] Further, he states, 'the ability to cast out demons per se is not an indication of any peculiar ontological status, but is indicative of possessing an authority or power of such a sort as human beings can exercise'.[127] This is uncontroversial; the Gospel of Mark itself indicates that exorcisms could be performed by other people, without any suggestion they might be divine (e.g. Mark 6:7; 9:38).

Kirk goes on to argue, 'power over demons fits easily within a royal framework in early Judaism'.[128] Further, 'In the case of David, it is a signal of his empowerment by the spirit; in the case of Solomon, it is an extension of his wisdom'.[129] This paradigm is not a good fit for Jesus, however. In the case of David, both the biblical record (1 Sam 16:14–23) and the traditions that followed (e.g. 4Q510; 4Q511; 11Q5 xxvii.9–10; LAB 60:1–3), require the instrumental use of song. Even then, David's power over demons is limited and his cures only temporary.[130] Likewise, in the case of Solomon traditions (e.g. Jos. *Ant.* 8:47; *T. Sol.* 13), Jennifer Nyström has shown that it is,

> not probable that the contemporaries would have recognized a Solomonic exorcism technique when witnessing Jesus' exorcisms ... the contemporaries, if knowing about the Solomonic technique, should have noticed that Jesus' exorcisms rather transcended the Solomonic in each of its components; no *tool* is used in the deed, no *incantation* is used among the words and no *name* (Solomon's) is invoked.[131]

---

[124] See, for example, the discussion of Mark 12:35–37 in Marcus 2008: 136–40.
[125] Kirk 2016: 415–30, 421–25.
[126] Kirk 2016: 415, 423.
[127] Kirk 2016: 416, see also 425.
[128] Kirk 2016: 416.
[129] Kirk 2016: 417.
[130] Cf. LAB 60:3, 'As long as David sang, the spirit spared Saul'.
[131] Nyström 2016: 91, emphasis original; also Meier 1991: 593.

In these David traditions, neither the name nor person of David have any effect on demons, nor even his possession of God's spirit, only his songs. Likewise, Solomon requires a magical ring (e.g. *T. Sol.* 1:6) and only once long dead does his name become powerful (Jos. *Ant.* 8:47). As Kirk notes, Jesus' disciples 'do not have the authority simply because they are humans, but because they are acting in the name and with the authority of the idealized authoritative human [i.e. Jesus]'.[132] What Kirk does not note is that there is no precedent for such an authority being given to a person without them first becoming a legendary figure. And even in the case of Solomon, who does accrue some such authority, his name alone is not enough to perform an exorcism but the correct technique and tools must also be used (Josephus, *Ant.* 8:47).[133]

When Herod hears of the disciples performing exorcisms and healings there are three possible interpretations offered: John the Baptist raised from the dead, Elijah, or a prophet like the prophets of old (Mark 6:14–15; cf. 8:28). For Kirk this demonstrates that performing exorcisms does not indicate divinity, because none of the interpretations suggests a divine identity but only human possibilities.[134] But it is not the fact of exorcisms that is the problem for Herod. It is that these exorcisms are *not* being attributed to various individual everyday healer-exorcists, but that all these things (despite also being performed by others) are being attributed to Jesus: 'for his name had become known' (Mark 6:14).

This leads us to the significance of naming, observed earlier in Mark 5:1–20. The power of Jesus' name and identity as son of God was so great that Legion attempted to use it against Jesus (Mark 5:7). My exegesis agrees with Kirk that a royal David typology is at work behind the exorcisms. However, when Mark 5:1–20 is compared with the David story of 1 Sam 16–17 a contrast appears. That is, David relies on the name of YHWH/the Lord while Jesus does not. Jesus' name is sufficient. This demands an interpretation of Jesus beyond the similarity with David to ask how he is also different from David. The typology of Mark 5:1–20 both points to David as the paradigmatic king (exorcist and conqueror), but also to the name that David invoked in conquering Goliath, the name of YHWH.

For Kirk it is enough that Jesus is an exorcist like David and Solomon, but Kirk does not reckon with the details of the accounts that suggest Jesus is something more. Again, when the paradigm is examined closely, Jesus does not conform to it. He needs no tool or incantation, and invokes no higher authority than his own.

§6.6.3 Jesus as the Lord of Hosts

There is an ambiguity towards the end of Mark 5:1–20 which raises the question of Jesus' assimilation to David's God. The one point where the healed demoniac could be said to have disobeyed Jesus is in his substituting the name of Jesus for ὁ κύριος in his testimony of receiving mercy (Mark 5:19–20). As Feneberg writes, 'Jesus wollte, dass er das Große, das der Herr ihm getan hat, weiter berichtet. Mit 'der Herr' meint er nicht

---

[132] Kirk 2016: 426.
[133] 'The power to exorcize belonged to the techniques, not to the exorcist' (Bauckham 2017a: 29).
[134] Kirk 2016: 426.

sich, sondern Gott.'¹³⁵ But is this a failure on the healed man's part, or a deliberate Christological transposition? France does not consider that Jesus equates to Lord here.¹³⁶ Yet Stein is able to go as far as to say, 'There exists between God and Jesus a unique relationship and unity. Jesus in his actions and deeds is the Lord (5:19), and what Jesus has done (5:20) is what God the Lord has done (5:19)'.¹³⁷ Joshua Leim suggests this indirect identification of Jesus with the Lord is part of a cryptic Markan pattern (e.g. Mark 1:2-3; 13:20-27).¹³⁸ Kirk recognizes that Mark 5:19-20 suggests a 'close proximity between God and Jesus as God's agent' but considers it too ambiguous to straightforwardly identify Jesus with the Lord.¹³⁹

In my view, the parallelism between Mark 5:19 and 20 suggests a deliberate conflation of Jesus and Lord.

In particular, the change in order from 'how much the Lord for you had done' to 'how much did, for him, Jesus' creates the effect of a punch-line in the parallel phrase. It is formed by the delayed identification of the subject and unexpected substitution of Jesus for Lord. The distinctiveness of Jesus' use of ὁ κύριός for God also cues the audience to what Mark is doing.¹⁴⁰ So Stein is right to say that it is 'clear' that the Lord of 5:19 is Jesus.¹⁴¹

However, this interpretation is further reinforced by the recognition of a David typology. In 1 Sam 17:45-47 David refers four times to the Lord (YHWH, LXX κύριος x5): the Lord of hosts (armies), the Lord as deliverer (to death), the Lord as saviour, and the Lord as the one to whom the battle belongs. David's emphasis on the identity of the Lord during his confrontation with Goliath renders Mark's conflation of Jesus with 'lord' here, significant. At the very least it is identifying Jesus with the warrior God of Israel, 'who does not save by sword and spear' (1 Sam 17:47).

In Mark 2:23-28 Jesus, picking grain in typological correspondence with David,¹⁴² proclaims the Son-of-Man (himself) 'Lord, even of the Sabbath'. In Mark 11:1-11 when

Table 4 Parallelism in Mark 5:19 and 20

5:19	5:20
καὶ οὐκ ἀφῆκεν αὐτόν, ἀλλὰ λέγει αὐτῷ·	
ὕπαγε εἰς τὸν οἶκόν σου πρὸς τοὺς σοὺς καὶ ἀπάγγειλον αὐτοῖς ὅσα ὁ κύριός σοι πεποίηκεν καὶ ἠλέησέν σε.	καὶ ἀπῆλθεν ... ἐν τῇ Δεκαπόλει καὶ ἤρξατο κηρύσσειν ὅσα ἐποίησεν αὐτῷ ὁ Ἰησοῦς,
	καὶ πάντες ἐθαύμαζον.

---

¹³⁵ 'Jesus wanted him to continue reporting the great things the Lord has done to him. By "the Lord" he did not mean himself, but God' (Feneberg 2000: 144).
¹³⁶ France 2002: 232.
¹³⁷ Stein 2008: 261. See also Marcus 1992: 40; Garland 1996: 207; 2000a: 354; Hartman 2010: 219.
¹³⁸ Leim 2013: 226-7.
¹³⁹ Kirk 2016: 208.
¹⁴⁰ Jesus only calls God ὁ κύριός twice in Mark (5:19 and 13:20). For discussion see Bauckham 2019: 87-105, especially 88.
¹⁴¹ Stein 2008: 260.
¹⁴² Evans 1992: 863.

Jesus enters Jerusalem on a donkey in typological correspondence with the Davidic messiah of Zech 9:9, his disciples commandeered a donkey on the basis that 'the Lord' needed it. In Mark 12:35–37 Jesus denies that the messiah can be the son-of-David because David calls the messiah 'Lord' in Psalm 110. In fact, there is only one use of the name David in Mark which does not have a corresponding use of 'Lord' for Jesus (Mark 10:46–52). It is almost as if Mark struggles to mention David without reinforcing that Jesus is not David, or his son, but 'Lord'. Thus recognizing a David typology in Mark 5:1–20 strengthens the case for the reading of Jesus as Lord in Mark 5:19.

What, then, is the significance of Mark's designation of Jesus as Lord? While the title Lord can be understood as a cipher for YHWH it by no means has to be. Stein is representative of those who infer a proto-Nicene Christology: 'Although no one should read into 5:19–20 a fully developed Nicene Christology, Mark's understanding of Jesus in the account goes far beyond such descriptions as "prophet" or even "messiah".'[143] On the other hand, for Kirk, Jesus' power over demons 'fits squarely within an idealised human paradigm'.[144] The demons recognize Jesus as a human agent of God who 'plays the role of exercising divine authority on earth'.[145] Because David and Solomon were remembered as exorcists, Jesus' exorcisms merely portray him as a king, like David and Solomon.[146] It is thus not enough to show that Jesus is greater than David and Solomon, there must be a fundamental difference between them if we are to argue that in some way Jesus is being portrayed as divine.

Kirk argues that Jesus having authority to do works of power places him in the category of biblical human agents of divine power like Moses.[147] Such agents had delegated authority and power from YHWH without any need to assert divinity of them. Kirk also argues that the ability to cast out demons cannot indicate divinity because the disciples also cast out demons.[148]

However, this comparison fails because no *agent* of divine power in the Jewish scriptures ever delegates his power to another. The closest we get is Elijah and Elisha, but Elijah has to be translated before Elisha received the double portion of his spiritual power. Anyway, Elisha was God's choice rather than Elijah's (1 Kgs 19:16). Yet in Mark 3:15 and 6:7–13 the disciples derive their authority to drive out demons and heal from Jesus, he delegates it to them. Presumably the disciples also cast demons out in Jesus' name, hence the behaviour of the copycat exorcist in 9:38–41.

So, in Mark, deeds of power are done by disciples and others in Jesus' name (9:39). Kirk is correct that casting out demons does not connote divinity, but having demons cast out in your name is somewhat different. While the account of Josephus suggests Solomon's name was incorporated into the exorcism ritual of Eleazar, this was alongside use of a certain root and incantations (Jos. *Ant.* 8.2.5. §§45–49). Solomon's name on its own was not sufficient. On the other hand, the fragment 4Q560 1:4 describes an exorcism formula where the demon is cast out 'by the Name of Him who forgives sins

---

[143] Stein 2008: 261.
[144] Kirk 2016: 206.
[145] Kirk 2016: 206.
[146] Kirk 2016: 207.
[147] Kirk 2016: 208.
[148] Kirk 2016: 209.

and transgressions'.¹⁴⁹ If the disciples used Jesus' name, Eleazar used Solomon's name, and the Essenes used God's name, then whose name did Jesus use?

This is where a perplexing feature of the story comes into focus. Legion's use of Jesus' name and of God must be seen, in the context of an exorcism, as an attempt to control Jesus.¹⁵⁰ As Pesch argues, 'Der Besessene schleudert dem Exorzisten eine Abwehrformel entgegen (vgl. zu 1,24) und versucht, mit seinem Wissen um Jesu Namen und Würde Macht über ihn zu gewinnen'.¹⁵¹ The use of powerful names to control spirits is well attested (Lucian, *Men.* 9; *Philops.* 12; Pliny the Elder, *Nat.* 28, 4.6; PGM VIII, 20f; 4.1609–11).¹⁵² The demons already know who Jesus is but seem to think that their use of 'God' will allow them to control him (5:7).¹⁵³ Jesus' request for their identity is not a sign of ignorance but of superiority. Jesus is famous; the demons are just Satan's foot soldiers. This compares with David's disdainful refusal to use the name of Goliath, instead referring to him throughout 1 Sam 17 as just another (uncircumcised) Philistine.¹⁵⁴ Then David comes against Goliath 'in the name of the Lord' (17:45) after Goliath curses him by his own gods (17:43). It is in the name of the LORD that David expects victory and achieves it. This focus on the name of the LORD is emphasized in the Qumran War Scroll: 'you delivered [Goliath] into the hand of David, your servant, because he trusted in your great name and not in sword and spear' (1QM 11.2).¹⁵⁵ In LXX 1 Sam 17:36 God is also referred to by David as θεος ζῶν, the Living God, perhaps reflecting its use in other passages where God's people contend with Gentiles.¹⁵⁶

Jesus does not mention God at all.¹⁵⁷ The only Lord in this episode is Jesus. Jesus conquers Legion standing on his own authority. His name as the son of the Most High God has already been invoked (by the demons), but that is inconsequential for the task of deliverance. Jesus, in himself, is sufficient for the deed.¹⁵⁸ Just as 1 Sam 17:41–47 serves to reveal the powerlessness of the Philistine gods against Israel's God, so in Mark 5:7 the demons are revealed as powerless against the Lord, Jesus.

Neither Bauckham nor Hays discuss this exorcism story in regard to either its scriptural background or its possible contribution to divine identity Christology.

---

[149] Collins 2007: 167. 'Interestingly, any indication of the use of incantations by Jesus (or his disciples) in the exorcism pericopes is glaringly absent considering their apparent use in other groups in Judaism (e.g, Qumran)' (Wright 2016: 240).

[150] Twelftree 1993: 81; Garland 1996: 204; Dunn 2003: 675–6; Collins 2007: 268; Hartman 2010: 197; Kirk 2016: 205; Theissen 2020: 144–45; *pace* Guelich 1989: 57–8, 279. For a response to Guelich see Osborne 1994: 151–2.

[151] 'The possessed hurls a defensive formula at the exorcist (cf. 1:24) and tries to gain power over him with his knowledge of Jesus' name and rank' (Pesch 1979: 1.287).

[152] Theissen 1983: 64.

[153] The demonic ability to identity Jesus is a significant departure from the convention of exorcism stories. Nyström 2016: 78.

[154] When Goliath sees David the disdain is mutual (1 Sam 17:42).

[155] Evans 1997: 188.

[156] Josh 3:10; 2 Kgs 19:4, 16; LXX Ezra 6:13; 3 Macc 6:28; Isa 37:4, 17; Dan θ 6:27; Bell θ 1:24–5; Acts 14:15; 1 Thess 1:9.

[157] Collins 2007: 167.

[158] 'One notices all the signs of sovereignty on the side of Jesus; the imperative statement, the question (both in direct style), the permission to enter into the body of the animals (in indirect style) are expressed with extreme economy' (Starobinski 1973: 343). Correspondingly, Carter (2014: 147) suggests the demons' language casts Jesus as a military commander.

Arguably, however, this miracle assimilates Jesus to Israel's God in a similar manner to the miracles discussed previously, which they do see as indicating divine identity.

Mark recounted the story of Jesus calming the storm to display Jesus as an antitype of Jonah with the Christological twist that Jesus, in place of God, stilled the storm. In Mark 5:1-20 another typological correspondence between Jesus and a scriptural character, this time David, also contains a Christological twist. Jesus plays the role of both anointed warrior and the one in whose name the warrior expects victory, the role of the human agent of God and the role of the God Israel.

§ 6.64 Jesus and the Gentile mission

Mark 5:1-20 is set 'on the other side of the sea' in specifically Gentile territory (5:1), and demonstrates that Jesus' healing ministry is not for Jews alone.[159] Wefal makes the plausible suggestion that the Geresene exorcism begins a Gentile mission for Jesus which then proceeds parallel to Jesus' Jewish mission.[160] Both missions begin with an exorcism (Mark 1:21-28). Both exorcisms result in Jesus' fame being spread. John the Baptist prepares the way for Jesus in Judea and the healed demoniac prepares the way for Jesus in the Decapolis. The demoniac also parallels the disciples in hearing and obeying the call of Jesus.[161] I would add that Jesus' detailed battle with Legion parallels the testing by Satan (1:13) which preceded Jesus' mission in Galilee.

I have already noted David's 'evangelistic' goal (1 Sam 17:47, see above). The result of Jesus' exorcism is the proclamation of Jesus' mercy and power within the Decapolis (Mark 5:20). Under David, the Israelites plundered the Philistine tents (1 Sam 17:53) but under Jesus the very house of Beelzebul is being plundered (Mark 3:27). That is, not only God's chosen people but the Gentiles are being delivered from demonic oppression and receiving the good news. Jesus' refusal to allow the healed demoniac to be 'with him' (5:18-19)[162] is not a rejection of the man but is instead a) for the purpose of mission;[163] b) for the man's healing re-inclusion with his own people;[164] c) 'a real alternative avenue for fulfilment;'[165] and d) 'the offering of a genuine responsibility, a sign of trust'.[166]

The direction of the Gentile mission, anticipated by the Jonah typology in the preceding episode, now finds concrete expression in the deliverance and sending of a Gentile evangelist preacher.[167] There is no adversative between verses 19 and 20. The healed man does not disobey Jesus. In obedience to Jesus he goes to his house (in the

---

[159] Twelftree 1999: 71.
[160] Wefal 1995.
[161] Wefal 1995: 13-14; Broadhead 1992: 100; against this see Klinghardt 2007: 43.
[162] Presumably as a disciple, cf. Mark 3:14. Broadhead 1992: 99-100; Twelftree 1993: 79.
[163] Marcus 2000a: 353-54; France 2002: 232.
[164] Guth 2008: 67-8.
[165] Derrett 1979a: 4.
[166] Mainwaring 2014: 176.
[167] Kertelge 1979: 267. Although Dormandy (2000: 335) and Watts (1997: 164) argue for a Jewish identity for the demoniac, I would follow the majority of scholars in seeing that the Gentile geographical and agricultural setting and the man's home in the Decapolis all assume a Gentile identity. E.g. Theissen 1983: 254; Broadhead 1992: 98-102; Marcus 2000a: 342.

Decapolis) and there proclaims to his people (the Gentile inhabitants) his deliverance.[168] The healed demoniac becomes a paradigm both for the early church's proclamation to the Gentiles,[169] and for Mark's first readers, who cannot 'be with Jesus' as the first disciples were, but who are still called to proclaim him.[170]

The movement of the populace from fear to wonder is the second transformation of the episode (the first being the exorcism itself), this time effected by the healed man faithfully responding to Jesus' commission.[171] That the man's mission was successful is implied, not just in the amazement of 5:20, but by the fact that when Jesus goes to the region of the Decapolis in 7:31 he is famous enough to attract a crowd of four thousand (8:1-9). Thus, while David was content for the assembly of Israel to know YHWH as conquering Lord (1 Sam 17:47), Jesus sends the man to reveal the Lord's mercy and goodness to other nations as well.

§6.7 Conclusion

I have argued that 1 Samuel 16-18 is more significant to Mark 5:1-20 than other suggested allusions like LXX Isaiah 65 and the Watcher Tradition. These previous suggestions were shown to depend on tenuous evidence. The significance of 1 Samuel 16-18 was shown in both the number of correspondences and the comprehensive coverage of the whole episode. That it is the hermeneutical key for the episode is argued by the fruitfulness of the referent text in addressing contested issues regarding the Gospel text, especially the Christological import of the exorcism.

1 Samuel 16-18 has not to my knowledge been previously identified as a referent text for Mark 5:1-20. The recent scholarly interest in the Watcher tradition as a background to Mark 5:1-20 provided a way of conceiving how Mark could associate exorcism of demonic spirits with David's battle against Goliath, a descendant of the Nephilim in scriptural tradition. Close reading revealed many correspondences between the two narratives which further discussion showed to have considerable interpretive value. The real correspondence between David and Jesus is indicated by a literary typology which pervades the pericope. This scriptural allusion is thus additional evidence for a Markan typology of Jesus as the antitype of David. At the same time, the comparison with 1 Sam 16-17 brings to light theomorphic features of the exorcism account, that Jesus is also 'the Lord' in whose name the battle against evil forces is won. Against the background of 1 Samuel 16-18, the exorcism portrays Jesus as Davidic eschatological victor and gentle shepherd king, but also highlights the apparently divine authority that Mark's Gospel attributes to Jesus.

In the series of three superlative miracles in Mark 4:35-5:43 we have seen a consistent typological use of scripture. Firstly, a scriptural miracle with a surface resemblance to the Jesus story appears to have been used as a model either in the

---

[168] Derrett 1979a: 4; contra Theissen 1983: 147-8.
[169] Guelich 1989: 288-89; Schnabel 1994: 52; Schneck 1994: 148.
[170] Twelftree 1999: 72.
[171] Lahurd 1990: 158-9.

original act itself, or the composition of the story. This modelling is visible in terms of unconventional narrative features and similarity in narrative forms. As part of this there is lexical evidence of influence from the scriptures to the Gospel. However, going further than such potentially unconscious influence, there appears to be deliberate lexical clues in Mark's stories which are not only distinctive references to the respective scriptural miracles but also appear to carry some considerable Christological freight. These phrases or terms are unique in Mark and also unique or highly distinctive in the LXX. The presence of a consistent pattern across these three miracles seems to me beyond the realm of coincidence and must be considered to be there by authorial intent. There is one further extended miracle account in Mark which seems to evince a similar, although modified, approach to scriptural typology. And it is to this miraculous feeding miracle that we now turn.

§7

Shepherd, Moses and Elisha typology in Mark 6:30–44 and 8:1–10

This is the rule for the overseer of a camp. He must teach the general membership about the works of God, instruct them in his mighty miracles, relate to them future events coming to the world with their interpretations; he should care for them as a father does his children, taking care of all their problems as a shepherd does for his flock.

CD XIII:7–9

This chapter is the final exegetical chapter of the study. In previous chapters I have argued that Mark uses the miracle stories of Mark 4:35–41; 5:1–20 and 5:21–43 to relate Jesus typologically to particular scripture characters and narratives. This will continue to be the case in the feeding miracles. The walking on water (Mark 6:45–52), also discussed above, does not use scripture narrative in the same way, although it does arguably allude to LXX Job 9:8. Significantly, in 4:35–41; 5:1–20 and 5:21–43 we encounter a *Christological twist* whereby Jesus is not just compared to human characters of scripture, but also assumes the role of Israel's God from those same scriptural stories. As I will argue, the pattern of scriptural narrative use and lexical indication seen in 4:35–41; 5:1–20 and 5:21–43 appears modified in the Markan feeding miracles (6:30–44 and 8:1–10), but with enough similarities to suggest a consistent approach to typology across these miracle accounts.

I will examine the feeding miracle of Mark 6:30–44 as well as its counterpart in 8:1–10. After an initial discussion of the story and then analysis of the conventions of Jewish and Graeco-Roman 'gift' miracles, I will then examine the literary and historical context of the passage which help frame Mark's acount. I will argue that in the feeding of the five thousand there are three complementary scriptural typologies present, that of Elisha (2 Kings 4:42–44), the Shepherd (e.g. Ps 23) and Moses (Num 11). Each of these typologies also serve to place Jesus in the narrative role of YHWH, further contributing to Mark's divine Christology. I will also argue that the second feeding miracle employs the same Elisha typology but omits the Shepherd and Moses typologies to develop the theme of Gentile inclusion through several means including an allusion to Josh 9.

§7.1 Mark's miraculous meals

The hinge that holds the two halves of the Gospel of Mark together is Peter's declaration in Mark 8:29, 'You are the Christ'.[1] While the disciples' discovery of Jesus' identity has been, and will continue to be, an ongoing process of discovery, Peter's declaration marks a turning point. Once Peter confesses that Jesus is the Christ, Jesus' instruction of the disciples will move on to suffering, rejection, death and resurrection (8:30).[2] So what precipitates Peter's acclamation and what particular understanding of the title 'Christ' should we attribute to Peter?

Peter's conclusion that Jesus is the Christ (8:29) is arrived at after a sequence of miracles (4:35–8:26), in the first of which the disciples explicitly pose the question 'who is this?' (4:41). Those miracles are presented as part of the ongoing process of revelation that is symbolically represented in the incremental healing of the blind man of Bethsaida (8:22–26).[3] Thus the goal of Jesus' teaching and miracles is for the disciples to 'see everything clearly' (8:25). And so France argues, 'The medium of Jesus' gradual revelation is miracles'.[4] The term *Christ*, denoting the Jewish hope of a messiah, is a partial cipher that needs further explication.[5] In the Gospel narrative the miracles inform the disciples of what, in part, it means for Jesus to be the Christ. The narration of the miracles is intended to have the same revelatory impact on the reader.[6]

Not all the miracles prior to Peter's declaration are directly focused on Christology. Within Mark's narrative the healing of the deaf man and of the blind man (Mark 8:31–37, 22–26) are symbolic of discipleship.[7] The interaction with the Syro-Phoenecian Woman is focused on Gentile inclusion.[8] These two healings and the exorcism are all ordinary and unspectacular within the context of Jesus' ministry. They add nothing to the previous accounts of Jesus as a wonder worker, but use Jesus' works to illustrate other developing themes. That leaves the calming of the storm (4:35–41), the exorcism of Legion (5:1–20), the healing of Jairus' daughter and the haemorrhaging woman (5:21–43), the feeding of the five thousand (6:30–44), the walking on water (6:45–52) and the feeding of the four thousand (8:1–10). These miracles share in being more extended in description and more spectacular, and are without close parallel in Jesus' earlier or later ministry. This sequence of extraordinary acts of power leads up to Peter's Christological declaration.

---

[1] 'Most scholars concur that the pericope of Caesarea Philippi represents the turning point that divides the Gospel into at least two major sections' (Guelich 1989: xxxvi; also Pesch 1979: 1.410; Dunn 1989: 47; Bauckham 2017a: 26).

[2] One partcular clue to this is ἔρξατο διδάσκειν (Mark 8:31) which 'is not the normal Markan semitism but indicates a particular point of time at which for the first time the repeated teaching referred to by the διδάσκειν received a concrete content ... Having at last got over to them the message that He is Messiah, He must now explain what kind of Messiah' (Dunn 1970: 103–4).

[3] Richardson 1941: 86–87; Schweizer 1970: 161; Pesch 1979: 1.420; Marcus 2000b: 589.

[4] France 2002: 259.

[5] Boring 2006: 248–9; Marcus 2000b: 609.

[6] Van Oyen 1999: vii.

[7] '[T]he Blind Man at Bethsaida ... functions as a summary of Jesus' ministry for his disciples'. So Guelich 1989: xxxvi–xxxvii; see also Marcus 2000b: 597; Boring 2006: 233; *pace* Stein 2008: 390–4.

[8] Boring 2006: 208–9.

There are other differences between the feedings and the earlier miracles which need to be considered. Mark 4:35–41; 5:1–20; 5:21–43 and 6:45–52 all take place in front of a small group of people but generate reactions of amazement or fear. On the other hand, the feeding miracles take place in front of huge groups of people and yet no reaction is recorded.[9] Possibly, the implication is that only the disciples witness the miracle.[10] Yet they are sufficiently unimpressed by it that they still show concern when bread supplies are insufficient again, later in the Gospel (8:4, 16).

The first feeding miracle also contains a clear quotation of scripture, 'they were like sheep without a shepherd' (6:34). Such overt scripture use was conspicuous by its absence in the earlier miracles.

In the earlier miracles the dialogue focused on the recipients of the miracles: the disciples (4:35–41), the demoniac (5:1–20), and Jairus and the woman in the crowd (5:21–43). This, with parents standing in for their children, is the pattern of miracle accounts throughout Mark. In the feeding miracles the crowd benefit from the miracle but the focus is on the dialogue between Jesus and the disciples.

Finally, Mark 4:35–41; 5:1–20; 5:21–43 and 6:45–52 all contain a sense of urgency and threat: the storm will overwhelm the boat, the demoniac may use his strength (cf. Matt 8:28), Jairus' daughter will die, and so on. In the feeding of the four thousand there is the possibility that some will 'faint' (ἐκλύομαι) going home (Mark 8:3), but this does not imply that they will not reach home: ἐκλύομαι can equally be translated as become exhausted or weary.[11] In the feeding of the five thousand even this danger is not apparent (Mark 6:36). In both feedings it is not the crowd but, 'Es sind die Jünger, die immer wieder den Mangel an Nahrung wahrnehmen und kommunizieren'.[12] While the former miracles were in response to dire human need, the first feeding appears as a continuation of Jesus' prior presentation in the role of compassionate 'shepherd' (6:34). Arguably, then, the Christological focus is even more acute because these miracles stem not from the situation at hand as much as Jesus' narrated messianic identity in relation to the gathered crowds.

That the feeding miracles are intended to be interpreted together is confirmed by Jesus' dialogue with the disciples in 8:14–21 as well as by numerous similarities between the accounts.[13] That these feeding miracles are a key to Jesus' identity is confirmed by the narrator's comment of 6:52, 'they did not understand about the loaves',[14] and Jesus' words in 8:21, 'Do you not yet understand?' In the first, the disciples' failure to understand the loaves left them unable to understand the walking on the water. In the second, while it is clear the disciples do not understand the meaning of the two feeding miracles, it is not immediately apparent what exactly it is they are consequently failing to understand (is it, e.g., the yeast of the Pharisees or is it Jesus' ability to produce bread miraculously?).

---

[9] Koch 1975: 103; Hübenthal 2014: 407.
[10] Feneberg 2000: 166.
[11] BDAG, 306.
[12] 'It is the disciples who repeatedly notice and communicate the lack of food' (Hübenthal 2014: 403).
[13] To be discussed in detail below.
[14] Theissen 1983: 169.

That said, the feeding miracles also connect strongly with the immediate narrative context, especially the preceding account of Herod's birthday banquet. Additionally, the relation between the two feeding miracles must also be assessed. Therefore the treatment of the feeding miracles, while following the same approach as the previous chapters, will contain additional sections to properly situate the feeding miracles in the Markan context and towards each other.

§7.2 Exploring the conventions

Bultmann categorizes the feedings as 'nature miracles'.[15] Perhaps more usefully, Theissen categorizes them as 'gift miracles'.[16] Such gift miracles are characterized by spontaneity, that is the absence of a request, and with no account given of the actual mechanism, only the result.[17] Similar miracles in the Jewish scriptures are 1 Kgs 17:8–16; 2 Kgs 4:1–7, 42–44. All three of those miracles have elements in common with Jesus' feeding miracles, in particular, the use of limited resources which are then multiplied. However, 1 Kgs 17:8–16 and 2 Kgs 4:1–7 only benefit an individual and their family and appear to be private affairs. Only 2 Kgs 4:42–44 takes place in public and feeds a large group, like the Markan feedings. Further parallels with this text will be discussed in detail.[18]

Luke 5:1–11 is also comparable in character. In Luke 5:1–11 a large quantity of fish is produced; however, it is not ready to eat, no one is fed and the fish may have already been present in the water. That is, the fish themselves are not necessarily miraculous, only their behaviour in swimming into the net. Additionally, the symbolic meaning of the fish is made explicit within the narrative episode (5:10) and Simon Peter, James and John respond accordingly (5:11), whereas in Mark 6:30–45 the symbolic meaning is not referred to until later (8:19–20) and the disciples (or at least Peter) do not respond until even later (8:29).

Collins suggests two Graeco-Roman parallels to the feeding miracles. In Euripides (*Bacch.* 704–13), 'a god provides his followers with water, wine, milk, and honey. These gifts are spontaneously given'.[19] In Philostratus (*Vit. Apoll.* 3.27), Apollonius comes across an Indian village where magical tripods produced dried fruit, bread, vegetables, and dessert and wine and hot and cold water; also they apparently generated soft grass for reclining as they moved.[20] In comparison, Jesus' miracles serve humble fare indeed, and there is no indication that Jesus is responsible for the green grass, only that he instructs the people to recline upon it (5:39). Notably, neither of Collins' suggested parallels involve a human figure performing the miracle of abundant food. Instead they are performed by a power or divinity not described in the narrative. In comparison

---

[15] Bultmann 1963: 217.
[16] Theissen 1983: 103–6; also Pesch 1979: 1.348.
[17] Gnilka 1998: 1.257; Marcus 2000a: 415.
[18] §7.7 below.
[19] Collins 2007: 321.
[20] Collins 2007: 321–2.

with the other works of power discussed in the previous chapters, there are no close Graeco-Roman parallels to the feeding miracles. As I will show, they very much follow in the tradition of the Jewish scriptures. As Gnilka states regarding Mark 6:30–44: 'Die vorliegende Speisungsgeschichte ist von mehreren alttestamentlichen Anspielungen und Motiven erfüllt, auf die in der Interpretation zu achten ist.'[21]

David Sick argues that 'neither Mark's audience nor the 5,000 or more diners would have been especially amazed that a large crowd had been fed'.[22] Large feedings of public groups with bread, wine, and sometimes fish, were 'a well known means of euergetism [i.e. public good works] in the Greco Roman world'.[23] This might account for the surprising lack of reaction from the disciples or crowd regarding the miraculous feeding.[24] Sick argues at length that Mark 6:30–45 corresponds to the conventions of a publicly given Graeco-Roman symposium. One Epaminondas is recorded as giving baskets of bread, wine and condiments, possibly fish relish, to male citizens of his town to celebrate the establishment of games (IG 7.2712). The rules of the cult of Diana and Antinous required wine, bread, sardines, tablecloths and warm water to be distributed to its members for a feast six times a year (CIL 14.2112.2.11–13). Emperors Antiochus IV and Ptolemy II Philadephus both held opulent public feasts after grand processions (*Deipn.* 5.193d1–3; Polybius, *Hist.* 5.195d).[25] Certainly, in the free distribution of food, outdoor setting and arrangement into smaller συμπόσια (Mark 6:39) the feeding miracle is reminiscent of a Graeco-Roman public banquet. However, unlike the Graeco-Roman patrons listed by Sick, Jesus was not a man of great wealth and influence, nor would the wilderness be a feasible location for such 'euergetism'. Therefore, even without the miraculous element, the wilderness feedings would have been extraordinary. The witnesses should have been amazed. The problem of the lack of reaction is not solved. Finally, all the elements possibly evocative of Graeco-Roman symposia also evoke certain scriptural narratives and so the Graeco-Roman background of public symposia is not necessarily primary here.

§7.3 The banquet of death

The first feeding account is preceded by an episode unique to Mark's gospel. 'Only here is there an extended story in which Jesus does not appear and not directly concerned with him.'[26] In his portrayal of Herod, Mark sets up a contrast between two 'kings', Herod and Jesus.[27] Two points concern this study in particular. First, Herod's discussion of Jesus' identity closely parallels Jesus and Peter's later discussion.[28] This can be seen in

---

[21] 'The present feeding story is filled with several Old Testament allusions and motifs, which should be taken into account in the interpretation' (Gnilka 1998: 258).
[22] Sick 2015: 26.
[23] Sick 2015: 1.
[24] For the lack of reaction see Garland 1996: 256; France 2002: 268; Hartman 2010: 256.
[25] Sick 2015: 17–19.
[26] Boring 2006: 176.
[27] Boring 2006: 177.
[28] Masuda 1982: 213; Marcus 2000b: 611.

the following comparison of the two discourses with corresponding words and phrasing marked in bold.

Comparison of Mark 6:14–16 and Mark 8:28–29:

Mark 6:14–16	Mark 8:28–29
Καὶ ἤκουσεν ὁ βασιλεὺς Ἡρῴδης, φανερὸν γὰρ ἐγένετο τὸ ὄνομα αὐτοῦ,	οἱ δὲ εἶπαν αὐτῷ
καὶ **ἔλεγον**	**λέγοντες**
ὅτι Ἰωάννης ὁ βαπτίζων ἐγήγερται ἐκ νεκρῶν καὶ διὰ τοῦτο ἐνεργοῦσιν αἱ δυνάμεις ἐν αὐτῷ.	[**ὅτι**] **Ἰωάννην τὸν βαπτιστήν**,
ἄλλοι δὲ **ἔλεγον** **ὅτι Ἠλίας ἐστίν·** **ἄλλοι δὲ** ἔλεγον **ὅτι** προφήτης ὡς **εἷς τῶν προφητῶν.**	**καὶ ἄλλοι** **Ἠλίαν,** **ἄλλοι δὲ** **ὅτι εἷς τῶν προφητῶν.** καὶ αὐτὸς ἐπηρώτα αὐτούς· ὑμεῖς δὲ τίνα με λέγετε εἶναι;
ἀκούσας δὲ ὁ Ἡρῴδης ἔλεγεν· ὃν ἐγὼ ἀπεκεφάλισα **Ἰωάννην, οὗτος ἠγέρθη.**	ἀποκριθεὶς ὁ Πέτρος λέγει αὐτῷ σὺ εἶ ὁ χριστός.

The striking similarity between the two conversations presents them as an *inclusio*, whereby Herod's false conclusion prepares the reader for Peter's later insight.[29] It is within this *inclusio*, concerning Jesus' identity, that we find both the feeding miracles.

Second, Herod's conversation is followed by a description of a meal where Herod gives a banquet for his 'courtiers and officers and for the leaders of Galilee' (6:21).[30] In the typical form of a Graeco-Roman banquet, the meal, δεῖπνον (6:21), would usually be followed by a drinking party, συμπόσιον, during which entertainment such as music and dancing could also occur (Plut. *Quaest. conv.* 612E–F).[31] During the entertainment following Herod's banquet, Herodias' daughter dances for the guests and John the Baptist's fate is sealed. His head is presented on a platter like a macabre part of the feast (6:22–28).

In 6:21 Herodias finds an opportune time (εὔκαιρος) to dispose of John, while in contrast the disciples have no opportunity to eat (οὐδὲ φαγεῖν εὐκαίρουν, 6:31).[32] When Jesus makes the crowd recline (ἀνακλίνω) and organizes them into 'banquets' (συμπόσιον) in 6:39 this evokes a banquet and so links back to Herod's birthday dinner.[33] Indeed, Herod's δεῖπνον (6:21), main meal, finds a complement in Jesus'

---

[29] Feneberg 2000: 145.
[30] Birthday celebrations were a regular part of the Graeco-Roman patronage system; see Argetsinger 1992: 175–93.
[31] Smith 2003: 31, 34–6, 49.
[32] Collins 2007: 318.
[33] Collins 2007: 324.

συμπόσιον, drinking party. However, it should be noted both δεῖπνον and συμπόσιον could metonymically denote the whole banquet.[34] Thus Herod's banquet of death both provides a contrast to and sets the scene for Jesus' feeding miracle.[35] This juxtaposition creates a narrative analogy between the adjacent Gospel pericopae, 'through which one part of the text provides oblique commentary on another'.[36]

Reinforcing this connection is a possible allusion to 1 Kings 18:4. As Pesch argues, there is a strong parallel between the story of John, Herod and Herodias, and the story of Elijah, Ahab and Jezebel.[37] Just as John opposes Herod because of Herodias, so Elijah opposed Ahab because of Jezebel (1 Kgs 21). Just as Herodias seeks the life of John, so Jezebel sought the life of Elijah (1 Kings 19:2). Drewermann finds both Jezebel and Herodias are linked by the motif of 'der verhängnisvollen Allmacht einer Frau über die Königsgewalt ihres Gatten'.[38] John, of course, has already been identified with Elijah (Mark 1:6).

As will be discussed below, the 'groups of hundreds and fifties' of Mark 6:40 evoke Moses' arrangement of the people of Israel in Exod 18:21, 25; Deut 1:15. However, 1 Kgs 18:4, καὶ ἔλαβεν Αβδιου ἑκατὸν ἄνδρας προφήτας καὶ ἔκρυψεν αὐτοὺς κατὰ πεντήκοντα, presents a closer, albeit less prominent scriptural correspondence to 'hundreds and fifties' (Mark 6:40). Obadiah, Ahab's steward, rescues a hundred prophets in groups of fifty in 1 Kings 18:4 and then sustains them with bread and water. These prophets are specifically men, ἀνήρ (LXX 18:4), which corresponds to Mark 6:44. Importantly, the immediate narrative context for Obadiah's act is, 'when Jezebel was killing off the prophets of the Lord' (1 Kgs 18:4,) which corresponds with Herodias having John killed (Mark 6:14-29).[39] Immediately following, Ahab divides up the land between himself and Obadiah so that they can find grazing for the animals (1 Kgs 18:5-6). Thus Obadiah is portrayed as a pastoral herder of horses and mules who finds a way (ὁδός) to save them. As will be discussed below, shepherding (as in Psalm 23) and the Exodus are two significant biblical themes recognized as present in Mark 6:30-45. Given the strong parallel in 6:14-29 to the Elijah story, the mention of hundreds and fifties in 6:40 could possibly be an allusion to Obadiah (and by extension Ahab). This would serve to reinforce the contrast between Jesus and Herod, already implied by the juxtaposition of the murder of John at Herod's banquet and Jesus' feeding miracle.

§7.4 A revolutionary gathering?

The occasion of John's death provides a plausible narrative reason for public interest in Jesus suddenly to reach fever pitch.[40] The first-century reader of Mark may well have

---

[34] Smith 2003: 49.
[35] Aus 2010: 131-2; Collins 2007: 324; Garland 1996: 254; Witherington 2001: 217; Sick 2015: 14. On the socio-economic significance of this contrast see Batten 2017: 11.
[36] Alter 1981: 21.
[37] Pesch 1979: 1.339; also Collins 2007: 307; Hatina 2006: 42.
[38] 'The fateful omnipotence of a woman over the royal power of her husband' (Drewermann 1989: 407). This in no way absolves Herod of guilt for John's murder, however. See Hatina 2006: 39-40.
[39] Guelich 1989: 331.
[40] Montefiore 1962: 140.

been aware that the public reason John was executed was the possibility he could lead an uprising (Josephus, *Ant.* 18.118).[41] While John was in prison 'the whole Judean country side and all the people of Jerusalem' (Mark 1:5) who had gone to him in the wilderness would have been on tenterhooks. With his unjust death at the hands of king Herod all eyes would fall upon John's apparent successor, Jesus. Herod's character confirms this sense of Jesus' succession of John in Mark 6:16.

Hugh Montefiore suggests that the 'many coming and going' of 6:31 may well have been political activists seeking out Jesus and his disciples in the wake of John's decapitation.[42] His solution to the problem of the crowd arriving on foot before Jesus did by boat is 'a widespread concerted movement' that had been 'premeditated'.[43] Furthermore, he argues that, 'The phrase "sheep without a shepherd" means, according to Old Testament usage; not a congregation without a leader, but "an army without a general, a nation without a national leader". Mark here probably intends a reference to Num. xxvii. 16 ff.'[44]

Jesus' response to the crowd 'to teach them' (6:34) is similar to his response to Peter in 8:31 and may reflect a similar misunderstanding on the part of the crowd to Peter's regarding the nature of Jesus' messiahship.[45] The combination of number and orderliness in 6:40 is suggestive of the military divisions of the Israelites.[46] Mark's emphasis that the multitude is composed of men (ἀνήρ, 6:44) is also suggestive of a military gathering rather than one for the purpose of healing and teaching.[47] That there are no healings or exorcisms described may suggest that these were able-bodied men, suitable to form an army. Indeed, they would need to be fit and healthy in order to have run ahead of Jesus's boat (6:33). For Montefiore, at the end of the narrative, Jesus' abrupt forcing (ἀναγκάζω) of his disciples to leave suggests he wants them gone before they are influenced by the messianic fervour of the crowd.[48] Of course, John 6:15 ('they were about to come and take him by force to make him king') supports Montefiore's hypothesis, even as it highlights Mark's omission of such details, and it is possible that such a gathering is part of the historical background of the events described in Mark 6:30–44. As Hans Bayer states, 'Die Gefahr, dass Jesus in die populäre, zeitgenössische Messiaserwartung gepresst wird, ist tatsächlich akut'.[49] Finally, as James Dunn has argued, Jesus' retreat to prayer suggests he was himself in some sense tempted by the crowd.[50]

Further corroboration comes from Josephus, who records a number of first-century Palestinian 'ostensible prophets who, following a more or less fixed scenario, led people into the desert, where miracles of deliverance like those of Moses and his imitator,

---

[41] Boring 2006: 178.
[42] Montefiore 1962: 135.
[43] Montefiore 1962: 136.
[44] Montefiore 1962: 136; Collins 2007: 319.
[45] Montefiore 1962: 136.
[46] Montefiore 1962: 137.
[47] Montefiore 1962: 137; Marcus 2000a: 414.
[48] Montefiore 1962: 138; Dunn 1970: 102.
[49] 'The danger that Jesus will be pressed into the popular, contemporary messianic expectation is indeed acute' (Bayer 2008: 74). See also Bruce 1961: 344; Dunn 1970: 102; France 2002: 261.
[50] Dunn 1970: 103.

Joshua, were to be enacted'.⁵¹ I have already discussed these prophets in Chapter 2. Here, it should suffice to be reminded that the conjunction of a crowd (ὄχλος) gathered around a prophetic leader (cf. Mark 6:15; 8:28) in the wilderness (ἐρημία) was one that was consistently met with deadly armed response from the Romans. That is, whatever the intent of the crowd or of Jesus, such a gathering could be expected to be interpreted by the Romans as an insurrection. While the sign prophets in Josephus post-date Jesus, the relevant point here is that any reader around 70 BCE, aware of recent events in Palestine, would have been able to recognize this 'revolutionary' aspect as an implication of the account.

With internal and external evidence taken together it seems likely that at least some of the gathered crowd believed themselves to be part of a messianic uprising and that any such act would be seen as provocative by the Roman authorities. That said, Mark does not explicitly acknowledge this aspect of the gathering. Rather than the reason that these men gather to Jesus, Mark focuses his reader on what Jesus does with them.

§7.5 Transformation of a revolution

As France observes, 'The whole story reads more like an ad hoc picnic than a military manoeuvre'.⁵² Likewise, Marcus suggests that Jesus is described as 'throwing a banquet rather than raising an army'.⁵³ Of course even the provision of food could be a prelude to an armed uprising, the supply of food to campaigning or besieged troops was (and still is) a large part of any successful war.⁵⁴ Indeed, Jesus orders (ἐπιτάσσω, 6:39) the crowd about much like Herod giving an order (ἐπιτάσσω, 6:27) to his soldiers. So, Jesus appears a little like Herod. But whereas Herod is manipulated to order death and motivated by the approval of others, Jesus orders a banquet motivated by compassion (6:34).

Jesus orders the crowd into groups, not in military terms, but συμπόσια συμπόσια (6:39) and πρασιαὶ πρασιαὶ (6:40). A συμπόσιον, a NT *hapax* (literally a 'drinking-party' but 'better understood as "banquet"'), does not imply military seriousness but festivity and 'sparkling conversation'.⁵⁵ Indeed, 'Greco-Roman Symposium literature, of which Plato's *Symposium* is the most famous example, combines the banquet setting with a philosophical discussion'.⁵⁶ Consequently the symposium was not just a meal but also a literary form with established conventions.⁵⁷ It could be that the philosophical symposium and its association with decency and refinement is here intended to contrast with Herod's δεῖπνον.⁵⁸ Given that Jesus has just been teaching the crowd it is reasonable to suggest that the potentially revolutionary gathering was transformed by Jesus into a meal for his disciples to celebrate and discuss his teaching.

---

⁵¹ Allison 1993: 81.
⁵² France 2002: 262.
⁵³ Marcus 2000a: 421.
⁵⁴ See, e.g., Rao 2012.
⁵⁵ BDAG 959.
⁵⁶ Marcus 2000a: 408.
⁵⁷ Smith 2003: 48.
⁵⁸ Having his niece/stepdaughter dance for the pleasure of his guests was hardly decent, and a human head on a plate speaks for itself. See Boring 2006: 178, 182.

Even more surprising is the use of πρασιά in 6:40. The KJV translates it as 'ranks' and the NAS as 'companies'. It seems wrong to translate into military terminology a word derived from such an inoffensive vegetable as the leek (πράσον), and meaning 'garden plot, garden bed'.[59] Far better is Marcus' suggestion that the 'unprecedented' use of 'this agricultural image invites comparison with rabbinic texts in which pupils are compared to plants arranged in lines before their teacher', for example in *y. Ber.* 4:1 and also 1 QH 8:5–11 (16) where the elect end-time community are figured as a garden.[60]

Perhaps, however, a closer parallel comes from the Gospel of Mark itself. The parables of Mark 4:1–32 figuratively depict people as seeds which respond to the word in different ways (4:1–20) and the kingdom of God as a field in which seed grows (4:26–29).[61] The πρασιά are not *flower* garden beds, but agricultural, *vegetable* garden beds from which a harvest can be expected.[62] By arranging the crowd into garden beds (πρασιά) Mark's Jesus can be seen as inserting the crowd into the parables of the kingdom. They are the seeds who must respond to the word (4:13–20; 6:34). To my knowledge this connection not been previously suggested.

What supports my suggestion here is that the *miracle* of multiplication of food corresponds to the *parables* of multiplication (Mark 4:8, 4:30–32). As Andrew Salzmann observes, 'Each of these [feeding miracle] stories, it must be noted, is an illustration of the Kingdom of God. The fragments of bread again become symbolic of the Kingdom of God in their superabundance.'[63] The small beginning of a mustard seed (Mark 4:31) that becomes a great plant (4:32) or the single seed that reproduces a hundredfold (4:8) find an analogy in the five loaves and two fish that feed a multitude. In the parables Jesus tells the disciples what the kingdom of God is like (4:11, 26, 30). In the feeding miracles he shows them that same multiplying power of divine abundance at work.

Whether or not the five thousand men arrived in the wilderness to form a revolt, Jesus turns them into something else: disciples sharing in a meal, individual seeds hearing the word, God's field from which the harvest will come.

§7.6 The repeated miracle

While there are a number of healings and exorcisms recounted in Mark, no two are exactly alike. For example, the water miracles (4:35–41; 6:45–52) share some common themes but differ in structure, content and lexicon. The two feeding miracles, however, are so alike that they are considered by some to be two versions of the same story.[64] The following comparison shows overlaps in word choice in the parallel stories marked in bold:

---

[59] BDAG, 860; LSJ, 1460; GE, 1735.
[60] Marcus 2000a: 408.
[61] Jesus' parables in Mark 4 all revolve around 'Vegetationsmetaphern' rather than 'soziomorphe Metaphern'; see Guttenberger 2004: 73.
[62] This difference should not be overdrawn. Leeks, of course, can flower if allowed to go to seed, and πρασιά could denote flower beds. On the later point see GE, 1735. My point is with regard to the Markan πρασιά.
[63] Salzmann 2009: 132.
[64] E.g. Gnilka 1998: 1.255.

Mark 6:30–44	Mark 8:1–10
34 ... **πολὺν ὄχλον** ...	1 ... **πολλοῦ ὄχλου** ...
34 ... **ἐσπλαγχνίσθη ἐπ'** ...	2 **σπλαγχνίζομαι ἐπὶ** ...
34 ..., **ὅτι** ἦσαν ὡς πρόβατα μὴ ἔχοντα ποιμένα, καὶ ἤρξατο διδάσκειν αὐτοὺς πολλά. 35 Καὶ **ἤδη** ὥρας πολλῆς γενομένης	2 ... **ὅτι ἤδη** ἡμέραι τρεῖς προσμένουσίν μοι
35 ... οἱ **μαθηταὶ αὐτοῦ** ἔλεγον ...	4 ... ἀπεκρίθησαν αὐτῷ οἱ **μαθηταὶ αὐτοῦ** ...
36 **ἀπόλυσον αὐτούς**, ἵνα ἀπελθόντες **εἰς** ...	3 καὶ ἐὰν **ἀπολύσω αὐτοὺς** νήστεις **εἰς** ...
36 ... **τί φάγωσιν.**	2 ... **τί φάγωσιν·**
37 ὁ δὲ **ἀποκριθεὶς** εἶπεν αὐτοῖς ...	4 καὶ **ἀπεκρίθησαν** αὐτῷ ...
38 ὁ δὲ λέγει αὐτοῖς· **πόσους ἄρτους ἔχετε;** ...	5 καὶ ἠρώτα αὐτούς· **πόσους ἔχετε ἄρτους;** ...
39 καὶ ἐπέταξεν αὐτοῖς **ἀνακλῖναι** πάντας συμπόσια συμπόσια **ἐπὶ** τῷ χλωρῷ χόρτῳ.	6 καὶ παραγγέλλει τῷ ὄχλῳ **ἀναπεσεῖν ἐπὶ** τῆς γῆς·
40 καὶ **ἀνέπεσαν** πρασιαὶ πρασιαὶ ...	
41 καὶ **λαβὼν** τοὺς πέντε **ἄρτους** καὶ τοὺς δύο **ἰχθύας** ἀναβλέψας εἰς τὸν οὐρανὸν **εὐλόγησεν** καὶ **κατέκλασεν** τοὺς ἄρτους **καὶ ἐδίδου τοῖς μαθηταῖς** [αὐτοῦ] ἵνα **παρατιθῶσιν** αὐτοῖς, καὶ τοὺς δύο **ἰχθύας** ἐμέρισεν πᾶσιν.	6 ... καὶ **λαβὼν** τοὺς ἑπτὰ **ἄρτους** εὐχαριστήσας **ἔκλασεν καὶ ἐδίδου τοῖς μαθηταῖς** αὐτοῦ ἵνα **παρατιθῶσιν**, καὶ παρέθηκαν τῷ ὄχλῳ.
	7 καὶ εἶχον **ἰχθύδια** ὀλίγα· καὶ **εὐλογήσας** αὐτὰ εἶπεν καὶ ταῦτα **παρατιθέναι.**
42 **καὶ ἔφαγον** πάντες **καὶ ἐχορτάσθησαν,**	8 **καὶ ἔφαγον καὶ ἐχορτάσθησαν,**
43 **καὶ ἦραν κλάσματα** δώδεκα κοφίνων πληρώματα ...	8 ... **καὶ ἦραν** περισσεύματα **κλασμάτων** ἑπτὰ σπυρίδας.
44 καὶ **ἦσαν** οἱ φαγόντες [τοὺς ἄρτους] πεντακισχίλιοι ἄνδρες.	9 **ἦσαν** δὲ ὡς τετρακισχίλιοι ...
45 **Καὶ εὐθὺς** ἠνάγκασεν τοὺς **μαθητὰς αὐτοῦ ἐμβῆναι εἰς τὸ πλοῖον** καὶ προάγειν **εἰς** τὸ πέραν πρὸς Βηθσαϊδάν ...	10 **Καὶ εὐθὺς ἐμβὰς εἰς τὸ πλοῖον** μετὰ τῶν **μαθητῶν αὐτοῦ** ἦλθεν **εἰς** τὰ μέρη Δαλμανουθά.
45 ... ἕως αὐτὸς **ἀπολύει** τὸν ὄχλον.	9 ... καὶ **ἀπέλυσεν** αὐτούς.

There is an undeniable overlap in vocabulary and structure. Despite the clear similarity, which is unique among the other miracle narratives in Mark, the stories do display differences. Firstly, all the features that suggested 6:30–45 may have been a gathering of revolutionary minded men, as discussed above, are absent in 8:1–10.

Secondly, were they to be two separate accounts of the same tradition which Mark has now brought together (in, e.g., a hypothesis like that of Achtemeier 1970; 1972) it would elicit the question as to why the lesser miracle – four thousand people instead of five and a lesser multiplication of food – was reported second.[65] The natural order would have been to place the lesser miracle first, to show an escalation in Jesus' popularity and power.

Third, each feeding miracle is followed by a boat voyage (6:45-52; 8:14-21) both of which refer back to the previous feeding miracle(s) (6:52; 8:19-20) but only the first of which contains a spectacular miracle. The second boat journey contains only a (non-miraculous) stinging rebuke to the disciples.

Fourth, many of the scriptural allusions of the first account are missing in the second: 'in der zweiten Episode die Erzählfiguren nicht auf einem dichten intertextuellen Teppich sitzen'.[66]

Finally, regardless of speculative constructions of tradition history, from the point of view of interpreting Mark, the clear intent is to portray two different events, both of which contribute in some esoteric way to the disciples' and consequently the readers' comprehension of who Jesus is (8:14-21).[67] If they are not two stories based on the same event, Mark's typological use of a sciptural narrative may provide an alternative explanation for their similarity.

§7.7 2 Kgs 4:42-44

The close resemblance between Mark 6:30-45 and 8:1-10 is not just to each other, but also to a much shorter scriptural story. A number of commentators note that 2 Kgs 4:42-44 shares themes and structure with the Markan feeding miracles.[68] Despite its comparatively short length, a mere three verses, the Markan stories find many correspondences in the Elisha account, as is shown in the following table.

The key narrative correspondences are a hungry crowd, the command of the prophet to feed the crowd, the protest of the helper(s), an account of the small amount of available food, the giving out of the food, everyone eating, the presence of leftovers and numbering those who had eaten.[69] For Collins, the miracles themselves are 'almost identical'.[70] For Marcus the feature of producing greater food from a small amount derives from 2 Kgs 4:42-44.[71] France concludes, 'there can be little doubt that Mark had the story [of 2 Kgs 4:42-44] in mind'.[72]

---

[65] For a survey and critique of the history of this question, see Fowler 1981: 5-90.
[66] 'In the second episode, the narrative figures are not sitting on a tightly-woven intertextual carpet' (Hübenthal 2014: 410).
[67] Pesch 1979: 1.411, 1.348; Fowler 1981: 148; Oyen 1999: 192; Stein 2008: 310.
[68] E.g., Richardson 1941: 95; Haenchen 1968: 284; Gray 1970: 502; Guelich 1989: 344; Stegner 1989: 60; Schneck 1994: 155-56; Schnackenburg 1995: 31; Garland 1996: 256; Dechow 2000: 214; Feneberg 2000: 165-66; Marcus 2000a: 415; Witherington 2001: 217; Dunn 2003: 686; Fritz 2003: 256; Boring 2006: 185; Collins 2007: 320; Hartman 2010: 248-49; Focant 2012: 258-59.
[69] Pesch 1979: 1.354; Marcus 2000a: 415-16; Hartman 2010: 254-5.
[70] Collins 2007: 320.
[71] Marcus 2000a: 407.
[72] France 2002: 262.

Table 5 Comparison of Mark's feeding miracles and Elisha's feeding miracle

	Mark 6	Mark 8		2 Kgs 4
Disciples gathered	31	1b	Prophets with Elisha	38
Description of crowd	33	1a	Company/100 people	38, 43
Jesus' compassion on crowd	34	2		
Need for food explained	35	3	Famine in land	38
Jesus wants crowd fed	37	3	Elisha wants people fed	42
Disciples protest	35	4	Servant protests	43
Jesus requests and receives stock take	38	5	Offering described	42
Jesus orders crowd to lie down	39	6a		
Jesus takes, blesses, gives for distribution	41	6b–7	Elisha sets before (not LXX)	44a
All eat and are filled	42	8a	All eat	44b
There are leftovers	43	8b	Leftovers (not specified)	44c
The crowd is numbered	44	9a	Servant reports 100 people	43
Immediate embarkation	45a	10		
Crowd dismissed	45b	9b		

From the LXX a number of words also help link the stories: ἄρτους (2 Kgs 4:42; Mark 6:37, 38 41 (x2) 8:4,5,6); ἐσθίω (2 Kgs 4:42–44 (x4); Mark 6:31, 36, 37 (x2), 42, 44; 8:1, 2, 8); ἀνήρ (2 Kgs 4:42, 43; Mark 6:44); and δίδωμι (2 Kgs 4:42, 43; Mark 6:37 (x2), 41; 8:6). However, all of these words are very common. Another common word that might have been expected is καταλείπω (2 Kgs 4:43, 44) which Mark uses elsewhere (10:7; 12:19, 21; 14:52) but does not use in the feeding accounts. There are no shared words that are unusual enough to confirm literary dependence, but the structural similarities in this instance are sufficient to suggest influence. Consequently, many similarities in the two Markan feeding narratives can be explained by their both being influenced by the same scriptural story, 2 Kgs 4:42–44, with which they share themes, structure and some common words.

However, Hartman rightly notes that the Elisha parallel does not account for the prominence of the shepherd motif in the Markan feeding miracles.[73] This too can be shown to have a scriptural background.

§7.8 The shepherd motif

Psalm 23 (LXX 22) is not prominent in the NT and early Christian literature. For example, in the Apostolic Fathers only 1 Clement 26:2 cites it, and briefly at that (ὅτι σὺ μετ' ἐμοῦ εἶ, LXX Ps 22:4). However, Dale Allison observes that it is alluded to in Rev

---
[73] Hartman 2010: 263.

7:17.⁷⁴ He also finds that 'both [Revelation and 1 Clement] use the psalm as a prophecy of eschatological future'.⁷⁵ The third place Allison argues allusions to Psalm 23 are present is Mark 6:30–45, and he suggests the following correspondences: 'The Lord is my shepherd' (Ps 23:1) corresponds to 'They were like sheep without a shepherd' (Mark 6:34); 'I shall not want' (Ps 23:1) corresponds to 'They all ate and were satisfied' (Mark 6:42); 'He makes me to lie down in green pastures' (Ps 23:2) corresponds to 'He commanded them all to sit down by companies upon the green grass' (Mark 6:39); and 'He leads me beside still waters' (Ps 23:2) corresponds to the fact that the feeding took place at the seashore in the evening (34, 35).⁷⁶

Others have also suggested that themes of compassion (Ps 23:6; Mark 6:34; 8:2), teaching (Ps 23:3; Mark 6:34) and preparing a table (Ps 23:5; Mark 6:39–41; 8:6–7) serve to link Ps 23 with Mark 6:30–44.⁷⁷ The theme of 'rest' is also a possible link (Mark 6:31; LXX Ps 22:2, ὕδατος ἀναπαύσεως ἐξέθρεψέν με).⁷⁸ In particular, σπλαγχνίζομαι is infrequently used in Mark (1:41; 6:34, 8:2; 9:22) but is used in both feeding miracles, and presents Jesus as a compassionate shepherd for the 'sheep'.⁷⁹ The verb only occurs in the LXX in 2 Mac 6:8, but semantically corresponds to the description of the shepherd of Psalm 23 comforting, guiding and showing goodness and mercy/loving-kindness (חסד/ἔλεος, Ps 23:6/LXX 22:6).

Stein discounts the influence of Psalm 23 because τόπον χλόης (LXX Ps 22:2) and τῷ χλωρῷ χόρτῳ (Mark 6:39) are not exactly the same.⁸⁰ However, the power of an allusion is not dependent on using the exact same words. Here there is considerable semantic and motific overlap. Comparable, for example, is the way in which 'green grass', 'verdant pasture' or 'lush fields' could all evoke the same image for an English reader despite using different vocabulary.

Secondly, without access to the exact Hebrew and Greek texts of the scriptures that Mark was using, it does not stretch the imagination to suppose that a Greek manuscript of Ps 23 could use χλωρός instead of χλόη. Indeed, Mark's τῷ χλωρῷ χόρτῳ is a closer translation of the Hebrew דשא of Ps 23:2 than the Septuagint's τόπον χλόης.⁸¹ As Pesch writes, 'die Lagerung "auf dem grünen Gras" (V 39) ruft Ps 23,2 in Erinnerung'.⁸² It is both unique and otherwise unnecessary for Mark to make a reference to colour. It is also possible that Mark chose χόρτος because of its relation to χορτάζω, which he uses for fullness in Mark 6:42; 7:27; 8:4, 8. With their associations with animal feed,⁸³ χόρτος and χορτάζω serve to reinforce the figuration of the crowd as sheep and Jesus as good shepherd. Consequently, this evocative allusion to Psalm 23:2 should be considered deliberate. However, the other correspondences listed are rather tenuous and are best

---

⁷⁴ Allison 1983: 133.
⁷⁵ Allison 1983: 134.
⁷⁶ Allison 1983: 134; see also Garland 1996: 255–56; Du Toit 2006: 100.
⁷⁷ Masuda 1982: 209; Derrett 1985:1.124; Hartman 2010: 259–60; see also Owen 2015: 54; Pesch 1979: 1.350.
⁷⁸ Donahue and Harrington 2005: 204; Hübenthal 2014: 403.
⁷⁹ France 2002: 265.
⁸⁰ Stein 2008: 315.
⁸¹ Focant 2012: 260.
⁸² 'Camping "on the green grass" (V 39) calls to mind Ps 23:2' (Pesch 1979: 1.352).
⁸³ BDAG: 1087.

explained by the presence of a more general theme of 'shepherd', rather than allusions to Psalm 23 specifically.

What most concretely confirms the Shepherd motif is the expression 'they were like sheep without a shepherd'.[84] While this may evoke Psalm 23, it is close to a quotation of several other LXX passages.[85] Compare:

Mark 6:34	ὡς πρόβατα μὴ ἔχοντα ποιμένα
Num 27:17	ὡσεὶ πρόβατα οἷς οὐκ ἔστιν ποιμήν
1 Kgs 22:17	ὡς ποίμνιον ᾧ οὐκ ἔστιν ποιμήν
2 Chr 18:16,	ὡς πρόβατα οἷς οὐκ ἔστιν ποιμήν
Jdt 11:19,	ὡς πρόβατα οἷς οὐκ ἔστιν ποιμήν

With the exception of Judith, all these scriptures use the expression to refer to Israel. Thus this allusive phrase figures the crowd as Israel, the people of God (also see Ezek 34:5–6; Zech 10:2).[86] If the people lack a shepherd, then, in his teaching and feeding of them, Jesus is presented as the shepherd they need (Mark 6:34, 42).[87]

The image of shepherd is applied in a number of ways in the Jewish scriptures.[88] God is described as having been a shepherd (Ps 78:52). God also promises to be a shepherd to his people (Jer 31:10). The shepherd is also a typological image, as 'The figures of Moses, Joshua, and David are all painted with pastoral colors in the OT: They shepherd Israel on God's behalf'.[89] In particular Moses and David are (literal) shepherds who become (figurative) shepherds of God's people. So the shepherd motif potentially evokes Moses and/or David.

Alongside this, in the scriptures God promises to provide an eschatological shepherd, and this becomes part of the messianic hope (e.g. Ps 78:70–72; Ezek 34:23; Micah 5.4; *Pss. Sol.* 17.45(40)) of which the NT holds Jesus to be the fulfilment.[90]

So it can be argued that the shepherd motif complements and reinforces some themes from 2 Kgs 4:42–44 and provides background for some places in the Mark narratives which did not link to the Elisha story, especially Jesus making the crowd lie down and Jesus' compassion.

Despite the prominence of David typology elsewhere in Mark, here the image of bread in the wilderness combined with the shepherd motif inescapably places the emphasis on a Moses typology.[91]

---

[84] Guelich 1989: 340.
[85] Pesch 1979: 1.350.
[86] Kee 1987: 196; Witherington 2001: 217.
[87] See also Masuda 1982: 209; France 2002: 265; Stein 2008: 313.
[88] For an overview see Baxter 2009: 210–13.
[89] Hartman 2010: 259.
[90] See Mark 14:27, 28; John 10:1–18; Heb 13:20; 1 Pet 2:25; 5:4; Rev 7:17; Matt 10:6; 15:24; Luke 19:10; see further Allison 1983: 135–6.
[91] Baxter 2009: 214.

§7.9 Moses

Regarding Mark 6:30–45, Gnilka states, 'Nicht ist Jesus als zweiter Mose vorgestellt'.[92] On the contrary, given the clear link with 2 Kgs 4:42–44 where Elisha is shown as 'another Moses' through his bread miracle,[93] and the irrefutable presence of shepherd motif (Mark 6:34), it seems clear that Jesus is being portrayed in a way intended to bring Moses to mind,[94] and possibly also the promise of Deut 18:15-18.[95] Moses has been brought to mind from the very beginning of the Gospel in its allusions to the Exodus (e.g. Mark 1:2-3).[96] Marcus finds this section of the Gospel, 6:6b-8:21, to contain 'a pronounced Mosaic typology'.[97] In Mark 6:30-45 specifically, the wilderness setting, the arrangement of the crowd, the numerical symbolism, and the teaching and compassion in the wilderness combine to strongly evoke Moses.[98] Moreover, just as the later sign prophets would seek to imitate Moses, by leading crowds into the wilderness with the promise of miracles, so too Jesus' miracle working for a crowd in the desert inescapably evokes Moses.[99]

The Moses typology of Mark 6:30-45 can be further explicated with reference to specific scriptural passages:

1. Most commentators find the 'groups of hundreds and fifties' of Mark 6:40 reflect Moses' arrangement of the people of Israel in Ex 18:21, 25; Deut 1:15.[100] Significantly, in Exodus these groups are not formed for military purposes but for the purpose of pastoral care, i.e. 'judging' (Exod 18:22, 26). However, the role of teacher remained solely with Moses (Exod 18:19-20). In Mark 6:34 Jesus teaches in response to seeing the crowd 'like sheep without a shepherd' (cf. Num 27:17) and prior to forming the groups. Thus Jesus is presented as a teacher in the wilderness and as the one whose teaching the sheep of Israel need, doubly evoking Moses.[101]
2. The motif of miraculous bread in the desert recalls the story of the manna of Exodus 16 (LXX 16:8, 12, 15 ἄρτους; 16:1, ἔρημος) when the Lord gives (16:8, 15, δίδωμι) Israel food.[102] In Mark 6:39, Jesus commands (ἐπιτάσσω) the people to lie down to be fed. In Exodus 16:16, 24, 34 the Lord and Moses command

---

[92] 'Jesus is not presented as a second Moses' (Gnilka 1998: 1.259).
[93] Carroll 1969: 411-12; Brueggemann 2000: 326, 329.
[94] Du Toit 2006: 100.
[95] Collins 2007: 319.
[96] Omerzu 2011: 83.
[97] Marcus 2000a: 417.
[98] Marcus 2000a: 417-19.
[99] The evocation of Moses does not necessarily conflict with the figuring of Jesus as Davidic messiah. The Apocryphon of Moses C (4Q377 2.ii.5), 'Moses his (God's) messiah', perhaps provides precedent for association of Davidic messiah with Moses (Bowley 2001: 175). Regardless, inter alia, Deut 33:5; Isa 63:11; Exod 4:20 LXX all present Moses as a king (Horbury 1998: 31). Thus the conflation of hopes for a new Moses and a new David in one kingly figure could easily occur.
[100] E.g. Stegner 1989: 57; Schneck 1994: 159; Marcus 2000a: 408; Witherington 2001: 217, 219; Du Toit 2006: 100; Hartman 2010: 248, 261.
[101] See Ps 119:176; Philo, *Post.* 67-69; 2 Bar 76:13-14. So, Marcus 2000a: 406; also Hartman 2010: 247.
[102] Hooker 1991: 164; Garland 1996: 254.

(συντάσσω) Israel regarding the manna. It is also possible that the five loaves symbolize the five books of Moses.[103]

3. The recounting of the Exodus in Psalm 78 (LXX 77) reads καὶ ἐφάγοσαν καὶ ἐνεπλήσθησαν σφόδρα (LXX 77:29) which Collins rightly suggests 'has an important similarity' to Mark 6:42, καὶ ἔφαγον πάντες καὶ ἐχορτάσθησαν.[104] Psalm 78 also evokes the shepherd motif (Ps 78:52, 70–72) using the image of shepherd for both God and David. As a nexus of both Exodus feeding and shepherd imagery the likelihood of Psalm 78 being in the background of Mark 6:42 is increased. Mark does not use any Greek terms for fullness that link to the LXX feeding passages. However, the language of 'fullness' is very much part of the Markan feeding accounts (χορτάζω, Mark 6:42 & 8:4; πλήρωμα, 6:43; περίσσευμα, 8:8),[105] and surely links to similar language in the LXX (πλησμονή, Exod 16:3, 12; ἐμπίπλημι, Ps 77:29).[106]

4. The narrative setting for Num 27:17, 'like sheep without a shepherd' (cf. Mark 6:34), is the appointment of Joshua (in Greek: Jesus) son of Nun as Moses' successor. Thus Jesus could be being figured as Moses' successor Joshua.[107] Sanae Masuda makes the intriguing suggestion that Mark 8:1–10 omits Δότε αὐτοῖς ὑμεῖς φαγεῖν of 6:37, to minimize the connection with Elisha found in Mark 6:30–45 and instead links to Joshua 9 through ἡμέραι τρεῖς (Mark 8:2; cf. Jos 9:16) and ἀπὸ μακρόθεν ἥκασιν (Mark 8:3, cf. LXX Jos 9:6, 9, 22). Thus for Masuda both Joshua and Jesus receive Gentiles 'from afar' who stay with them for 'three days', but while Joshua makes them slaves, Jesus invites them to share in the same shepherding care and provision as the nation of Israel received.[108] More tentatively, the Gibeonites of Josh 9 use bread, ἀρτός, in their deception, and are one of the seven nations described in Deut 7:1–2, which fact may correspond to the seven baskets collected in 8:8.[109] Masuda's suggestion is plausible. However, the expressions are too common to be decisive. Such an allusion, however, would not detract from Jesus being a type of Moses, as Joshua was himself a type of Moses.[110]

5. The disciples' responses to Jesus' plan to feed the crowds (Mark 6:37; 8:4) also finds a counterpart in Moses' words in Numbers 11:13 and 11:21–22, 'Where am I to get meat to give to all this people? ... Are there enough flocks and herds to slaughter for them? Are there enough fish in the sea to catch for them?'[111] The numbering of the people on foot in Num 11:21, ἑξακόσιαι χιλιάδες πεζῶν ὁ λαός, may connect to Mark 6:33, πεζός, and 6:44; 8:9. The account of gathering the quails and

---

[103] Hooker 1991: 166; Hübenthal 2014: 404.
[104] Collins 2007: 326.
[105] See also comment on περίσσευμα in Masuda 1982: 206–7.
[106] Note, both Exod 16:33 and the Byzantine tradition of Mark 6:43 use πλήρης.
[107] Marcus 2000a: 406.
[108] Masuda 1982: 211; see also Danker 1963: 215; Derrett 1985:1.143; Guelich 1989: 404.
[109] Danker 1963: 215–16; Marcus 2000a: 487.
[110] As argued in §2.
[111] Hooker 1991: 164; Garland 1996: 253; Marcus 2000a: 418–19.

numbering the homers (Num 11:32) may connect with the gathering of the pieces in Mark 6:43 and 8:8.[112]

6. Numbers 11 may also provide the background for another detail in the Markan feeding miracles. As France notes, Mark keeps fish prominent in the feeding accounts (Mark 6:38, 41 (x2), 43; 8:7).[113] This is seen in contrast to Matthew and Luke who reduce the number of fish references in their parallel accounts.[114] In Num 11:5 the Israelites complain of their lack of free fish (ἰχθύς) that they had enjoyed in Egypt. In Num 11:22 Moses complains that all the fish in the sea (πᾶν τὸ ὄψος τῆς θαλάσσης) would not suffice to feed the people. Thus if we see a link to Moses and to Numbers 11 in particular then we can conclude with Garland that the significance of the fish is that 'Jesus is therefore able to provide the people in the desert what Moses could not'.[115]

7. There is a repeated reference to the wilderness (Mark 6:31, 32). This wilderness is reached after a sea crossing (6:32) and then followed by the miraculous feeding with bread in the wilderness on the other side of the sea. Stegner notes that this sets up a parallel with the order of events in the Exodus, as does Mark's double account of feedings which may even be in imitation of the twin accounts of the manna in Exodus 16 and Numbers 11.[116]

Thus a variety of background texts from the Pentateuch as well as Joshua 9 and Psalm 78 provide scriptural background that reflects a Moses typology at work. Numbers 11 provides the most points of narrative contact as well as some significant lexical correspondences.

§7.9.1 A unique indicator

Further confirmation of Mark's intention to signal an attentive reader towards Numbers 11 is the use of the NT *hapax* πρασιά (6:40 x2). The significance of this distinctive word has been missed by scholarly focus on its unprecedented and awkward use to describe the groupings into which Jesus forms the crowd.[117] We have already discussed its rarity and etymology as a bed of leeks above. However, having observed the elements of Moses typology in Mark's feeding miracle accounts I would argue that this NT *hapax* is a deliberate word-play on a related LXX *hapax*.[118]

---

[112] It has also been suggested that Mark may have drawn upon Num 11:26–29 for Mark 9:38 (Garland 1996: 368; France 2002: 376).
[113] France 2002: 260.
[114] Batten 2017: 11.
[115] Garland 1996: 255.
[116] Stegner 1989: 58.
[117] Schneck (1994: 161–3) considers πρασιά to be a reference to Sirach 24:31, which is a metaphorical passage about Ben Sira's wisdom spreading to others. Whilst this provides a parallel with Jesus' teaching reaching the crowds, it should be noted that the πρασιά of Mark 6:40 are not related to his teaching but the feeding. Moreover, there are no undisputed links to Sirach in the Markan text.
[118] Having come to this idea independently, I was interested to find the same conclusion reached by a more circuitous route (via the irrigation of vegetables in Egypt and the Song of Songs) in Derrett 1975: 101–3. I consider my argument to be simpler and more plausible than Derrett's.

In Num 11:5 where the Israelites complain about their lack of fish they also mention a number of other foodstuffs they miss; among them are 'leeks', in the MT חָצִיר, in the LXX πράσον. Numbers 11:5 is the only place in 22 MT instances of the Hebrew חָצִיר where it is translated in the LXX by πράσον. Usually חָצִיר simply means 'grass' and the LXX translates with βοτάνη (1 Kgs 18:5, Job 8:12), χλόη (2 Kgs 19:26; Ps 95, etc.), and most commonly χόρτος (Job 40:15; Ps 37:2, etc.).[119] The significance of χόρτος and χορτάζω to the feeding miracles (Mark 6:39, 42; 8:4, 8), already noted above, may have drawn Mark to this distinctive Septuagintal *hapax*. Given the possible allusion to the story of Obadiah in 6:40,[120] the use of חָצִיר in association with Obadiah in 1 Kgs 18:5 may also have attracted Mark to this cryptic allusion. It is a tiny etymological step from πράσα (LXX Num 11:5) to πρασιά (Mark 6:40). In my view, nothing else accounts for Mark's use of πρασιά. An allusion to Num 11:5 both explains an otherwise awkward word and reinforces the evident Moses typology.

While the pattern of typology observed in previous chapters has not been used as consistently in the feeding miracles, Mark's playful use of distinctive words and expressions continues to subtly indicate his narrative allusions to scriptural miracle accounts.

§7.10 Reading Mark 6:30–44 and 8:1–10 with Elisha/Moses/Joshua Typology

It remains to discuss how recognising the scriptural allusions in Mark 6:30–45 and 8:1–10 informs our understanding of Mark's Christology.

§7.10.1 Jesus as a greater Elisha and Moses

With regards to 2 Kgs 4:42–44 Jesus performs a greater miracle than Elisha.[121] There is less food to begin with and a greater number of people are fed. After Elisha's miracle they only 'had some left' (4:44). Mark goes into detail about the huge amounts of food left over from Jesus' feedings (Mark 6:43; 8:8). Elisha implies that he is performing the miracle on the basis of a prediction from the Lord (2 Kgs 4:43). In contrast, Mark presents Jesus as the initiator of the miracles.

With regards to the manna in the desert the situation is more complicated. Numbers 11:21 describes the feeding of six hundred thousand people. Jesus thus feeds far fewer people. Yet in the Exodus story people are told not to collect the leftovers which will otherwise spoil (Exod 16:19–20). When Jesus' disciples collect the leftovers, the implication by contrast is that the food he gives will not spoil.[122] Also there were no fish

---

[119] HALOT 343–4.
[120] Discussed above, §7.3.
[121] Guelich 1989: 344; Schneck 1994: 156; Schnackenburg 1995: 31–32; Dunn 2003: 687; Fritz 2003: 256; Boring 2006: 185.
[122] Masuda 1982: 207; Marcus 2000a: 421.

provided during Israel's wilderness journey, but Jesus does provide fish, and so Jesus surpasses the miracle of the manna in that way also.[123] In Exod 16:4 the initiative for the manna is YHWH's and Moses takes no active part in the miracle's performance, he only proclaims it to the people (16:6–8). In contrast, Jesus is both the initiator and performer of the miracles. There is no mention of God during Mark's accounts of the miracles. Jesus is thus presented as being in the line of Moses and Elisha but greater than them both.

It seems likely that behind this literary typology is a real typology which sees Jesus as the eschatological fulfilment of these preceding prophetic figures. Regarding the act of feeding crowds bread in the wilderness, Feneberg states, 'Es handelt sich um eine zeichenhafte Vorwegnahme des endzeitlichen Freudenmahls in der Herrschaft Gottes'.[124] A number of features support this assertion.

In other early Christian uses of Psalm 23 there is a clear eschatological orientation to the use of the psalm (Rev 7:17; 1 Clement 26:2).[125] Additionally, Marcus notes that several Rabbinic texts interpret Psalm 23 eschatologically and messianically (*Gen. Rab.* 88.5; *Exod. Rab.* 25.7; 50.5; *Num. Rab.* 21.21).[126] This raises the strong possibility as to whether the use of Psalm 23 in Mark 6:30–45 also has eschatological connotations.

Several scriptures use the shepherd motif for a messianic figure. Ezekiel 34:23 reads, 'I will set over them one shepherd, my servant David, and he shall feed them: he shall feed them and be their shepherd'.[127] LXX Psalm 131:15 also combines the hope for a Davidic messiah with provision of food and with which Mark 6:42; 8:4 & 8 share the word, χορτάζω.[128] Micah 5:4–5 reads, 'And he shall stand and feed his flock in the strength of the LORD, in the majesty of the name of the LORD his God. And they shall live secure, for now he shall be great to the ends of the earth; and he shall be the one of peace'.[129] The Psalms of Solomon describe the coming eschatological son of David (17:21) as 'faithfully and righteously shepherding the Lord's flock, he will not let any of them stumble in their pasture'.[130]

Likewise, the presentation of Jesus as a second but greater Moses and Elisha bears implications of eschatological significance. As the greatest of all prophets Jesus is endued with significance beyond discrete miracles as the 'harbinger of the messianic age'.[131] In particular, the return of the manna was a recurrent theme in Jewish eschatological texts (2 Bar 29:8; *Mek. Exod* 16:25; *Tanḥ. Exod* 16:33 (*Beshalach Siman* 21); *Eccl. Rab* 1:9).[132] While the Rabbinic texts are too late to have influenced Mark, they demonstrate the plausibility of similar traditions existing among first-century Jews and Jewish Christians. They show the evocative power of Psalm 23 and the manna tradition within the context of eschatological messianic expectation. Jesus' production of

---

[123] Garland 1996: 255; Marcus 2000a: 419.
[124] 'It is a symbolic anticipation of the eschatological banquet in the reign of God' (Feneberg 2000: 165).
[125] Allison 1983: 132–4.
[126] Marcus 1992: 408.
[127] Hartman 2010: 248, 259; Owen 2015: 54–5; see especially discussion in Block 1998: 297–301.
[128] Collins 2007: 322–3.
[129] Note the messianic use of Micah 5:2 in Matt 2:6.
[130] Trans. R. B. Wright, OTP 2.668.
[131] Allison 1983: 135; Marcus 2000a: 419.
[132] Cranfield 1972: 222; Marcus 2000a: 410; France 2002: 262 n. 44.

miraculous bread in the wilderness would thus carry a strong eschatological significance.

Thus the use of the shepherd motif and manna traditions set the Markan feeding miracles within the context of eschatological messianic expectation. The miracles are recapitulations of former miracles by former prophets. The former prophets have been exceeded and fulfilled by their antitype, Jesus the messiah.

§7.10.2 Kirk's paradigm of messianic banquets

Kirk concludes, regarding the feeding miracle in Mark 6:30–44, that 'what is unfolding is the life-giving banquet of the true king of Israel, in contrast to the death-feast of Herod the pretender'.[133] For Kirk, the feeding miracles present Jesus as both a new David and new Moses.[134] Mark does not have in mind the 'divine shepherd' of Psalm 23 and Ezek 34:11–16 but a 'faithful human king [who] represents the divine shepherd through his tending of the flock (e.g. Ezek 34:23–24)'.[135] As argued earlier, Psalm 23 does appear to have influenced Mark 6:30–45.[136] However, the issue at stake here is not a particular background text but whether Kirk's paradigm can explain the presentation of Jesus in the feeding miracles.

Kirk returns to an argument from his discussions of Jesus' exorcisms and healings, that, 'if a human does the things that Jesus does, then Jesus's performance of such actions is no indication of ontological distinction. In Mark's Gospel, the disciples participate in the feeding'.[137] He further explains, 'Jesus does not reserve this miracle for himself as one indicating his unique divine authority or ontology, but instead extends the authority to his disciples as those capable of doing the same'.[138]

Again, however, the disciples' actions are not equivalent to Jesus'. The miracle is initiated, commanded and enacted by Jesus. The disciples only participate under Jesus' authority, not as autonomous powerful individuals. Unlike the healings and exorcisms (Mark 6:7–13), there is no point at which the disciples are empowered to multiply food when away from Jesus. Rather, the feeding miracles are something the disciples are supposed to reflect on in terms of Jesus' identity (Mark 8:17–21).

Regarding 2 Kgs 4:42–44 Kirk states, 'Jesus in the synoptic Gospels initiates the same type of miracle while amplifying its abundance to proportions befitting the eschatological advent of God's anointed'.[139] His interest is in the type of miracle and his analysis stops there. He does not pay attention to the way the narrative also diverges from the type. However, as my exegesis has shown, while the similarities are important, and indeed signal Mark's intended subtext, the differences in detail are equally important. The feeding miracles in the Gospels are indeed like the feeding miracles in Exodus and 2 Kings but which role is Jesus playing? Is he just playing the role of human

---

[133] Kirk 2016: 451.
[134] Kirk 2016: 452.
[135] Kirk 2016: 453.
[136] See also Allison 1983; Garland 1996: 255–6.
[137] Kirk 2016: 453.
[138] Kirk 2016: 454.
[139] Kirk 2016: 455–6.

prophet or does he also perform the role of YHWH? The paradigm provided by the scriptural miracle accounts reveals the profound difference between Jesus and those prophets.

§7.10.3 Jesus and the God of Israel

France writes,

> this narrative has echoes ... both of past miracles and of the future eucharistic feast ... [but] surely the primary purpose in Mark's inclusion of this story [is] the sheer wonder of an 'impossible' act, and the testimony which this provides in answer to the growing Christological question.[140]

I would argue, however, that the superlative nature of the miracle is less Christologically significant for Mark than the typological aspect.

To begin with, as already noted, feeding five thousand and four thousand hardly compares to the six hundred thousand of the Exodus narrative (Num 11:21). Yes, it is an extraordinary act of power and far surpasses Elisha (2 Kgs 4:42–44), but, as I have argued, given Mark's choice to lexically link to Numbers 11, comparison of power cannot be the primary motive.

On the other hand, consideration of the three scriptural typological *topoi* identified above generates another possible emphasis. Firstly, the shepherd motif has the potential for some ambiguity. While Moses, Joshua and David are all cast as shepherds, frequently in prophetic literature the true good shepherd of Israel is YHWH. A pertinent example of this is Ps 23:1, יהוה רעי, 'YHWH is my shepherd'. By assuming the role of shepherd and making the people lie down on the green grass and satisfying them with abundant food Jesus steps into the role of YHWH in Ps 23.

Second, the narrative that the feeding accounts most closely resemble in structure, 2 Kgs 4:42–44, twice emphasizes that the miracle is performed according to the word of YHWH using the formulas, כה אמר יהוה (4:43), and כדבר יהוה (4:44). Yet in Mark there is no such emphasis, rather the miracles are performed at the initiative and behest of Jesus (Mark 6:37–41; 8:2–6). As well as playing the role of Elisha, the prophet, Jesus also steps into the role of Israel's God.

Third, the narrative of Numbers 11, linked to by the fish and the word play on πράσον/πρασιά, and the manna miracles in general, are miracles not performed by a prophet, but by God. Again, in the accounts there is an emphasis on God's word (e.g. Exod 16:4, 11–12, 28–29; Num 11:23, 24). Not only so, but the purpose of the manna is twofold: to feed the people and to teach them that YHWH is their God (Exod 16:12).[141] When Numbers 11 is read against Mark 6:30–45 and 8:1–10, a surprising feature is that the disciples, not Jesus, take Moses' role in their complaints:

---

[140] France 2002: 263; also Stein 2008: 318–19.
[141] Collins 2007: 322.

Num 11:13 'Where am I to get meat for all these people?'	Mark 8:4 'How can we feed these people with bread here in the desert?'
Num 11:22 'Are there enough flocks and herds to slaughter for them? Are there enough fish in the sea to catch for them?'	Mark 6:37 'Are we to go and buy two hundred denarii worth of bread, and give it to them to eat?'

In comparison with Numbers 11, Jesus, in both provoking and answering the disciples' questions, and in miraculously providing the food, plays the narrative role, not of Moses, but of YHWH.

With the use of each typological *topos* there is to be found a Christological twist, whereby Jesus takes on the role, not just of the human prophets from the scriptural narratives, but also of Israel's God. I can now argue that this pattern is consistently applied across the miracle catena of Mark 4:35–6:45. By the use of literary typology and key scripturally allusive words, Mark identifies the messiah Jesus with the scriptural portrayal of Israel's Lord. In many of these instances the twist is subtle. However, the consistent pattern argues for a deliberate and significant feature for interpretation.

§7.10.4 Divine identity in the feeding miracles

Hays discusses the feeding of the five thousand in two places. In the first, he recognizes that Mark 6:34, 'they were like sheep without a shepherd', 'metaleptically evokes two key passages'. The first passage is Moses' plea to God in Num 27:17. However, after a brief discussion of how this depicts Jesus as another Joshua, successor of Moses, he then asserts, 'Mark does not develop a sustained picture of Jesus as the new Moses'.[142] He then turns to discuss Ezek 34:2–6, 23–24 and especially its promise of a davidic shepherd.[143]

In the second place, he again focuses on Ezek 34, but this time verses 11–15, particularly the promise that 'I myself [i.e. the LORD] will be the shepherd of my sheep, and I will make them lie down' (34:15). He suggests that Jesus may be symbolically declaring, 'You are my sheep, the sheep of my pasture, and I am your God' (34:31).[144] However this seems problematic, in that his earlier discussion saw the echoing of Ezekiel 34 as entailing Jesus Davidic status, now it asserts his 'divine identity'. If Ezekiel 34 is evoked by Mark's story, and Hays presents no evidence that Mark intends to evoke it, then there seems to be no reason why a reader would relate *both* divine and Davidic identities to Jesus. God's identity as shepherd is worked out in Ezekial 34 by his establishing of his 'servant David' (34:23, 24). Thus, Jesus would be God's Davidic servant with no suggestion of divinity.

There is, perplexingly, no consideration by Hays of the feeding miracles of the Jewish scriptures, even despite recognizing the evocation of Moses. He does not discuss how the Elisha or Manna stories might be behind some of the imagery, despite the fact

---

[142] Hays 2016: 49.
[143] Hays 2016: 49–50.
[144] Hays 2016: 70.

that his own criteria would show them to be stronger intertextual resonances for the Gospel episode. Instead, a text not alluded to by Mark's narrative or word choices (Ezek 34) is centred in interpretation. As with Mark 4:35–41, the impression is given that the pursuit of a divine identity for Jesus has obscured the search for 'echoes of scripture', and the rich allusions to human characters and miracles of the scriptures, made by Mark, have been missed.

§7.10.5 Jesus and the Gentile mission

The puzzle remains as to why there are two very similar feeding miracles, what their cumulative effect is intended to be and what we are to make of Jesus' conversation with the disciples in Mark 8:14–21? That dialogue presents itself as the key to understanding the significance of the feeding miracles.[145] Yet it must be acknowledged that the solution is still not obvious. Jesus' warning in Mark 8:15, 'beware the yeast of the Pharisees and the yeast of Herod', serves to keep the contrast with Herod, established in Mark 6,[146] prominent. The contrast is initially between the two banquets. Herod feeds only 'his courtiers and officers and ... the leaders of Galilee' (Mark 6:21) and his banquet ends in the death of a prophet, who figuratively becomes a part of the meal by having his head put on a plate. The Pharisees, on the other hand, had just been rebuked during a meal (7:2) with the words of Isaiah 29:13 (Mark 7:6–7). In contrast to the Pharisees and their teaching, which voids the word of God and brings people in danger of death (Mark 7:9–13), Jesus will go on to enact Isaiah 29:18–19.

> 18 On that day the deaf (κωφοί) shall hear the words of a scroll, and as for those who are in the darkness and those who are in the fog, the eyes of the blind (τυφλοί) shall see. 19 And the poor shall be glad with joy because of the Lord, and those despairing among people shall be filled (ἐμπίπλημι) with joy.
>
> LXX Isa 29:18–19, NETS

Thus the healing of the deaf man (κωφός) in Mark 7:31–37 corresponds to the deaf (κωφοί) in Isa 29:18. The healing of the blind man (τυφλός) in Mark 8:22–29 corresponds to the blind (τυφλοί) in Isa 29:18. Note also the reference to being filled (Isa 29:19, ἐμπίπλημι; cf. LXX Ps 77:29).

We thus have four meals in Mark 6–8, grouped in contrasting pairs. Herod's birthday is contrasted with the feeding of the five thousand, and the Pharisees' hand-washing controversy meal is contrasted with the feeding of the four thousand. Both Herod and the Pharisees are portrayed as those whose meals result in death (Mark 6:16, 27–29; 7:10). By contrast, then, it is implied that Jesus' meals bring life. These contrasts are then reviewed in the dialogue of Mark 8:13–21.

How, then, does the feeding of the four thousand contrast with the Markan Pharisees' traditions and hypocrisy? When the feeding of the four thousand is compared

---

[145] Boobyer 1952: 168; Salzmann 2009: 130.
[146] See §7.3 above.

with the feeding of the five thousand, two factors are distinctive. These same two factors are what Jesus highlights in his dialogue with the disciples (8:14–21). First is the numbers. Twelve baskets full (6:43; 8:19) is most likely a reference to Israel, as are the other times that the number twelve is mentioned in Mark (e.g. 3:14; 5:25, 42).[147] Thus the twelve baskets suggest 'the eschatological fullness of the people of God'.[148]

The seven baskets full, like the seven days of creation, suggest completion and fullness;[149] or 'God's vigilance over the whole earth',[150] as in the seven 'eyes of the LORD, which range through the whole earth' (Zech 4:10); or even 'der 7 noachischen Gebote'.[151] Perhaps, as seven churches represented the whole church in Asia Minor (Revelation 2–3), and seven deacons represented the Hellenist Christ-believers (Acts 6:1–7),[152] the seven baskets here suggest the whole region of the Decapolis where the feeding takes place. As with the number of days of creation, the fullness is not restricted to Israel but to all humanity.[153] Correspondingly, the four thousand people in Mark 8:9 would then represent the four winds of heaven (Zech 6:5, cf. Mark 13:27) which come from the ends of the earth.[154]

Stein, however, denies the numerological significance of the baskets, 'Mark gives no hint to his readers that the numbers … possess any symbolic significance. It is best therefore not to find any symbolic significance in them.'[155] Similarly, Gnilka states, 'Auf sehr unsicheren Boden begibt man sich bei einer symbolischen Deutung der Zahlen'.[156] Such a view is hard to account for given the dialogue of 8:14–21, but the numbers on their own, especially the seven baskets, are indeed too vague to draw any firm conclusions.[157]

The second factor is the word choice around 'baskets'. In Mark 6:43 and 8:19 κόφινος is used. In Mark 8:8 and 8:20 σπυρίς is used. Both terms refer to baskets of indeterminate size in which provisions could be carried.[158] While semantically they may appear to be interchangeable words, what is noticeable is that Mark does not treat them interchangeably but maintains the distinction between them in the feeding narratives and the later dialogue about them.[159] It seems possible that κόφινος was particularly associated with Jews, as Juvenal twice uses a Latinized form of κόφινος as a part of his caricature of Jews.[160]

---

[147] Broadhead 1992: 122; Chilton et al. 2009: 251; for a discussion and literature on the significance of the number 12 in Greek contexts, see Mayr 2008: 127–30.
[148] Marcus 2000a: 411; see also Collins 2007: 326; Salzmann 2009: 130.
[149] Mayr 2008: 120.
[150] Chilton et al. 2009: 251.
[151] Pesch 1979: 1.403.
[152] Wefal 1995: 22–3.
[153] Cf. Philo, *De Opificio Mundi*, 90.
[154] Chilton et al. 2009: 251.
[155] Stein 2008: 314, also 317.
[156] 'One goes onto very insecure ground with a symbolic interpretation of the numbers' (Gnilka 1998: 1.262).
[157] Guelich 1989: 343.
[158] For κόφινος, see BDAG, 563; LSJ, 988; GE, 1169. For σπυρίς, see BDAG, 940; LSJ, 1631; GE, 1950.
[159] Richardson 1941: 98.
[160] LSJ, 988; Wefal 1995: 18; Marcus 2000a: 413; Salzmann 2009: 132.

Even so, it is hardly clear, as the only other biblical or patristic use of either of these words outside of the feeding miracles is Acts 9:25 where Paul is let down a wall in a σπυρίς by other Jews, albeit in Damascus. That is, there are no other NT, LXX, or Apostolic texts that suggest an ethnic differentiation between κόφινος and σπυρίς should be made. LSJ, which suggests 'used especially by Jews', only gives Juvenal (cited above) and Matt 16:9 in support.[161] Indeed, Josephus' single use of κόφινος, in his description of a Roman soldier's equipment (J.W. 3:95), rather argues the opposite. Additionally, the fact that Matthew preserves the distinction between baskets despite otherwise editing away from the other possible Gentile markers in the second feeding in Mark (including changing the location) suggests that it did not have the same significance for Matthew (Matt 14:20; 15:39; 16:9, 10).[162] At best the numbers, and to a lesser extent the baskets, provide a vague hint that the second feeding is given to Gentiles and is symbolic of Gentile inclusion in the eschatological people of God.[163]

One further hint was mentioned above, following Danker and Masuda: 'three days' (Mark 8 2; cf. Jos 9:16) and 'from afar' (Mark 8:3, cf. LXX Jos 9:6, 9, 22) create a link with Josh 9 and are thus also suggestive of gentiles.[164] Mark's only use of ἥκω (8:3) may also serve to link to Josh 9:6, 9. However, such a tentative interpretation is made more secure by attention to the narrative context of the story. After Jesus' confrontation with the Pharisees he sets out to the region of Tyre (Mark 7:24). Now in Gentile territory he encounters a woman, 'a Gentile, of Syrophoenecian origin' (7:26). This introductory pleonasm is no mere hint, but sets the scene for the ensuing dialogue which is entirely about the right of the Gentiles to 'eat' the blessings of Jesus' ministry (7:28). Initially it seems uncertain as to whether Jesus will help the woman's daughter, but in response to her confident and playful responses he does, thus demonstrating that the kingdom blessings which Jesus brings are for all people. Jesus then returns to the Gentile region of the Decapolis (7:31), where he heals another presumed Gentile (in accordance with Isaiah 29:18 and 35:5–6 and probably Isa 56 as well; Mark 7:32–37). Then without any change in location he feeds the four thousand (8:1–9), before returning to Dalmutha where he once again encounters the Pharisees who demand a sign (8:10–12). Salzmann astutely writes of the woman in Mark 7:24–30, 'When she is denied his ministry, she asks for "a crumb" fallen from the table: the daughter is healed, and soon seven baskets of bread crumbs will be offered to the reader—perhaps as Jesus' ultimate answer to the faith-filled plea of the gentile woman'.[165]

The strongest indications of the Gentile identity of the crowd in 8:1–10 come from the narrative geographical markers which place the second feeding miracle in Gentile territory.[166] In contrast to the first feeding the location of the second is in the Decapolis region, on the other side of the sea, and in the wilderness. A further difference in the feeding stories is that Jesus' response to the crowd does not emerge from recognizing

---

[161] LSJ, 988.
[162] *Pace* Salzmann 2009: 133. See detailed discussion in Cousland 1999: 8–23.
[163] Cousland 1999: 4.
[164] Masuda 1982: 205; Danker 1963; also Guelich 1989: 404; *pace* Koch 1975: 109.
[165] Salzmann 2009: 131; see also Wainwright 1971: 29.
[166] Broadhead 1992: 136; Wefal 1995: 20; Feneberg 2000: 130, 140–41, 152–73; Boring 2006: 219.

them as the lost sheep of Israel (6:34) but as hungry humans.[167] Wefal also suggests the disciples' apparent reluctance to feed them results from the Gentile character of the crowd,[168] and that the number four thousand represents the four corners of the earth.[169]

Boobyer, reading the feedings in their narrative context, seems justified to conclude, 'All the nations of the earth are hungry and in need of the bread which God gives, so that although it has been thought of as pre-eminently the children's bread it must be shared with Gentiles'.[170] That is all to say that the strong implication of the narrative context is that the four thousand are to be understood as residents of the Decapolis, and Gentiles.[171] Thus the numbers and possibly baskets, which on their own are just vague hints, clearly align with the Jewish–Gentile contrast established by the narrative and geographical settings of the two feeding miracles.[172]

This narrative progression can be seen clearly by following the word χορτάζω, which served the shepherd motif. In Mark 6:42 it describes the Jewish crowd being filled. However, in Mark 7:27 Jesus tells the Syrophoenecian woman that the 'dogs' cannot eat until the 'children' have been fed, or filled, χορτάζω. The irony here, of course, is that the reader and Jesus know that the 'children' have just been filled. Hence Jesus does heal her daughter and then goes on to feed/fill the Gentiles. In 8:4 the disciples question how the crowd is to be satisfied, χορτάζω. If their question seems incongruous after the first feeding it serves Mark's purpose in showing the feeding of the Gentiles as a new problem, not solved by the feeding of the Jews, but ultimately with the same solution. So, in 8:8 the Gentile crowd are also filled, χορτάζω, by Jesus. These are the only four uses of χορτάζω in Mark. The shepherd is bringing fullness to God's people from both the Jewish and Gentile flocks.

Jesus' bread is also to be contrasted with the leaven of the Pharisees and of Herod (Mark 8:5). Herod's meal is socially exclusive. The Pharisees' meals are ritually exclusive. Jesus' meals are of a different nature altogether.[173] In the second feeding miracle, shared with the Gentiles, he confirms that his messiahship is one which will call and embrace the Gentiles into God's kingdom (cf. Isa 60:6–12; 49:6).[174]

With all the factors taken together it seems fair to conclude that meaning of the second feeding miracle was Gentile inclusion in Jesus' eschatological kingdom feast. Thus, part of what was to be understood by the term 'Christ' in Mark 8:29 was that Jesus was the messiah who would include the Gentiles in God's eschatological people.

If this is so, one might ask the question, why is Mark's Jesus not more direct in embracing Gentiles? For Salzmann, 'The answer seems to lie between, on the one hand, the historical fact that the apostles did extend their ministry to the gentiles, and, on the other hand, their initial resistance to do exactly that'.[175] An alternative reply is that Mark

---

[167] Guelich 1989: 402–3; Wefal 1995: 19; Boring 2006: 219.
[168] Wefal 1995: 19.
[169] Wefal 1995: 24.
[170] Boobyer 1952: 171; also Wefal 1995: 25.
[171] Bosenius 2014: 233.
[172] See also Boring 2006: 180.
[173] Boobyer 1952: 168.
[174] Salzmann 2009: 130.
[175] Salzmann 2009: 132.

may well have been direct for those among Mark's original readers who were able to parse correctly the meaning of the numbers, names of baskets, and intertextual and narrative clues. What is cryptic to us now may have been obvious to them.

However, by recognizing the scriptural typology within the passage this conclusion may be further reinforced. As Salzmann observes, messianic expectation, while diverse, generally anticipated a significant change in the way God's people related to the Gentiles.[176] This would either be in terms of military conquest and imperial dominion over the Gentiles (*Pss. Sol.* 17) or inclusion of them in the people of God and the covenant blessings (e.g. Isa 60:1–6). The latter hope became a significant factor in the spread of Christianity beyond its Jewish roots.[177]

More pertinent here is the Elisha typology. While in 2 Kgs 4:42–44 Elisha miraculously feeds a hundred prophets there is a later miracle when a marauding army of Arameans is blinded (2 Kgs 6:8–23). These Arameans are not slain but taken to the king of Israel. Elisha commands the king, 'Set (παρατίθημι) food and water before them so that they may eat and drink' (6:22) and the king 'prepared (παρατίθημι) for them a great feast' (6:23). It is possible that this account influenced Mark 6:41 which has Jesus give the broken loaves to his disciples to set (παρατίθημι) before the people. But the significantly shorter account of 8:1–10 uses παρατίθημι three times, the second and third times of which appear redundant. Even if we attribute the extra uses of παρατίθημι to Mark's poor editing, the Elisha typology corresponds well to a Gentile feeding as Elisha is the only scriptural prophet to have set a feast before Gentiles. Additionally, Elisha's healing of Naaman and Naaman's conversion to the Lord (2 Kgs 5:1–19) present him as a prototypical prophet of Gentile inclusion. In Mark 8:1–10 then, the Moses typology is much reduced from the earlier feeding miracle, but the Elisha typology becomes more significant. Thus recognizing the Elisha typology present in the feeding miracles strengthens the Gentile inclusion interpretation of Mark 8:1–10.

§7.11 Conclusion

In this chapter I have sought to demonstrate the significance of the scriptural background to the Markan feeding miracles. Not only does recognizing 2 Kgs 4:42–44, the shepherd motif, Numbers 11, Josh 9 and 2 Kgs 6:22–23, help explain a number of peculiarities in the text but it also sheds light on other interpretive issues, not least Gentile inclusion. Importantly, the analysis reveals two pertinent features which have also been found in the miracles of Mark 4:35–6:45. That is, rare words or phrases from the LXX are used to confirm the link to typological scriptural narratives. Those same narratives illuminate a Christological twist when read beside their Markan counterparts which consistently depict Mark's Jesus to be acting in the roles of Israel's God from the corresponding scriptural stories.

---

[176] Salzmann 2009: 130.

[177] It is perhaps worth noting that Moses' marriage to an Ethiopian (Num 12:1) was considered a type of the Gentile 'in-grafting' (cf. Rom 11:17) to God's people in the early church (Iren. *Haer.* IV.20.12; Origen *Hom. Num.* 6.4.2; *Hom. Song.* 1.6). On this see Shuve 2012: 85–6; Westerholm and Westerholm 2016: 57.

§8

Mark's typological christology

Again, behold Jesus, not son of man, but son of God, by type and in flesh revealed.[1]

In this final chapter I will summarize the results of the preceding exegetical chapters, summarise my conclusions regarding previous approaches to divinity in the Markan miracles, and then present my own constructive analysis of Mark's typological presentation of Christ's divinity.

§8.1 Summary of results

§8.1.1 Jesus as typological fulfilment of human agents of salvation history

In each Markan miracle narrative considered I have argued that Jesus is typologically figured after the pattern of a significant character from the scriptures: in Mark 4:35–41 Jesus played the part of Jonah; in Mark 5:1–20 Jesus played the part of David; in Mark 5:21–43 Jesus played the part of Elisha; and in Mark 6:30–44 and 8:1–10 Jesus played the part of Moses and of Elisha.

By presenting Jesus as a new Jonah, David, Elisha or Moses, Mark enlists scriptural authority for Jesus. Jesus is like these scriptural figures and should be accorded the respect due to them. Further, by aligning Jesus with these scriptural characters Mark provides an implicit commentary on who Jesus is and what he means. The recent events of Jesus' ministry and death and the community's experience of his resurrection require interpretation. The natural framework by which Jesus should be interpreted is the Jewish scriptures, and Mark does this via typology. Perhaps most importantly, Mark demonstrates his concern to show Jesus in continuity with the scriptural past. He presents Jesus as a continuation of God's work begun in earlier times. As one like Jonah, David, Elisha and Moses, he is an agent of God as they were. He is performing momentous and significant deeds as did. His life will give identity, inspiration and instruction to God's people, just as they did.

However, I have also argued that in each miracle Mark has been concerned to show Jesus as one greater than those scriptural characters. If Jesus is the one who 'fulfils the time' then there is a need for Jesus' deeds to surpass those of his predecessors. This is no

---

[1] Barn 12:10, author's translation

easy task for Mark. Jesus has not physically delivered an entire people group from slavery and led them across a desert like Moses. Jesus has not become a popular and militarily successful king like David. Jesus has not brought an entire city to repentance like Jonah. Jesus has not decisively dealt with foreign invaders like Elisha.

Because Mark's Jesus cannot compete with the scale of the scriptural miracles, Mark uses his scriptural typology to show how Jesus is greater in other ways. So, Jesus is greater than Jonah because he calms the storm himself. Jesus is greater than David because he casts out many evil spirits, not just one, and then destroys them, never to return. Jesus is greater than Elisha because the hem of his garment heals when Elisha's staff failed to do so. Jesus is greater than Elisha because Jesus heals on his own word, while Elisha has to pray. Jesus is also greater than Elisha because he feeds more people (though less than Moses did), but he is greater than Moses because he can give fish in the wilderness as well as bread, and to both Jew and Gentile.

Placing analogous narrative figures in simultaneous comparison and contrast is a key function of typology. By calling to mind specific stories from the Jewish scriptures for his readers, Mark alerts them to the comparisons he wishes to draw. For Mark, Jesus is both the continuation and culmination of God's work in salvation history. Although the coming kingdom appears to have small beginnings – that is, the limited scale of Jesus' ministry and miracles – it will in fact prove to be the greatest of all God's works (cf. Mark 4:30–32).

§8.1.2 Jesus as typologically theomorphic

There is a further implication of the way that Mark portrays Jesus as greater than the scriptural heroes. In addition to portraying Jesus according to the pattern of human agents of God, Jesus also appears to take on the narrative role of God. This is most apparent in Mark 4:35–41 where Jesus and not God calms the storm. The obviously divine role played by Jesus in Mark 4:35–41 primes the reader for more subtle implications in the following miracles. In Mark 5:1–20 Jesus assumes the authority that the divine name played in David's encounter with Goliath. In Mark 5:21–43 it is Jesus' lack of prayer in contrast to Elisha which implies that he is himself the source of healing power. In Mark 6:30–45 and 8:1–10 it is both that the miracle is performed according to Jesus' word, not God's as in 2 Kgs 4:42–44 and Exodus 16, and that the disciples' dialogue places them in relation to Jesus as Moses was in relation to God. The sequence of superlative miracles is completed by Jesus walking on the water in 6:45–52, another more direct evocation of divinity, alluding to Job 9, and the counterpart to the storm stilling which began the sequence. In all the Gospel miracles, neither prayer nor divine intervention are the narrated source of power but rather it is Jesus. Likewise, in the miracles where supplication is present it is from others to Jesus, in place of God.

Perhaps it could be argued that such subtle implications are simply an unintended consequence of Mark's escalated typological figuring of Jesus. It is subtle. However, a couple of points mitigate against this being an unintended by-product of different concerns. First, we have to reckon with the observable tendency in early Jewish writing to protect the agency of God against the impression that human technique or influence was responsible for a miracle.[2] Rabbinic miracles, for example, are consistently and explicitly the result of prayer rather than allowing any suggestion the source of power could be the rabbi himself.[3] Against such a background it seems unlikely that a Jewish author would unintentionally write narratives that give the opposite suggestion: that Jesus is the source of power and that God is not invoked or petitioned in the performance of any of his miracles. The most likely explanation is that Mark intended to give this effect because it reflected his convictions about Jesus.

The second consideration is how this narrative identification of Jesus with the God of Israel can be observed throughout the Gospel, displaying a similar level of subtlety throughout. The same indentification with God that we observed in the structural and Christological highpoints of the Gospel in §3 has again been present throughout these miracles. The consistency of the pattern suggests intention, its subtlety suggests nuance or ambiguity. The most likely conclusion is that Mark intends his readers to perceive something profound about Jesus' relationship to God and something beyond simply being another, or even the superlative, agent of God, in a line of similar agents. This conclusion will require further discussion before this study is complete.

§8.1.3 Jesus' prototypical Gentile mission

Alongside of the fulfilment and theomorphic typologies, a third theme has been consistently present, albeit to varying degrees. Jesus' identification with Jonah in Mark 4:35–41 creates an expectation that he is heading into Gentile territory. While there is some controversy in the literature as to whether or not the Gerasene demoniac would have been a Jew or a Gentile, this question is not directly germane to the literary use to which Mark puts him. Figured as a Philistine and narrated as a citizen of the Decapolis, the demoniac becomes the beachhead for Jesus' proclamation outside of the border of Galilee and Judea and the ethno-religious boundary of Judaism.

The David typology in Mark 5:1–20 raises the question of Jesus' relation to the Gentiles. David was a conqueror of the nations, but also a diplomat – his reign was remembered as bringing peace (2 Sam 10:19; 1 Chron 19:19; 22:18; 23:25). So, when Jesus is figured as David the question emerges, what will Jesus' relationship be to the nations? Messianic expectation was highly varied but in general a common core was the expectation the messiah would destroy Israel's enemies, the Gentile nations (Pss. Sol. 17:21–25; 4QpIsa^a [4Q161] 8–10.3.11–24; 4 Ezra 12:31–34; 2 Bar 72:1–6).[4] Mark's

---

[2] This case is made at length by Zakovich 1990. One example, given on pp. 90–1 is that of Exod 14:31 where Moses, along with the God of Israel, is a recipient of faith because of the crossing of the Red Sea miracle. However, in subsequent scriptural reflections God alone is accredited for the miracle (Exod 15:1; 10; 12; Josh 2:10; 4:23; Neh 9:11. Ps 66:5–6; 114:1–3; 78:13; 106:9–11; 136:13–15).
[3] Note, for example, how in the cases of Onias/Honi (Josephus, *Ant.* 14 2.1 (21); *m. Ta'an.* 3:8) and Gamaliel (*b. B. Meṣi'a* 59b) the rabbis are explicitly depicted as praying and the miracle is God's. The rabbis' achievement is to have such piety that God listens to them, but they do not have power in themselves.
[4] Collins 2010: 52–78. At the same time this view was complicated by the hope that Gentiles would come to worship the God of Israel (e.g. Isa 2:2–3; 45:6) and share in Israel's salvation (e.g. Tob 14:6–7; 1 Enoch 90:30–33). See further Sanders 1987: 213–18; Schnabel 1994: 41.

Jesus, however, does not set himself up in opposition to the Gentiles. He is opposed to the Pharisees, scribes and Herodians and, in the testing in the wilderness and his exorcisms, to the house of Satan (Mark 3:20–30). Through the typology of the account of the Gerasene demoniac, the messiah's destruction of the enemies of Israel is transposed from a war against human, gentile enemies, into a war against spiritual, demonic enemies.

In the *Sitz im Leben* of Mark's Gospel the Gentile question doubtlessly remains a significant one. The letters of Paul, especially Galatians and Romans, show that Gentile inclusion was a controversial issue in the early Church.[5] Mark portrays a Jesus who was inclusive of Gentiles but his typology also connects that inclusivity with God's actions in the past. And so, the stories of Elisha interacting with Gentiles are brought to mind. But to make his point further, the second feeding miracle – this time of a crowd from the Decapolis – evokes both Elisha and the Arameans (2 Kgs 6:8–23) and Joshua and the Gibeonites (Joshua 9). Mark presents Jesus' mission to the Gentiles as *typological fulfilment* of Jonah, David and Elisha, but also as the *prototype* for the early church's own missionary activity among the nations.

§8.1.4 The Function of typology in the Gospel of Mark

This study has argued that a *literary typology* is at work in the Markan miracles of 4:35–6:45 (and 8:1–10). This typology is extensive, relating whole narratives to whole narratives. It is a typology which employs narrative motifs, lexical borrowing and thematic inversions. Despite this manifold use of correspondences, it is a subtle and cryptic typology, frequently missed by interpreters. Mark's use of distinctive phrases and unique words from the LXX reveal an intimate acquaintance with the scriptures, quite probably in both Hebrew and Greek and with attention to unusual and distinctive wording. These correspondences between Gospel miracles and scripture miracles, when examined together, suggest not coincidence but deliberate authorial allusions which convey significant meaning. The fact that they are *meaningful* further strengthens the probability that they are intentional.

Analysis shows that this literary feature is indicative of three different *real* typologies. That is, typologies where there is a genuine, real world and not just literary, connection between the two figures of the typology in the mind of the author. *Fulfilment typology* relates Jesus to characters and events of salvation history as their continuation and culmination. *Theomorphic typology* reveals a divine Jesus who acts in the narrative role of the God of the Jewish scirptures. *Exemplary typology* portrays Jesus as the prototype that the Church will imitate in its own Gentile mission. Typology is thus vital to Mark's Christological presentation and is a channel for Mark's hermeneutical, theological and ethical convictions. Typology functions for Mark as a means of conveying traditions about Jesus, as one way to interpret scripture, as one way to convey the significance and identity of Jesus, and as one way to influence and form the Gospel's reading/listening community.

---

[5] Cf. Schnabel 1994: 41–3.

Fulfilment and exemplary typologies are not in themselves controversial, even if not all readers will be convinced by my presentation. However, theomorphic typology brings us directly into the early high Christology debate. Hence, the recognition of a thoroughgoing theomorphic typology now requires further discussion. Mark's portrayal of Jesus as in *some sense* divine is a key issue in present-day debates about early Christology. In what way might this study of Markan typology inform these discussions? I will seek to apply the foregoing exegesis to answer this question: first with critical reference to the idealized human figure, divine identity and pre-existence approaches to Jesus' divinity; then I will outline what can be said constructively about Christ's divinity from the perspective of scriptural typology in the miracles of Mark 4:35–6:45.

§8.2 Regarding previous approaches to divinity in Mark's miracles

§8.2.1 Mark's Jesus does not fit the paradigm of exalted human figure

Daniel Kirk writes, 'the Gospels offer a unique combination of various abilities in one person, as well as a unique focus on such powers'.[6] If Mark's presentation of Jesus is unique against the background of figures in early Jewish literature, and I would agree that it is, then the validity of applying 'paradigms' based on prior literature is undermined.[7] Its very uniqueness precludes the ability to be neatly categorized in pre-existing paradigms.

Kirk's classification of Mark's Jesus within an early Jewish paradigm of exalted human figures has not been upheld by the foregoing typological exegesis of the miracles. Indeed, Mark does want to associate Jesus with particular human figures. However, this is not as a class or paradigm, but in terms of the typological resemblance of corresponding moments in scriptural story to Jesus' own story. A paradigm such as Kirk's does not help us get closer to Mark's intent, but may well obscure the actual Christological point intended because the paradigmatic method requires thinking in terms of generalities not specifics. Mark's deliberate typologies, by contrast, are richer and more productive because they focus a particular narrative for comparison, not all narratives of a certain (scholar-contructed) category.

While Jesus may do the kinds of things that had been done in the past by human figures, the detail of the narratives, especially when compared to the texts that Mark specifically alludes to, reveal how Jesus also diverges from the pattern in ways that take him far beyond his human precursors. Mark's scriptural typology, while it specifically relates Jesus to human prototypes, also distinguishes Jesus from them in profound ways.

---

[6] Kirk 2016: 487.
[7] In case the obvious needs to be stated: drawing on *parallels* in selected contextually relevant texts is not the same as constructing a *paradigm* from an entire (and impressively diverse) body of literature. Of course early Jewish texts are valuable for early Christology; that is not in question. The question is one of appropriate method.

§8.2.2 Mark's Jesus does not fit the category of divine identity

The typological exegesis of my earlier chapters reveals that Jesus' power, actions and relations strongly resemble those of God in the Jewish scriptures. Bauckham's divide requires that a divine Jesus be understood as included in the identity of God as creator. However, within Mark's Gospel, Jesus' evident humanity and subordination to God define him as a creature.[8] Within the conceptual framework of divine identity, Jesus must be identified as being solely on the creature side of Bauckham's line. Mark's Jesus both meets the criteria for a creature and fails to satisfy Bauckham's criteria for being divine. Nothing occurs in the miracle accounts that contradicts this conclusion. If Mark is understood to be working within a framework of divine identity, then Mark's Jesus is not divine.

Furthermore, the category of divine identity appears to work to obscure Mark's intended scriptural referent, even for Hays' work with a specifically scriptural intertextual focus. By focusing on possible signs of divine identity (specifically in Mark 4:35–41 and 6:30–44), it appears an exegete can miss stronger scriptural allusions present in the text. Further, the focus on creational-sovereignty may cause the exegete to miss the Christological significance of a moment like the transfiguration which evokes Sinai, not creation. For Hays, for example, this is solely a 'prefiguration of Jesus' heavenly glory' and does not warrant discussion as evoking scripture, despite the appearance of Elijah and Moses in the episode.[9]

For Bauckham it is Jesus' role in the creation of all things (1 Cor 8:6) which confirms his participation in the divine identity. He writes, 'This is what defines him as the one and only true God, distinguished from all other reality, which was created by him and is subject to his rule. There are only God and all things. This is a binary distinction that allows for no ambiguous semi-divine beings.'[10] Paula Fredriksen considers this an anachronistic projection of *creatio ex nihilo* onto the Pauline text, and that no such distinction between the creator and all things existed in Paul's lifetime.[11] Whether or not that is the case, the pre-cosmic existence of Jesus and his role in creation are simply not on the horizon of Mark's Gospel.

As April DeConick has forcefully argued, easy association of the universal transcendent God of Greek philosophy with the God of Israel should not be assumed for New Testament authors.[12] While Bauckham's category is something of a 'philosophical taxonomy',[13] or even 'a free-floating set of categories concerning God's relation to all existence',[14] Mark's narrative typology does not seek to relate Jesus to such abstractions, but rather to miraculous storied moments in scriptural history. Bauckham's divine identity criteria, rightly or wrongly, serves to identify Jesus with the universal *pre*-cosmic creator. Mark's typology identifies Jesus with the God of Israel and his actions *in* the cosmos.

---

[8] See also Hays 2016: 77–8.
[9] Hays 2016: 62.
[10] Bauckham 2020: 146.
[11] Fredriksen 2020: 309.
[12] DeConick 2020: 264.
[13] Novenson 2020: 5.
[14] Tilling 2015: 61.

A further reason Bauckham argues that Mark's miracles reveal divine identity is their display of inherent transcendent power.[15] I would agree that Jesus' power appears inherent rather than attained. Jesus in Mark is never *given* authority over sin, the Sabbath, or creation. Mark simply portrays this authority as inherent to Jesus. While Jesus receives the Spirit in Mark 1:10, the words from heaven (1:11) only mention being pleased with Jesus, not imparting any authority to him (compare Mark 6:7). The consistent pattern noted in the miracles, is that Jesus does not invoke God or pray, but is instead invoked and petitioned, and that Jesus is the source of power in each situation. This suggests that Jesus' power is qualitatively different from those who receive their power from God. To put it in certain terminology, Jesus acts in God's own role as a 'bearer of numinous power'.[16] Nevertheless, it does not necessitate a divine identity. Even if Jesus' numinous power did not derive from God at all, bearing such power does not satisfy the criteria of either absolute sovereignty or responsibility for creation.

Finally, creational-sovereignty for Jesus is only logically possible along with preexistence. Without pre-existence Mark's Jesus cannot have performed a role in the creation of all things.

§8.2.3 Pre-existent christology in Mark's miracle accounts

Allthough divine identity requires pre-existence for Jesus to have been involved with creation, pre-existence is separate from and does not necessitate divine identity. Simon Gathercole and Mike Bird have argued that implicit in Mark's presentation of Jesus is his pre-existence as a divine entity prior to his incarnation as Jesus of Nazareth.[17] Pertinent to this study is the way the evidence of the miracles has been brought to bear on this discussion and whether the typological approach strengthens one side of the debate or another? Gathercole, for example, argues that the sea miracles show Jesus 'acting *as* God himself' rather than 'as one uniquely endowed by God in a *representative* function'.[18] On the one hand, the discovery of scriptural narrative typology at work in the sea miracles certainly confirms that Jesus is portrayed by the narrative acting *as* God in those situations. On the other hand, acting as God in a situation does not require that Jesus had always been divine, but only that at some point divine prerogatives had been granted to him.

In addition, Gathercole appears to assume that there would be some observable difference between Jesus acting as God or only being a uniquely endowed representative. In Mark, Jesus' power goes beyond that of the human scriptural figures of the past. But if God can do something, then God is also able to grant a person equal ability whether temporarily or permanently, just as any human sovereign could delegate their authority to others. Mark's Jesus fails to invoke or acknowledge God in any of his miracles (except perhaps 7:34 where he looks to heaven in the healing of the deaf man) which might imply Jesus' power is independent of God's.[19] Yet, Jesus' dependence upon God is seen

---

[15] Bauckham 2008: 265 n. 41.
[16] Eve 2002: 386; Grindheim 2011: 42.
[17] Gathercole 2006; Bird 2017.
[18] Gathercole, 2006: 61, emphasis original.
[19] Grindheim 2011: 41–3.

in his reception of the Spirit (1:10; cf. 3:29) and his prayer (1:35; 6:46). It cannot be argued that, in Mark, Jesus' power is independent of or in addition to God's power. Rather, his power is an extension of God's power. Thus, the data from the Markan miracles are ambiguous in respect of Jesus' pre-existence. Jesus' inherent power raises the question of origin, but it is not one addressed by Mark's miracle accounts.

§8.2.4 Typology and pre-existence

Typology, however, may provide an alternative way to think about Jesus' pre-existence. Hengel writes, 'the problem of "pre-existence" necessarily grew out of the combination of Jewish ideas of history, time and creation with the certainty that God had disclosed himself fully in his Messiah Jesus of Nazareth'.[20] These Jewish ideas of history, time and creation find one form of expression in what I have termed typology. Because early Christians saw Jesus as the fulfilment of scriptural history, he could be understood to be in some sense already present in those characters and events which typologically prefigured him. This tendency is explicit in 1 Cor 10:4, where a Jewish tradition concerning the Exodus (LAB 10:7; 11:15) becomes a tradition about *Christ's* presence in the Exodus. Arguably, 1 Cor 10:9; John 12:41; Matt 23:37; and Jude 5, all show a similar tendency.[21] In the NT early Christians transferred the significance and meaning of the saving events of Israel's history to Jesus and his work.[22]

Once Jesus is understood in this way, his life, death and resurrection become the necessary prerequisite for the stories of the scriptures. For the Christian typologist, it is Jesus Christ who gave shape to the story, characters and message of the Jewish scriptures. This influence of Christ could of course be eschatological: the influence of the coming future drawing the past and present towards itself. Combined with belief in God's foreknowledge (an assumption of Jewish prophecy, e.g. Isa 48:3), such an eschatological influence would also require a prior ideal existence; that is, existence as an idea, in the mind of God.

An ideal existence in God's mind could be represented figuratively as a real presence in heaven, which could easily then be understood literally by a reader.[23] Such an ideal existence may well be implied for the son of man in 1 Enoch 48 who is given a name before time (48:2). Before the creation of the sun, moon, stars or earth (48:3, 6), he was the 'chosen one' and was concealed in God's presence (48:6). The hiddenness of the Enochic son of man probably implies an ideal existence only, but could easily be read as a real pre-existence; that is, substantial and actual, in heaven.[24] The messiah figure/s of 4 Ezra 11–13 also imply some form of pre-existence: for the lion, 'this is the Messiah whom the Most High has kept until the end of days' (12:32) and for the figure of a man, 'this is he whom the Most High has been keeping for many ages' (13:26).[25]

---

[20] Hengel 1976: 72.
[21] See further, Gathercole 2006: 210–21; Gathercole 2005: 40–1.
[22] Gathercole 2005: 40–1; Hengel 1976: 68.
[23] Hengel 1976: 69.
[24] Collins 1992: 455.
[25] Collins 1992: 464.

Similarly, in a later Jewish text (*Pesiq. Rab.* 36.1) Satan requests to see the messiah, identified with the light of Gen 1:4, who is hidden under God's throne.[26] When Satan sees the messiah he sees his own forthcoming judgement and annihilation. Here, there is a connection between eschatology (Satan's judgement), a liminal existence in heaven (hidden under God's throne), and creation (Gen 1:4). Although the messiah's existence is 'contemplated' by God and therefore ideal, he is nonetheless seen by both God and Satan, and later converses with God concerning his coming suffering. The *Pesiqta Rabbati* is centuries older than Mark (550–650 CE), but serves as an illustration of how the division between real and ideal existence is easily blurred.

Some rabbis also read the messiah into the creation story via the hovering of the spirit of God in Gen 1:2 and Isa 11:2, 'the Spirit of the Lord will rest upon him' (*Pesiq. Rab.* 33.6).[27] The eschatological promise of the Spirit's rest in Isa 11:2 required that the Spirit's rest in Gen 1:2 implied the presence of the messiah. This is 'the proof that the king Messiah existed from before the creation of the world' (*Pesiq. Rab.* 33.6).[28] Likewise, in *Genesis Rabbah* 1.4 the messiah was 'decided to be created' (citing Ps 93:2), and at creation 'the name of the messiah was' (citing Ps 72:17). And in *Gen. Rab.* 1:6 the 'light' of creation is the messiah (citing Isa 60:1). We can see in those texts how eschatological belief in a messiah motivated a creational complement. The beginning was made to reflect the end. In ancient Jewish contexts, belief in an eschatological messiah could result in speculation towards that messiah's pre-existence. Early Christian speculation about Jesus' pre-existence could follow the same lines.

Gathercole objects to the category of ideal pre-existence, because, he argues, it would extend to everything that ever was, is, or will be, because of God's omniscience.[29] This objection fails on two counts. First, ideal pre-existence of the messiah is clearly present in Jewish writing, as discussed above, and is a concept distinct from God's general omniscience. Secondly, even if a classical definition of omniscience is appropriate here, the eggs on toast I had for breakfast this morning may preveniently exist in God's mind without there being any need for it to be discussed by or visually represented to any Jewish sage or angel who visited God's throne in heaven or had a vision. In contrast, the eschatological importance of the messiah would make him essential viewing for a heavenly being or enraptured prophet who wanted to know about the end times.

Chris Tilling argues that pre-existence is not a 'first principle' that organizes the New Testament but is instead 'logically derivative' from Christ's transcendence.[30] In doing so he echoes Hengel's earlier argument that there was an 'inner necessity' to the development of pre-existence Christology.[31] Markan typology confirms this logical progression. If Jesus is the antitype of the scriptural miracle workers then in some way his reality influenced those pre-figuring types. This could be conceptualized as taking

---

[26] Hengel 1976: 71.
[27] Hengel 1976: 70.
[28] Nemoy 1968: 2.642.
[29] Gathercole 2006: 287.
[30] Tilling 2014: 121.
[31] Hengel 1976: 71.

place either on the horizontal plane, eschatologically or on the vertical plane, as the ideal or real heavenly existence of the messiah from before creation. By anachronizing narrative in order to say 'this is that', as typology does, chronology ceases to be absolute. We see Moses and Elijah – prophets long gone – talking on the mountain with Jesus (Mark 9:2-7). When we read the Jewish scriptures through Mark's eyes we 'see' Jesus – who is yet to come – calming storms, walking on the water, delivering from evil spirits, healing the sick and raising the dead, and sharing bread in the wilderness.

A typological mind-set logically necessitates either Jesus' pre-existence in some form, or at least a view of reality where time is not unidirectional but in which the future can in some sense influence the past. Pre-existence is neither the goal nor the motivation for Mark's typology. But, once Jesus is established as the fulfilment of scripture, typology in some sense implies his pre-existence, whether real or ideal. It is ambiguous as to whether or not the author of Mark had arrived at this conclusion. The most we can say is that Mark's use of scriptural typology supports the development of pre-existence Christology, even though the Gospel itself is silent on the matter. That said, there is still a further (large) step to make from being pre-existent to being co-creator of the cosmos, but speculating on that is beyond the bounds of this study.

§8.3 Mark's typological portrayal of Jesus' divinity

§8.3.1 How does typology portray divinity?

The early high Christology debate presents us with several possibilities as to how Mark could have chosen to depict Jesus' divinity.

1. Mark might have chosen to depict Jesus' divinity in terms of creational sovereignty, including Jesus within what Bauckham terms divine identity. However, Mark does not do so within the miracles or the wider Gospel.
2. Mark might have chosen to depict Jesus as pre-existing in some form of divinity, as logos, hyspostasis or angel. But Mark does not.
3. Mark might have chosen to depict Jesus' divinity in terms of ontological change, the human, mortal and earthly body being transformed into a divine, immortal, celestial one, or even vice versa. The only possible evidence of this is in Mark 9:2; however, the lack of commentary means this event is frustratingly vague in terms of ontological significance, even as it effectively evokes an important scriptural narrative.
4. Mark might have depicted Jesus receiving cultic worship.[32] Although he does receive prostration and supplication (e.g. Mark 4:38; 5:6, 22–23, 33), he does not receive anything in the category of cultic worship. This is congruous with the respect shown to a high-status human (e.g. ironically, Mark 15:19).

---

[32] On this, Hurtado 2003.

Whether or not those things were already present in the Christ-believing communities of the first century CE, we must respect the fact that Mark does not advocate or assume any of those things in his Gospel portrayal. In what sense, then, can we describe Mark's Jesus as divine?

Mark's depiction of Jesus' divinity is via narrative typology. It is consequently reliant on allusion, and so it is implicit and not explicit. A further consequence is that it is reliant on interpretation, and so it is not direct, precise and propositional but is indirect, evocative and ambiguous. From Mark's point of view, typology is the perfect vehicle to convey a divine Christology which will be opaque to those outside the kingdom and available only to those who are part of the mystically empowered interpretive community (ὑμῖν τὸ μυστήριον δέδοται τῆς βασιλείας τοῦ θεοῦ, 4:11). Mark's Christology is then always and only for those with 'ears to hear' (4:9) and who know 'the scriptures' and 'the power of God' (12:24).

That said, the most direct Christological moment is perhaps Mark 6:45–52 when Jesus walks on the sea in allusion to Job 9, which Hays terms 'the signature image of Markan Christology'.[33] However, within the structure of the Gospel, we must recognize that this miracle is not as key Christologically as Jesus' baptism, transfiguration and passion; neither is it referred to again or its distinctive terminology repeated.[34] If this is the main point at which Jesus' divinity is revealed, then that divinity has only a marginal role in Mark's overall Christology.

A second direct moment, however, is that of the transfiguration in 9:2–8. Here, rather than an allusion to the *Chaoskampf* creation myth, Jesus is typologically figured as YHWH of the Exodus meeting his prophets, Moses and Elijah, on the mountain. It is this image, structurally central to the Gospel, the hinge around which its narrative turns, which affirms the identification of Jesus as the coming Lord of Isaiah's new exodus (Mark 1:2–3) and as Jerusalem's judge looking in vain for the fruit of righteousness (Mark 11:12–24). This same identification with YHWH then makes sense of theomorphic typology displayed in the epiphanic miracles of 4:35–6:52. Mark's identifcation of Jesus with YHWH is not with the universal creator, according to a philosophical binary, but with the God of Israel at work in miraculous power, judgement and salvation, according to the history of God's people written in the scriptures. We have here, then, a manner of 'divine identity' distinct from that proposed by Bauckham, although not necessarily in conflict with it.

However, if we examine this as an instance of typology in the tradition of Jewish scriptural typology we must acknowledge something novel, not in typological method, but in the use to which that method is put. In all the examples of typological exegesis we examined in Chapter 2, typology always served to assimilate people and events to other people and events. The one possible exception is 1 Cor 10:9, where Paul may assert that the Israelites put Christ to the test.[35] However, this is not an assimilation of the human Jesus to YHWH, but an insertion of Paul's (pre-existent/risen?) Christ into the Exodus

---

[33] Hays 2016: 72.
[34] It may also be significant that it is not a YHWH text, but refers simply to God (אֱלוֹהַּ ,אֵל, Job 9:2; 9:13).
[35] This is of course only one possible rendering as the clause καθώς τινες αὐτῶν ἐπείρασαν lacks an object and θεός (cf. 1 Cor 10:5) may be implied.

narrative. In literary terms, this is the opposite direction of travel to Markan typology. In Christological terms, though, it is far closer. That said, Paul's repeated, strongest and most developed typological relationship is between Adam and Christ (see §2.4). To my knowledge, the tradition of Jewish typology did not assimilate *humans* to YHWH.

Yes, humans could be portrayed as becoming divine through ontological bodily change,[36] but this is not typology but transformation of substance. The identity of the human remained, whether Enoch or Moses, for example, and they take on divine aspects such as radiance, but they are in no way confused with YHWH in this process. However high they ascend, the distinction of identity remains. What is apparently novel about Mark's approach is that he typologically assimilates the human Jesus to YHWH and in doing so identifies Jesus with YHWH to a far greater extent than could be achieved through accounts of celestial transformation. Celestial transformation could only turn a human Jesus into an exalted figure. Theomorphic typology reveals Mark's belief that Jesus can and should be identified with YHWH long before his promised exaltation takes place.

§8.3.2 The divinity of Mark's human Christ

France argues that one fundamental difference between Christian and Jewish exegesis was the belief that scripture had been fulfilled in the recent past, i.e. the life, death and resurrection of Jesus, and not only the distant past or coming future.[37] Likewise, it is one thing to speculate about the heavenly journeys of Moses or Enoch and quite another to do so about the fate of a near-contemporary doctrinally controversial figure who died a shameful death at the hands of the Romans. Moreover, in Markan typology, Jesus' assimilation to God does not wait for a heavenly journey or a post-mortem exaltation. In his earthly human life, we are shown Jesus already acting as if divine.

As if he were the creator God, Jesus commands the wind and waves and they obey him (Mark 4:35–41). As if he were Israel's Lord, Jesus is shown to be the one in whose name the armies of Satan are challenged, and they are defeated (Mark 5:1–20). As if he were God, Jesus heals in his own power and without prayer (Mark 5:21–43). As if he were Israel's Lord, Jesus feeds Israel and the Gentiles with miracle bread in the wilderness (Mark 6:30–45; 8:1–10). As if he were YHWH, Jesus walks upon the sea as if walking on dry land (Mark 6:45–52). Yet, apart from the brief moment of possible ontological change in Mark 9:2, *Mark's Jesus is portrayed as ontologically human throughout.*

Patrick Counet observes:

> Still there is a clear difference between, on the one hand, the categories of beings that were deified [in Second Temple Judaism], and on the other hand, Jesus of Nazareth. The deified and glorified beings from early Judaism are beings in which God is so explicitly present that their own identity falls away. They represent God *not as* individual persons, but in their professional or mythical appearance ... The

---

[36] As discussed in §3.2.3.
[37] France 1981: 123–4.

venerators do not see this or that high-priest nor that prophet, they see God represented in them ... [Jesus of Nazareth], he remains ... a man with a human face and a personal history ... The authors of the New Testament have never spirited off Jesus' humanity.[38]

Unfortunately, Counet's essay is rather cursory and does not really establish his conclusions. However, Sellin comes to a similar conclusion in his study of Philo's Logos:

> Fast alle neutestamentlichen christologischen Entwürfe aber gehen in zwei Punkten über die Logos-Konzeption Philos hinaus: 1. durch ihre Konzentration auf eine historische Person – wobei das Ereignis der Logos-Offenbarung als solches gar nicht oder nur noch in abgeleiteter Form wiederholbar wird – und 2. durch den Aspekt des Leidens und Sterbens (neben der Passionsgeschichte in Mk vor allem in Hebr 5,1–10 und Phil 2,6 ff). Beide Unterschiede lassen sich konfundieren in dem einen: Der philonische Logos-Mensch, der ἄνθρωπος θεοῦ ist – jedenfalls im Zustand seiner Logos-Existenz – kein Mensch mehr. Christus aber ist gerade als Mensch das Antlitz Gottes.[39]

To Sellin's first point, the divinity of Mark's Jesus does not provide a model that other pious humans could follow. He is unique in power and authority which is inherent to him and not attained. By contrast the disciples' acts of power are derivative from Jesus' authority (Mark 6:7).

To Sellin's second point, the role of the epiphanic miracles in the Gospel is to determine Jesus' messianic identity (8:29) prior to the subsequent explication of the messianic mission of suffering, rejection, death and resurrection (8:31). The sufferings of the messiah are essential to his mission, but the divinity of the messiah is essential to his identity, so that the reader will know *who* this human is that walks the way of the cross to Jerusalem.

I would argue, then, that it is not so much Jesus' divinity that defies convention, but his assimilation to God while remaining, in terms of ontology, human. Typological exegesis has exposed in Mark's miracle narratives the feature of NT Christology indicated by Counet and Sellin: in Jesus' particular and historical human life and actions he personifies God. That is, without ontological change from human to divine, he nonetheless appears as Israel's God – not simply as God's agent. He does not simply function as God in the miracles, but this is the identity he takes all the way to the cross.

---

[38] Counet 2009: 51–2.
[39] 'Almost all New Testament Christological frameworks, however, go beyond Philo's conception of Logos in two ways: 1. Through concentration on a single historical person – whereby the event of the Logos revelation as such does not become repeatable at all or only in a derivative form – and 2. through the aspect of suffering and dying (especially in Hebrews 5:1–10 and Phil 2:6ff, in addition to the Passion story in Mark). Both differences consist in one thing: Philo's Logos-man, the ἄνθρωπος θεοῦ is – at least in the state of his Logos existence – no longer a human being. But Christ, precisely as a human being, is the face of God' (Sellin 1992: 36).

§8.3.3 Mark's divine Jesus and Jewish monotheism

In my view, the best solution that has been offered as to how Jesus could be so identified with the God of Israel without compromising the Jewish idea of their God's uniqueness is to see Jesus as God's authorized representative, a mediator between the divine and human, who brings God's rule, authority and power to earth while God continues to reign over heaven and earth from heaven. What makes Jesus different from an ideal king, such as David, is that his rule on behalf of God and his representation of God is eschatological, universal and eternal, rather than historical, partial and temporary.

This idea is brought out by Marcus in his study on the *Shema* in Mark.[40] There he argues that Zech 14:9 provides an interpretation of the *Shema* that considers the oneness of YHWH and his name to be made eschatologically manifest through his rule over the earth. Mark's use of the word εἷς, 'one', instead of μόνος, 'alone', in discussions of God's prerogative to forgive sins (2:7) and unique goodness (10:18) are strong hints that it is Jesus who manifests the forgiveness and goodness of the *one* God on earth.[41] This, then, is a manner of 'incarnational' Christology which does not require pre-existence. Jesus is the earthly, human and ultimate instantiation of God's rule and goodness.

A parallel idea is also arguably present in the parable of the tenants in Mark 12:1–12. In that parable the 'only son' is both a type of the slaves, being sent to Israel and suffering abuse at the hands of the wicked tenants, but also a type of the father, his own flesh and blood. The 'son' of the parable is a more authoritative and complete representative of the father because, while he performs the same function as the slaves, he more perfectly fulfils the role because he more completely manifests the father's image and authority. So, Jesus is a *type* of the prophets who have gone before, but unlike the prophets who have gone before he is also a *type* of the Father (the God of Israel) who sent them.

The double typology of the parable's son is exactly what we have found in the miracle accounts. Although questions of pre-existence and divine identity are underdetermined, we can discern a sophisticated theological agenda, whereby Mark portrays Jesus as the one God's unique and final human representative on earth. From the point of view of Mark's Christology, questions of pre-existence, divine identity or celestial ontology are immaterial. Mark's Christology is exegetical not philosophical, narrative not propositional, typological not ontological.

Jesus cannot simply be another agent of God in the paradigm of those who have gone before (*pace* Kirk). Mark's insistent emphasis on Jesus' uniqueness, 'only beloved son' (Mark 12:6; cf. 1:11; 9:7), is what necessitates Mark's approach to scriptural typology. As much as Mark employs the techniques of earlier Jewish exegetes, his aim in doing so is radically different, as he ties the identity of the one God of Israel to the human Jesus. For Mark, it is not that Jesus is included in the divine identity (*pace* Bauckham, Hays), but that he represents God to such an extent that it is as if *the God of Israel has gained a human identity*, Jesus the Christ the son of God.

---

[40] Marcus 1994: 196–211.
[41] A distinction lost in most English translations.

§8.4 Conclusion

Mark does not write to present a 'systematic' Christology, at least not using credal categories. As Joseph Ernst puts it, 'Die Christologie des [Markusevangeliums] sperrt sich gegen vorschnelle Systematisierungen'.[42] In this sense Mark's narrative resembles the Jewish scriptures that he has incorporated into it.[43] Horsley's dictum concerning magic and miracle, applies equally to Christology: 'An important consideration in using the sources, then, is to discern interpretive concepts and language appropriate to the sources in their historical, cultural context.'[44]

Yet debates around Jesus' pre-existence and his divine or human nature as he is presented in the earliest canonical Gospel persist. Because these debates use categories which are alien to Mark's text they will likely continue. These debates are essentially unresolvable, asking a question the Gospel of Mark refuses to answer. Here I have argued that both divine identity and exalted human figure Christological paradigms tend to obscure Mark's text through the imposition of abstract conceptual categories. Rather, by restricting ourselves to the categories and terms that emerge from Mark's typological presentation of Jesus we can arrive at a robust Markan Christology, identifying Jesus as God's final and most complete representative; the new and final Moses, Elisha, David and Jonah; the ruler of the wind and waves; the conqueror of Satan's house; the healer of Israel; the one who provides for and saves both Jew and Gentile; the culmination of scriptural history; the eschatological instantiation of God's sovereignty and goodness; a suffering human of the recent past who nonetheless manifests the God of Israel; he is YHWH's human identity. At the same time this radical message is concealed within cryptic allusions. Mark's divine human Jesus can be grasped only by those with 'ears to hear' – a challenge that confronts every reader of Mark's Gospel, even today.

---

[42] 'The Christology of Mark's Gospel closes itself off against rash systematisations' (Ernst 1981: 44).
[43] Sternberg 1985: 38.
[44] Horsley 2014: 21.

Bibliography

Achtemeier, Elizabeth. 1963. 'Jesus Christ the Light of the World: The Biblical Understanding of Light and Darkness'. *Int* 17: 439–49.
Achtemeier, Paul J. 1962 'Person and Deed: Jesus and the Storm-Tossed Sea'. *Int* 16: 169–76.
Achtemeier, Paul J. 1970. 'Toward the Isolation of Pre-Markan Miracle Catenae'. *JBL* 89: 265–91.
Achtemeier, Paul J. 1972. 'The Origin and Function of the Pre-Marcan Miracle Catenae'. *JBL* 91: 198–221.
Aitken, James K. 2015. 'Introduction'. In *T&T Clark Companion to the Septuagint*, edited by James K. Aitken, 1–12. London: Bloomsbury.
Alfaro, María Jesús Martínez. 1996. 'Intertextuality: Origins and Development of the Concept'. *Atlantis* 18: 268–85.
Allen, David. 2020. 'The Use of Criteria: The State of the Question'. In *Methodology in the Use of the Old Testament in the New: Context and Criteria*, edited by David Allen and Steve Smith, 129–41. LNTS 579. London: T&T Clark.
Allison, Dale C. 1983. 'Psalm 23 (22) in Early Christianity: A Suggestion'. *IBS* 5: 132–7.
Allison, Dale C. 1993. *The New Moses: A Matthean Typology*. Minneapolis, Minn.: Fortress Press.
Allison, Dale C. 2000. *The Intertextual Jesus: Scripture in Q*. London: Trinity Press International.
Allison, Dale C. 2005. *Studies in Matthew: Interpretation Past and Present*. Grand Rapids, Mich.: Baker Academic.
Allison, Dale C. 2015. 'The History of Interpretation of Matthew: Lessons Learned'. *IDS* 49: 1–13.
Alter, Robert. 1981. *The Art of Biblical Narrative*. New York: Basic Books.
Anderson, Joel Edmund. 2012. 'Jonah in Mark and Matthew: Creation, Covenant, Christ, and the Kingdom of God'. *BTB* 42: 172–86.
Annen, Franz. 1976. *Heil für die Heiden*. Frankfurt: Joseph Knecht.
Argetsinger, Kathryn. 1992. 'Birthday Rituals: Friends and Patrons in Roman Poetry and Cult'. *Classical Antiquity* 11: 175–93.
Atkinson, Kenneth R. 2000. 'On the Use of Scripture in the Development of Militant Davidic Messianism at Qumran: New Light from Psalm of Solomon 17'. In *The Interpretation of Scripture in Early Judaism and Christianity*, edited by Craig A. Evans, 106–23. JSPS 33. Sheffield: Sheffield Academic Press.
Aus, Roger David. 2000. *The Stilling of the Storm: Studies in Early Palestinian Judaic Traditions*. Binghampton, NY: Global.
Aus, Roger David. 2003. *My Name Is Legion: Palestinian Judaic Traditions in Mark 5:1–20 and Other Gospel Texts*. Lanham, Md.: UPA.
Aus, Roger David. 2010. *Feeding the Five Thousand : Studies in the Judaic Background of Mark 6:30–44 Par. and John 6:1–15*. Lanham, Md.: University Press of America.
Avioz, Michael. 2015. *Josephus' Interpretation of the Books of Samuel*. LSTS 86. London: Bloomsbury.

Baarlink, Heinrich. 1977. *Anfängliches Evangelium: Ein Beitrag zur näheren Bestimmung der theologischen Motive im Markusevangelium*. Kampen: J. H. Kok.

Barker, Margaret. 1999. 'The High Priest and the Worship of Jesus'. In *The Jewish Roots of Christological Monotheism*, edited by C. C. Newman, James R. Davila, and Gladys S. Lewis, 93–111. JSJSup 63. Leiden: Brill.

Barnett, P. W. 1981. 'The Jewish Sign Prophets – A.D. 40–70: Their Intentions and Origin'. *New Testament Studies* 27: 679–97.

Barrett, C. K. 1978. 'The House of Prayer and the Den of Thieves'. In *Jesus und Paulus: Festschrift für Werner Georg Kummel zum 70. Geburstag*, edited by E. Earle Ellis and Gräßer, 13–20. Göttingen: Vandenhoeck & Ruprecht.

Batten, Alicia J. 2017. 'Fish Tales'. *BTB* 47: 5–14.

Bauckham, Richard. 1981. 'The *Liber Antiquitatum Biblicarum* of Pseudo-Philo and the Gospels as "Midrash"'. In *Studies in Midrash and Historiography*, edited by R. T. France and David Wenham, 33–76. Gospel Perspectives, Ill. London: Bloomsbury.

Bauckham, Richard. 1998. 'For Whom Were Gospels Written?' In *Gospels for All Christians*, edited by Richard Bauckham, 9–48. London: Bloomsbury Academic.

Bauckham, Richard. 1999. 'The Throne of God and the Worship of Jesus'. In *The Jewish Roots of Christological Monotheism*, edited by C. C. Newman, J. R. Davila, and G. S. Lewis, 43–69. JSJSup 63. Leiden: Brill.

Bauckham, Richard. 2004. 'Biblical Theology and the Problems of Monotheism'. In *Out of Egypt: Biblical Theology and Biblical Interpretation*, edited by Craig Bartholomew, Mary Healy, Karl Möller and Robin Parry, 187–232. Milton Keynes: Paternoster.

Bauckham, Richard. 2008. *Jesus and the God of Israel: God Crucified and Other Studies on the New Testament's Christology of Divine Identity*. Grand Rapids, Mich.: Eerdmans.

Bauckham, Richard. 2012. 'Moses as "God" in Philo of Alexandria: A Precedent for Christology?' In *The Spirit and Christ in the New Testament & Christian Theology*, edited by I. Howard Marshall, Volker Rabens, and Cornelis Bennema, 246–65. Grand Rapids, Mich.: Eerdmans.

Bauckham, Richard. 2017a. 'Markan Christology According to Richard Hays: Some Addenda'. *JTI* 11, 21–36.

Bauckham, Richard. 2017b. 'A Case for High Human Christology', *Expository Times* 129, no. 3, 121–4.

Bauckham, Richard. 2017c. 'Is "High Human Christology" Sufficient? A Critical Response to J. R. Daniel Kirk's A Man Attested by God'. Bulletin for Biblical Research 27, no. 4, 503–25.

Bauckham, Richard. 2019. 'Jesus' Use of "Father" and Disuse of "Lord"'. In *Son of God: Divine Sonship in Jewish and Christian Antiquity*, edited by Garrick V. Allen, Kai Akagi, Paul Sloan and Madhavi Nevader, 87–105. University Park, Pa.: Eisenbrauns.

Bauckham, Richard. 2020. 'Confessing the Cosmic Christ (1 Corinthians 8:6 and Colossians 1:15–20)'. In *Monotheism and Christology in Greco-Roman Antiquity*, edited by Matthew V. Novenson, NovTestSup 180, 139–171. Leiden: Brill.

Baxter, Wayne. 2009. 'The Extending of the Shepherd Metaphor in Early Jewish and Christian Writings'. In *Early Christian Literature and Intertextuality*, edited by Craig A. Evans and H. Daniel Zacharias, Volume 1: Thematic Studies, 208–24. LNTS 391. London: T&T Clark.

Bayer, Hans F. 2008. *Das Evangelium nach Markus*. HTA 5. Gießen: SCM R. Brockhaus.

Beavis, Mary Ann. 2010. 'The Resurrection of Jephthah's Daughter: Judges 11:34–40 and Mark 5:21–24, 35–43'. *Catholic Biblical Quarterly* 72: 46–62.

Becker, Eve-Marie. 2013. 'The Reception of 'Mark' in the 1st and 2nd Centuries C.E. and Its Significance for Genre Studies'. In *Mark and Matthew II*, edited by Eve-Marie Becker and Anders Runesson, 15–36. WUNT 304. Tübingen: Mohr Siebeck.

Becking, Bob. 2009. 'The Boundaries of Israelite Monotheism'. In *The Boundaries of Monotheism: Interdisciplinary Explorations into the Foundations of Western Monotheism*, edited by Anne-Marie Korte and Maaike De Haardt, 9–27. Leiden: Brill.

Ben-eliyahu, Eyal. 2016. '"On That Day, His Feet Will Stand on the Mount of Olives": The Mount of Olives and Its Hero between Jews, Christians, and Muslims'. *Jewish History* 30: 29–42.

Berg, Shane. 2011. 'Religious Epistemology and the History of the Dead Sea Scrolls Community'. In *The 'Other' in Second Temple Judaism: Essays in Honor of John J. Collins*, edited by Daniel C. Harlow, Karina Martin Hogan, Matthew Goff and Joel S. Kaminsky. Grand Rapids, Mich.: Eerdmans.

Bermejo-Rubio, Fernando. 2016. 'The Day of the Lord Is Coming: Jesus and the Book of Zechariah'. In *Jesus and the Scriptures: Problems, Passages and Patterns*, edited by Tobias Hägerland, 111–31. LNTS 552. London: Bloomsbury.

Best, Ernest. 1990. *The Temptation and the Passion: The Markan Soteriology*. 2nd edn. SNTSMS 2. Cambridge: Cambridge University Press.

Bieler, Ludwig. 1967. *Theios Anēr: Das Bild des 'Göttlichen Menschen' in Spätantike und Frühchristentum*. Darmstadt: Wissenschaftliche Buchgesellschaft.

Bird, Michael F. 2017. *Jesus the Eternal Son: Answering Adoptionist Christology*. Grand Rapids, Mich.: Eerdmans.

Blackburn, Barry. 1991. *Theios Anēr and the Markan Miracle Traditions*. WUNT 2. 40. Tübingen: Mohr Siebeck.

Blenkinsopp, Joseph. 1999. 'Miracles: Elisha and Hanina Ben Dosa'. In *Miracles in Jewish and Christian Antiquity: Imagining Truth*, edited by John C. Cavadini, 57–82. Notre Dame Studies in Theology 3. Notre Dame, Ind.: University of Notre Dame Press.

Blinzler, Josef. 1969. *Der Prozess Jesu*. 4th edn. Regensburg: Friedrich Pustet.

Block, Daniel I. 1998. *The Book of Ezekiel: Chapters 25–48*. NICOT. Grand Rapids, Mich.: Eerdmans.

Blomberg, Craig L. 2007. 'Matthew'. In *Commentary on the New Testament Use of the Old Testament*, edited by G. K. Beale and D. A. Carson, 1–110. Grand Rapids, Mich.: Baker Academic.

Bock, Darrell L. 2000. *Blasphemy and Exaltation: The Charge against Jesus in Mark 14:53–65*. Grand Rapids, Mich.: Baker.

Bock, Darrell L. 2006. 'The Function of Scripture in Mark 15:1–39'. In *Biblical Interpretation in Early Christian Gospels, Volume 1: The Gospel of Mark*, edited by Thomas R. Hatina, 8–17. LNTS 304. London: T&T Clark.

Bock, Darrell L. 2007. 'Blasphemy and the Jewish Examination of Jesus'. *BBR* 17: 53–114.

Bond, Helen K. 2015. 'Was Peter behind Mark's Gospel?' In *Peter in Early Christianity*, edited by Helen K. Bond and Larry W. Hurtado, 46–61. Grand Rapids, Mich.: Eerdmans.

Bond, Helen K. 2016. 'Josephus and the New Testament'. In *A Companion to Josephus*, edited by Honora Howell Chapman and Zuleika Rodgers, 147–58. BCAW. Chichester: Wiley Blackwell.

Bond, Helen K. 2019. 'A Fitting End? Self-Denial and a Slave's Death in Mark's Life of Jesus'. *NTS* 65: 425–42.

Boobyer, G. H. 1952. 'The Eucharistic Interpretation of the Miracles of the Loaves in St Mark's Gospel'. *JTS* 3: 161–71.

Boomershine, Thomas E. 1989. 'Epistemology at the Turn of the Ages in Paul, Jesus, and Mark: Rhetoric and Dialectic in Apocalyptic and the New Testament'. In *Apocalyptic and the New Testament: Essays in Honor of J. Louis Martyn*, edited by Joel Marcus and Marion L. Soards, 147–68. JSNTSup 24. Sheffield: JSOT Press.

Boring, M. Eugene. 1999. 'Markan Christology: God-Language for Jesus?' *NTS* 45: 451–71.

Boring, M. Eugene. 2006. *Mark: A Commentary*. Louisville, Ky.: Westminster John Knox.

Bosenius, Bärbel. 2014. *Der literarische Raum des Markusevangeliums*. WMANT 140. Göttingen: Vandenhoeck & Ruprecht.

Bostock, Gerald. 1980. 'Jesus as the New Elisha'. *Expository Times* 92: 39–41.

Botner, Max. 2017. 'The Messiah Is the Holy One'. *JBL* 136: 417–33.

Botner, Max. 2018. 'Has Jesus Read What David Did? Probing Problems in Mark 2:25–26'. *JTS* 69: 484–99.

Bowley, James E. 2001. 'Moses in the Dead Sea Scrolls: Living in the Shadow of God's Anointed'. In *The Bible at Qumran: Text, Shape, and Interpretation*, edited by Peter W. Flint, 159–81. SDSS. Grand Rapids, Mich.: Eerdmans.

Boyarin, Daniel. 2011. 'How Enoch Can Teach Us about Jesus'. *Early Christianity* 2: 51–76.

Bradshaw, Paul F. 2010. *Reconstructing Early Christian Worship*. Collegeville, Minn.: Liturgical Press.

Bradshaw, Paul F., and Maxwell E. Johnson. 2012. *The Eucharistic Liturgies: Their Evolution and Interpretation*. Collegeville, Minn.: Liturgical Press.

Broadhead, E. K. 1992. *Teaching with Authority: Miracles and Christology in the Gospel of Mark*. JSNTSup 74. Sheffield: Sheffield Academic Press.

Brodie, Thomas L. 1981. 'Jesus as the New Elisha: Cracking the Code'. *ExpTim* 93: 39–42.

Brodie, Thomas L. 2000. *The Crucial Bridge: The Elijah–Elisha Narrative as an Interpretive Synthesis of Genesis-Kings and a Literary Model for the Gospels*. Collegeville, Minn.: Liturgical Press.

Brodie, Thomas L. 2001. 'Towards Tracing the Gospels' Literary Indebtedness to the Epistles'. In *Mimesis and Intertextuality in Antiquity and Christianity*, edited by MacDonald, Dennis R., 104–16. Harrisburg, PA: Trinity Press International.

Brooke, George J. 1995. '4Q500 1 and the Use of Scripture in the Parable of the Vineyard'. *DSD* 2: 268–94.

Brooke, George J. 1997. '"The Canon within the Canon" at Qumran and in the New Testament'. In *The Scrolls and the Scriptures: Qumran Fifty Years After*, edited by Stanley E. Porter and Craig A. Evans, 242–66. JSPSup 26. Sheffield: Sheffield Academic Press.

Brooke, George J. 2009. 'New Perspectives on the Bible and Its Interpretation in the Dead Sea Scrolls'. In *The Dynamics of Language and Exegesis at Qumran*, edited by Devorah Dimant and Reinhard G. Kratz, 19–37. WUNT 2. 35. Tübingen: Mohr Siebeck.

Brooke, George J. 2010. 'Shared Exegetical Traditions between the Scrolls and the New Testament'. In *The Oxford Handbook of the Dead Sea Scrolls*, edited by Timothy H. Lim, John J. Collins, 565–92. Oxford: Oxford University Press.

Brower, Kent. 2009. '"Who Then Is This?" – Christological Questions in Mark 4:35–5:43'. *EvQ* 81: 291–305.

Brown, Raymond. 1971. 'Jesus and Elisha'. *Perspective* 12: 85–104.

Brown, Raymond. 1993. *The Birth of the Messiah: A Commentary on the Infancy Narratives in the Gospels of Matthew and Luke*. New York: Doubleday.

Brown, Raymond. 1994. *The Death of the Messiah*. 2 vols. ABRL. New York: Doubleday.

Bruce, F. F. 1961. 'The Book of Zechariah and the Passion Narrative'. *Bulletin of the John Rylands Library* 43: 336–53.

Bruce, F. F. 1981. 'Biblical Exposition at Qumran'. In *Studies in Midrash and Historiography*, edited by R. T. France and David Wenham, 77–98. Gospel Perspectives, III. London: Bloomsbury.

Brueggemann, Walter. 2000. *1 & 2 Kings*. SHBC. Macon, Ga.: Smyth & Helwys.

Buchanan, George W. 1994. 'Withering Fig Trees and Progression in Midrash'. In *The Gospels and the Scriptures of Israel*, edited by Craig A. Evans and W. Richard Stegner, 249–89. JSNTSup 104. Sheffield: Sheffield Academic Press.

Bultmann, Rudolf. 1952. *Theology of the New Testament*. 2 vols. Translated by Kendrick Grobel. London: SCM.

Bultmann, Rudolf. 1963. *The History of the Synoptic Tradition*. Translated by John Marsh. Oxford: Blackwell.

Burnett, David A. 2015. '"So Shall Your Seed Be": Paul's Use of Genesis 15:5 in Romans 4:18 in Light of Early Jewish Deification Traditions'. *JSPL* 5: 211–36.

Burnett, David A. 2019. 'A Neglected Deuteronomic Scriptural Matrix for the Nature of the Resurrection Body in 1 Corinthians 15:39–42?' In *Scripture, Texts, and Tracings in 1 Corinthians*, edited by Linda L. Belleville and B. J. Oropeza, 187–212. Scripture and Paul. Lanham, Md.: Lexington/Fortress.

Burridge, Richard A. 1992. *What Are the Gospels? A Comparison with Graeco-Roman Biography*. SNTSMS 70. Cambridge: Cambridge University Press.

Buth, Randall, and Brian Kvasnica. 2006. 'Temple Authorities and Tithe-Evasion: The Linguistic Background and Impact of the Parable of the Vineyard, Tenants and the Son'. In *Jesus' Last Week: Jersualem Studies in the Synoptic Gospels—Volume One*, edited by R. Steven Notley, Marc Turnage and Brian Becker, 53–80. Jewish and Christian Perspectives 11. Leiden: Brill.

Cahill, Michael. 1998. *The First Commentary on Mark: An Annotated Translation*. Oxford: Oxford University Press.

Cain, Rebecca Bensen. 2012. 'Plato on Mimesis and Mirrors'. *Philosophy and Literature* 36: 187–95.

Capes, David B. 2018. *The Divine Christ: Paul, the Lord Jesus, and the Scriptures of Israel*. Grand Rapids, Mich.: Baker Academic.

Caragounis, Chrys C. 1993. 'History and Supra-History: Daniel and the Four Empires'. In *The Book of Daniel: In the Light of New Findings*, edited by A. S. Van der Woude, 387–97. Bibliotheca Ephemeridum Theologicarum Lovaniensium, CVI. Leuven: Leuven University Press.

Carroll, R. P. 1969. 'The Elijah–Elisha Sagas: Some Remarks on Prophetic Succession in Ancient Israel'. *VetT* 19: 400–15.

Carter, Warren. 2014. 'Cross-Gendered Romans and Mark's Jesus: Legion Enters the Pigs (Mark 5:1–20)'. *JBL* 134: 139–55.

Cary, Phillip. 2008. *Jonah*. BTC. Baker Books.

Casey, Maurice. 1991. *From Jewish Prophet to Gentile God: The Origins and Development of New Testament Christology*. Louisville, Ky.: Westminster John Knox.

Chapman, Dean W. 1993. *The Orphan Gospel: Mark's Perspective on Jesus*. Sheffield: Continuum.

Chapman, Stephen B., and Laceye C. Warner. 2008. 'Jonah and the Imitation of God: Rethinking Evangelism and the Old Testament'. *JTI* 2: 43–69.

Charlesworth, James H. 2014. 'Jesus and the Temple'. In *Jesus and the Temple: Textual and Archaeological Explorations*, edited by James H. Charlesworth, 145–82. Minneapolis, Minn.: Fortress.

Chester, Andrew. 2011. 'High Christology: Whence, When and Why?' *Early Christianity* 2: 22–50.
Chilton, Bruce, Darrell L. Bock, Daniel M. Gurtner, Jacob Neusner, Lawrence H. Schiffman and Daniel Oden, eds. 2009. *A Comparative Handbook to the Gospel of Mark: Comparisons with Pseudepigrapha, the Qumran Scrolls, and Rabinic Literature*. NTGJC 1. Leiden: Brill.
Chou, Marie-Christine. 2011. 'Parole et silence, chemins de foi: Une lecture de Mc 5, 21–43 selon la méthode narrative'. *BLE* CXII: 363–90.
Clark, Donald Lemen. 1957. *Rhetoric in Greco-Roman Education*. New York: Columbia University Press.
Clemens, Samuel L., and Charles Dudley Warner. 1874. *The Gilded Age, a Tale of Today*. Hartford, Conn.: American Publishing Company
Cohen, Shaye J. D. 1982. 'Josephus, Jeremiah, and Polybius'. *History and Theory* 21: 366–81.
Collins, Adela Yarbro. 2006. 'The Charge of Blasphemy in Mark 14:64'. In *The Trial and Death of Jesus: Essays on the Passion Narrative in Mark*, edited by Geert Van Oyen and Tom Shepherd, 149–70. Contributions to Exegesis and Theology 45. Leuven: Peeters.
Collins, Adela Yarbro. 2007. *Mark: A Commentary*. Hermeneia. Minneapolis, Minn.: Fortress.
Collins, Adela Yarbro, and John J. Collins. 2008. *King and Messiah as Son of God: Divine Human, and Angelic Messianic Figures in Biblical and Related Literature*. Grand Rapids, Mich : Eerdmans.
Collins, John J. 1992. 'The Son of Man in First-Century Judaism'. *NTS* 38: 448–66.
Collins, John J. 1994 'The Works of the Messiah'. *DSD* 1: 98–112.
Collins, John J. 2010. *The Scepter and the Star: Messianism in Light of the Dead Sea Scrolls*. 2nd edn. Grand Rapids, Mich.: Eerdmans.
Colson, F. H., and G. H. Whitaker. 1949. *Philo I*. LCL. London: William Heinemann.
Colson, F. H., and G. H. Whitaker. *Philo IV*. LCL. London: William Heinemann.
Cotter, Wendy J. 1999. *Miracles in Greco-Roman Antiquity: A Sourcebook*. London: Routledge.
Cotter, Wendy J. 2010. *The Christ of the Miracle Stories: Portrait Though Encounter*. Grand Rapids, Mich.: Baker.
Counet, Patrick Chatelion. 2009. 'The Divine Messiah: Early Jewish Monotheism and the New Testament'. In *The Boundaries of Monotheism: Interdisciplinary Explorations into the Foundations of Western Monotheism*, edited by Anne-Marie Korte and Maaike De Haardt, 9–27. Leiden: Brill.
Cousland, J. R. C. 1999. 'The Feeding of the Four Thousand Gentiles in Matthew? Matthew 15:29–39 as a Test Case'. *NovT* 41: 1–23.
Cranfield, C. E. B. 1972. *The Gospel According to St Mark*. CGTC. Cambridge: Cambridge Univeristy Press.
Crossan, John Dominic. 2009. *Jesus: A Revolutionary Biography*. San Fransisco, Calif.: HarperCollins.
Cummings, J. T. 1980. 'The Tassel of His Cloak: Mark, Luke, Matthew – and Zechariah'. In *Studia Biblica 1978*, II. Papers on the Gospels, 47–61. JSNTSup 2. Sheffield: JSOT Press.
Currie, Bruno. 2016. *Homer's Allusive Art*. Oxford: Oxford University Press.
D'Angelo, Mary Rose. 1999. 'Gender and Power in the Gospel of Mark: The Daughter of Jairus and the Woman with the Flow of Blood'. In *Miracles in Jewish and Christian Antiquity: Imagining Truth*, edited by John C. Cavadini, 83–109. Notre Dame Studies in Theology 3. Notre Dame, Ind.: University of Notre Dame Press.
Danker, Frederick William. 1963. 'Mark 8:3'. *JBL* 82: 215–16.

Daube, David. 1980. 'Typology in Josephus'. *JJS* 31: 18–36.
Daube, David. 1990. 'On Acts 23: Sadducees and Angels'. *JBL* 109: 493–7.
Davidson, Richard M. 2014. 'Did Mathew "Twist" the Scriptures? A Case Study in the New Testament Use of the Old Testament'. In *Hermeneutics, Intertextuality and the Contemporary Meaning of Scripture*, edited by Paul Petersen and Ross Cole, 51–73. ATF Press.
Davies, P. R., and B. D. Chilton. 1978. 'The Aqedah: A Revised Tradition History'. *CBQ* 40: 514–46.
Davila, James R. 1999. 'Of Methodology, Monotheism and Metatron: Introductory Reflections on Divine Mediators and the Origins of the Worship of Jesus'. In *The Jewish Roots of Christological Monotheism*, edited by C. C. Newman, James R. Davila, and Gladys S. Lewis, 3–18. JSJSup 63. Leiden: Brill.
Dawson, Audrey. 2008. *Healing, Weakness and Power: Perspectives on Healing in the Writings of Mark, Luke and Paul*. Milton Keynes: Paternoster.
Dawson, David. 1992. *Allegorical Readers and Cultural Revision in Ancient Alexandria*. Berkeley, Calif.: University of California Press.
Day, John. 1985. *God's Conflict with the Dragon and the Sea: Echoes of a Canaanite Myth in the Old Testament*. University of Cambridge Oriental Publications 35. Cambridge: Cambridge University Press.
De Boer, Martinus C. 2011. *Galatians*. NTL. Louisville, Ky.: Westminster John Knox.
De Jonge, Henk Jan. 2003. 'The Cleansing of the Temple in Mark 11:15 and Zechariah 14:21'. In *The Book of Zechariah and Its Influence*, edited by Christopher Tuckett, 87–100. Aldershot: Ashgate.
Dechow, Jens. 2000. *Gottessohn und Herrschaft Gottes: Der Theozentrismus des Markusevangeliums*. WMANT 86. Neukirchen-Vluyn: Neukirchener Verlag.
DeConick, April D. 2020. 'The One God Is No Simple Matter'. In *Monotheism and Christology in Greco-Roman Antiquity*, edited by Matthew V. Novenson, NovTestSup 180, 263–92. Leiden: Brill.
Dehn, Gunther. 1953. *Der Gottessohn. Eine Einführung in das Evangelium des Markus*. Hamburg: Im Furche-Verlag.
Dell, Katharine J. 2020. 'Genre versus Intertextuality: Linking Wisdom Texts, Themes and Contexts with the Wider Old Testament and with the Sayings of Jesus'. In *Methodology in the Use of the Old Testament in the New: Context and Criteria*, edited by David Allen and Steve Smith, 40–52. LNTS 579. London: T&T Clark.
Derrett, J. Duncan. 1975. 'Leek-Beds and Methodology'. *BZ* 1: 101–3.
Derrett, J. Duncan. 1979a. 'Contributions to the Study of the Gerasene Demoniac'. *JSNT* 3: 2–17.
Derrett, J. Duncan. 1979b. 'Spirit-Possession and the Gerasene Demoniac'. *Man* 14: 286–93.
Derrett, J. Duncan. 1982. 'Mark's Technique: The Haemorrhaging Woman and Jairus' Daughter'. *Biblica* 63: 474–505.
Derrett, J. Duncan. 1985. *The Making of Mark: The Scriptural Bases of the Earliest Gospel*. 2 vols. Shipston-on-Stour: Drinkwater.
Desogus, Paolo. 2012. 'The Encyclopedia in Umberto Eco's Semiotics'. *Semiotica* 192: 501–21.
Dibelius, Martin. 1971. *From Tradition to Gospel*. Translated by Bertram Lee Woolf. Cambridge: James Clarke.
DiTomasso, Lorenzo. 2009. 'Giants- Judaism'. *Encyclopaedia of the Bible and Its Reception* Berlin: Walter de Gruyter: 202.
Dodd, Charles Harold. 1965. *According to the Scriptures: The Sub-Structure of New Testament Theology*. London: Collins.

Donahue, John R., and Daniel J. Harrington. 2005. *The Gospel of Mark*. Collegeville, Minn.: Liturgical Press.
Dormandy, Richard. 2000. 'The Expulsion of Legion: A Political Reading of Mark 5:1-20'. *ExpTim* 111: 335-7.
Drewermann, Eugen. 1989. *Das Markusevangelium: Erster Teil: Mk 1,1 bis 9,13*. 4th edn. Olten un Freiburg im Breisgau: Walter-Verlag.
Drury, John. 1985. *The Parables in the Gospels: History and Allegory*. New York: Crossroad.
Drury, John. 1990. 'Mark'. In *The Literary Guide to the Bible*, edited by Robert Alter and Frank Kermode, 402-17. Cambridge, Mass.: Harvard University Press.
Du Toit, David S. 2006. *Der abwesende Herr: Strategien im Markusevangelium zur Bewältigung der Abwesenheit des Auferstandenen*. WMANT 111. Neukirchen-Vluyn: Neukirchener Verlag.
Dunn, James D. G. 1970. 'The Messianic Secret in Mark'. *Tyndale Bulletin* 21: 92-117.
Dunn, James D. G. 1988. *Romans*. WBC. 2 Vols. Dallas, Tex.: Word Books.
Dunn, James D. G. 1989. *Christology in the Making: A New Testament Inquiry into the Origins of the Doctrine of the Incarnation*. 2nd ed. Grand Rapids, Mich.: Eerdmans.
Dunn, James D. G. 1994. 'The Making of Christology—Evolution or Unfolding?' In *Jesus of Nazareth: Lord and Christ: Essays on the Historical Jesus and New Testament Christology*, edited by Joel B. Green and Max Turner, 437-52. Grand Rapids, Mich.: Eerdmans.
Dunn, James D. G. 1998. *The Theology of Paul the Apostle*. Grand Rapids, Mich.: Eerdmans.
Dunn, James D. G. 2003. *Jesus Remembered*. Christianity in the Making, vol 1. Grand Rapids, Mich.: Eerdmans.
Dunn, James D. G. 2004. 'Was Jesus a Monotheist? A Contribution to the Discussion of Christian Monotheism'. In *Early Jewish and Christian Monotheism*, edited by Loren T. Stuckenbruck and Wendy North, 104-19. JSNTSup 263. London: T&T Clark.
Dwyer, Timothy. 1993. 'Prominent Women, Widows, and Prophets: A Case for Midrashic Intertextuality'. *Essays in Literature* 20: 23-30.
Dwyer, Timothy. 1996. *The Motif of Wonder in the Gospel of Mark*. JSNTSup 128. Sheffield: Sheffield Academic Press.
Eco, Umberto. 1981. 'The Theory of Signs and the Role of the Reader'. *The Bulletin of the Midwest Modern Language Association* 14: 35-45.
Eco, Umberto. 1986. *Semiotics and the Philosophy of Language*. Bloomington, Ind.: Indiana University Press.
Edwards, James R. 1989. 'Markan Sandwiches: The Significance of Interpolations in Markan Narratives'. *NovT* 31: 193-216.
Ehrman, Bart D. 2014. *How Jesus Became God: The Exaltation of a Jewish Preacher from Galilee*. New York: HarperCollins.
Elder, Nicholas. 2016. 'Of Porcine and Polluted Spirits: Reading the Gerasene Demoniac (Mark 5: 1-20) with the Book of Watchers (1 Enoch 1-36)'. *CBQ* 78: 430-47.
Ellis, E. Earle. 1994. 'Deity-Christology in Mark 14:58'. In *Jesus of Nazareth: Lord and Christ: Essays on the Historical Jesus and New Testament Christology*, edited by Joel B. Green and Max Turner, 192-203. Grand Rapids, Mich.: Eerdmans.
Emadi, Samuel. 2015. 'Intertextuality in New Testament Scholarship: Significance, Criteria, and the Art of Intertextual Reading'. *CBR* 14, no. 1: 8-23.
Engberg-Pedersen, Troels. 2009. 'Complete and Incomplete Transformation in Paul – a Philosophical Reading of Paul on Body and Spirit'. In *Metamorphoses: Resurrection, Body and Transformative Practices in Early Christianity*, edited by Turid Karlsen Seim and Jorunn Økland, 1: 123-46. Ekstasis: Religious Experience from Antiquity to the Middle Ages. New York: Walter de Gruyter.

Ernst, Joseph. 1981. *Das Evangelium nach Markus*. RNT. Regensburg: Verlag Friedrich Pustet.
Evans, Craig A. 1984. 'On the Vineyard Parables of Isaiah 5 and Mark 12'. *BZ* 28: 82–6.
Evans, Craig A. 1992. 'Typology'. In *Dictionary of Jesus and the Gospels*, edited by Joel B. Green, Scot McKnight and I. Howard Marshall, 862–66. Downers Grove, Ill.: IVP.
Evans, Craig A. 1997. 'David in the Dead Sea Scrolls'. In *The Scrolls and the Scriptures: Qumran Fifty Years After*, 183–97. JSPSup 26. Sheffield: Sheffield Academic Press.
Evans, Craig A. 1999. 'Jesus and Zechariah's Messianic Hope'. In *Authenticating the Activites of Jesus*, edited by Bruce Chilton and Craig A. Evans, 2: 373–88. NTTS, XXVIII. Leiden: Brill.
Evans, Craig A. 2001a. *Mark 8:27–16:20*. WBC 34b. Nashville, Tenn.: Thomas Nelson.
Evans, Craig A. 2001b. 'Abraham in the Dead Sea Scrolls: A Man of Faith and Failure'. In *The Bible at Qumran: Text, Shape, and Interpretation*, edited by Peter W. Flint, 149–58. SDSS. Grand Rapids, Mich.: Eerdmans.
Evans, Craig A. 2001c. *Jesus and His Contemporaries: Comparative Studies*. Leiden: Brill.
Evans, Craig A. 2002. 'The Baptism of John in a Typological Context'. In *Dimensions of Baptism: Biblical and Theological Studies*, edited by Stanley E. Porter and Anthony R. Cross, 45–71. JSNTSup 234. London: Sheffield Academic Press.
Evans, Craig A. 2005. *Ancient Texts for New Testament Studies: A Guide to the Background Literature*. Peabody, Mass.: Hendrickson.
Evans, Craig A. 2006. 'The Beginning of the Good News and the Fulfilment of Scripture in the Gospel of Mark'. In *Hearing the Old Testament in the New Testament*, edited by Stanley E. Porter, 83–103. Grand Rapids, Mich.: Eerdmans.
Evans, Craig A. 2006. 'Zechariah in the Markan Passion Narrative'. In *Biblical Interpretation in Early Christian Gospels, Volume 1: The Gospel of Mark*, edited by Thomas R. Hatina, 64–80. LNTS 304. London: T&T Clark.
Evans, Craig A. 2015. 'Why Did the New Testament Writers Appeal to the Old Testament?' *JSNT* 38: 36–48.
Eve, Eric. 2002. *The Jewish Context of Jesus' Miracles*. JSNTSup 231. London: Sheffield Academic Press.
Eve, Eric. 2008. 'Spit in Your Eye: The Blind Man of Bethsaida and the Blind Man of Alexandria'. *NTS* 54: 1–17.
Farrer, Austin. 1951. *A Study in St Mark*. Westminster: Dacre.
Fassnacht, Martin. 2003. 'Das Verhältnis von Wissen und Rettung dargestellt an der Wundergeschichte Mk 5, 21–43'. In *Die Weisheit – Ursprünge und Rezeption: Festschrift für Karl Löning zum 65. Geburtstag*, edited by M. Fassnacht, A. Leinhäupl-Wilke and S. Lücking, 105–24. Neutestamentliche Abhandlungen 44. Münster: Aschendorff Verlag.
Fee, Gordon D. 2014. *The First Epistle to the Corinthians*. Rev. edn. NICNT. Grand Rapids, Mich.: Eerdmans.
Feneberg, Rupert. 2000. *Der Jude Jesus und die Heiden: Biographie und Theologie Jesu im Markusevangelium*. HBS 4. Freiburg: Herder.
Fishbane, Michael. 1985. *Biblical Interpretation in Ancient Israel*. Oxford: Clarendon.
Fisher, Kathleen. 1981. 'The Miracles of Mark 4:35–5:43: Their Meaning and Function in the Gospel Framework'. *BTB* 11: 13–16.
Fisk, Bruce N. 2000a. 'Offering Isaac Again and Again: Pseudo-Philo's Use of the Aqedah as Intertext'. *CBQ* 62: 481–507.
Fisk, Bruce N. 2000b. 'Rewritten Bible in Pseudepigrapha and Qumran'. In *Dictionary of New Testament Background*, edited by Craig A. Evans and Porter, Stanley, 947–53. Downers Grove, Ill.: IVP.

Fisk, Bruce N. 2001. *Do You Not Remember? Scripture, Story and Exegesis in the Rewritten Bible of Pseudo Philo*. JSPSup 37. Sheffield: Sheffield Academic Press.
Fitzmyer, Joseph A. 1993. *Romans*. AB 33. New York: Doubleday.
Fitzmyer, Joseph A. 2002. 'The Sacrifice of Isaac in Qumran Literature'. *Biblica* 83: 211–29.
Fitzmyer, Joseph A. 2003. *Tobit*. CEJL. Berlin: Walter de Gruyter.
Fitzmyer, Joseph A. 2008. *First Corinthians*. AYB 32. New Haven, Conn.: Yale University Press.
Focant, Camille. 2012. *The Gospel According to Mark*. Translated by Leslie Robert Keylock. Eugene, Oreg.: Pickwick.
Fossheim, Hallvard. 2001. 'Mimesis in Aristotle's Ethics'. In *Making Sense of Aristotle: Essays in Poetics*, edited by Øivind Andersen and Jon Haarberg, 73–86. London: Duckworth.
Foster, Paul. 2015. 'Echoes without Resonance: Critiquing Certain Aspects of Recent Scholarly Trends in the Study of the Jewish Scriptures in the New Testament'. *JSNT* 38: 96–111.
Foulkes, Francis. 1994. 'The Acts of God: A Study of the Basis of Typology in the Old Testament'. In *The Right Doctrine from the Wrong Texts? Essays on the Use of the Old Testament in the New*, edited by G. K. Beale, 342–71. Grand Rapids, Mich.: Baker.
Fowler, Robert M. 1981. *Loaves and Fishes: The Function of the Feeding Stories in the Gospel of Mark*. SBL Dissertation Series 54. Ann Arbor, Mich.: Scholars Press.
Fowler, Robert M. 1991. *Let the Reader Understand: Reader-Response Criticism and the Gospel of Mark*. Minneapolis, Minn.: Fortress.
France, R. T. 1971. *Jesus and the Old Testament: His Application of Old Testament Passages to Himself and His Mission*. Downers Grove, Ill.: IVP.
France, R. T. 1981. 'Jewish Historiography, Midrash, and the Gospels'. In *Studies in Midrash and Historiography*, edited by R. T. France and David Wenham, 99–127. Gospel Perspectives, III. London: Bloomsbury.
France, R. T. 2002. *The Gospel of Mark: A Commentary on the Greek Text*. NIGTC. Grand Rapids, Mich.: Eerdmans.
Fredriksen, Paula. 2007. 'Mandatory Retirement: Ideas in the Study of Christian Origins Whose Time Has Come to Go'. In *Israel's God and Rebecca's Children: Christology and Community in Early Judaism and Christianity*, edited by D. Capes, A. D. Deconick, H. Bond and T. MIller, 25–38. Waco, Tex.: Baylor University Press.
Fredriksen, Paula. 2020. 'How High Can High Christology Be?' In *Monotheism and Christology in Greco-Roman Antiquity*, edited by Matthew V. Novenson, NovTestSup 180, 293–320. Leiden: Brill.
Freeman, H., and M. Simon, eds. 1939. *Midrash Rabbah*. Vol. 3. 9 vols. London: Soncino.
Frei, Hans W. 1974. *The Eclipse of Biblical Narrative: A Study in Eighteenth and Nineteenth Century Hermeneutics*. New Haven, Conn.: Yale University Press.
Frieden, Ken. 1990. 'The Language of Demon Possession: A Key Word Analysis'. In *The Daemonic Imagination: Biblical Text and Secular Story*, edited by Robert Detweiler and William G. Doty, 41–52. AAR Studies in Religion 60, Atlanta, Ga.; Scholars Press.
Fritz, Volkmar. 2003. *1 & 2 Kings*. Translated by Anselm Hagedorn. Continental Commentaries. Minneapolis, Minn.: Fortress.
Fung, Ronald. 1994. *The Epistle to the Galatians*. Grand Rapids, Mich.: Eerdmans.
Galbraith, Deane. 2019. 'Jeremiah Never Saw That Coming: How Jesus Miscalculated the End Times'. In *Jeremiah in History and Tradition*, edited by Jim West and Niels-Peter Lemche, 150–75. Abingdon: Routledge.
Gardner, Helen. 1959. *The Business of Criticism*. Oxford: Clarendon Press.
Garland, David E. 1996. *Mark*. NIVAC. Grand Rapids, Mich.: Zondervan.

Garner, Richard. 1990. *From Homer to Tragedy: The Art of Allusion in Greek Poetry*. London: Routledge.
Garnet, Paul. 1980. 'The Baptism of Jesus and the Son of Man Idea'. *JSNT* 9: 49–65.
Garroway, Joshua. 2009. 'The Invasion of a Mustard Seed: A Reading of Mark 5.1–20'. *JSNT* 32: 57–75.
Gathercole, Simon. 2005. 'Pre-Existence, and the Freedom of the Son in Creation and Redemption: An Exposition in Dialogue with Robert Jenson'. *International Journal of Systematic Theology* 7: 38–51.
Gathercole, Simon. 2006. *The Preexistent Son: Recovering the Christologies of Matthew, Mark, and Luke*. Cambridge: Eerdmans.
Geddert, Timothy J. 2009. 'The Use of Psalms in Mark'. *Baptistic Theologies* 1: 109–24.
Gheorghita, Radu. 2009. 'The Influence of the Septuagint on the New Testament: Toward a More Objective Assessment'. In *Early Christian Literature and Intertextuality*, edited by Craig A. Evans and H. Daniel Zacharias, Volume 1: Thematic Studies, 165–83. LNTS 391. London: T&T Clark.
Gieschen, Charles A. 1998. *Angelomorphic Christology: Antecedents and Early Evidence*. AGJU, XLII. Leiden: Brill.
Ginzberg, Louis. 1998. *The Legends of the Jews*. 7 Vols. Baltimore, Md.: Johns Hopkins University Press.
Girard, René. 1990. 'The Demons of Gerasa'. In *The Daemonic Imagination: Biblical Text and Secular Story*, edited by Robert Detweiler and William G. Doty, 77–98. AAR Studies in Religion 60, Atlanta, Ga.; Scholars Press.
Glasswell, M. E. 1965. 'The Use of Miracles in the Markan Gospel'. In *Miracles*, edited by C. F. D. Moule, 149–62. London: A. R. Mowbray & Co.
Gnilka, Joachim. 1998. *Das Evangelium nach Markus*. EKK, II. Zürich: Benziger Verlag.
Goldingay, John. 2007. *Psalms: Psalms 42–89*. Grand Rapids, Mich : Baker.
Goldingay, John. 2008. *Psalms: Psalms 90–150*. Grand Rapids, Mich.: Baker.
Goldstein, Jonathan A. 1976. *1 Maccabees*. AB 41. New York: Doubleday.
Goodacre, Mark. 2006. 'Scripturalization in Mark's Crucifixion Narrative'. In *The Trial and Death of Jesus: Essays on the Passion Narrative in Mark*, edited by Geert Van Oyen and Tom Shepherd, 33–48. Contributions to Exegesis and Theology 45. Leuven: Peeters.
Goodenough, Erwin R. 1935. *By Light, Light: The Mystic Gospel of Hellenistic Judaism*. New Haven, Conn.: Yale University Press.
Goppelt, Leonhard. 1982. *Typos: The Typological Interpretation of the Old Testament in the New*. Translated by Donald M. Madvig. Grand Rapids, Mich.: Eerdmans.
Goulder, M. D. 1964. *Type and History in Acts*. London: SPCK.
Grabbe, Lester L. 2000. *Judaic Religion in the Second Temple Period: Belief and Practice from the Exile to Yavneh*. London: Routledge.
Gray, John. 1970. *I & II Kings*. 2nd rev. edn. OTL. London: SCM.
Grindheim, Sigurd. 2011. *God's Equal: What Can We Know about Jesus' Self-Understanding in the Synoptic Gospels*. LNTS 446. London: T&T Clark.
Grindheim, Sigurd. 2012. *Christology in the Synoptic Gospels: God or God's Servant?* London: T&T Clark.
Guelich, Robert A. 1989. *Mark 1–8:26*. WBC 34A. Nashville, Tenn.: Thomas Nelson.
Gundry, Robert H. 1967. *The Use of the Old Testament in St Matthew's Gospel: With Special Reference to the Messianic Hope*. NovTSup 18. Leiden: Brill.
Gundry, Robert H. 1976. *Soma in Biblical Theology: With Emphasis on Pauline Anthropology*. SNTSMS 29. Cambridge: Cambridge University Press.

Gundry, Robert H. 1993. *Mark: A Commentary on His Apology for the Cross*. Grand Rapids, Mich.: Eerdmans.
Guth, Christine J. 2008. 'An Insider's Look at the Gerasene Disciple (Mark 5:1–20)'. *Journal of Religion, Disability & Health* 11: 61–70.
Guttenberger, Gudrun. 2004. *Die Gottesvorstellung im Markusevangelium*. BZNW 123. Berlin: Walter de Gruyter.
Haenchen, Ernst. 1968. *Der Weg Jesu: Eine Erklärung des Markus-Evangeliums und der kanonischen Parallelen*. 2nd edn. dGl. Berlin: Walter de Gruyter.
Halliwell, Stephen. 2001. 'Aristotelian Mimesis and Human Understanding'. In *Making Sense of Aristotle: Essays in Poetics*, edited by Øivind Andersen and Jon Haarberg, 87–108. London: Duckworth.
Halton, Charles. 2012. 'An Indecent Proposal: The Theological Core of the Book of Ruth'. *Scandinavian Journal of the Old Testament* 26: 30–43.
Hamori, Esther J. 2008. *When Gods Were Men: The Embodied God in Biblical and near Eastern Literature*. BZAW 384. Berlin: De Gruyter.
Hart, J. H. A., ed. 2012. *Ecclesiasticus, the Greek Text of Codex 248: Edited with a Textual Commentary and Prolegomena*. Cambridge: Cambridge University Press.
Hartman, Lars. 1966. *Prophecy Interpreted: The Formation of Some Jewish Apocalyptic Texts and the Eschatological Discourse, Mark 13 Par*. Translated by Neil Tomkinson. Lund: CWK Gleerup.
Hartman, Lars. 2010. *Mark for the Nations: A Text- and Reader-Oriented Commentary*. Eugene, Oreg.: Wipf and Stock.
Hatina, Thomas R. 2006. 'Embedded Scripture Texts and the Plurality of Meaning: The Announcement of the 'Voice from Heaven' in Mark 1.11 as a Case Study'. In *Biblical Interpretation in Early Christian Gospels, Volume 1: The Gospel of Mark*, edited by Thomas R. Hatina, 81–99. LNTS 304. London: T&T Clark.
Hays, Richard B. 1989. *Echoes of Scripture in the Letters of Paul*. New Haven, Conn.: Yale University Press.
Hays, Richard B. 2005. *The Conversion of the Imagination: Paul as Interpreter of Israel's Scripture*. Grand Rapids, Mich.: Eerdmans.
Hays, Richard B. 2016. *Echoes of Scripture in the Gospels*. Waco, Tex.: Baylor University Press.
Heil, John P. 1981. *Jesus Walking on the Sea: Meaning and Gospel Functions of Matt 14:22–33, Mark 6:45–52 and John 6:15b–21*. Analectica Biblica. Rome: Biblical Institute.
Helyer, L.R. 2000. 'Tobit', *Dictionary of New Testament Background*. Downers Grove, Ill.: IVP: 1238-39
Hengel, Martin. 1976. *The Son of God: The Origin of Christology and the History of Jewish-Hellenistic Religion*. Translated by John Bowden. London: SCM.
Hengel, Martin. 1989. *The Zealots: Investigations into the Jewish Freedom Movement in the Period from Herod I until 70 A.D*. Translated by David Smith. Edinburgh: T&T Clark.
Hengel, Martin. 2001. *Studies in Early Christology*. Edinburgh: T&T Clark.
Himmelfarb, Martha. 1993. *Ascent to Heaven: In Jewish and Christian Apocalypses*. Oxford: Oxford University Press.
Himmelfarb, Martha. 2013. *Between Temple and Torah*. Texts and Studies in Ancient Judaism 151. Tübingen: Mohr Siebeck.
Hollander, H. W., and M. de Jonge. 1985. *The Testaments of the Twelve Patriarchs: A Commentary*. Leiden: Brill.
Hollenbach, Paul W. 1981. 'Jesus, Demoniacs, and Public Authorities: A Socio-Historical Study'. *Journal of the American Academy of Religion* 49: 567–88.

Hooker, Morna D. 1991. *The Gospel According to Saint Mark*. Peabody, Mass.: A & C Black.
Horbury, William. 1985. '"Like One of the Prophets of Old": Two Types of Popular Prophets at the Time of Jesus'. *CBQ* 47: 435–63.
Horbury, William. 1998. *Jewish Messianism and the Cult of Christ*. London: SCM.
Horbury, William. 2003. *Messianism among Jews and Christians: Biblical and Historical Studies*. London: T&T Clark.
Horbury, William. 2004. 'Jewish and Christian Monotheism in the Herodian Age'. In *Early Jewish and Christian Monotheism*, edited by Loren T. Stuckenbruck and Wendy North, 16–44. JSNTSup 263. London: T&T Clark.
Horbury, William. 2011. 'Die jüdischen Wurzeln der Christologie'. *Early Christianity* 2: 5–21.
Horsley, Richard A. 2001. *Hearing the Whole Story: The Politics of Plot in Mark's Gospel*. Louisville, Ky.: Westminster John Knox.
Horsley, Richard A. 2014. *Jesus and Magic: Freeing the Gospel Stories from Modern Misconceptions*. Eugene, Oreg.: Cascade.
Hübenthal, Sandra. 2014. *Das Markusevangelium als kollectives Gedächtnis*. FRLANT 253. Göttingen: Vandenhoeck & Ruprecht.
Huizenga, Leroy Andrew. 2009. *The New Isaac: Tradition and Intertextuality in the Gospel of Matthew*. Leiden: Brill.
Hurtado, Larry W. 1988. *One God, One Lord: Early Christian Devotion and Ancient Jewish Monotheism*. London: SCM Press.
Hurtado, Larry W. 1998. 'First-Century Jewish Monotheism'. *JSNT* 71: 3–26.
Hurtado, Larry W. 2003. *Lord Jesus Christ: Devotion to Jesus in Earliest Christianity*. Grand Rapids, Mich.: Eerdmans.
Hwang, Jin K. 2009. 'The Crises at Corinth and Paul's Use of Numbers in 1 Corinthians'. In *Early Christian Literature and Intertextuality*, edited by Craig A. Evans and H. Daniel Zacharias, Volume 1: Thematic Studies, 197–207. LNTS 391. London: T&T Clark.
Jacobson, Howard. 1996. *A Commentary on Pseudo-Philo's Liber Antiquitatum Biblicarum*. 2 vols. Arbeiten zur Geschichte des Antiken Judentums und des Urchristentums, XXXI. Leiden: Brill.
Janowski, Bernd. 2013. *Arguing with God: A Theological Anthropology of the Psalms*. Translated by Armin Siedlecki. Louisville, Ky.: Westminster John Knox.
Jewett, Robert. 2007. *Romans: A Commentary*. Hermeneia. Minneapolis, Minn.: Fortress.
John, Jeffrey. 2001. *The Meaning in the Miracles*. Grand Rapids, Mich.: Eerdmans.
Johnson, Nathan C. 2018. 'The Passion According to David: Matthew's Arrest Narrative, the Absalom Revolt, and Militant Messianism'. *CBQ* 80: 247–72.
Juel, Donald. 1977. *Messiah and Temple: The Trial of Jesus in the Gospel of Mark*. SBLDS 31. Missoula, Mont.: Scholars Press.
Juel, Donald. 1992. *Messianic Exegesis: Christological Interpretation of the Old Testament in Early Christianity*. Minneapolis, Minn.: Fortress Press.
Juel, Donald. 2003. 'Interpreting Israel's Scriptures in the New Testament'. In *A History of Biblical Interpretation*, edited by Alan J. Hauser and Duane F. Watson, Vol. 1: The Ancient Period, 283–303. Grand Rapids, Mich.: Eerdmans.
Kahl, Brigitte. 1996. 'Jairus und die verlorenen Töchter Israels: Sozioliterarische Überlegungen zum Problem der Grenzüberschreitung in Mk 5, 21–43'. In *Von der Wurzel Getragen: Christlich-Feministische Exegese in Auseinandersetzung mit Antijudaismus*, edited by Luise Schottroff and Marie-Theres Wacker, 61–78. Biblical Interpretation 17. Leiden: Brill.
Kampling, Rainer. 1992. *Israel unter dem Anspruch des Messias: Studien zur Israelthematik im Markusevangelium*. SBB 25. Stuttgart: Verlag Katholisches Bibelwerk.

Kanarek, Jane L. 2014. *Biblical Narrative and the Formation of Rabbinic Law*. New York: Cambridge University Press.
Kaufman, Stephen A. 1982. 'The Temple Scroll and Higher Criticism'. *Hebrew Union College Annual* 53: 29–43.
Kee, Howard Clark. 1978. 'The Function of Scriptural Quotations and Allusions in Mark 11–16'. In *Jesus und Paulus: Festschrift für Werner Georg Kummel zum 70. Geburstag*, edited by E. Earle Ellis and Erich Gräßer, 165–88. Göttingen: Vandenhoeck & Ruprecht.
Kee, Howard Clark. 1987. 'Christology in Mark's Gospel'. In *Judaisms and Their Messiahs at the Turn of the Christian Era*, edited by Jacob Neusner, William Scott Green and Ernest Frerichs, 187–208. Cambridge: Cambridge University Press.
Keim, Katharina E. 2016. *Pirqei de Rabbi Eliezer: Structure, Coherence, Intertextuality*. AJEC 96. Leiden: Brill.
Kelber, Werner H. 1974. *The Kingdom in Mark: A New Place and a New Time*. Minneapolis, Minn.: Fortress Press.
Kertelge, Karl. 1979. 'Die Epiphanie Jesu im Evangelium (Markus)'. In *Das Markus-Evangelium*, edited by Rudolf Pesch, 259–82. WdF, CDXI. Darmstadt: Wissenschaftliche Buchgesellschaft.
Kim, Hyn Chul Paul. 2007. 'Jonah Read Intertextually'. *JBL* 126: 497–528.
King, Daniel. 2014. *St Cyril of Alexandria: Three Christological Treatises*. Fathers of the Church 129. Washington, DC: Catholic University of America Press.
Kirk, J. R. Daniel. 2016. *A Man Attested by God: The Human Jesus of the Synoptic Gospels*. Grand Rapids, Mich.: Eerdmans.
Kirk, J. R. Daniel, and Stephen L. Young. 2014. "I Will Set His Hand to the Sea": The Relevance of Ps 88:26 LXX to Debates about Christology in Mark'. *JBL* 133: 333–40.
Kister, Menahem. 2006. 'Some Early Jewish and Christian Exegetical Problems and the Dynamics of Monotheism'. *Journal for the Study of Judaism* 37: 548–93.
Klinghardt, Matthias. 2007. 'Legionsschweine in Gerasa: Lokalkolorit und historischer Hintergrund von Mk 5,1–20'. *ZNW* 98: 28–48.
Knox, W. L. 1961. *St. Paul and the Church of the Gentiles*. Cambridge: Cambridge University Press.
Koch, Dietrich-Alex. 1975. *Die Bedeutung der Wundererzählungen für die Christologie des Markusevangeliums*. BZNW 42. Berlin: Walter de Gruyter.
Koch, Klaus. 1994. 'Monotheismus und Angelologie'. In *Ein Gott allein? JHWH-Verehrung und biblischer Monotheismus im Kontext der israelitischen und altorientalischen Religionsgeschichte*, edited by Walter Dietrich and Martin A. Klopfenstein, 565–81. Freiburg: Vandenhoeck & Ruprecht.
Kok, Michael J. 2015. *The Gospel on the Margins: The Reception of Mark in the Second Century*. Minneapolis, Minn.: Fortress.
Kowalski, Beate. 2020. 'Selective versus Contextual Allusions: Reconsidering Technical Terms of Intertextuality'. In *Methodology in the Use of the Old Testament in the New: Context and Criteria*, edited by David Allen and Steve Smith, 86–102. LNTS 579. London: T&T Clark.
Kraft, Robert A. 1994. 'The Pseudepigrapha in Christianity'. In *Tracing the Threads: Studies in the Vitality of Jewish Pseudepigrapha*, edited by John C. Reeves, 55–86. SBLEJL 6. Atlanta, Ga.: Scholars Press.
Kraus, Hans-Joachin. 1993. *Psalms 60–150*. Translated by Hilton C. Oswald. Minneapolis, Minn.: Fortress.
Krause, Deborah. 1994. 'Narrated Prophecy in Mark 11.12–21: The Divine Authorization

of Judgement'. In *The Gospels and the Scriptures of Israel*, edited by Craig A. Evans and W. Richard Stegner, 235–48. JSNTSup 104. Sheffield: Sheffield Academic Press.

Kreuzer, Siegfried. 2018. 'New Testament Quotations and the Textual History of the Septuagint'. In *Rewriting and Reception in and of the Bible*, edited by Jesper Høgenhaven, Jesper Tang Nielsen, and Heike Omerzu, 65–84. WUNT 396. Tübingen: Mohr Siebeck.

Kristeva, Julia. 1974. *La Révolution du langage poétique*. Paris: Seuil.

Kristeva, Julia. 1986. 'Revolution in Poetic Language'. In *The Kristeva Reader*, edited by Toril Moi, 90–136. Oxford: Basil Blackwell.

Küchler, Max. 1992. 'Gott und seine Weisheit in der Septuaginta (Ijob 28; Spr 8)'. In *Monotheismus und Christologie: Zur Gottesfrage in hellenistischen Judentum und im Urchristentum*, edited by Hans-Josef Klauck, 118–43. Quaestiones Disputatae 138. Freiburg: Herder.

Kugel, James L. 1998. *Traditions of the Bible: A Guide to the Bible as It Was at the Start of the Common Era*. Cambridge, Mass.: Harvard University Press.

Lacocque, André. 2018. *The Book of Daniel*. 2nd rev. ed. Eugene, Oreg.: Cascade.

Lahurd, Carol Schersten. 1990. 'Reader Response to Ritual Elements in Mark 5:1–20'. *BTB* 20: 154–60.

Lakoff, George. 1987. *Women, Fire, and Dangerous Things: What Categories Reveal about the Mind*. Chicago: University of Chicago Press.

Lamb, William R. S. 2012. *The Catena in Marcum: A Byzantine Anthology of Early Christian Commentary on Mark*. TENTS 6. Leiden: Brill.

Lampe, George. 1965. 'Hermeneutics and Typology'. *The London Quarterly & Holborn Review* 34: 17–25.

Lang, Bernhard. 1994. 'Der monarchische Monotheismus und die Konstellation zweier Götter im Frühjudentum: Ein neuer Versuch über Menschensohn, Sophia und Christologie'. In *Ein Gott allein? JHWH-Verehrung und biblischer Monotheismus im Kontext der israelitischen und altorientalischen Religionsgeschichte*, edited by Walter Dietrich and Martin A. Klopfenstein, 559–64. Freiburg: Vandenhoeck & Ruprecht.

Lapide, Pinchas. 1980. 'A Jewish Exegesis of the Walking on Water'. Translated by G. W. S. Knowles. *Concilium* 138: 35–40.

Larsson, Kristian. 2014. 'Intertextual Density, Quantifying Imitation'. *JBL* 133: 309–32.

Law, Timothy Michael. 2013. *When God Spoke Greek: The Septuagint and the Making of the Christian Bible*. Oxford: Oxford University Press.

Lee, Dorothy. 2004. *Transfiguration*. New Century Theology. London: Continuum.

Leim, Joshua E. 2013. 'In the Glory of His Father: Intertextuality and the Apocalyptic Son of Man in the Gospel of Mark'. *Journal of Theological Interpretation* 7: 213–32.

Levenson, Jon Douglas. 1993. *The Death and Resurrection of the Beloved Son: The Transformation of Child Sacrifice in Judaism and Christianity*. New Haven, Conn.: Yale University Press.

Levinson, Bernard M. 1997. *Deuteronomy and the Hermeneutics of Legal Innovation*. Oxford: Oxford University Press.

Lindars, Barnabas. 1961. *New Testament Apologetic*. Philadelphia, Pa.: Westminster.

Lindars, Barnabas. 1965. 'Elijah, Elisha and the Gospel Miracles'. In *Miracles*, edited by C. F. D. Moule, 61–80. London: A. R. Mowbray & Co.

Lindbeck, George A. 1984. *The Nature of Doctrine: Religion and Theology in a Post-Liberal Age*. Louisville, Ky.: Westminster John Knox.

Litwa, M. David. 2014a. *IESUS DEUS: The Early Christian Depiction of Jesus as a Mediterranean God*. Minneapolis, Minn.: Fortress.

Litwa, M. David. 2014b. 'The Deification of Moses in Philo of Alexandria'. *The Studia Philonica Annual* 26: 1–27.
Loke, Andrew Ter Ern. 2017. *The Origin of Divine Christology*. SNTSMS 169. Cambridge: Cambridge University Press.
Longenecker, Richard. 2016. *The Epistle to the Romans*. NIGTC. Grand Rapids, Mich.: Eerdmans.
Lyons, Michael A. 2015. 'Psalm 22 and the 'Servants' of Isaiah 54; 56–66'. *CBQ* 77: 640–56.
MacDonald, Dennis R. 2000. *The Homeric Epics and the Gospel of Mark*. New Haven, Conn.: Yale University Press.
MacDonald, Dennis R. 2001. 'Introduction'. In *Mimesis and Intertextuality in Antiquity and Christianity*, edited by Dennis R. MacDonald, 1–10. Harrisburg, Pa.: Trinity Press International.
MacDonald, Nathan. 2008. *Not Bread Alone: The Uses of Food in the Old Testament*. New York: Oxford University Press.
Mach, Michael. 1999. 'Concepts of Jewish Monotheism during the Hellenistic Period'. In *The Jewish Roots of Christological Monotheism*, edited by C. C. Newman, James R. Davila and Gladys S. Lewis, 21–42. JSJSup 63. Leiden: Brill.
Mainwaring, Simon. 2014. *Mark, Mutuality, and Mental Health: Encounters with Jesus*. SemeiaSt 79. Atlanta, Ga.: SBL.
Malbon, Elizabeth Struthers. 1984. 'The Jesus of Mark and the Sea of Galilee'. *Journal of Biblical Literature* 103, no. 3: 363–77.
Malbon, Elizabeth Struthers. 2014. *Mark's Jesus: Characterization as Narrative Christology*. Waco, Tex.: Baylor.
Marcus, Joel. 1992. *The Way of the Lord*. Louisville, Ky.: John Knox.
Marcus, Joel. 1994. 'Authority to Forgive Sins upon the Earth: The Shema in the Gospel of Mark'. In *The Gospels and the Scriptures of Israel*, edited by Craig A. Evans and W. Richard Stegner, 196–211. JSNTSup 104. Sheffield: Sheffield Academic Press.
Marcus, Joel. 2000a. *Mark 1–8: A New Translation with Introduction and Commentary*. AYB. New Haven, Conn.: Yale University Press.
Marcus, Joel. 2000b. *Mark: 8–16: A New Translation with Introduction and Commentary*. AYB. New Haven, Conn.: Yale University Press.
Marcus, Joel. 2008. 'Identity and Ambiguity in Markan Christology'. In *Seeking the Identity of Jesus: A Pilgrimage*, edited by Beverly Roberts Gaventa and Richard B. Hays, 133–47. Grand Rapids, Mich.: Eerdmans.
Martens, Peter W. 2008. 'Revisiting the Allegory/Typology Distinction: The Case of Origen'. *JECS* 16: 283–317.
Martin, Dale. 2010. *The Corinthian Body*. New Haven, Conn.: Yale University Press.
Martin, Dale. 'When Did Angels Become Demons?' *JBL* 129: 657–77.
Martínez, Florentino García, and Eibert J. C. Tigchelaar. 2000. *The Dead Sea Scrolls: Study Edition*. 2 vols. Leiden: Brill.
Marxsen, Willi. 1979. *The Beginnings of Christology: Together with The Lord's Supper as a Christological Problem*. Translated by Paul J. Achtemeier and Lorenz Nieting. Philadelphia, Pa.: Fortress.
Masuda, Sanae. 1982. 'The Good News of the Miracle of the Bread: The Tradition and Its Markan Redaction'. *NTS* 28: 191–219.
Maynard, Arthur H. 1985. 'ΤΙ ΕΜΟΙ ΚΑΙ ΣΟΙ'. *NTS* 31: 582–86.
Mayr, Florian. 2008. 'Epiphanen und Heilungen: Zur Konfiguration der Wunderzählungen im Markusevangelium'. *Münchener Theologische Zeitschrift* 59: 113–36.

Mays, James Luther. 2011. *Psalms*. Louisville, Ky.: Westminster John Knox.
McInerny, William F. 1996. 'An Unresolved Question in the Gospel Called Mark: "Who Is This Whom Even Wind and Sea Obey?" (4:41)'. *Perspectives in Religious Studies* 23: 255–68.
McLay, R. Timothy. 2003. *The Use of the Septuagint in New Testament Research*. Grand Rapids, Mich.: Eerdmans.
Meier, John P. 1991. *A Marginal Jew: Rethinking the Historical Jesus*. 5 vols. ABRL. New York: Doubleday.
Meier, Samuel A. 1999. 'Angel of Yahweh מלאך יהוה.' In *Dictionary of Deities and Demons in the Bible*, edited by Karel van der Toorn, Bob Becking and Pieter W. van der Horst, rev. edn, 53–59. Leiden: Brill.
Metzger, Bruce M. 1971. *Textual Commentary on the Greek New Testament*. London: United Bible Societies.
Meye, Robert. 1978. 'Psalm 107 as "Horizon" for Interpreting the Miracle Stories of Mark 4:35–8:26'. In *Unity and Diversity in New Testament Theology: Essays in Honour of George E. Ladd*, edited by Robert A. Guelich, 1–13. Grand Rapids, Mich.: Eerdmans.
Milinovich, Timothy. 2015. 'The Parable of the Storm: Instruction and Demonstration in Mark 4:1–41'. *BTB* 45: 88–98.
Millay, Thomas J. 2017. 'Septuagint Figura: Assessing the Contribution of Richard B. Hays'. *Scottish Journal of Theology* 70: 93–104.
Mirqin, M. 1981. *Midrash Rabbah*. Vol. 5. 11 vols. Tel Aviv: Yavneh.
Moberly, Walter. 1992. *The Old Testament of the Old Testament: Patriarchal Narratives and Mosaic Yahwism*. Minneapolis, Minn.: Fortress.
Montefiore, Hugh. 1962. 'Revolt in the Desert? (Mark VI.33ff.)'. *NTS* 8: 135–41.
Moo, Douglas J. 1983. *The Old Testament in the Gospel Passion Narratives*. Sheffield: Almond Press.
Moore, Carey A. 1996. *Tobit*. AB 40A. New York: Doubleday.
Morey, Ann-Janine. 1990. 'The Old In/Out'. In *The Daemonic Imagination: Biblical Text and Secular Story*, edited by Robert Detweiler and William G. Doty, 169–80. AAR Studies in Religion 60, Atlanta, Ga.; Scholars Press.
Moscicke, Hans. 2019. 'The Gerasene Exorcism and Jesus' Eschatological Expulsion of Cosmic Powers: Echoes of Second Temple Scapegoat Traditions in Mark 5.1–20'. *JSNT* 41: 363–83.
Moss, Candida R. 2010. 'The Man with the Flow of Power: Porous Bodies in Mark 5:25–34'. *JBL* 129: 507–19.
Moyise, Steve. 2000. 'Intertextuality and the Study of the OT in the NT'. In *The Old Testament in the New Testament: Essays in Honour of J. L. North*, edited by Steve Moyise, 14–41. JSNTSup 189. Sheffield: Sheffield Academic Press.
Moyise, Steve. 2005. 'Intertextuality and Biblical Studies: A Review'. *Verbum et Ecclesia* 23: 418–31.
Moyise, Steve. 2020. 'Concluding Reflections'. In *Methodology in the Use of the Old Testament in the New: Context and Criteria*, edited by David Allen and Steve Smith, 178–86. LNTS 579. London: T&T Clark.
Muddiman, John. 2003. 'Zechariah 13:7 and Mark's Account of the Arrest in Gethsemane'. In *The Book of Zechariah and Its Influence*, edited by Christopher Tuckett, 101–9. Aldershot: Ashgate.
Murcia, Thierry. 2016. 'La question du fond historique des récits évangéliques. Deux guérisons un jour de Kippour: l'hémorroïsse et la résurrection de la fille de Jaïre et le possédé de Gérasa/Gadara'. *Judaïsme Ancien* 4: 123–64.

Murphy, Frederick J. 1993. *Pseudo-Philo: Rewriting the Bible*. New York: Oxford University Press.
Myers, Ched. 2008. *Binding the Strong Man: A Political Reading of Mark's Story of Jesus*. Maryknoll, NY: Orbis Books.
Nemoy, Leon, ed. 1968. *Pesikta Rabbati*. Translated by William G. Braude. Yale Judaica, XVIII. New Haven, Conn.: Yale University Press.
Neusner, Jacob. 1977. *The Tosefta*. Vol. 3. 6 vols. Hoboken, NJ: Scholars Press.
Newsom, Carol A. 2005. 'Spying out the Land: A Report from Genology'. In *Seeking Out the Wisdom of the Ancients*, edited by Ronald L. Troxel, Kevin G. Freibel, and Dennis R. Magary, 437–50. Winona Lake, Ind.: Eisenbrauns.
Newsom, Carol A. 2014. *Daniel*. OTL. Louisville, Ky.: Westminster John Knox Press.
Nielsen, J. T. 1968. *Adam and Christ in the Theology of Irenaeus of Lyons*. Assen: Van Gorcum.
North, Wendy, and Loren T. Stuckenbruck. 2004. 'Introduction'. In *Early Jewish and Christian Monotheism*, edited by Loren T. Stuckenbruck and Wendy North, 1–13. JSNTSup 263. London: T&T Clark.
Novakovic, Lidija. 2007. '4Q521: The Works of the Messiah or the Signs of the Messianic Time?' In *Qumran Studies: New Approaches, New Questions*, edited by Michael Thomas Davis and Brent A. Strawn, 208–31. Grand Rapids, Mich.: Eerdmans.
Novenson, Matthew V. 2012. *Christ among the Messiahs: Christ Language in Paul and Messiah Language in Ancient Judaism*. New York: Oxford University Press.
Novenson, Matthew V. 2020. 'Introduction'. In Monotheism and Christology in Greco-Roman Antiquity, edited by Matthew V. Novenson, NovTestSup 180, 1–8. Leiden: Brill.
Nowell, Irene. 2005. 'The Book of Tobit: An Ancestral Story'. In *Intertextual Studies in Ben Sira and Tobit*, edited by Jeremy Corley and Vincent Skemp, 3–13. CBQM 38. Washington, D.C.: Catholic Biblical Association of America.
Nyström, Jennifer. 2016. 'Jesus' Exorcistic Identity Reconsidered: The Demise of a Solomonic Typology'. In *Jesus and the Scriptures: Problems, Passages and Patterns*, edited by Tobias Hägerland, 69–92. LNTS 552. London: Bloomsbury.
O'Brien, Kelli S. 2010. *The Use of Scripture in the Markan Passion Narrative*. LNTS 384. London: T&T Clark.
Omerzu, Heike. 2011. 'Geschichte durch Geschichten: zur Bedeutung jüdischer Traditionen für die Jesusdarstellung des Markusevangeliums'. *Early Christianity* 2: 77–99.
O'Neill, John. 1994. 'Adam Who Is the Figure of Him that Was to Come: A Reading of Romans 5:12–21'. In *Crossing the Boundaries: Essays in Biblical Interpretation in Honour of Michael D. Goulder*, edited by Stanely E. Porter, Paul Joyce and David E. Orton, 183–200. Leiden: Brill.
Osborne, Grant R. 1994. 'Structure and Christology in Mark 1:21–45'. In *Jesus of Nazareth: Lord and Christ: Essays on the Historical Jesus and New Testament Christology*, edited by Joel B. Green and Max Turner, 147–63. Grand Rapids, Mich.: Eerdmans.
Ounsworth, Richard. 2012. *Joshua Typology in the New Testament*. WUNT 2. 328. Tubingen: Mohr Siebeck.
Owen, Paul. 2015. 'Jesus as God's Chief Agent in Mark's Christology'. In *Mark, Manuscripts, and Monotheism: Essays in Honour of Larry W. Hurtado*, edited by Chris Keith and Dieter T. Roth, 40–57. LNTS 528. London: Bloomsbury.
Pearson, Birger. 1976. *The Pneumatikos-Psychikos Terminology in 1 Corinthians: A Study in the Terminology of the Corinthian Opponents of Paul and Its Relation to Gnosticism*. Dissertation Series 12. Missoula, Mont.: Scholars Press.
Perrin, Norman. 1976. 'The Interpretation of the Gospel of Mark'. *Interpretation* 30: 115–24.

Pesch, Rudolf. 1979. *Das Markusevangelium*. 2 vols. HThKNT 2. Freiburg: Herder.
Petersen, Norman R. 1978. 'Point of View in Mark's Narrative'. *Semeia* 12: 97–121.
Petterson, Anthony R. 2009. *Behold Your King: The Hope for the House of David in the Book of Zechariah*. LHBOTS 513. London: T&T Clark.
Pitts, Andrew W. 2016. 'The Origins of Greek Mimesis and the Gospel of Mark: Genre as Potential Constraint in Assessing Markan Imitation'. In *Ancient Education and Early Christianity*, edited by Matthew Ryan Hauge and Andrew W. Pitts, 107–36. LNTS 533. London: T&T Clark.
Porter, Stanley E. 1997. 'The Use of the Old Testament in the New Testament: A Brief Commentary on Method and Terminology'. In *Early Christian Interpretation of the Scripture of Israel: Investigations and Proposals*, edited by Craig A. Evans and James A. Sanders, 79–96. JSNTSup 148. Sheffield: Sheffield Academic Press.
Portier-Young, Anathea. 2005. '"Eyes to the Blind": A Dialogue between Tobit and Job'. In *Intertextual Studies in Ben Sira and Tobit*, edited by Jeremy Corley and Vincent Skemp, 14–27. CBQM 38. Washington, DC: Catholic Biblical Association of America.
Potolsky, Matthew. 2006. *Mimesis*. The New Critical Idiom. New York: Routledge.
Powell, Mark Allan. 2007. 'Echoes of Jonah in the New Testament'. *Word and World* 27: 157–64.
Putthoff, Tyson L. 2017. *Ontological Aspects of Early Jewish Anthropology: The Malleable Self and the Presence of God*. BRLJ 53. Leiden: Brill.
Rajkumar, Peniel Jesudason Rufus. 2007. 'A Dalithos Reading of a Markan Exorcism: Mark 5:1–20'. *ExpTim* 118: 428–35.
Ramsey, Arthur Michael. 1949. *The Glory of God and the Transfiguration of Christ*. London: Longmans, Green and Co.
Rao, D. Vijaya, ed. 2012. *Armies, Wars and Their Food*. New Delhi: Cambridge University Press India.
Reed, Annette Yoshiko. 2009. 'Beyond Revealed Wisdom and Apocalyptic Epistemology: Early Christian Transformations of Enochic Traditions about Knowledge'. In *Early Christian Literature and Intertextuality*, edited by Craig A. Evans and H. Daniel Zacharias, Volume 1: Thematic Studies, 138–64. LNTS 391. London: T&T Clark.
Reid, Robert S. 1994. 'When Words Were a Power Loosed: Audience Expectation and Finished Narrative in the Gospel of Mark'. *Quarterly Journal of Speech* 80: 427–47.
Rhoads, David. 1982. 'Narrative Criticism and the Gospel of Mark'. *Journal of the American Academy of Religion* 50: 411–34.
Rhoads, David. 2004. *Reading Mark: Engaging the Gospel*. Minneapolis, Minn.: Fortress.
Rhoads, David, and Donald Michie. 1982. *Mark as Story: An Introduction to the Narrative of a Gospel*. Philadelphia, Pa.: Fortress.
Richardson, Alan. 1941. *The Miracle Stories of the Gospels*. London: SCM.
Rindge, Matthew S. 2012. 'Reconfiguring the Akedah and Recasting God: Lament and Divine Abandonment in Mark'. *JBL* 131: 755–74.
Robinson, Jonathan Rivett. 2021 'Jonah's Gourd and Mark's Gethsemane: A Study in Messianic Allegorical Exegesis'. *Journal for the Study of the New Testament* 43.3: 370–88.
Robinson, Jonathan Rivett. Forthcoming (a). 'Reconsidering Psalm 89:25, Jewish Water Miracles, and Markan Christology'. *Journal of the Jesus Movement in its Jewish Setting*.
Robinson, Jonathan Rivett. Forthcoming (b). '"Listen to Him!": Angelic and Divine Typology in Mark's Transfiguration Account'. *Horizons in Biblical Theology*.
Rosch, Eleanor. 1975. 'Cognitive Representations of Semantic Categories'. *Journal of Experimental Psychology: General* 104: 192–233.

Roth, Wolfgang. 1988. *Hebrew Gospel: Cracking the Code of Mark*. Oak Park, Ill.: Meyer-Stone.
Rowland, Christopher. 1982. *The Open Heaven: A Study of Apocalyptic in Judaism and Early Christianity*. London: SPCK.
Rudd, Niall, trans. 1991. *Juvenal: The Satires*. Oxford: Clarendon.
Salzmann, Andrew Benjamin. 2009. "Do You Still Not Understand?' Mark 8:21 and the Mission to the Gentiles'. *BTB* 39: 129-34.
Sanders, E.P. *Jesus and Judaism*. 1987. Philadelphia, Phil.: Fortress.
Sanders, E.P. 2016. *Judaism: Practice and Belief, 63 BCE-66CE*. Minneapolis, Minn.: Fortress Press.
Sanders, John. 2007. *The God Who Risks*. Rev edn. Downers Grove, Ill.: IVP.
Sandmel, Samuel. 1962. 'Parallelomania'. *JBL* 81: 1-13.
Sandmel, Samuel. 1970. 'Prolegomena to a Commentary on Mark'. In *New Testament Issues*, edited by Richard Batey, 45-56. London: SCM.
Schenke, Ludger. 1974. *Die Wundererzählungen des Markusevangeliums*. SBB 5. Stuttgart: Katholisches Bibelwerk.
Schildgen, Brenda Deen. 1999. *Power and Prejudice: The Reception of the Gospel of Mark*. Detroit, Mich.: Wayne State University Press.
Schmücker, Reinold. 1993. 'Zur Funktion der Wundergeschichten im Markusevangelium'. *ZNW* 84: 1-26.
Schnabel, Eckhard J. 1994. 'Jesus and the Beginnings of the Mission to the Gentiles'. In *Jesus of Nazareth: Lord and Christ: Essays on the Historical Jesus and New Testament Christology*, edited by Joel B. Green and Max Turner, 37-58. Grand Rapids, Mich.: Eerdmans.
Schnackenburg, Rudolf. 1995. *Jesus in the Gospels: A Biblical Christology*. Translated by O. C. Dean. Louisville, Ky.: Westminster John Knox.
Schneck, Richard. 1994. *Isaiah in the Gospel of Mark, I-VIII*. Vallejo, CA: BIBAL.
Schniewind, Julius. 1958. *Das Evangelium nach Markus*. Berlin: Evangelische Verlaganstalt.
Scholtissek, Klaus. 1995. 'Der Sohn Gottes für das Reich Gottes'. In *Der Evangelist als Theologe: Studien zum Markusevangelium*, edited by Thomas Söding. Stuttgarter Bibelstudien 163. Stuttgart: Verlag Katholisches Bibelwerk.
Schroer, Sylvia. 1994. 'Die personifizierte Sophia im Buch der Weisheit'. In *Ein Gott allein? JHWH-Verehrung und biblischer Monotheismus im Kontext der israelitischen und altorientalischen Religionsgeschichte*, edited by Walter Dietrich and Martin A. Klopfenstein, 543-58. Freiburg: Vandenhoeck & Ruprecht.
Schweizer, Eduard. 1970. *Good News According to Mark*. London: SPCK.
Scott, Ian W. 2008. 'Epistemology and Social Conflict in Jubilees and Aristeas'. In *Common Judaism: Explorations in Second Temple Judaism*, edited by Wayne O. McCready and Adele Reinhartz, 195-214. Minneapolis, Minn.: Fortress.
Scott, Ian W. 2009. *Paul's Way of Knowing*. Grand Rapids, Mich.: Baker Academic.
Segal, Alan F. 1984. "'He Who Did Not Spare His Own Son . . .': Jesus, Paul and the Akedah'. In *From Jesus to Paul: Studies in Honour of Francis Wright Beare*, edited by P. Richardson and J. C. Hurd, 169-84. Waterloo: Wilfrid Laurier University Press.
Segal, Alan F. 2002. *Two Powers in Heaven: Early Rabbinic Reports about Christianity and Gnosticism*. Boston, Mass.: Brill.
Sellin, Gerhard. 1992. 'Gotterkenntnis und Gotteserfahrung bei Philo von Alexandrien'. In *Monotheismus und Christologie: Zur Gottesfrage in hellenistischen Judentum und im Urchristentum*, edited by Hans-Josef Klauck, 17-40. Quaestiones Disputatae 138. Freiburg: Herder.

Senior, Donald. 1984. 'The Struggle to Be Universal: Mission as Vantage Point for New Testament Investigation'. *CBQ* 46: 63–81.

Shively, Elizabeth E. 2018. 'Recognizing Penguins: Audience Expectation, Cognitive Genre Theory, and the Ending of Mark's Gospel'. *CBQ* 80: 273–92.

Shuve, Karl. 2012. 'Irenaeus' Contribution to Early Christian Interpretation of the Song of Songs'. In *Irenaeus: Life, Scripture, Legacy*, edited by Paul Foster and Sara Parvis, 81–8. Minneapolis, Minn.: Fortress Press.

Sick, David H. 2015. 'The Symposium of the 5,000'. *JTS* 66: 1–27.

Skemp, Vincent. 2005. 'Avenues of Intertextuality between Tobit and the New Testament'. In *Intertextual Studies in Ben Sira and Tobit*, edited by Jeremy Corley and Vincent Skemp, 43–70. CBQM 38. Washington, DC: Catholic Biblical Association of America.

Slater, Thomas B. 1995. 'One like a Son of Man in First-Century CE Judaism'. *NTS* 41: 183–98.

Smith, Dennis E. 2003. *From Symposium to Eucharist: The Banquet in the Early Christian World*. Minneapolis, Minn.: Fortress Press.

Smith, Jonathan Z. 1980. 'Fences and Neighbours: Some Countours of Early Judaism'. In *Approaches to Ancient Judaisms: Theory and Practice*, edited by William Scott Green, vol 2: 1–15. Brown Judaic Studies 1. Chicago: Scholars Press.

Smith, Steve. 2020. 'The Use of Criteria: A Proposal from Relevance Theory'. In *Methodology in the Use of the Old Testament in the New: Context and Criteria*, edited by David Allen and Steve Smith, 142–54. LNTS 579. London: T&T Clark.

Smothers, Colin. 2013. 'Miraculous Redemption: An Allusion to Psalm 107 Found in Mark 4:35–6:44'. Unpublished research paper, Southern Baptist Theological Seminary. https://colinsmothers.files.wordpress.com/2014/04/psalm-107-and-mark-final.pdf. Accessed 27/08/2021.

Snodgrass, Klyne R. 2018. *Stories with Intent: A Comprehensive Guide to the Parables of Jesus*. 2nd edn. Grand Rapids, Mich.: Eerdmans.

Sommer, Benjamin D. 1998. *A Prophet Reads Scripture: Allusion in Isaiah 40–66*. Stanford, CA: Stanford University Press.

Spilsbury, Paul. 2003. 'Flavius Josephus on the Rise and Fall of the Roman Empire'. *JTS* 54: 1–24.

Stamps, Dennis L. 2006. 'The Use of the Old Testament in the New Testament as a Rhetorical Device: A Methodological Proposal'. In *Hearing the Old Testament in the New Testament*, edited by Stanley E. Porter, 9–37. Grand Rapids, Mich.: Eerdmans.

Stanley, Christopher D. 1997. 'The Rhetoric of Quotations: An Essay on Method'. In *Early Christian Interpretation of the Scripture of Israel: Investigations and Proposals*, edited by Craig A. Evans and James A. Sanders, 44–58. JSNTSup 148. Sheffield: Sheffield Academic Press.

Starobinski, Jean. 1973. 'The Struggle with Legion: A Literary Analysis of Mark 5: 1–20'. Translated by Dan O. Via. *New Literary History* 4, no. 2: 331–56.

Stec, David M. 2004. *The Targum of Psalms*. Collegeville, Minn.: Liturgical Press.

Stegner, W. Richard. 1985. 'The Baptism of Jesus: A Story Modelled on the Binding of Isaac'. *Bible Review* 1: 36–46.

Stegner, W. Richard. 1989. *Narrative Theology in Early Jewish Christianity*. Louisville, Ky.: Westminster John Knox Press.

Stegner, W. Richard. 1997. 'The Use of Scripture in Two Narratives of Early Jewish Christianity (Matthew 4.1–11; Mark 9.2–8)'. In *Early Christian Interpretation of the Scriptures of Israel*, edited by Craig A. Evans and James A. Sanders, 98–120. LNTS 148. London: Bloomsbury.

Stein, Robert H. 2008. *Mark*. BECNT. Grand Rapids, Mich.: Baker.
Steinmetz, David. 1980. 'The Superiority of Pre-Critical Exegesis'. *Theology Today* 37: 27–38.
Sternberg, Meir. 1985. *The Poetics of Biblical Narrative: Ideological Literature and the Drama of Reading*. Indiana Studies in Biblical Literature. Bloomington, Ind.: Indiana University Press.
Strauss, David Friedrich. 1846. *The Life of Jesus Critically Examined*. Translated by George Eliot London: SCM Press.
Stuckenbruck, Loren T. 1995. *Angel Veneration and Christology*. WUNT 2. 70. Tübingen: Mohr Siebeck.
Stuckenbruck, Loren T. 1997. *The Book of Giants: Texts, Translation, and Commentary*. TSAJ 63. Tübingen: Mohr Siebeck.
Stuckenbruck, Loren T. 1999. 'Worship and Monotheism in the Ascension of Isaiah'. In *The Jewish Roots of Christological Monotheism*, edited by C. C. Newman, James R. Davila and Gladys S. Lewis, 70–89. JSJSup 63. Leiden: Brill.
Stuckenbruck, Loren T. 2004. ''Angels' and 'God': Exploring the Limits of Early Jewish Monotheism'. In *Early Jewish and Christian Monotheism*, edited by Loren T. Stuckenbruck and Wendy North, 45–70. JSNTSup 263. London: T&T Clark.
Stump, Eleonore. 2009. 'The Problem of Evil: Analytic Philosophy and Narrative'. In *Analytic Theology: New Essays in the Philospy of Theology*, edited by Oliver D. Crisp and Michael C. Rea, 251–64. Oxford: Oxford University Press.
Sugirtharajah, Rasiah S. 2002. *Postcolonial Criticism and Biblical Interpretation*. Oxford: Oxford University Press.
Talbert, Charles. 1977. *What Is a Gospel? The Genre of the Canonical Gospels*. Philadelphia, Pa.: Fortress Press.
Talbert, Charles. 2011. *The Development of Christology during the First Hundred Years: And Other Essays on Early Christian Christology*. NovTSup 140. Leiden: Brill.
Telford, William. 1995. 'Introduction: The Interpretation of Mark'. In *The Interpretation of Mark*, edited by William Telford, 2nd edn, 1–62. Studies in New Testament Interpretation. Edinburgh: T&T Clark.
Telford, William. 2009. *Writing on the Gospel of Mark*. Guides to Advanced Biblical Research. Blandford Forum: Deo Publishing.
Theissen, Gerd. 1983. *The Miracle Stories of the Early Christian Tradition*. Translated by John Kenneth Riches. Edinburgh: T&T Clark.
Theissen, Matthew. 2020. *Jesus and the Forces of Death: The Gospel's Portrayal of Ritual Impurity within First-Century Judaism*. Grand Rapids, Mich.: Baker.
Thompson, Thomas L. 1998. '4QTestamonia and Bible Composition: A Copenhagen Lego Hypothesis'. In *Qumran between the Old and New Testaments*, edited by Frederick H. Cryer and Thomas L. Thompson, 261–76. JSOTSup 290. Sheffield: Sheffield Academic Press.
Tilling, Chris. 2014. 'Problems with Ehrman's Interpretive Categories'. In *How God Became Jesus: The Real Origins of Belief in Jesus' Divine Nature*, edited by Michael F. Bird, Craig A. Evans, Simon J. Gathercole, Charles E. Hill and Chris Tilling, 117–33. Grand Rapids, Mich.: Zondervan.
Tilling, Chris. 2015. *Paul's Divine Christology*. Grand Rapids, Mich.: Eerdmans.
Tooman, William A. 2020. 'Scriptural Reuse in Ancient Jewish Literature: Comments and Reflections on the State of the Art'. In *Methodology in the Use of the Old Testament in the New: Context and Criteria*, edited by David Allen and Steve Smith, 23–39. LNTS 579. London: T&T Clark.

Tov, Emmanuel. 1999. 'The Composition of 1 Samuel 16–18 in Light of the Septuagint'. In *The Greek and Hebrew Bible: Collected Essays on the Septuagint*, 333–62. VTSup 72. Leiden: Brill.
Towner, W. Sibley. 1984. *Daniel*. Interpretation. Atlanta, Ga.: John Knox.
Treier, Daniel J. 2003. 'The Superiority of Pre-Critical Exegesis? Sic et Non'. *Trinity Journal* 24: 77–103.
Trocmé, Etienne. 1975. *The Formation of the Gospel According to Mark*. Translated by P. Gaughan. London: SPCK.
Trumbower, Jeremy A. 1994. 'The Role of Malachi in the Career of John the Baptist'. In *The Gospels and the Scriptures of Israel*, edited by Craig A. Evans and W. Richard Stegner, 28–41. JSNTSup 104. Sheffield: Sheffield Academic Press.
Twelftree, Graham H. 1993. *Jesus the Exorcist*. WUNT 2. 54. Tübingen: Mohr Siebeck.
Twelftree, Graham H. 1999. *Jesus the Miracle Worker: A Historical and Theological Study*. Downers Grove, Ill.: IVP Academic.
Twelftree, Graham H. 2003. 'The Miracles of Jesus: Marginal or Mainstream?' *JSHJ* 1: 104–24.
Ulrich, Eugene C. 1999. *The Dead Sea Scrolls and the Origins of the Bible*. Grand Rapids, Mich.: Eerdmans.
Van Iersel, Bas M. F. 1998. *Mark: A Reader Response Commentary*. Translated by W. H. Bisscheroux. JSNTSup 164. Sheffield: Sheffield Academic Press.
Van Oyen, Geert. 1999. *The Interpretation of the Feeding Miracles in the Gospel of Mark*. Collectanea Biblica et Religiousa Antiqua, IV. Brussels: Koninklijke Vlaamse Acaemie van België.
Vermès, Géza. 1983. *Scripture and Tradition in Judaism: Haggadic Studies*. 2nd rev. edn. Studia Post-Biblica 4. Leiden: Brill.
Viviano, Benedict T., and Justin Taylor. 1992. 'Sadducees, Angels, and Resurrection (Acts 23:8–9)'. *JBL* 111: 496–8.
Von Heijne, Camilla Hélena. 2010. *The Messenger of the Lord in Early Jewish Interpretations of Genesis*. BZAW 412. Berlin: De Gruyter.
Waetjen, Herman C. 1989. *A Reordering of Power: A Socio-Political Reading of Mark's Gospel*. Eugene, Oreg.: Wipf and Stock.
Wainwright, Geoffrey. 1971. *Eucharist and Eschatology*. London: Epworth Press.
Wall, Robert W. 2001. 'The Intertextuality of Scripture: The Example of Rahab (James 2:25)'. In *The Bible at Qumran: Text, Shape, and Interpretation*, edited by Peter W. Flint, 217–36. SDSS. Grand Rapids, Mich.: Eerdmans.
Wallace, Daniel B. 1996. *Greek Grammar beyond the Basics*. Grand Rapids, Mich.: Zondervan.
Walsh, Jerome T. 2001. *Style and Structure in Biblical Hebrew Narrative*. Collegeville, Minn.: Liturgical Press.
Warrington, Keith. 2015. *The Miracles in the Gospels*. Peabody, Mass.: Hendrickson.
Watts, Joel L. 2013. *Mimetic Criticism and the Gospel of Mark: An Introduction and Commentary*. Eugene, Oreg.: Wipf and Stock.
Watts, Rikki E. 1997. *Isaiah's New Exodus in Mark*. Grand Rapids, Mich.: Baker.
Watts, Rikki E. 2004. 'Jesus and the New Exodus Restoration of Daughter Zion: Mark 5:21–43 in Context'. In *The New Testament in Its First Century Setting: Essays on Context and Background in Honour of B. W. Winter on His 65th Birthday*, 13–29. Grand Rapids, Mich.: Eerdmans.
Watts, Rikki E. 2007. 'Mark'. In *Commentary on the New Testament Use of the Old Testament*, edited by G. K. Beale and D. A. Carson, 111–250. Grand Rapids, Mich.: Baker Academic.

Watts, Rikki E. 2020. 'Rethinking Context in the Relationship of Israel's Scriptures to the NT: Character, Agency and the Possibility of Genuine Change'. In *Methodology in the Use of the Old Testament in the New: Context and Criteria*, edited by David Allen and Steve Smith, 157–77. LNTS 579. London: T&T Clark.
Weeden, Theodore J. 1971. *Mark: Traditions in Conflict*. Fortress Press.
Wefal, Eric K. 1995. 'The Separate Gentile Mission in Mark: A Narrative Explanation of Markan Geography, the Two Feeding Accounts and Exorcisms'. *JSNT* 60: 3–26.
Wenham, David. 1995. 'How Jesus Understood the Last Supper: A Parable in Action'. *Themelios* 20: 11–16.
Westerholm, Stephen, and Martin Westerholm. 2016. *Reading Sacred Scripture: Voices from the History of Biblical Interpretation*. Grand Rapids, Mich.: Eerdmans.
Whitenton, Michael R. 2016. *Hearing Kyriotic Sonship: A Cognitive and Rhetorical Approach to the Characterization of Mark's Jesus*. BINS 148. Leiden: Brill.
Whitlatch, Lisa. 2016. 'The Attainment of Every Virtue: A Pindaric Allusion in Grattius' Cynegetica', *Classical Quarterly* 66: 807–12.
Wilpert, G. (=J.). 1903. *Roma sotteranea: Le pitture delle catacombe romane*. Rome.
Wilpert, J. 1895. *Fractio Panis: die älteste Darstellung des eucharistischen Opfers in der 'Cappela Graeca'*. Freiburg.
Wilpert, J. 1897. *Die Malerien der Sakramentskapellen in der Katacombe des hl. Callistus*. Freiburg.
Winn, Adam. 2010. *Mark and the Elijah-Elisha Narrative: Considering the Practice of Greco-Roman Imitation in the Search for Markan Source Material*. Eugene, Oreg.: Pickwick.
Winn, Adam. 2016. *Reading Mark's Christology under Caesar: Jesus the Messiah and Roman Imperial Ideology*. Downers Grove, Ill.: IVP Academic.
Winter, Paul, and Géza Vermès. 1974. *On the Trial of Jesus*. Berlin: Walter de Gruyter.
Witherington, Ben. 2001. *The Gospel of Mark: A Socio-Rhetorical Commentary*. Grand Rapids, Mich.: Eerdmans.
Witherington, Ben. 2017. *Isaiah Old and New: Exegesis, Intertextuality, and Hermeneutics*. Minneapolis, Minn.: Fortress.
Woodruff, Paul. 1992. 'Aristotle on Mimesis'. In *Essays on Aristotle's Poetics*, edited by Amélie Oksenberg Rorty, 73–96. Princeton, N.J.: Princeton University Press.
Wrede, Wilhelm. 1901. *Das Messiasgeheimnis in den Evangelien: Zugleich ein Beitrag zum Verständnis des Markusevangeliums*. Göttingen: Vandenhoeck & Ruprecht.
Wrede, William. 1971. *Messianic Secret*. Translated by J. C. G. Greig. Cambridge: James Clarke.
Wright, Archie. 2005. 'Some Observations of Philo's *De Gigantibus* and Evil Spirits in Second Temple Judaism'. *JSJ* 36: 471–88.
Wright, Archie. 2016. 'The Demonology of 1 Enoch and the New Testament Gospels'. In *Enoch and the Synoptic Gospels: Reminiscences, Allusions, Intertextuality*, edited by Loren T. Stuckenbruck and Gabriele Boccaccini, 215–44. EJL 44. Atlanta, Ga.: SBL.
Wright, Terence R. 1990. 'Margaret Atwood and St. Mark: The Shape of the Gaps'. In *The Daemonic Imagination: Biblical Text and Secular Story*, edited by Robert Detweiler and William G. Doty, 181–90. AAR Studies in Religion 60, Atlanta, Ga.; Scholars Press.
Young, Frances. 1987. 'Allegory and Atonement'. *Australian Biblical Review* 35: 107–14.
Young, Frances. 1989. 'The Rhetorical Schools and Their Influence on Patristic Exegesis'. In *The Making of Orthodoxy: Essays in Honour of Henry Chadwick*, edited by R. Williams. Cambridge: Cambridge University Press.
Young, Frances. 1997a. *Biblical Exegesis and the Formation of Christian Culture*. Cambridge: Cambridge University Press.

Young, Frances. 1997b. 'The Fourth Century Reaction against Allegory'. In *Studia Patristica*, 30: 120–5. Leuven: Peeters.
Young, Frances. 1999. 'The Confessions of St Augustine: What Is the Genre of This Work? (The 1998 St Augustine Lecture)'. *Augustinian Studies* 30: 1–16.
Young, Frances. 2002. 'Ministerial Forms and Functions in the Church Communities of the Greek Fathers'. In *Community Formation in the Early Church and in the Church Today*, edited by Richard Longenecker, 157–76. Peabody, Mass.: Hendrickson Publishers.
Youngblood, Kevin J. 2014. *Jonah: God's Scandalous Mercy*. Grand Rapids, Mich: Zondervan.
Zadorojnyi, Alexei V. 2012. 'Mimesis and the (Plu)Past in Plutarch's Lives'. In *Time and Narrative in Ancient Historiography: The 'Plupast' from Herodotus to Appian*, edited by Jonas Grethlein and Christopher B. Krebs, 175–98. Cambridge: Cambridge University Press.
Zakovich, Yair. 1990. *The Concept of the Miracle in the Bible*. Tel Aviv: MOD Books.
Zwiep, Arie W. 2015. 'Jairus, His Daughter and the Haemorrhaging Woman (Mk 5.21–43; Mt. 9.18–26; Lk. 8.40–56): Research Survey of a Gospel Story about People in Distress'. *CBR* 13, no. 3: 351–87.

Scripture Index

HEBREW BIBLE
Genesis
1 95
1–11 35
1:2 69, 189
1:4 189
1:9 41
6:1–4 129, 132
7–8 95
8:1 96
9:13 42
9:15 42
11 135
11:30 38
11:31 47
12 135
12:10–13:2 35
12:14 38
15:1–5 38
15:5 61
15:6 38
15:7 36
16:4 38
17:1 38
18:22–33 38
20:17 105
22 51, 80
22:1 38, 53
22:2–3 36
22:2 53, 59, 66, 69–70
22:3 53
22:5 69
22:11–12 53
22:12 36, 53, 66, 70
22:13–14 68
22:14 59, 69
22:16 53, 66, 70
22:17 62
22:18 59
24:40 38
25:7 38
25:21–23 38
25:29–34 135
26:1 135
27:1 38
27:33 111
29:4–6 38–9
42:8 41
48–49 38
49 40
49:10–11 72
51:1–14 40

Exodus
1:4 36
1:7 35
3 37
3:7–10 38
3:14 95
4:20 168
7–12 36
7:3 30
7:27 38
8:16–24 38
10:21–23 69
11:9–10 30
12 37
12:11 37
12:23 38
12:31 36
12:35 36
12:38 36
13:1 69
13:11–16 69
13:18 31
14 41, 92
14:21 30, 71
14:31 183
15 36
15:1 183
15:4 139
15:10 183
15:12 183
16 170, 182
16:3 169
16:4 172
16:6–8 172
16:8 168
16:11–12 174
16:12 168–9, 174
16:15 168
16:16 168
16:19–20 171
16:24 168
16:28–29 174
16:34 168
17 37
18:19–20 168
18:21 159, 168
18:22 168
18:25 159, 168
18:26 168
20:2 36
20:20 36, 95
20:24 36
23:21 57
24 37, 56–7
24:9–18 57
24:10 58
26:22 87
32:5 45
32:19–20 42
33:17–23 95
34 56–7
34:2–6 175
34:5 58
34:6 95
34:29–35 41, 63
34:29 57–8
34:35 57

Leviticus
12–15 113
16:21 131
16:22 131
17:7 127

Numbers
5 42
11 153, 170, 174, 180
11:5 170–1
11:13 169, 175
11:21–22 169
11:21 171, 174
11:22 170, 175
11:23 174
11:24 174
11:26–29 170
11:32 170
12:1 180
12:13 105
13 36
13:25–33 135
17:25 42
18:27 66
18:30 66
21:9 105
23:16–17 160
25:1–15 39–40
27:17 167–9, 175
33:24–25 111

Deuteronomy
1–34 37
1:15 159, 168
4:34 30
5:29 36
6:22 30
7:1–2 169
7:1 44
7:19 30

8:2 36
9 37
10:12-22 36
11:3 30
12:5 36
15:14 66
16:3 37
16:13 66
17:7 44
17:12 44
18:15-18 168
18:18-19 57
19:19 44
21:21 44
29:2 30
31-32 38
32:8 128
32:17 128
32:16-17 127
32:21 45
32:39 95
33:5 168
34:11 30

Joshua
2 36
2:10 183
3 92
3:7 37
3:14-17 30
4:14 37
4:22-24 37
4:23 183
5 37
6 31
7 37
9 170, 180, 184
9:6 169, 178
9:9 178
9:16 169, 178
9:22 169, 178
23-24 37
24:5 38

Judges
3:7-11 4
3:12-30 4
6:23 95

1 Samuel/
  1 Kingdoms
2:14 22
6:3 105
10:1 74
13:14 142
14:15 111
14:6 40
16:7 142
16:13 73
16:14-18:9 123, 133-51
16:14-23 126, 134-6, 144
16:14-15 138-9
16:14 142
17:1-18:9 136
17:3 136
17:4-11 135
17:4-10 136
17:4 137
17:5 137
17:8 137
17:16 136
17:28 137
17:34 137, 141
17:36 148
17:41-47 136, 148
17:42 148
17:43 136, 148
17:44-46 138
17:45-47 146
17:45 141, 148
17:46 142
17:47 142, 146, 149-50
17:48 136
17:49 137
17:51-53 138
17:52 142
17:53 142, 149
18:2 138
18:6-7 138
18:7 136-7
18:8-9 138
21:1-8 142
21:1-6 23
22:1-2 40
22:7-19 40

23:1-5 40
23:14 40
24:3 87
30:22-25 40

2 Samuel/
  2 Kingdoms
1:19 40
2:4-5 74
2:4 73
2:6-7 74
2:8 74
7:7 141
7:13-14 80
7:14 76
10:19 183
15 80
15:16-31 75
15:31 75
16:10 137
19:22 137
21:15-22 135

1 Kings/
  3 Kingdoms
1:8 20
15:11 4
17-2 Kgs 13 107
17:1-18:46 107
17:1-7 42
17:8-16 156
17:17-24 4, 101, 106, 108, 116
17:9 108
17:20 120
17:24 108, 116
18:4 56, 159
18:5-6 159
18:5 171
19:2 56, 159
19:8-18 56
19:8 57
19:11 95
19:16 147
19:19-21 42
21 159
21:1-22:40 107
22:17 167

2 Kings/4
  Kingdoms
2:8-14 92
2:9 106
2:19-22 114
3:4-27 114
4:1-7 114, 156
4:8-37 111
4:9 109
4:10 109
4:13 109, 111, 121
4:14 109
4:18-37 4, 64, 101, 106-22
4:22-25 109
4:23-26 111
4:23 109-10
4:26 110
4:27 108, 110, 116, 120
4:28 110-11
4:29 110
4:30 108-9
4:31 110
4:33 108, 120
4:37 108, 110
4:38-41 114
4:42-44 114-15, 153, 156, 164-5, 168, 171, 173-4, 180, 182
5:1-27 121
5:1-19 105, 114, 180
5:8 116
5:11 109
5:26 116
6:8-23 114, 180, 184
6:12 116
6:20-23 121
6:22 180
6:23 180
6:27 66
7:1-2 114
8:1-6 114
9:3 74
9:6 74

11:1–12:17 107
13:14–21 114
13:20–21 106, 110
14:25 97
18:13 4
19:26 171
20:7 105
22:2 4

1 Chronicles
19:19 183
22:18 183
23:25 183

2 Chronicles
3:1 69
18:16 167
30:20 105

Nehemiah
9:11 183

Job 38
8:12 171
9:2 191
9:8–13 95, 153, 182, 191
9:13 191
26 83–4
38 83–4
40:15 171

Psalms
2:1–2 138
2:7 47, 76
2:9 141
22 35, 70, 77
23 153, 159, 165–7, 172–4
23:1 174
LXX 22:4 165
24:3 69
37:2 171
41 75, 77, 80
42:6 90
42:12 90
43:5 90
44:23 98
55 75, 80

66:5–6 183
69 70
69:25 138
72:17 189
77:43 30
78 170
78:13 183
LXX 77:29 169, 176
78:52 167, 169
78:70–72 167
78:70–72 169
80:8–18 75
89 84
89:8–10 96
89:25 92–3
89:27–28 76
LXX 90:6 127
93:2 189
95 171
95:5 127
LXX 103:2 59
104:27 30
106 84
106:9–11 183
106:9 96
106:37 128
107 81, 83–6, 94, 101
107:23–32 83–6, 98
107:43 84
109:8 138
110:1 78–9, 147
110:4 79
114 37
114:1–3 183
118:19–20 66
118:22–23 66, 72
118:25–26 23, 72
118:27 66
119:176 168
LXX Psalm 131:15 172
134:9 30
136:13–15 183

Proverbs
3:10 66
29:25 111

Song of Solomon
1:3 74
1:4 74
2:5 74
4:10 74
4:14 74

Isaiah
2:2–3 1832:3 69
5:1–7 72
5:1–2 65–7
8:14 67
11:1ff 37
11:1–5 37
11:2 189
11:15–16 37
13:21 127
16:10 66
19:19–25 37
21:4 111
28:16 67
29:13 176
29:18–19 176
29:18 178
30:29 69
34:4 64–5
34:14 127
35:5–6 9, 178
40–55 35
40 84
40:3 18, 47, 52, 80
40:11 75
41:4 95
42:1 47
43:16–21 37
45:6 183
48:3 188
48:20–21 37
48:21 71
49:6 179
51 84
51:9–11 37
51:12 95
52:4 37
52:12 37
53 11
54 35
56–66 35
56:7 23, 64

57:19 114
60:1–6 180
60:6–12 179
60:1 189
61:8 37
63:11 168
64:1 47
65:3–5 123, 127–9, 140, 150
65:3 128
65:4 127
65:7 127
65:11 127
65:17ff 37
66:22 37
65:23ff 37

Jeremiah
6:26 53
7:1–4 65
7:11 23, 64–5, 80
7:34 33
8:7–12 65
8:13 65, 80
13:27 33
15:9 69
16:14–15 37
20:1–2 33
23:1–6 75
23:4 75
23:5 37
23:7–8 37
30:5 111
31:10 167
31:27–28 37
31:33–34 37
38:17–26 33
40:1–5 33
48:33 66

Ezekiel
9:2 58
16 42
16:8 120
20:34–36 37
26:16 111
27:35 111
32:10 111
34:5–6 167

34:11–16 173
34:11–15 175
34:23–24 75, 173, 175
34:23 167, 172
34:24 37
34:25ff 37
34:31 175
36:35 37
37:24 75
37:26 37
40–48 37

Daniel
2:16 32
2:19–30 47
2:45 67
4:3 78
4:34 78
6:26 78
7.9 58, 73–9
7:13–14 78–9
9:27 20
10:7 111
11:31 20
12:3 61
12:11 20

Hosea
2 42
2:12 64–5, 80
6:1–3 114
6:10 65
7:2 65
9:2 66
9:3 37
9:10–17 54–5, 80, 112
9:16 64
10:17 64
11:5 37
11:11 37

Joel
1:7 64–5
2:2 69
2:24 66
2:31 69
4:13 66

Amos
8:9 69
8:10 70

Jonah
1 81, 86–99, 101, 111, 142
1:1–2 87
1:1 98
1:3 87–8
1:4 87, 94
1:5 87, 89–90
1:6 88, 94
1:8 88
1:9–10 88
1:10 89
1:11–14 89
1:11 88, 96
1:12 88, 96
1:13 90
1:14 88
1:15 87–8, 96
1:16 89
2:2 96, 142
4:2 90
4:3 90–1
4:6–9 97
4:9 90
7:52 97

Micah
5:2 172
5:4–5 172
5.4 167
7:1 64–5
7:14 37, 141

Zephaniah
1:15 69

Haggai
2:16 66
2:19 64–5

Zechariah
4:7 67
4:10 177
6:5 177
8:23 120

9–14 71, 77, 134
9:9 72, 147
9:11 75
10:2 167
10:3–4 72
11 141
11:16 75
12:10 53
13:2 72, 134–5, 141
13:7 24, 75
14 73
14:1–2 73
14:4 30, 71–3, 75
14:5 73
14:9 134, 194
14:10 66
14:21 72

Malachi
3:1 18, 47, 52, 56
4:4–5 56
4:5 20, 37

APOCRYPHA
Tobit 38–9
3:8 128
3:17 128
2:10 103
3:10 53
6 126
6:8 128
6:15 128
6:16 128
6:17 128
7:3–5 39
8:3 128
14:6–7 183

Judith
8:26 55
11:19 167

Wisdom of Solomon
14:3 32
17:16 137

Sirach
17:17 128

24:31 170
44:21 62
48:12–14 106
50:1–20 14, 92

1 Maccabees
1:64 39
2:1–6 39
2:1 40
2:24 40
2:26 39
2:27–28 40
2:29–38 40
2:39–41 40
2:42–43 40
2:44–48 40
2:49–70 40
2:54 40
2:64–66 40
2:67–68 40
2:69 40
2:70 40
3:4 40
3:8 40
3:18 40
9:21 40
10:8 89

2 Maccabees
6:8 166

NEW TESTAMENT
Matthew
1:1 143
1:20 72
2:6 172
8:32 139
9:38 98
10:6 167
12:38–41 89
12:41 92
13:7 139
13:58 118
14:20 178
15:24 167
15:39 178
16:4 89
16:9 178

Scripture Index

16:10 178
17:2 59
18:6 139
18:28 139
21:4–5 72
23:37 188
26:24 32
26:36 69

Mark
1:1–15 51–5, 56, 59, 68
1:1–7 20
1:1 51, 56, 74, 77
1:2–3 18, 32, 47, 52, 56, 73, 146, 168, 191
1:2 107
1:3 80
1:4–9 70
1:5 118, 160
1:6 106, 159
1:9–11 47, 106
1:10–11 73
1:10 53, 55, 56, 71, 143, 187–8
1:11 47, 52–3, 55, 71, 187, 194
1:13 53, 55, 149
1:14 56, 70
1:15 56
1:16–20 20
1:21–28 141, 149
1:24 126, 142, 148
1:26 134
1:27 144
1:31 109
1:35 94, 188
1:40 107
1:41 109, 143, 166
1:42 107
2:5 104, 118
2:6–8 116
2:7 194
2:13–17 20
2:19–20 74
2:23–28 142–4, 146
2:23–26 71
2:25–26 142

2:25 23
3:1–6 118
3:6 56
3:10 105
3:11 52–3, 125
3:14 98, 177
3:15 147
3:16 137
3:17 137
3:20–30 184
3:22–23 126
3:27 142, 149
3:29 188
4:1–32 162
4:5 123
4:9 20, 191
4:11 191
4:30–32 182
4:35–8:26 154
4:35–6:45 1, 7, 8, 25, 119, 175, 180, 184–5, 191
4:35–5:43 123, 150
4:35–5:20 116
4:35–41 81–99, 111, 123, 133, 140, 153–5, 162, 181–3, 186, 192
4:35 87, 98
4:36 85–8, 124
4:37 85, 87–8
4:38 85, 97, 190
4:39 85, 88, 94, 96, 124
4:40 97
4:41 81–2, 84–5, 87–9, 94–5, 97, 102, 116, 124, 154
5:1–43 102
5:1–20 14, 113, 123–51, 153–5, 181–3, 192
5:1 123
5:2–5 136
5:2 102, 124, 129, 136
5:3–5 141
5:3–4 137

5:3 129
5:4 126, 132
5:5 127, 129, 132, 136–7
5:6 102, 124–5, 136, 190
5:7–13 136
5:7 52, 124–6, 137–9, 141, 144, 148
5:8 102, 124, 129, 134
5:9 137
5:10–12 102
5:10 128
5:11–13 132, 142
5:11 129, 136
5:12–13 138
5:13–14 138
5:13 125, 129, 139, 142
5:14–16 138
5:15 102, 116
5:17–18 102
5:18–19 138, 149
5:19–20 125, 145–7, 149
5:19 129, 147
5:20 116, 137, 149–50
5:21–43 64, 101–22, 133, 153–5, 181–2, 192
5:22–23 190
5:22 102, 108–10, 137
5:23 102, 105, 109–10
5:24 108–10
5:25–26 124
5:25 102, 177
5:26 103
5:27–30 105
5:27–29 115, 118, 143
5:27 109
5:28 105, 118
5:29 109
5:30 118

5:31 102, 105, 108, 110
5:33 102, 110, 120, 190
5:34 110, 118
5:35 109, 118
5:36 104, 108, 118
5:39 106, 156
5:40 108–9
5:41 104, 105, 110
5:42 108–10, 116, 177
6:1–6 118
6:3 119
6:5 109
6:6–8:21 168
6:6–13 115, 118
6:6 119
6:7–13 147, 173
6:7 98, 144, 187, 193
6:8 115
6:13 118
6:14–29 4, 56, 70, 159
6:14–16 121, 158
6:14–15 145
6:14 118, 145
6:15 161
6:16 160, 176
6:21 158, 176
6:22–28 158
6:27–29 176
6:27 161
6:30–44 153–80, 181–2, 186, 192
6:31 158, 160, 165, 170
6:32 170
6:33 160, 169
6:34 155, 160–2, 166–8, 175, 179
6:35 166
6:36 155, 165
6:37–41 174
6:37 165, 169, 175
6:38 165, 170
6:39 157, 158, 161, 166

6:39 158, 166, 168, 171
6:40 159-62, 168, 170-1
6:41 165, 170, 180
6:42 165-7, 169, 171, 179
6:43 169-71, 177
6:44 159-60, 165, 169
6:45-52 81-2, 90, 94-7, 153-5, 162, 164, 182, 191-2
6:46 94, 97, 188
6:48-49 97
6:48 90, 95, 138
6:49 90, 95
6:50 95, 97, 104
6:52 95, 155
6:56 105
7:1-23 143
7:2 176
7:4 22
7:6-7 176
7:6 18
7:8 53
7:9-13 176
7:10 176
7:24-30 115, 118, 121, 178
7:24 178
7:26 178
7:27 166, 179
7:28 178
7:29 104
7:30 105
7:31-37 121, 176, 178
7:31 150, 178
7:32 109
7:33 104
7:34 187
8:1-10 153-80, 178, 181-2, 184, 192
8:1-9 150, 178
8:1 165
8:2-6 174
8:2 165-6, 169, 178

8:3 155, 169
8:4 155, 166, 169, 171, 175, 179
8:5 179
8:6 165
8:7 170
8:8 165-6, 169-71, 177, 179
8:9 169, 177
8:10-12 178
8:13-21 176
8:14-21 155, 164, 176-7
8:15 176
8:16 155
8:17-21 173
8:19-20 156, 164
8:19 177
8:20 177
8:21 155
8:22-29 176
8:22-26 119, 154
8:23 104, 109
8:25 109, 154
8:27-30 121
8:28-29 158
8:28 145, 155, 161
8:29 74, 77, 154, 156, 179, 193
8:30 154
8:31-16:8 56
8:31-9:1 56
8:31-38 56
8:31-37 154
8:31 56, 66, 70, 77, 154, 160, 193
8:32-33 56
8:38-9:1 14, 59
8:38 73
9:1-7 2
9:1 53
9:2-8 56-63, 68, 107, 191
9:2-7 14, 80, 190
9:2 63, 102, 190, 192
9:4 56, 58, 71
9:7 52-3, 56, 59, 63, 71, 194
9:8 63

9:9-13 121
9:11-13 4
9:12-13 18
9:13 4, 23, 56, 70-1, 106
9:14-29 105
9:18 115, 125, 194
9:22 166
9:23 104
9:24-27 118
9:24 118
9:29 94
9:31 66, 70, 77
9:37 98
9:38-41 147
9:38 144, 170
9:39 147
10:7 165
10:33-34 66, 70
10:34 77
10:38 53
10:45 52
10:46-52 119, 143, 147
10:47-48 71
10:49 104
11-12 63-7
11 66
11:1-11 47, 63, 72, 146
11:2 72
11:4 72
11:9 23
11:10 71
11:12-25 63-4, 72, 80, 112, 191
11:12-14 63
11:13 65
11:15-19 63
11:15 134
11:17 18, 23, 47, 65
11:20-25 63
11:23 71
11:24 94
11:25 94
11:27-33 72
11:27-29 65
11:27 66
11:29-30 65

12:1-12 47, 65-7, 72, 194
12:6 52-3, 80, 98, 194
12:19 165
12:21 165
12:24 21, 191
12:34 72
12:35-37 72, 144, 147
12:35 74
12:37 80
12:42 144
13 66, 73
13:2 98
13:3 102
13:14 20
13:20-27 146
13:20 146
13:22 30
13:24-26 47
13:26 14
13:27 14, 98, 177
13:32 52, 116
14-15 68-71
14:1-2 73
14:1 68
14:3-9 73
14:3 74
14:7 74
14:8 74
14:9 74
14:10-42 75
14:10 74
14:15 76
14:17-19 76
14:18 74-5, 116
14:20 75
14:21 18
14:22 68
14:24 68, 75
14:25 4, 75
14:26 75
14:27-28 167
14:27 18, 24
14:30 116
14:32-42 68, 90-1
14:32-39 94
14:32 69, 90, 137

14:33 102
14:34 75, 90
14:35–6 97
14:35 90
14:36 54, 69, 90–1
14:38 90
14:39 90
14:43–46 75
14:57 70
14:49 18
14:52 165
14:61–62 52, 76–7
14:61 68, 74, 80
14:62 14, 47, 78–9, 97
15:2 76
15:9 76
15:12 76
15:16–20 71, 77
15:8 76
15:19 190
15:20 70
15:24 70
15:26 76
15:27 70
15:29 70
15:32 70, 74, 76
15:33 68–9, 71
15:34 68, 70
15:35 70
15:36 70–1
15:38 68, 71
15:39 52, 68, 71, 121

Luke
1:27 72
1:32 72
1:69 72
2:4 72
2:9 89
2:11 72
4:21 32
5:1–11 157
8:31–33 142

8:33 139
9:28–36 4
9:29 59
10:2 98
11:29 89
11:32 92
19:10 167
20:13 66
24:50–53 4

John
2:17 70
6:15 160
10:1–18 167
10:3–5 75
10:30 14
11 4
12:14 32
12:41 188
13:18 75
20 4

Acts
1:9–11 4
1:20 138
2:23 32
2:30 73
4:25–28 138
4:28 32
5:36 30
6:1–7 177
9:25 178
13:22 142
16:16–24 126
19:11–20 126
21:38 30

Rom
1:3–4 72
4:18 62
5:12–21 4, 45–6
5:14 46
6:4 53

6:17 48
8:29 32
9:11–18 32
10:19 23
11:17 180
12:17 32

1 Corinthians
2:7 32
5:1–5 44
5:6–8 44
8:6 14, 186
10:1–22 44–5, 46
10:4 188
10:5 191
10:6 46
10:9 188, 191
10:11 46
10:20 127
10:20–21 128
14:41–2 62
14:44 62
15:12–20 4, 14
15:21–22 45–6
15:45 46
15:45–49 45–6
15:49 62
15:51 62

2 Cor
8:21 32

Galatians
4 44, 46
4:1–7 67
4:25–5:1 43

Eph
1:10 6, 32

Philippians
2:6ff 193
3:17 48

1 Thessalonians
1:7 48

1 Tim
1:16 48
4:12 48
5:8 32
6:9

2 Tim
1:13 48
2:8 72

Hebrews
1:1–3 14
5:1–10 193
6:13–14 55
11:17–19 53, 55
11:29 139
13:20 167

James
2:21–23 55

1 Peter
2:25 167
3:21 53
5:3 48
5:4 167

Jude 5 188

Revelation
2–3 177
2:7 141
3:21 78
5:5 72
7:17 165–7, 172
15:6 58
22:16 72

Index of Other Ancient Sources

JEWISH
Apocalypse of
  Abraham.
14:6 131
20:3–5 62

2 Baruch
29:7 117
29:8 172
72:1–6 183
76:2 56
76:13–14 168
51:5–12 51

1 Enoch
1–31 129–32, 134
6–11 129
6 130
9:4 130
10 131
10:1 130
10:4 130
10:5 130
10:7–9 130
10:11–13 130
10:12 53
12:6 53
14:6 53
14:20 51, 58
15:3–4 129
15:8 123
15:7–10 130
39:5–7 61
46:5 78
48:2–6 188
48:5 78
55:4 126, 142
62:6 78
62:9 78
89:56 66

89:66–67 66
89:73 66
90:30–33 183
96:3 117
99:5 53
104:2–4 61

2 Enoch 22:8 J 58

3 Enoch 12:1–2 58

4 Ezra
4:26–32 20
6:26 56
8:37–45 20
8:52–54 117
9:31–37 20
12:31–34 183
12:32 188
13:3 78
13:10–11 78
13:26 188
13:32 78
13:37–28 78
14:9 56

Genesis
  Apocryphon
20:20–22 101, 105

Joseph and
  Asenath
15:5 60
16:16 60
18:5 60
18:9–11 60

Josephus
Against Apion
2.180 32
2.263 127

Antiquities
1.222–36 54
1.226 69
6.116–69 126
6.166 139
8.44–45 126–7
8.45–49 124, 143, 147
8.45 133
8.46–49 126
8.47 144–5
8.325–7 108
8.326 120
9.28–185 108
9.182 106
10 33
10:79 32
10.126–8 32
10.198–99 34
10.277–80 32
10.278 32
10.156–9 33
11.205 34
14.21 183
16.20 127
18.118 160
20:97 30
20:97 92
20:167 29–30
20:168 29–30, 32
20:169 30
20:170 31
20.172 31
20:188 31
Jewish War
1.69 127
1.233 127
1.613 127
2.258 32
2:259 30
2:261–3 30

3:95 178
3.351–4 33
3.391 32, 33
3.392–9 34
4.629 34
5.272 66
5.362 33
5.391–3 33
5:391 33
5:406 33
5:411 33
6.300–9 33
7.182 127
7.185 127
7:438–40 31
Life
15 32, 33
208–10 33
418–21 32
425 32, 33

Jubilees
7:21 129
10:1 129, 132
17:15–16 68
17:16 54–5
18:3 68
18:6 69
18:13 69
18:18–19 68
23:26–30 116
25:29–34 135
49:1 68

LAB (Pseudo-
  Philo)
6:1–18 47
9:5–6 29
8:10 41
10:7 45, 188
11:15 188

12:1 41
12:7 42
15:6 41
18:5 54
19:11 41
31:1–2 54
32:1–4 54
40:2 54
48:1 42
48:2 42
60 126
60:1–3 73, 133, 144
60:2–3 132

3 Maccabees
5:30 32

4 Maccabees
7:14 54
7:19 54
13:12 54
13:17 54
13:19 32
16:20–25 54
17:22 32

Pss. Sol.
17 180
17:21–25 183
17:21 172
17.45(40) 167

Tg. Isa. 5:1–7 66
Tg. Neof. Exod
 12:42 69
Tg. Onq. Gen 22:14
 69
Tg. Onq. Gen 22:7
 69
Tg. Ps 55:13–24 75
Tg. Ps. 118:22 67
Tg. Ps.–J. Gen 22:7
 69
Tg Ps.–J. Exod
 12:42 69
Tg. Ps.–J. Isa 5:2 66
Tg. Zech. 4:7 67

T. Ben 10:5–6 56

T. Naph 6:1–10 83,
 85

T. Sol
1:6 145
5:2–3 129
5:6 130
13 144

Philo 54
Abr. 1:175 69
Abr. 168 53
Abr. 172 54
Abr. 196 53
Alleg. Interp. 3.219
 55
Creation 69 61
Creation 77 61
Creation 134–5
 61
Deus 1.4 53
Dreams 1.173 55
Dreams 1.34 61
Gig 132
Gig 16 127
Good Person 130
 127
Heir 86–7 61
Leg. all. 3.203 53
Migr. 140 53
Names 131 55
Opif 171–2 32
Opif 90 177
Plant. 61 131
Plant. 17–20 61
Post. 67–69 168
QE 2.29, 40 14
QG 2.56 61
QG 4.181 61
Somn. 1.194–5 53
Worse 124 55

QUMRAN
1Q20 126
1 QH 8:5–11 (16)
 162
1QHa 10.6 117
1QHa [35]
 11:15–18 142

1QM 11.1–2 141,
 148
1QpHab 7 67
1QS 3:20–24 132
4Q161 141
4Q161 8–10.3.11–
 24 183
4Q203 7A 131
4Q225 54–5
4Q285 141
4Q377 2.ii.5 168
4Q432 3.3 117
4QHf [432] 4.I.3–7
 142
4Q500 66
4Q510 131, 144
4Q511 131, 144
4Q521 2.II.11–13
 117
4Q560 1:4 147
11Q5 27 133, 144
11Q11 5 133
11QTS 47
11QMelch [13] 79,
 117
CD 13:7–9 153

RABBINIC
b. H. ag. 14a 78
b. Me'il. 17b 126
b. Mes.i'a 59b 83, 92,
 183
b. Pesah. 112b 126
b. Sanh. 38b 78
b. Sanh. 106b–107a
 75
b. Ta'an 23a–23b 92
Beshalach Siman 21
 172
Eccl. Rab 1:9 172
Exod. Rab. 15:11 69
Exod. Rab. 21.6 41
Exod. Rab. 25.7 172
Exod. Rab. 50.5 172
Gen. Rab. 1:6 189
Gen. Rab. 56.10 69
Gen. Rab. 88.5 172
m. Abot 6.3 75
m. Ta'an. 3:8 183

m. Ta'an. 3:8 92
m. Yoma 6.6 131
Mek. Exod 16:25
 172
Mek. Ishmael 7 69
Mek. Ishmael 11
 69
Mek. R. Shimon 15
 78
Mek. R. Yishmael
 5.4 78
Mek. Shimon 6 69
Midr. Ps 41:7 75
Midr. Ps 55:1 75
Midr. Pss, parasha 4
 79
Num Rab. 9.45–9
 42
Num. Rab. 21.21
 172
P. Avot 5:6 132
Pesiq. Rab. 10.8.
 42
Pesiq. Rab. 21 78
Pesiq. Rab. 33.6
 189
Pesiq. Rab. 36:1 92,
 189
Pirqe R. El. 31.10
 53
Pirqe R. El. 42. 41
Tanh. Exod 16:33
 172
y. Ber. 4:1 162
y. Ber. 9 82

GREEK and LATIN
Apuleius
 Metam. 11.5 82

Aelius Aristides
 Heracles 40.12 103
 Regarding Serapis
 45.33 82

Apollodorus
 Epitome 3.17–20
 104
 Library 1.9.15 105

Library 3.10.3-4 105

Apuleius
Flor. 19 105

Athenaeus
Deipnosophistae (Deipn.)
5.193d1-3 157
15.576a-b 82

Aristotle
Nic. Eth. 1176a17f 48
Poetics, 4.1448b4-19 48

Calpurnius
Bucolica 4.97-100 81

Cicero
De Oratore
I.xxxiv.156 48
II.xxii-xxiii.92-6 48

Corpus Inscriptionum Latinorum (CIL)
14.2112.2.11-13 157

Dio Cassius
Roman History
46.1-4 83
65.8 104

Diodrus Siculus, Library of History
1.25.4-5 103
1.25.6 105
4.43.1-2 82
4.71.1-3 105

Diogenes Laertius
Empedocles

8.59 83
8.69 103

Euripedes
Alc. 1136-63 105
Bacch. 704-13 156

Homer
Odyssey 48
The Iliad 48
1.222 127

Horace
Ode 4.1 48
Ode 4.2 48

Iamblichus
Life of Pythagoras
28, 135-6 83

Inscriptiones Graecae
4.1.121-2: Stelai 1.3, 9, 15, 18; 2.35, 36 103
4.2.128 104
7.2712 157

Isocrates
Panegyricus 10 48

Longinus
IV.xii-xiv 48

Lucien
Men. 9 148
False Philosopher (Philops.)
9 104
11 104
12 148
15-16 124
16 125
Salt. 45 105

Pausanias
Descr.1.27.4-5 106

PGM
VIII, 20f 148
VIII, 4.1609-11 148

Philodemus
Piety 52 105-6

Philostratus
Vit. Apoll.
2.4 125
3.27 156
3.38 104, 125
3.39 104
4:10 104
4.13.5-13 83
4.20 125
4.25 125-6
4.45 104, 106
6:43 104
7.38 104

Plato
Cratylus 398 b 127
Phaedrus, 263-4 48
Rep. 393-8 48
Rep. 596-9 48
Symposium 161
202d-e 127
Tim. 47b-c 48

Pliny the Elder
The Natural History
28.4.6 148
29.1.3 106

Plutarch
De cap ex inin, 92.e-f 48
De glor. Ath. 346f; 348b 48
Def. Orac. 417 125, 127

Def. Orac. 419 127
Life of Aratus 1.5 48
Marc. 20.5f 125
Peri, 1.4; 2.2; 48
Quaest. conv. 612E-F 158

Polybius
History 5.195d 157

Quintilian
Institutio Oratoria
v.vii.28 48
x.ii.2-8 48

Seneca
Ep 84 48
Controversiae 1. Praef. 6 48

Suetonius
Divine Vespasian 7.2 104

Tacitus
Hist. 4.81 104

Virgil
Aeneid 48

PATRISTIC

Barn 12:10 181

Did 9:2 75

1 Clement
7:7 89
26:2 165, 172

Gregory Palamas
The Triads 2.3.18 59

Irenaeus
Haer. IV.20.12 180

Justin
Dialogue 107 89

Origen
Cels. 1.68 125

Comm. John 10.16
102
Comm. Rom. 4.6.7
61

Hom. Num. 6.4.2
180
Hom. Song. 1.6
180

Ps. Jerome
Com. Marcum. 1:8
73

Author Index

Achtemeier, E. 69, 195
Achtemeier, P. 9, 81, 83–4, 89, 95–6, 102, 123, 163, 195
Allison, D.C. 3, 6–7, 20–1, 26, 29, 31, 36–7, 46, 57, 161, 165–7, 172–3, 211
Alter, R. 159, 197
Anderson, J.E. 87–8, 197
Annen, F. 127, 197
Atkinson, K. 133, 197
Aus, R.D. 86–7, 89, 92, 94, 124, 143, 159, 197
Avioz, M. 136, 197

Baarlink, H. 6, 198
Barnett, P.W. 31–2, 198
Barrett, C.K. 63, 72, 196
Batten, A.J. 159, 170, 198
Bauckham, R 2, 6, 8, 10, 13–15, 22, 41–2, 52, 58, 61–2, 77–9, 96–8, 121, 134, 145–8, 154, 186–7, 190–1, 134, 198
Baxter, W. 167, 198
Bayer, H.F. 97, 160, 198
Beavis, M.A. 108, 198
Becker, E. 25, 199
Bermejo-Rubio, F. 72–3, 75, 199
Best, E. 4, 53, 69, 77, 199
Bieler, L. 10, 199
Bird, M. 8, 187, 199, 218
Blackburn, B. 10, 199
Block, D.I. 172, 199
Bond, H. 19–20, 32, 199
Boobyer, G.H. 176, 179, 199
Boomershine, T.E. 19, 200
Boring, M.E. 8, 11, 18, 52, 56–7, 73–7, 81, 84, 88, 93, 101–2, 113, 120–1, 143, 154, 157, 160–1, 164, 171, 178–9, 200
Bosenius, B. 179, 200
Bostock, G. 107, 116, 200
Broadhead, E.K. 10, 12, 17, 95, 102, 136, 149, 177–8, 200
Brodie, T.L. 19, 47, 107, 200

Brooke, G. 1, 46, 47, 66, 200
Brower, K. 82–3, 86, 96, 200
Brown, R. 54, 69, 75, 77, 106–7, 200
Bruce, F.F. 72–3, 75, 77, 138, 160, 201
Brueggemann, 109–10, 121, 168, 201
Bultmann, R. 10, 17, 21–2, 82, 101, 109, 124, 156, 201
Burnett, D. 61–2, 201
Burridge, R. 19, 201
Buth, R. and Krasnica, B. 65–6, 201

Cahill, M. 26, 73, 201
Cain, R.B. 48, 201
Capes, D.B. 14, 201, 206
Carroll, R.P. 168, 201
Carter, W. 124, 131, 135, 148, 201
Chapman D.W. 20, 201
Chapman, S.B. and Warner, L.C. 98, 201
Charlesworth, J.H. 63, 66–7, 201
Chester, A. 14, 202
Chilton, B., Bock D., Gurtner, D., Neusner, J., Schiffman, L. and Oden, D. 66, 133, 142, 147, 177, 202
Chou, M.C. 102, 115, 120, 202
Clemens, S. 1, 202
Cohen, S.J.D. 33, 202
Collins, A.Y. 11, 19, 73–5, 82, 84, 86, 89–90, 93, 95, 102–3, 108–9, 123–5, 129–30, 137, 142–3, 148, 156, 158–60, 164, 168–9, 172, 174, 177, 202
Collins, J.J. 31, 72, 73, 76, 78, 117, 133, 135, 183, 188, 200, 202
Cotter, W.J. 82–3, 103–4, 126–7, 142, 202
Counet, P.C. 192–3, 202
Cousland, J.R.C. 178, 202
Cranfield, C.E.B. 70, 172, 202

Danker, F.W. 169, 178, 202
Daube, D. 33–4, 203
Davidson, R.M. 89, 203
Davies, P.R and Chilton, B.D. 54, 203

Dawson, A. 143, 203
Dawson, D. 2, 5, 43, 203
De Boer, M.C. 43–4, 203
De Jonge, H.J. 72, 75, 203
Dechow, J. 65, 82, 88, 90, 94–5, 119, 164, 203
Deconick, A.D. 186, 203
Dehn, G. 16–7, 203
Dell, K.J. 18, 21, 203
Derrett, J.D. 83, 86, 90, 98, 114, 120, 123–4, 127–8, 131, 134, 143, 149–50, 166, 169–70, 203
Desogus, P. 24, 203
Dibelius, M. 10, 12, 21–2, 82, 124–5, 203
DiTomasso, L. 135
Dodd, C.H. 11, 75, 77, 203
Donahue, J.R. and Harrington, D.J. 3, 11, 16, 57, 69–71, 73, 77, 88, 124, 127, 166, 203
Dormandy, R. 149, 204
Drewermann, E. 83–4, 86, 96, 159, 204
Drury, J. 20, 204
Du Toit, D.S. 86, 90, 92, 166, 168, 204
Dunn, J.D.G. 9, 51, 54, 57, 59, 62, 76, 92, 148, 154, 160, 164, 171, 204
Dwyer, T. 108, 204

Eco, U. 24, 204
Edwards, J. 16, 63, 101, 204
Elder, N. 124, 129–31, 134, 204
Emadi, S. 5, 22, 204
Engberg-Pedersen, T. 62, 204
Ernst, J. 195, 204
Evans, C.A. xii, 6–7, 9–10, 22, 29, 47, 56–9, 65–7, 69, 70, 72–3, 75–7, 79, 93, 133, 141, 146, 148, 205
Eve, E. 30–1, 103, 108, 117, 187, 205

Farrar, A. 17, 205
Fassnacht, M. 109, 205
Feneberg, R. 9, 84, 92, 127, 141, 145–6, 155, 158, 164, 172, 178, 205
Fishbane, M. 2, 6–7, 36–8, 135, 205
Fisher, K. 9, 102, 205
Fisk, S. 5, 40–2, 46, 54, 135, 205
Fitzmyer, J.A. 38–9, 45–6, 54, 206
Focant, C. 3, 86, 95, 124, 127, 164, 166, 206
Fossheim, H. 48, 206
Foster, P. 11, 19, 21, 22, 206, 217

Foulkes, F. 6, 37, 206
Fowler, R.M. 20–1, 164
France, R.T. 7, 56, 71–2, 81–3, 97, 102, 109, 118, 124–5, 141–2, 146, 149, 154, 157, 160–1, 164, 166–7, 170, 172, 174, 192, 198, 201, 206
Fredriksen, P. 26, 136, 206
Frei, H. 2
Frieden, K. 127–8, 206
Fritz, V. 120–1, 164, 171, 206
Fung, R. 43, 206

Gardner, H. 17–18, 206
Garland, D.E. 11, 73, 77, 83, 87, 90, 93, 127, 146, 148, 157, 159, 164, 166, 168–9, 170, 172–3, 206
Gathercole, S. 8, 14, 58, 84, 95, 187–9, 207
Gheorghita, R. 26, 207
Gieschen, C.A. 61, 207
Ginzberg, L. 110, 207
Girard, R. 137, 207
Glasswell, M.E. 109, 207
Gnilka, J. 8, 57, 75, 81, 86, 94, 95, 108, 124, 127, 156–7, 162, 168, 177, 207
Goldstein, J.A. 39–40, 207
Goppelt, L. 1, 43, 86, 134, 143, 207
Goulder, M.D. 4, 29, 40, 46, 207, 214
Gray, J. 106, 109–10, 164, 207
Grindheim, S. 14, 117, 187, 207
Guelich, R.A. 3, 8, 26, 52–3, 55, 86, 102, 104, 109, 148, 150, 154, 159, 164, 167, 169, 171, 177–9, 207, 213
Gundry, R. 56, 62, 76, 102, 110, 124–6, 142, 207
Guth, C.J. 141, 149, 208
Guttenberger, G. 51–2, 162, 208

Haenchen, E. 1145, 142, 164, 208
Halliwell, S. 48, 208
Halton, C. 120, 208
Hartman, L. 19, 73, 84, 86, 95, 102, 109, 120, 141, 146, 148, 157, 164–8, 172, 208
Hatina, T.R. 159, 208
Hays, R. 2, 5, 6, 14–15, 20–3, 26, 44–6, 83–6, 95–8, 121, 148, 175, 186, 191, 194, 198, 208
Heil, J.P. 82, 208
Hengel, M. 10, 30–1, 73, 78, 188–9, 208

Himmelfarb, M. 60-1, 208
Hooker, M. 53, 56-7, 66, 69-71, 136, 141, 168-9, 208
Horsley, R.A. 30-3, 103, 121, 126, 195, 209
Hübenthal, S. 155, 164, 166, 169, 209
Huizenga, L.A. 22, 24, 51, 54-5, 68-9, 209
Hwang, J.K. 44-5, 209

Jacobson, H. 41-2, 209
Janowski, B. 70, 75, 77, 209
Jewett, R. 45, 209
John, J. 102, 209
Johnson, N.C. 72, 75-6, 209
Juel, D. 6, 10, 22, 49, 65-6, 70, 76, 209

Kampling, R. 52-3, 209
Kanarek, J.L. 69, 209
Kaufman, S.A. 47, 209
Kee, H. 9, 35, 46, 59, 69, 72, 73-4, 115, 167, 170, 176, 188, 210
Kelber, W.H. 98, 210
Kertelge, K. 149, 210
King, D. 5, 210
Kirk, D. 2, 8, 13, 15-16, 21, 62, 92-3, 116-19, 133-4, 144-8, 173-4, 185, 194, 198, 210
Klinghardt, M. 127, 149, 210
Koch, K. 81, 94-5, 124, 155, 178, 210
Kok, M.J. 25, 210
Kowalski, B. 22-4, 210
Krause, D. 64, 210
Kristeva, J. 21-2, 211
Kugel, J.L. 22, 211

Lacocque, A. 61, 211
Lahurd, C.S. 142-3, 150, 211
Lamb, W.R.S. 25, 115, 211
Lampe, G. 6, 211
Lapide, F. 89-90, 211
Law, T.M. 26, 211
Leim, J.E. 146, 211
Levenson, J. 68-9, 211
Levinson, B.M. 5, 211
Lindars, B. 11, 106, 211
Lindbeck, G. 2, 211
Litwa, M.D. 56-9, 61, 211
Longenecker, R. 54, 212
Lyons, M.A. 23, 34-5, 212

MacDonald, D.R. 47-212
McInerney, W.F. 90, 94, 212
McLay, R.T. 26, 213
Mainwaring, S. 149, 212
Malbon, E.S. 10, 86-7, 89, 143, 212
Marcus, J. 8, 11, 20, 33, 47, 52, 56-7, 63, 66-72, 75-9, 84, 86-8, 94, 97-8, 101-5, 118, 124-7, 131, 134, 136, 143-6, 149, 154, 156-7, 160-4, 168-9, 171-2, 177, 194, 200, 212
Martens, P.W. 2, 43, 212
Martin, D. 62, 128, 212
Marxsen, W. 17, 212
Masuda, S. 157, 166-7, 169, 171, 178, 212
May, F. 177, 212
Mays, J.L. 66, 79, 84, 212
Meier, J.P. 57, 82, 93, 95, 104, 144, 213
Meye, R. 83-4, 213
Millay, T. 2, 213
Moberly, W. 36, 213
Moo, D. 11, 66, 68, 213
Montefiore, H. 159-60, 213
Morey, A.J. 125, 213
Moscicke, H. 124, 128-32, 139, 213
Moss, C. 110, 113, 116, 120, 213
Moyise, S. 5, 20, 22-4, 213
Murcia, T. 129, 131, 213
Murphy, F.J. 42, 213

Nemoy, L. 189, 214
Newsom, C. 18, 61, 214
Novakovic, L. 117, 214
Novenson, M.V. 72, 186, 214
Nowell, I. 38-9, 214
Nyström, J. 124, 143-4, 148, 214

O'Brien, K. 11, 89, 214
Omerzu, H. 6-7, 52, 56, 58, 107, 168, 211, 214
Osborne, G.R. 148, 214
Ounsworth, R. 2-4, 6, 48, 214
Owen, P. 166, 172, 214

Pearson, B. 62, 214
Perrin, N. 17, 214
Pesch, R. 8-9, 56-9, 75, 83, 86-9, 92-8, 103-8, 111, 120, 124, 127, 148, 154, 156, 159, 164, 166-7, 177, 210, 214
Porter, S.E. 21, 22, 215

Portier-Young, A. 38, 215
Potolsky, M. 47–8, 215
Powell, M.A. 86, 215
Putthof, T. 60–1, 215

Ramsey, A.M. 56, 59, 215
Rao, D.V. 161, 215
Reid, R.S. 18–19, 215
Rhoads, D. 17, 20, 215
Rhoads, D. and Michie, D. 10, 18, 20, 215
Richardson, A. 9, 83, 154, 164, 177, 215
Rindge, M. 53–4, 59, 69–70, 215
Robinson, J.R.R. 91–2, 57–8, 215
Rosch, E. 18, 215
Roth, W. 19, 107, 114, 215

Salzmann, A.B. 162, 176–80, 216
Sanders, E.P. 183, 216
Sandmel, S. 22, 216
Schildgen, B.D. 25, 216
Schmücker, R. 9, 216
Schnabel, E.J. 183–4, 216
Schnackenburg, R. 59, 95, 143, 164, 171, 216
Schneck, R. 127, 143, 150, 164–8, 170–1, 216
Schweizer, E. 101, 124, 154, 216
Segal, A.F. 54, 78, 216
Sellin, G. 193, 216
Shively, E.E. 18, 216
Shuve, K. 180, 217
Sick, D. 157, 159, 217
Slater, T.B. 78, 217
Smith, D.E. 158–9, 161, 217
Smith, S. 24, 217
Smothers, C. 83–5, 217
Snodgrass, K.R. 66–7, 217
Sommer, B.D. 5, 217
Spilsbury, P. 32, 217
Stamps, D. 1, 5, 217
Stanley, C.D 3, 20, 217
Starobinski, J. 124–5, 135, 148, 217
Stec, D.M. 67, 217
Stegner, W.R. 53–4, 57, 164, 168, 170, 217
Stein, R.H. 556, 59, 69, 81, 86–9, 91, 93, 124, 129, 146–7, 154, 164, 166–7, 174, 177, 217

Steinmetz, D. 2, 217
Sternberg, M. 195, 217
Strauss, D.F. 9–10, 102, 125, 218

Telford, W. 12, 17, 21, 26, 218
Theissen, G. 82, 104, 109, 150, 156, 218
Theissen, M. 103, 107–8, 113–14, 116, 128–9, 143, 148–9, 218
Thompson, T. 1, 218
Tilling, C. 14, 186–9, 218
Tooman, W.A. 34–5, 38, 218
Treier, D. 2, 218
Trocmé, E. 17, 219
Trumbower, J.A. 33, 219
Twain, M. 1
Twelftree, G. xii, 9–10, 18, 83, 87, 92, 124–8, 136, 141, 148–50, 219

Van Iersel, B.M.F. 52–3, 57–8, 70, 72, 219
Van Oyen, G. 154, 219
Vermès, G. 54, 69, 219, 220
Von Heijne, C. 57, 219

Waetjen, H.C. 86, 219
Wallace, D.B. 142, 219
Warrington, K. 116, 219
Watts, R. 1, 6, 11, 25, 47, 67, 102, 114, 114, 127, 149, 219
Weeden, T. 10. 12, 219
Wefal, E.K. 87, 127–8, 149, 177–9, 220
Wenham, D. 68, 220
Westerholm S. and M. 37, 180, 220
Winn, A. 10, 17–19, 47, 107, 220
Witherington, B. 86, 89, 159, 164, 167–8, 220
Woodruff, P. 48, 220
Wrede, W. 12, 17, 63, 220
Wright, A. 128, 130–2, 136, 148, 220
Wright, T.R. 20, 220

Young, F. 2–3, 5, 7, 21, 43, 45, 48, 220
Young, S. 13, 76, 92–3, 210
Youngblood, K.J. 86, 221

Zadorojnyi, A.V. 48, 206
Zakovich, Y. 183, 221

Subject Index

Abraham 36–8, 43, 47, 53–5, 61–2, 68–71, 105, 126, 135
Adam 4–5, 16, 35, 45–6, 62, 89, 192, 214
Ahab and Jezebel 138, 159
Ahithopel 75–6
Allegory 2–3, 43, 204, 212, 220
Angel/s 14, 54, 57–9, 73, 98, 132, 189

Baptism 26, 44–5, 47, 51, 53–4, 73, 79–80, 106, 191

Daniel (*see also* scripture references) 60–1, 70, 78–9
David (King) 4–5, 7, 16, 23–4, 33, 36–7, 40, 46, 51, 67, 71–80, 92–3, 123–51, 165–9, 172–5, 181–4, 194–5
Demon/s/iac/evil spirits 14, 52, 84, 105, 113, 116, 121–50, 155, 183–4, 190
Divine Identity 2, 8, 13–16, 52, 62–3, 77–9, 97, 121, 145, 148–9, 175–6, 165, 167, 190–1, 194–5, 198

Elijah 4–5, 7, 20, 36–7, 42, 56–70, 80, 92, 101, 106–9, 111, 113–14, 116, 120–2, 145, 147, 159, 186, 190–1
Elisha 4, 9, 42, 92, 101, 105–22, 133, 147, 153, 164–5, 167–9, 171–2, 174–5, 180–2, 184, 195
Enoch 53, 192 (*see also* ancient sources)
Esther 33–4
Eucharist/Last Supper 4, 45, 68, 74–5, 174, 199, 200, 212, 217, 219–20
Exodus 20, 30–1, 35–7, 41–2, 45–7, 57–8, 96, 159, 168–71, 174, 188, 191
Exodus, New 11, 37–8, 114

Feeding miracle 8, 45, 64, 114, 117, 121, 141, 151, 153–80, 184
Fish 156–7, 162, 169–71, 174–5, 182
Flood 41, 47, 84, 95–6, 129–30, 132

Gehazi 105, 110, 114

Healing 8–9, 16, 82, 93–4, 101–22, 126–8, 131, 143, 145, 149, 154, 160, 132, 173, 180, 182, 187, 190
Human Figures, Idealized/Exalted 2, 8, 15–16, 62, 92–3, 117, 185, 195

Imperial propaganda 10
Intercalation/sandwich 63–5, 101–2, 107, 111–12
Isaac (Akedah) 36–8, 43, 51–5, 59, 66, 68–70, 79–80

Jairus and daughter 101–2, 106, 108–10, 112, 115, 118–19, 121
Jeremiah 33, 36, 65, 67
John the Baptist 4–5
Jonah 24, 46, 81, 86–99, 111, 121, 133, 142, 149, 181–4, 195
Joshua 29, 31, 33, 67, 92–3, 107, 161, 167, 169–70, 174–5, 184
Judas (disciple) 74, 76, 138
Judas (Maccabeus) 40

Lazarus 4
Leek/s 162, 170–1
Leprosy/lepra 105, 107

Mimesis 47–9
Moses 5, 7, 9, 14, 29–31, 33, 36–7, 41–2, 44, 56–9, 62–3, 80, 92–3, 105, 107, 147, 153, 159–60, 167–75, 180–3, 186, 190–2, 195

Nephilim/giants 123, 129–31, 133, 135–6, 144, 150
Noah 35, 41

Ontology 4, 60–3, 173, 193–4

Paul 15, 29, 43–6, 49, 53, 61–3, 89, 126, 178, 184, 186, 191–2
Purity 108, 113–14, 122, 129, 142–3

Resurrection 4, 6–8, 10, 12, 32, 46, 53–4, 59, 62, 70, 101–3, 105, 108–10, 111–12, 114, 117, 120–1, 130, 154, 181, 188, 192–3

Shunamite woman 108–12, 115, 121
Solomon 74, 126, 133, 137, 143–5, 147–8

Transfiguration 4, 26, 51, 56–63, 71, 79–80, 102, 107, 186, 191

Typology, Definition 2–5
Typology, Fulfillment 1, 4–5, 7–8, 12, 16, 19, 51, 55, 80, 99, 122, 167, 172, 181, 183–4, 185, 188, 190
Typology, Literary 1–2, 4–5, 8, 11–12, 18, 21, 29, 34, 39, 42, 48–9, 89, 91, 99, 122, 141, 150, 172, 175, 184
Typology, Theomorphic 1, 5, 7–8, 12, 60, 80, 89, 150, 182–5, 191–2

Watcher tradition 123, 129–32, 133, 135–6, 140, 150
Woman in the crowd 102–3, 109–16, 118, 120–1, 143, 154–5

www.ingramcontent.com/pod-product-compliance
Lightning Source LLC
Chambersburg PA
CBHW062137300426
44115CB00012BA/1959